THE HISTORY OF THE VIOLIN
Its Ancestors and Collateral Instruments

Archangelo Corelli, from the Frontispiece of his Sonatas op. V, engraved by Van der Gucht, from a portrait by H. Howard.

THE HISTORY OF THE VIOLIN

Its Ancestors and Collateral Instruments

FROM EARLIEST TIMES
TO THE PRESENT DAY

by

E. VAN DER STRAETEN

Author of " The History of the Violoncello, etc."
" The Romance of the Fiddle," "The Revival of the Viols," etc.

With 48 Plates and numerous illustrations in text

VOL. I

CASSELL
and Company, Ltd.
London, Toronto, Melbourne
and Sydney

Edmund van der Straeten:

History of the Violin, Its Ancestors and Collateral Instruments from the Earliest Times to the Present Day.

Vol. 1.

First published by Cassell & Co., 1933.

Republished Travis & Emery 2009.

Published by
Travis & Emery Music Bookshop
17 Cecil Court, London, WC2N 4EZ, United Kingdom.
(+44) 20 7240 2129
neworders@travis-and-emery.com

Hardback: ISBN10: 1-904331-83-1   ISBN13: 978-1904331-83-4
Paperback: ISBN10: 1-904331-84-X   ISBN13: 978-1904331-84-1

Edmund Sebastian Joseph van der Straeten, composer, cellist and author, born 29 April 1855, Düsseldorf, Germany, died 17 September 1934, London, England.

Bibliography:
 The Technics of Violoncello playing. London, The Strad, 1898.
 The Romance of the Fiddle. The origin of the Modern Virtuoso and the Adventures of his Ancestors. London, Rebman, 1911.
 History of the Violoncello, the Viol da Gamba, their precursors and collateral instruments. With biographies of all the most eminent players of every country. London: William Reeves, 1915
 A handbook of musical form for instrumental players and vocalists. London, William Reeves, 1911.
 Well-known Violoncello Solos. London, William Reeves, 1926.
 History of the Violin, Its Ancestors and Collateral Instruments from the Earliest Times to the Present Day. London, Cassell, 1933.
 Also an unpublished opera.

© Travis & Emery 2008.

THE
HISTORY OF THE VIOLIN
Its Ancestors and Collateral Instruments

FROM EARLIEST TIMES
TO THE PRESENT DAY

by

E. VAN DER STRAETEN

Author of " The History of the Violoncello, etc."
" The Romance of the Fiddle," "The Revival of the Viols," etc.

With 48 Plates and numerous illustrations in text

VOL. I

CASSELL
and Company, Ltd.
London, Toronto, Melbourne
and Sydney

First Published . . . *1933*

PRINTED IN GREAT BRITAIN
BY BUTLER AND TANNER LTD., FROME AND LONDON
F7.5.833

To My Friend
NEWMAN FLOWER
who alone made this book possible

Preface

FOR many years the idea of writing a History of the Violin has been in my mind, as the few existing English works on the subject (Dubourg, Sandys and Forster, Mason Clarke) are either out of date or quite inadequate. I therefore kept collecting material for the purpose, as I found it in the course of research work for my "History of the Violoncello," and for other works on musical history. I then began to peruse all the works on the subject accessible to me, German, French, and Italian, including Musical Dictionaries, Eitner's "Quellenlexikon," memoirs, letters, periodicals, and any other works (sometimes unconnected with music) that might supply information on the subject. As this was continued for a period of more than twenty years it would be impossible for me to give a complete bibliography, for, apart from the fact that I sometimes omitted to keep a record of the sources of minor details, such a list would add too much to the already considerable bulk of the work.

In this work, as in the "History of the Violoncello," I have adhered to the chronological order, rather than that of schools, as in Wasielewski's "Die Violine," because, thereby, a clearer picture of the progress is gained. As the history of the violin is essentially the history of its masters, and vice versa, I have, especially in the early 17th century, sometimes given the names of violinists of whom nothing more, except perhaps the place where they were engaged, is known for the reason that their record supplies us with the fact that the violin at that time was cultivated at such-and-such a place, giving also the nationality of the respective violinists. Moreover, the attention of other historians may be drawn to these names, and result in interesting discoveries, for there is practically no finality in historical research. Many errors have been rectified within quite recent years, and many gaps in the biographies of important violinists have been filled,

Preface

while others are still awaiting discovery. Although great care has been taken in collecting the biographies of all the older violinists I could discover, yet their number is so great that I cannot be certain that some may not have escaped my attention.

Of living artists the number has grown to such proportions that anything even approaching their complete inclusion appeared beyond accomplishment, especially as it was almost impossible to obtain particulars. Those, therefore, who have been omitted I beg to feel assured that this was quite unintentional, and shall be remedied, as far as possible, in any future edition.

To the many friends who have supplied me with valuable information I beg to tender my sincerest thanks: especially to the authorities of the British Museum who accorded to me every facility and assistance in the use of their incomparable library, especially also to Mr. W. C. Smith, the keeper of the printed music; to Mr. K. Parker, of the Print room; and to the Controller of H.M. Stationery Office for sketches based upon illustrations in "Musical Instruments" (Engel, V. and A. Museum). To Mr. Frank T. Arnold special thanks are due for sacrificing much of his valuable time in helping me to arrange the material, instituting special research into various matters in Italy, and in contributing the interesting portraits of Torelli, Tom. Vitali, and the brothers Somis, which he obtained, by the kind permission of Sig. Vatielli, from the Bologna library, who possesses the original portraits, hitherto, as far as we know, never published; particularly also to Messrs. Alfred E. and Arthur F. Hill (of Messrs. E. W. Hill & Sons), who gave their kind permission for the reproduction of the unique portraits of Joachim, Paganini, Nicolas Mori, W. Ernst and P. Sainton, all painted from life; of Spohr, Campagnoli, Vieuxtemps and Tessarini, from engravings; of the unique Lyra da Braccio by Giovan Maria, the "Blunt" Stradivari (1721), the violin by A. Amati, and the collection of bows. Again, to Miss Schlesinger (W. Reeves); to the proprietors of *The Strad*, for illustration-material; and to Mr. W. Howard-Head, for the Tartini bow. To the Right Honourable the Marquess of Salisbury for his gracious permission of the reproduction of his most interesting picture by J. Hoefnagel, the Rev.

Preface

Canon F. W. Galpin for pictures of early English violinists, and much valuable information; Prof. O. E. Deutsch for portraits; Prof. Joh. Wolf, of the Berlin State library, and many kind friends for sundry contributions and courtesies. Dr. Georg Kinsky, former curator of the Heyer Museum, Cologne, has also kindly supplied me with much valuable information.

LONDON, *July* 1933

Contents: Vol. I

PART I
ORIGIN AND EARLY HISTORY OF THE VIOLIN TO 1700

CHAP.		PAGE
1.	PRECURSORS OF THE VIOLIN FAMILY FROM THE EARLIEST TIMES TO THE APPEARANCE OF THE PERFECT VIOL	1
2.	THE FIDDLE, FIDULA OR VIELLE, AND THE GUITAR-FIDDLE	11
3.	INTRODUCTION OF THE BOW	17
4.	THE VIOLS	24
5.	THE LYRA	29
6.	THE VIOLIN	35
7.	THE EVOLUTION OF VIOLIN PLAYING	46
8.	THE VIOLIN IN ITALY FROM 1600 TO CIRCA 1650	49

VIOLINISTS FROM c. 1550 TO 1700

9.	ENGLAND	57
10.	FRANCE	75
11.	GERMANY: I. To 1650	94
12.	II. To 1700	109
13.	ITALY: I. To 1650	121
14.	II. To 1700	136
15.	NETHERLANDS	172
16.	POLAND AND SCANDINAVIA	174

PART II
HISTORY OF THE VIOLIN FROM 1700 TO 1800

17.	HISTORY OF THE VIOLIN FROM 1700 TO 1800	179

VIOLINISTS OF THE PERIOD

18.	AUSTRIA	185
19.	BELGIUM	199
20.	BOHEMIA: I. To 1750	208

Contents

CHAP.			PAGE
21.	BOHEMIA: II. To 1800	.	224
22.	FRANCE: I. To 1725	.	235
23.	II. To 1750	.	248
24.	III. To 1775	.	264
25.	IV. To 1800	.	285
26.	GERMANY: I. To 1725	.	299
27.	II. To 1750	.	321
28.	III. To 1775	.	347
29.	IV. To 1800	.	379
30.	GREAT BRITAIN: I. To 1750	.	399
31.	II. To 1800	.	408
32.	HUNGARY	.	416

List of Illustrations
PLATES

ARCHANGELO CORELLI	*Frontispiece*

FACING PAGE

FAMOUS BOWS	22
TARTINI'S TOURTE BOW	23
LYRA DA BRACCIO, 1540, BY GIOVAN MARIA	40
THE GILLING CASTLE PANELS	41
VIOLIN BY ANDREAS AMATI	64
A MARRIAGE FÊTE BY JORIS HOEFNAGEL, 1590	65
DETAIL OF VIOLINISTS AND INSTRUMENTS	65
WILLIAM CORBETT	98
JEAN FERRY REBEL	98
ADALBERT GYROWETZ	98
THOMAS PINTO	98
JOHN BANISTER, The Younger	99
MICHEL CORRETTE	99
NICOLA COSIMI	128
JEAN BAPTISTE LULLY	128
GIUSEPPE TORELLI	129
TOMMASO ANTONIO VITALI	129
GIOVANNI BATTISTA SOMIS	152
ANTONIO VIVALDI	153
FRANCESCO MARIA VERACINI	153
PIETRO NARDINI	153
P. SPAGNOLETTI	153
LORENZO SOMIS	162
FRANCESCO GEMINIANI	162
VIOLIN BY ANTONIUS STRADIVARI, 1721	163
ANTON WRANITZKY	163

List of Illustrations

	FACING PAGE
KARL DITTERS VON DITTERSDORF	192
IGNAZ SCHUPPANZIGH	192
FRANZ KROMMER	192
FRANZ BENDA	193
JOHANN PETER SALOMON	193
FRANÇOIS FRANCOEUR	272
JEAN JOSEPH CASSANEA DE MONDONVILLE	272
PIERRE RODE	272
RODOLPHE KREUTZER	272
JEAN MARIE LECLAIR	273
LEOPOLD MOZART	273
HEINRICH I. F. BIBER VON BIBERN	336
CHRISTIAN CANNABICH	336
JOHANN WENZEL ANTON STAMITZ	336
FRIEDRICH WILHELM PIXIS	336
WILHELM CRAMER	337
FRIEDRICH WILHELM RUST	337

DRAWINGS AND DIAGRAMS

FIG.		PAGE
	Evolution of the Violin: Genealogical Table	2
1.	Cithara	2
2.	German Rotta: 5th and 7th Century	4
3.	French Crouth (Rotta): 11th Century	4
4.	Welsh Crwth: 18th Century	5
5.	Lyra: 13th Century	6
6.	Rebec: 16th Century	7
7.	Italian Giga: 15th Century	9
8.	13th-century Fiddle with Bow	13
9.	13th-century Guitar-Fiddle	13
10.	Guitar-Fiddle: 11th Century	15
11.	Reinmar's Fiddle with Bow: 13th Century	16
12.	Fiddle from Reinmar's Helmet: 13th Century	16
13.	Bow in use: 8th to 16th Centuries	18

List of Illustrations

FIG.		PAGE
14.	Crwth Bow: 9th Century	18
15.	9th-century Bow	19
16.	Knobbed Bow: 12th Century	19
17.	13th-century Bow	19
18.	Notched Bow: 14th Century	19
19.	Bow with *Crémaillière*: 15th Century	20
20.	Detail showing 17th-century *Crémaillière*	20
21.	Gigue with Bow: 16th Century	20
22.	Detail of early Bow showing detached Nut	21
23.	17th-century Kit Bow	21
24.	17th-century Violin Bow	21
25.	Italian Fidel: *c.* 1500	24
26.	Pareia's Viol: 1482	25
27.	Viol of 1542	25
28.	Tenor Viol da Gamba: 1699 ("The Perfect Viol")	27
29.	Lyra da Braccio and Bow: 1505	30
30.	Lyra da Braccio and Bow: 1499	30
31.	Lyra da Braccio: 1550	31
32.	Viol da Gamba: 1540	42

PART I
ORIGIN AND EARLY HISTORY OF THE VIOLIN TO 1700

CHAPTER 1

Precursors of the Violin Family from the Earliest Times to the Appearance of the Perfect Viol

MANY and various are the theories that have been advanced in connexion with the origin of the violin, but the majority are based upon myths, fables and conjectures which have no solid foundation, and with which, therefore, we need not concern ourselves.

In trying to find the real ancestor of the violin, it is evident that we must look for an instrument possessing the same fundamental characteristics, i.e. the triplicity of the sound-body, composed of a table and a back joined together by ribs which form a separate part.

The task of discovering that instrument, and of showing its gradual evolution into the modern violin, appears to us to have been accomplished in the most convincing manner by Miss Kathleen Schlesinger in her book "The Precursors of the Violin Family" (London, Wm. Reeves). In this work she shows that the violin proceeded from the Egyptian Kithara, while the chrotta, crwth, and other instruments of dual form, viz. a table fixed to a rounded back which is carved out of a solid block of wood, are descendants of the Egyptian lyre, and on p. 425 she gives the genealogical table appearing on next page, with her kind permission.

Pear-shaped instruments as the rebec and the gigue, although of dual construction like the chelys, with a vaulted back and flat soundboard, glued together without ribs, did not descend from the latter instrument, but from an ancient Persian instrument which developed into the Moorish rebab, the immediate precursor of the rebec, of which the gigue was but an improved species. It is evident therefore that they cannot be regarded as ancestors of the violin, although

The History of the Violin

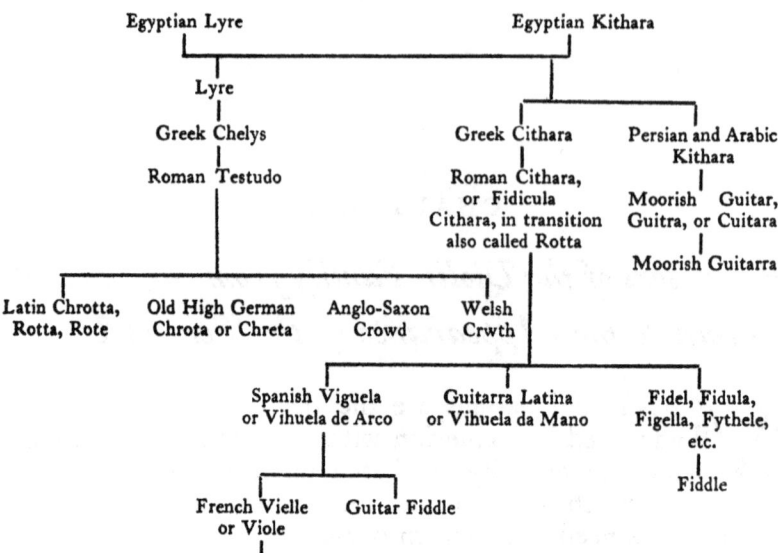

they played their part in its evolution, as we shall see later on.

From the above table we see that the Roman cithara (Fig. 1), was also called fidicula, which word was changed to fidula, fidel, etc., and eventually to fiddle in Anglo-Saxon and German countries; to viguela and vihuela in Spain; which became vielle and viole in France, and viola in Italy, the diminutive of viola being "violina," which was applied at first to the smaller viols such as the lyra da braccio, as may be seen from the title page of the rare chap-book "La violina con la sua risposta" by Giulio Grotto, Brescia, ca. 1550, on which a man is represented playing the lyra da braccio. The title page is reproduced in E. van der Straeten's "The Romance of the Fiddle" from the copy in possession of Mr. Edward Heron-Allen. The male gender of "la violina" is "il violino," and this was eventually applied to the violin proper.

FIG. 1.—Cithara.

Precursors of the Violin Family

We find moreover that the cithara in its transition was also called rotta, and that the chrotta, which was related to the crowd and the crwth, and, as well as these, descended from the Egyptian lyre, was likewise called rotta. Not unfrequently there exists, unfortunately, a good deal of confusion in the nomenclature of musical instruments in mediæval works, which proves very embarrassing to the student of musical history.

The various phases of the transition from the Roman cithara to the guitar fiddle of the Troubadours, the first application of the neck to the cithara, and the gradual modifications of the sound-body until it arrived at the guitar shape, have been fully explained by Miss Schlesinger in her above-named book, from illustrations contained in the 9th-century Utrecht Psalter. It is believed that these miniatures were copied by a Greek artist from Oriental sources of a much earlier date, probably about the 4th century A.D. They show figures of men carrying instruments of the cithara type in various stages of transformation. Some have rounded-off corners and a short neck, others have a long fretted neck, and approach the guitar form. Unfortunately the drawings of most of them are so small that it is impossible to see whether the strings were fixed to a tailpiece or to a bar glued to the table as on the lute and on the guitar; nor do they show any bridge or soundholes. That these, however, were known already to the Greeks and Romans, may be seen in an Etruscan lyre, from d'Harcanville's "Collection of Etruscan, Greek and Roman Antiquities," p. 109 (reproduced in Miss Schlesinger's "The Precursors" etc., p. 290), possessing all three features. All these instruments were played with a plectrum or by plucking the strings with the fingers.

As the history of the mediæval stringed instruments has been fully dealt with in "The Viols and their Revival" (E. v. d. Str., partly published in *The Strad*, Feb. 1909, etc.), this work will briefly indicate their place in the evolutionary chain of the violin family.

It has already been shown in the above genealogical table, that the first stage of transition from the Roman lyre (testudo = turtle) was the Rotta (Fig. 2), old High-German Hrôta, Hrôtta, or Chrotta, which means a toad, also turtle, thus clearly indicating its origin, as the chelys or lyre was originally

The History of the Violin

constructed from the shell of a turtle, the hollow being covered with a skin. The Berlin Museum für Völkerkunde contains a specimen of a rotta which was found in the tomb of an Allemanic warrior, 5th to 7th centuries, in the Black Forest, described and illustrated in the above-mentioned book. Apart from strings and pegs, it is in a perfect state of preservation. The six pegholes prove beyond doubt that it was a six-stringed instrument. It is of the dual construction of the lyre, the ribs and back being carved out of a solid plank of oak, which has become almost black and very hard with age, like the Irish bog-oak. The rotta underwent many modifications in

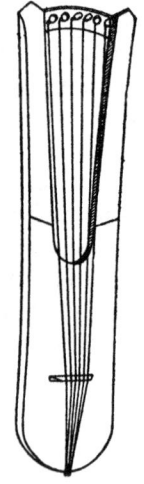

Fig. 2.—German Rotta: 5th and 7th Century.

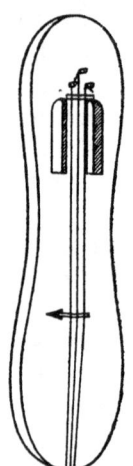

Fig. 3. — French Crouth (Rotta): 11th Century.

its outward form, and was a favourite instrument to which the bow was applied on the European Continent from the 11th century; in Ireland and England from about the 12th century. In the Celtic countries (Brittany and Ireland) the name was modified into "crot" or "cruit," in Old English it became "crûdh," middle English "crud," "crowde," "crowd," and in Cymry "crwth." The crwth was merely a chrotta to which a fingerboard had been added. In France it was called "crouth" (Fig. 3). On the Continent it disappeared entirely towards the end of the 14th century, but in Great Britain and Ireland it survived until much later times, and in Wales as the crwth (Fig. 4) even to the beginning of the 19th century. What has been said before shows that this rotta had no direct part in the evolution of the sound-body of the violin, and the crwth, instead of being its ancestor was the last member of a now extinct family.

On the other hand, it is in some chrottas, as those depicted in two Bibles transcribed and illustrated for Charles the Bald about the middle of the 9th century, that we find not only the application of the fingerboard, which was present already in the presumably earlier instruments of the Utrecht Psalter, but also three small soundholes on either side of the bridge, which are not to be met with in the latter pictures; neither has the above-mentioned original rotta in the Berlin Museum, nor even a French Crouth, depicted in a miniature of an 11th-century Codex from the Abbey of St. Martial de Limoges, any sound holes (Dr. G. Kinsky's "Heyer Catalogue," p. 377). We may therefore look upon those appearing in the above-mentioned Bibles (Schlesinger, "Precursors," etc., p. 337) as probably the first rottas, or chrottas, with soundholes.

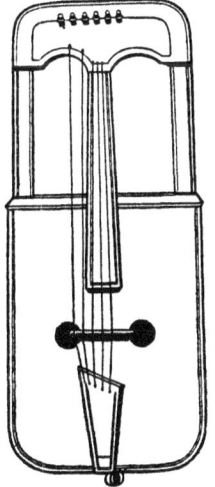

FIG. 4.—Welsh Crwth 18th Century.

Of the tripartite rotta not a single original instrument has come down to us, and as the name of cithara as well as rotta, chrotta, etc., was applied indiscriminately to both kinds, which in their outward appearance resembled each other, while the illustrations and even sculptural representations are by no means clear and exact, it is practically impossible to decide which of the two kinds is meant in any particular instance, except that in the Utrecht Psalter most if not all of the transition forms belong to the tripartite rottas, as they show almost step by step the various forms leading to the guitar fiddle, which was undoubtedly of the latter type.

M. Gerbert in his "De Cantu," etc., gives a drawing of a one-stringed instrument from a MS. formerly believed to date from the 9th century, but afterwards found to belong to the 13th century. It is evidently a pear-shaped instru-

The History of the Violin

ment, the back and neck of which were of one piece. It had a bridge, two semicircular soundholes by the side of the feet of this, a tailpiece and apparently also a fingerboard which ran on into the head. It was played with a bow and is called "Lyra" (Fig. 5) in this as well as in a 12th-century MS., the "Hortus deliciarum," by Herrad von Landsberg, which perished unfortunately in the destruction by fire of the Strassburg library in the Franco-Prussian War in 1870–71, while the original of the former MS. was lost in a fire at the Abbey of St. Blaise in the Black Forest. Representations of the lyra are met with in the sculptures of several French Norman churches of the 12th and 13th centuries. A notable example is that to be seen at the church of Moissac, in the South of France, where over the western door are bold sculptures of the three old men of the Apocalypse each holding a lyra, that of the middle figure having flame-shaped soundholes which we do not meet with again until a much later period, and which in the early 18th century became a characteristic feature of the Viol d'amour. The lyra disappeared about the end of the 13th century, except in Greece, where it still exists as a three-stringed instrument tuned: d', g', b', which according to Curt Sachs ("Reallexikon") is called the Cretan tuning. Both the lyra and the fidula are mentioned as early as A.D. 868, in Otfried of Weissenburg's "Liber Evangeliorum," but no illustrations are given.

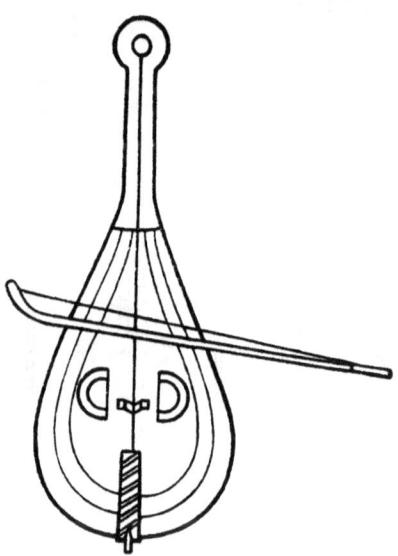

FIG. 5.—Lyra: 13th Century.

From the 13th century the rubeba and the rebec took the place of the lyre, from which apparently they originated. Of the rubeba we know very little, as we have no authentic pictorial or sculptural record of the instrument, unless we accept an illustration in Grillet's "Les Ancêtres" (i., p. 138)

Precursors of the Violin Family

as such, although it is mentioned frequently in the works of poets and prose writers from the 13th to the latter part of the 15th century. Sandys and Forster give quotations from Lydgate, Chaucer and others, while Grillet ("Les Ancêtres," etc.) quotes passages from the Roman de la rose, E. Deschamp, Molinet, Guilleaume Machaut, and passages from the "Lettres de Remission" (1391, 1395, 1458), the latter showing that it was chiefly used for dance music. Hieronymus of Moravia (13th century) gives the tuning as c, g. Dr. G. Kinsky (Heyer Catalogue) thinks that it was a larger instrument than the rebec, and that the name of the latter is derived from the Italian diminutive of Rubeba, viz. Rubecchino, Rebecchino, shortened into rebec.

The Rebec was of greater importance than the rubeba, as it continued in use from the 8th or 9th century to the beginning of the 19th century, and in Russia it is still popular in a variety called the gudock (pron. goodock). Originally, there existed two kinds of rebecs, one descending from the above-mentioned mediæval lyra, whose shape it retained in all essential parts, the other from the Moorish "rabé" or "rebab." Both are still mentioned by Jan Ruiz, arch-priest of Hita in the 14th century, but about this time a fusion of the two types took place which resulted in the standard form

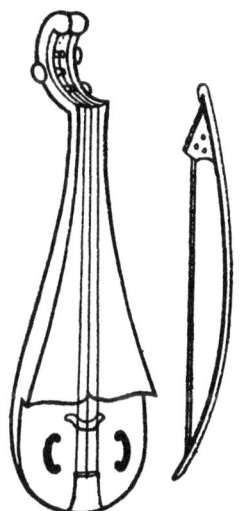

FIG. 6.—Rebec: 16th Century, from Kastner's "Danses des Morts" (1852).

of the rebec. It then became the pear-shaped instrument seen in Fig. 6 with a fingerboard, widening out into the shape of the table, over which it was raised sufficiently to allow the bow to touch each of the three strings separately. In this form it became a favourite instrument, chiefly used for dance music, but never by the troubadours or minstrels of a higher order. Its tone was harsh and dry, and on the Continent it was early relegated to fairs and taverns, although we find John Severnake (Severnac) as a rebec player at the English Court from 1518 until after 1553, while in 1538 we find apart from him also Thomas Evans as a second rebec player, who however is dispensed with again from the time of Edward VI. In the list of Elizabeth's Court musicians we find one rebec player mentioned in 1588, but without the name, but no rebec player appears in the lists from that time onward, when probably the violin took the place of the rebec for dances at the Court. At the French Court likewise, one rebec is to be found among the Court musicians of the 15th and 16th centuries, at least as late as 1559, when Jehan Cavalier filled that post, vide "Dictionnaire Critique de Biographie et d'Histoire," Paris, 1867. From the 17th century it became an instrument of the street musicians, as may be seen from an order of the governor of Paris of the year 1628, according to which the use of all kinds of violins, except the rebec, was forbidden in cabarets and "mauvais lieux," and Guignon, king of the minstrels, in a decree given in Paris, 1741, forbade the use of a four-stringed violin to all professional musicians who were not members of the guild.

The rebec already exhibited several features which were afterwards adapted to the violin. It had no frets, and in two 14th-century four-stringed rebecs from the "Liber Regalis," of Westminster Abbey (Schlesinger, "Precursors," etc., p. 390), we find already a primitive sort of scroll. The tuning was either

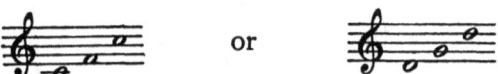

This tuning, however, must be taken as relative, as the rule was to pull up the first string as high as it would bear without breaking and then tune the two others from it in accordance with the given intervals.

In Germany we find from the latter part of the 15th century a kind of rebec, or rather gigue, known as the "Polnische kleine Geigen" (Polish small fiddles), which were constructed in three different sizes, tuned according to Martin Agricola ("Musica deudsch," Wittenberg, 1528 and 1545) and Hans Gerle ("Musica teusch," etc., Nürnberg, 1532):

Treble   Alto and Tenor   Bass

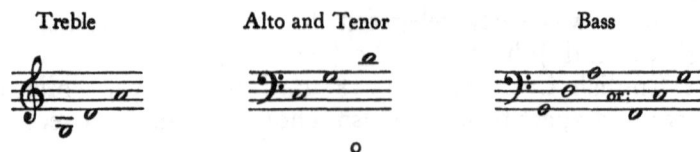

Precursors of the Violin Family

They were merely an improved form of the older rebec with the adaptation of a few features of the already greatly advanced viols. In Italy they were known as "Violette da arco senza tasti" (small viols with a bow, without frets), described by Giovan Maria Lanfranco ("Scintille di Musica," Brescia, 1533), and by Silvestro Ganassi ("Lettione seconda," Venice, 1543). The bass of the Italian instruments had, however, four strings and they were of more elegant proportions in their outline than the "kleine Geigen." These instruments disappeared as early as the middle of the 16th century to make room for the more perfect viols. The word "Geige" is derived from the old Nether-German "Geiga" = to go backward and forward, and the middle high-German "Gîgen" = to tremble, to vibrate; in Italian it became "giga" (Fig. 7), and in French "gigue," which words were used more particularly to designate a kind of rebec of more slender and elegant shape, which in Italy was mounted with four strings, and from this, and the fact that it is often represented in Italian paintings of the late 15th and early 16th centuries as a very artistic instrument, often richly decorated with carved head, finely cut rosettes, etc., it appears safe to assume that it held an important position among the musical instruments of its time.

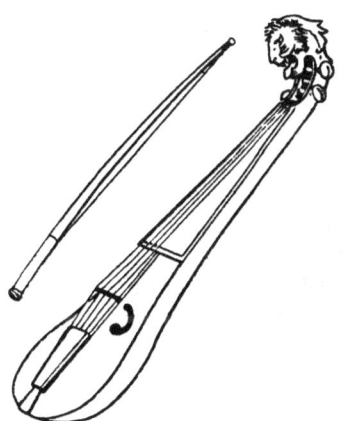

FIG. 7.—Italian Giga: 15th Century.

In all other European countries the gigue was a three-stringed instrument. It survived in a miniature form to the end of the 18th century as the "kit" or dancing master's fiddle; French "pochette," German "Taschengeige," which latter names it received because dancing masters, who chiefly used the instrument, could carry it in the coat pocket.

The German word Geige, which in the 16th and 17th centuries was applied indiscriminately to all instruments played with a bow, while from the 18th century onward it was only used for the violin, was originally the name of the rebec, and its first use in that sense occurs in works of the 12th century. Miss Schlesinger ("Precursors," etc., p. 415) quotes an instance from "Judith," a poem of that time in which "gîgen" (gigues) are mentioned in conjunction with "vigelen" (viols), rottas, liras, and harps. These were among the instruments most frequently mentioned in the romances and other works of the 12th to the 14th centuries, and we find them in the "Parcival" of Wolfram von Eschenbach, "Tristan," by Gottfried von Strassburg, the "Prise d'Alexandrie," by Guillaume de Machault, Dante's "Divina Commedia," etc., etc. In view of this fact we may safely relegate the derivation of the word gigue from the French "gigot" = a leg of mutton, on account of their supposed similarity of form, which is still generally to be met with, into the realm of fiction, for according to Godefroy's dictionary of the old French language the word gigot designated: (1) a small copper coin of the value of about a farthing which was minted at Tournay in Flanders in the 14th century; (2) a kind of nail or peg, called "clou de gigot" used in the 16th century. Apparently not until the 17th century was the word applied to the leg of mutton, according to the French dictionary by Littré, who says that it was first used in that sense by Madame de Maintenon, and later still by Marmontel. As the words "gîge," "giga," "gigue" were used for the instrument as early as the 12th century, it will be seen that the derivation given above is no doubt the correct one. As the gigue was chiefly used, like the rebec, for dance music, it is more than probable that the dance form known as jig, French "gigue," Italian "giga," received its name from the instrument.

CHAPTER 2

The Fiddle, Fidula or Vielle, and the Guitar-Fiddle

AFTER having discussed the pear-shaped instruments of dual construction, which descended from the lyre, we return now to the instruments of a triple form which descended from the Kithara, as the real ancestors of the violin.

We have mentioned above Miss Schlesinger's important discovery of the various stages in the evolution of the fiddle from the Kithara as illustrated in the Utrecht-, and other ancient Psalters. She presumes, with apparently very good reason, these illustrations to be copies from earlier MSS. by Eastern scribes, whose workmanship they resemble very closely in style, and that probably they represent instruments used during the early centuries of our era in Asiatic Greece and Northern Egypt, before the destruction of Alexandria by the Arabs in A.D. 638. We have seen that Otfried von Weissenburg mentions both fidula and lyra as early as in A.D. 868 (p. 6), and Egidius Parisiensis, in his Carolinus, states that the deeds of Charlemagne were sung in the streets to the sounds of the fiddle (vielle) (Grillet, i, 40). There is every reason to suppose that the instrument found its way into Germany and France through the Byzantine Empire. Grillet discovered in the portal of the church of Anzy-le-Duc (Saône et Loire) a sculpture of the early 11th century (ca. 1000 to 1025) in which the three old men of the Apocalypse are represented each holding a five-stringed vielle, resting with the lower end on the legs. Unfortunately the right arms of two of the figures are missing, and the bow is missing from the hand of the third, who was represented in the act of playing. This is the earliest representation we have so far of the fiddle.

Curt Sachs ("Real-Lexikon") considers these instruments to be lyras, and thinks it unsafe to form a judgment of the form of the ribs and backs from such primitive sculptures, while he declares the number of strings to be only a secondary criterion. Their front view certainly presents a striking likeness to the lyra, but they are of distinctly larger proportions and have longer necks, and in this the sculptures from Anzy-le-Duc tally exactly with others from Saint-Georges de Boscherville and Moissac, both of the 12th century, as advanced by Grillet. In the latter, although it has ornamental sound-holes similar to those of the middle one of the three lyras from the church of Moissac (p. 6), yet it shows the flat, separate ribs most distinctly; it is moreover in an excellent state of preservation, and the sculptor has evidently paid attention to every detail, as even the attachment of the tailpiece to the lower part of the ribs is clearly indicated. It shows moreover that one of the five strings, on the right side, is a bourdon (a drone running alongside of the fingerboard), of which mention is made by Hieronymus de Moravia, who moreover tells us that the vielle (fiddle) *must* have five strings which by different players are tuned in three different ways:

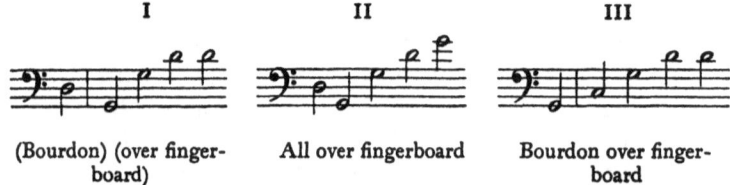

(Bourdon) (over fingerboard)   All over fingerboard   Bourdon over fingerboard

The vielle or fiddle existed in the 12th century in at least two different sizes, as is clearly shown in two figures, one from the cathedral of Chartres, the other from the Abbey of Saint-Denis. Grillet (Ib., pp. 46 and 47) gives the full figures, Schlesinger ("Precursors," etc., pp. 443, fig. 170, and 473, fig. 193) gives only part of the sculptures, showing however the details of the instruments more clearly. The vielle of the Chartres figure, with a large round soundhole in the centre of the table, no bridge, and reminiscent, in the outline of the table, of the lyra. It is held against the left collar-bone, while the one from Saint-Denis is of evidently larger size resting on the left shoulder. This vielle has elongated sound-

Fiddle, Fidula or Vielle, and Guitar-Fiddle

holes in the upper part of the table, which has an elaborately decorated edging, a bridge, and a tailpiece with ornamental purfling, showing the artistic care bestowed on some of these instruments. In Schlesinger's drawing the outer string on the right side is a little apart from the other four strings, which seems to point it out as the bourdon.

There has been much discussion as to the introduction of corner blocks. Fétis credited German makers with their first use, but if we but look at the instruments from the Utrecht Psalter which Schlesinger calls citharas in the third stage of transition, it becomes evident that they could not possibly be made without corner blocks which therefore must have been known already in the 4th century when these instruments were used in the Orient.

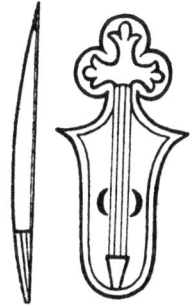

FIG. 8.—13th-century Fiddle with Bow.

FIG. 9.—13th-century Guitar-Fiddle.

There is in a window of Bourges Cathedral the representative of a 13th-century fiddle with four strings (Fig. 8), which appears carefully drawn to nature, except for the neck, which is impossibly short, and the shape of the head, which is conventionalized for decorative purposes. It has slight incurvations of the sides and strongly projecting corners at the upper end of the body, and but for the difference in the head and the neck it is almost identical with the cithara in third transition as shown in the miniatures from the Utrecht Psalter, and this resemblance is still more pronounced in a four-stringed guitar-fiddle (Fig. 9) of the end of the 13th century with a well-defined fingerboard and a disc-shaped head from Add. MS. 16975 in the British Museum. Both appear also in Schlesinger (Ib., pp. 473 and 474). The time of the Renaissance, which was so fertile in the creation of new forms, brought to life a great number of variations in the shape of the oval vielle or fiddle during the 13th and 14th centuries, and even added one the body of which is absolutely circular. But as these have no part in the evolution of the violin, we must refer those who wish further to acquaint themselves therewith to E. van der Straeten's "The Viols," etc., as well as the frequently quoted works by Schlesinger, Grillet, and Kinsky.

The form of the fiddle which concerns us more closely is that which resembles the model of the ancient Egyptian guitar, and which Miss Schlesinger therefore very appropriately calls the guitar-fiddle, and it was this latter instrument which we find pre-eminently in the hands of the Troubadours and the Minnesingers. There exists still a great deal of confusion in the classification of mediæval stringed instruments, as their names were not infrequently used indiscriminately by the ancient writers, and still more rarely do we meet with the description of an instrument accompanied by an illustration, or an illustration of an instrument giving its name, as in the MS. of Herrad von Landsberg mentioned on p. 6. The result is that historians often differ in their classification; but if we accept the guitar-shaped body constructed of a table, ribs, back, and a neck, in separate parts as criteria, though the table may sometimes be prolonged into a facing of the neck, serving as a fingerboard, we shall not be in doubt as to whether an instrument is a guitar-fiddle or not. Sometimes of course it may be difficult to decide from a sculpture or illustration whether the ribs really *are* separate, or carved together with the back from one block. There are moreover sometimes mixed forms which present great difficulties for classification, but this is a question which cannot be dealt with here. More will be found in E. van der Straeten's "The Viols." In any case we cannot follow Grillet's reasoning when he describes as "rotas" instruments which look like large guitar-fiddles, but have no resemblance to the rota (or rotta) as drawn in ancient miniatures. Miss Schlesinger evidently concurs in this view at least in the cases of the 13th-century fiddle from Saint-Georges de Boscherville and the 13th-century four-stringed instrument with deep and elongated incurvations, in the hands of a crowned figure from a painted window in Troyes Cathedral which she describes as a fiddle.

Fiddle, Fidula or Vielle, and Guitar-Fiddle

With regard to the incurvations of the sound-body, it is evident from the above-mentioned Egyptian guitar (1100 to 1200 B.C.) that they were in the first instance not made to facilitate the use of the bow, but probably from æsthetic reasons, though they were afterwards deepened for the former purpose.

The tuning for the four-stringed guitar-fiddle is given in an anonymous 14th-century MS. treatise on stringed instruments in the library of Gand (Belgium) as:

The instrument ascribed to Albinus to which this tuning is applied has very deep incurvations and very short lower bouts in which the c-chaped soundholes are set right and left of the tailpiece (Illustration and particulars, see E. v. d. Str., "The Viols"). The deep incurvations are also noticeable in a 12th-century fiddle of far better proportions with the c-shaped soundholes between the middle bouts, as in modern instruments; the bridge however is in the lower bouts.

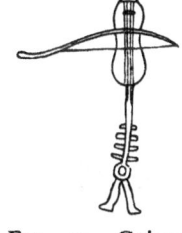

FIG. 10.—Guitar-Fiddle: 11th Century.

There is apparently no earlier representation of a guitar-fiddle than that (Fig. 10) which Miss Schlesinger discovered (Ib., p. 448) in a Greek Psalter written and illuminated by the arch-priest Theodorus of Caesarea, A.D. 1066, a fact which makes it probable that the instrument found its way into Western Europe through the Byzantine Empire, although it may have been likewise introduced by the Moors through Spain. It has a long neck with four pegs going laterally right through the neck. The strings are fixed to a tailpiece and run over a straight bridge, but there is no indication of soundholes, which is evidently an omission on the part of the artist, as the thin soundboard would otherwise not be able to withstand the pressure of the strings. The guitar-fiddle soon took the form of the instruments which we find in the sculptures and miniatures of all European countries, from the 11th century onward. These forms have been fully illustrated in the above-named works and the reproduction of two representative Minnesinger fiddles (Figs. 11 and 12) in a picture of "Reinmar der Videller" from the Manessische Sammlung in the National Library, Paris, will serve our present purpose. Note the fiddle on Reinmar's helmet, which appears also on his shield.

The earliest instrumental music, contained in a MS. of

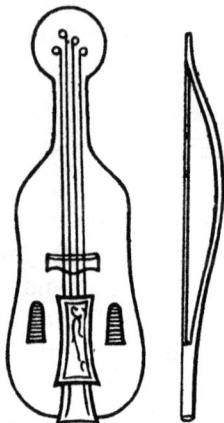
FIG. 11.—Reinmar's Fiddle with Bow: 13th Century.

FIG. 12.—Fiddle from Reinmar's helmet: 13th Century.

ca. 1200 (H. J. Moser, "Geschichte des Violinspiels"), is for the Minnesinger or Troubadour fiddle.

The guitar-fiddle continued with only minor modifications, in the form of additional soundholes in the shape of rosettes, variations in the number of strings from two to six, although four remained the general rule, and occasional modifications in its outline and the shape of the head, until the middle of the 15th century.

CHAPTER 3

Introduction of the Bow

MANY theories have been advanced with regard to the origin of the bow, none of which bear scientific investigation, and therefore need not concern us in this place. The only facts which appear fairly certain are that it originated in India, whence it was taken to Persia. When the Arabs conquered that country in the 6th century of our era they proved very apt pupils of its highly civilized people, from whom they adopted among their more perfect instruments, also the rebab and the bow, and both of these, together with the lute, and the Moorish guitar they brought with them into Spain early in the 8th century when they defeated the Goths, and Roderick their last King was slain. Charlemagne, who fought the Moors in many battles towards the end of that century, in one of which his nephew the famous Knight Roland was killed in an ambush at Ronzeval in 778, was the most enlightened ruler of his time, ready to garner the fruits of the superior knowledge and civilization of his enemies, and use them for the benefit of the people of his vast empire, which extended practically over the whole of Europe. As this great Emperor was interested in spreading the knowledge of music as well as that of all other arts, and for that purpose founded schools of music at Metz, St. Gall, and Soissons, it appears fairly certain that at that period the western world became acquainted also with the Moorish lute, and the rebab which was played with a bow. It is significant, at any rate, as Miss Schlesinger ("Precursors," etc., p. 280) points out, that one of the earliest illustrations of an instrument played with a bow is to be found in a translation of the Psalms by Labeo Notker, a monk of St. Gall, who died in 1022. The MS., preserved in the library of that monastery, contains an illustration in pen and ink of King David playing a seven-stringed lyre with a plectrum. He is surrounded by four musicians playing a harp, a cithara, a dulcimer, and a rebec. The latter is played with a bow which has a handle (Ib., p. 281, fig. 63, reproduction of the whole picture in Plate IV, facing p. 371). There is also a bow in the hand of King David in an ivory plaque from the binding of the Psalter of Lothair, which was presented by Charles le Débonnaire to the monastery of St. Hubert in the Ardennes in 825. The plaque (Schlesinger, "Precursors," etc., Plate I) is, however, of a later time, probably the 11th century, and the bow already of the much advanced *crémaillère* type. Both the lyra and the fidula mentioned in Otfried von Weissenburg's "Liber Evangeliorum," 868, were no doubt played with a bow, although there is of course no record of one in that place, where they are spoken of as instruments used in praise of God.

The introduction of the bow into Europe may have been

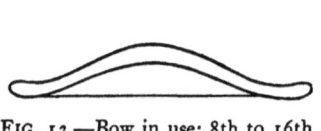

Fig. 13.—Bow in use: 8th to 16th Centuries.

Fig. 14.—Crwth Bow: 9th Century.

effected also from Asia Minor through the Byzantine Empire, independently from that of the Moors via Spain. The intercourse between Constantinople and Rome through Lombardy and the neighbouring countries was constantly maintained throughout the Middle Ages, and nothing is more likely than that the musical instruments of the Persians and Arabs were brought over by the Greeks of Asia Minor. There is at all events in the National Museum (Palazzo del Podesta) in Florence an ivory jewel-box of Byzantine workmanship of the 10th century which in its decorations exhibits a rebab and a bow. A representation of a bow, supposed to be from an illustration of the 8th century, given in Herbé's "Costumes Français," cannot be regarded as authentic, as Herbé is by no means reliable.

The first bows were not much more than the weapon from which they derived their name, and for a long time they remained in a more or less primitive condition (Figs. 13, 14,

Introduction of the Bow

15). In the 12th century, however, we find them already provided with a handle and sometimes with a knob at the point into which the hair was fixed (Fig. 16). A 13th-century bow (Fig. 17) from the Musician's House in Reims shows an approach, especially in the shape of the head, to the form of the modern bow. This bow is given in Schlesinger, "Precursors," etc., p. 283, fig. 71, in which,

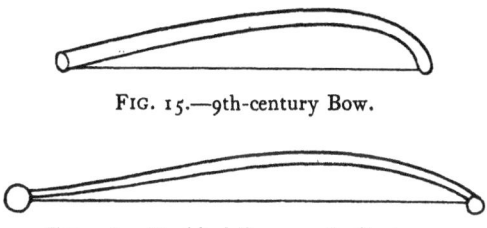

FIG. 15.—9th-century Bow.

FIG. 16.—Knobbed Bow: 12th Century.

too, on p. 474, fig. 197, the whole figure appears. Such solitary phenomena, which are to be met with also in the form and construction of the instruments themselves, are children born before their time, and are not followed up until at a much later period. On the other hand, we find here and there a return to more primitive forms when the majority had already advanced a step in the evolutionary

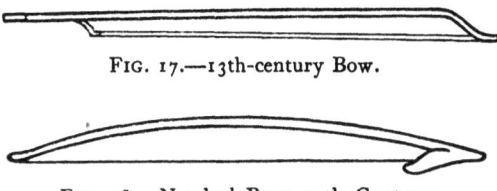

FIG. 17.—13th-century Bow.

FIG. 18.—Notched Bow: 14th Century.

chain. No real progress in the construction of the bow is noticeable during the 14th century, in spite of endless variations in minor detail, except perhaps the bow with notches in the end part of the stick (Fig. 18), foreshadowing of the *crémaillère* in a bow given in Schlesinger's "Precursors," etc., p. 283, fig. 72, taken from a 14th-century book on astronomy (Sloane MS. 3,983) of the British Museum. This device appears in a more perfected form in a 15th-century bow (Ib., p. 283, fig. 73), which clearly shows the strip of metal with little cogs (the *crémaillère*) (Fig. 19) on the top of the bow, near the end, by which, through the medium of a wire loop, the hair could be tightened. Fig. 20 shows the *crémaillère* of a late 17th-century bow. This device was used until the end-screw was introduced. When the latter took place is

FIG. 19.—Bow with *Crémaillère*: 15th Century.

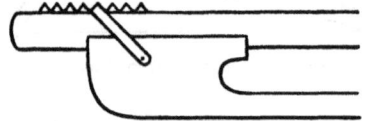

FIG. 20.—Detail showing 17th-century *Crémaillère*.

uncertain. Ottomar Luscinius' (Nachtigall) "Musurgia" (Strasburg, 1536), gives an illustration of a German gigue, with a bow which appears to have a kind of nut, and a round knob at the end of the stick which seems to indicate that it was at the end of a screw which moved the nut backwards and forwards. The illustration, which is here reproduced from the above-mentioned "Musurgia" of 1536, certainly seems to indicate this arrangement, although that would be very early for so elaborate a device, and there is no other instance known to us before we come to the viol da gamba bows in Mersenne's "Harmonie Universelle" (1634), which show it unmistakably. It is an interesting point in the history of the evolution of the bow.

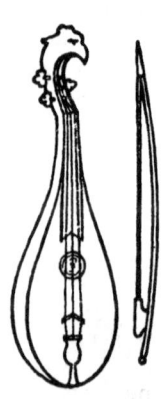

FIG. 21.—Gigue with Bow: 16th Century.

In a head ornament on p. 127 of "Les Ancêtres," etc., Grillet gives a picture of 15th-century musicians from a MS. in the Paris National Library. The first of these plays on a large fiddle with a bow which recalls the shape of that given in Fig. 17, and a figure from a stained-glass window at the Grey friars of the rue de Lourcine, Paris (Ib., p. 104), of the same period, plays a fiddle with a bow, the head of which is not unlike that of a 19th-century double-bass bow, while the attachment of the hair at the lower end

Introduction of the Bow

seems to be as in Fig. 19. Similar forms continue with occasional lapses into atavism until we come to the beginning of the 17th century, when a rapid advance shows itself.

In some bows about this period we meet with a curious device. The hair, being fixed in the bow-stick at the lower end as well as at the point, was tightened by placing a nut between the hair and the stick, which after being pressed into a slot cut in the stick, was held in place by the pressure of the hair. This is best explained by Fig. 22.

In a picture by Jan Breughel, "Hearing," ca. 1620, part of which appears as frontispiece to vol. ii of the Wm. Heyer museum catalogue by Dr. G. Kinsky, we see some viols with their bows which are of an elegant shape, with but slight outward curvature of the stick.

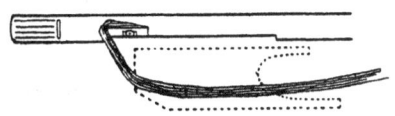

FIG. 22.—Detail of early Bow showing detached Nut.

One of these shows a light tip at the end which seems to indicate an end-screw.

Michael Prætorius in his "Theatrum Instrumentorum," 1620, gives an exact replica of Luscinius' gigue which he calls "Kleine Posche" (small pochette, or kit). The bow in this case shows no indication of the end-screw seen in Fig. 21. His viol da gamba bows, however, have little knobs at the end which seem to point to its presence. The bows themselves are of the same shape as those in Breughel's picture.

In order to obtain a clear idea of the evolution of the bow from ca. 1600 to modern times, we give the following illustrations which serve to show its general progress, without however taking notice of minor variations, or occasional atavistic forms.

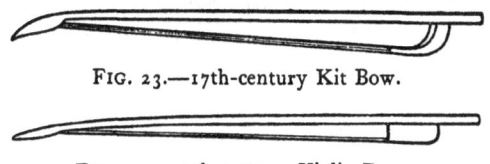

FIG. 23.—17th-century Kit Bow.

FIG. 24.—17th-century Violin Bow.

After having mentioned the bows in Prætorius we begin with two bows from Mersenne's "Harmonie Universelle' (1634), which represent, however, the first decades of the century (Figs. 23 and 24).

The History of the Violin

It has often been asserted that Corelli was instrumental in improving the shape of the bow; this appears, however, very doubtful if we accept as Corelli's the shape of the bow given by Fétis (Stradivari) as authentic. Bows of a far more advanced type, especially with regard to the shape of the head, and even showing the *cambre*, having existed already in the late 17th century. This also disposes of the legend that it was Tartini who first introduced the latter feature. As we know that he was a keen student of the technical as well as the scientific side of his art, it is quite possible that he may have conceived some improvement of the bow, of which we possess no authentic record, and this may have led to the above-mentioned tradition (see Plate, Tartini's bow). Geminiani in his "The Art of Playing on the Violin" (London, 1740), is represented playing the violin with an elegant bow of normal length, with a modern-looking hatchet and a nut with end-screw, but the stick appears to have no *cambre*.

In Leopold Mozart's famous tutor, which appeared at Augsburg in 1756, there are two portraits of the author playing the violin[1]; in both of these he is using bows of a much more primitive type, resembling those of the late 17th century; they do not even appear to have been provided with an end-screw, unless the engraver omitted to indicate it.

The bow was brought to its highest perfection by François Tourte, born in Paris 1747, and died there 1835, who may be justly looked upon as the Stradivari of the bow, for he gave it the greatest elasticity, combined with perfect balance, appropriate weight, elegance of form, and the addition of the slide and ferrule. Another important innovation of his was the adaptation of Pernambuco- or Brazil-wood for all bow-sticks, which henceforward superseded the use of all other woods. It has been stated that Viotti suggested to him the idea of the slide and the ferrule, which is so essential to obtain a straight and even surface of the hair; but important inventions lie in the universal consciousness when their time has come, and thus it often has happened that individuals in different countries, capable of contacting that consciousness, brought the same ideas into manifestation without the slightest knowledge of one another. So it happened that John Dodd,

[1] These as well as Geminiani's above-mentioned portrait appear in E. van der Straeten's "The Romance of the Fiddle."

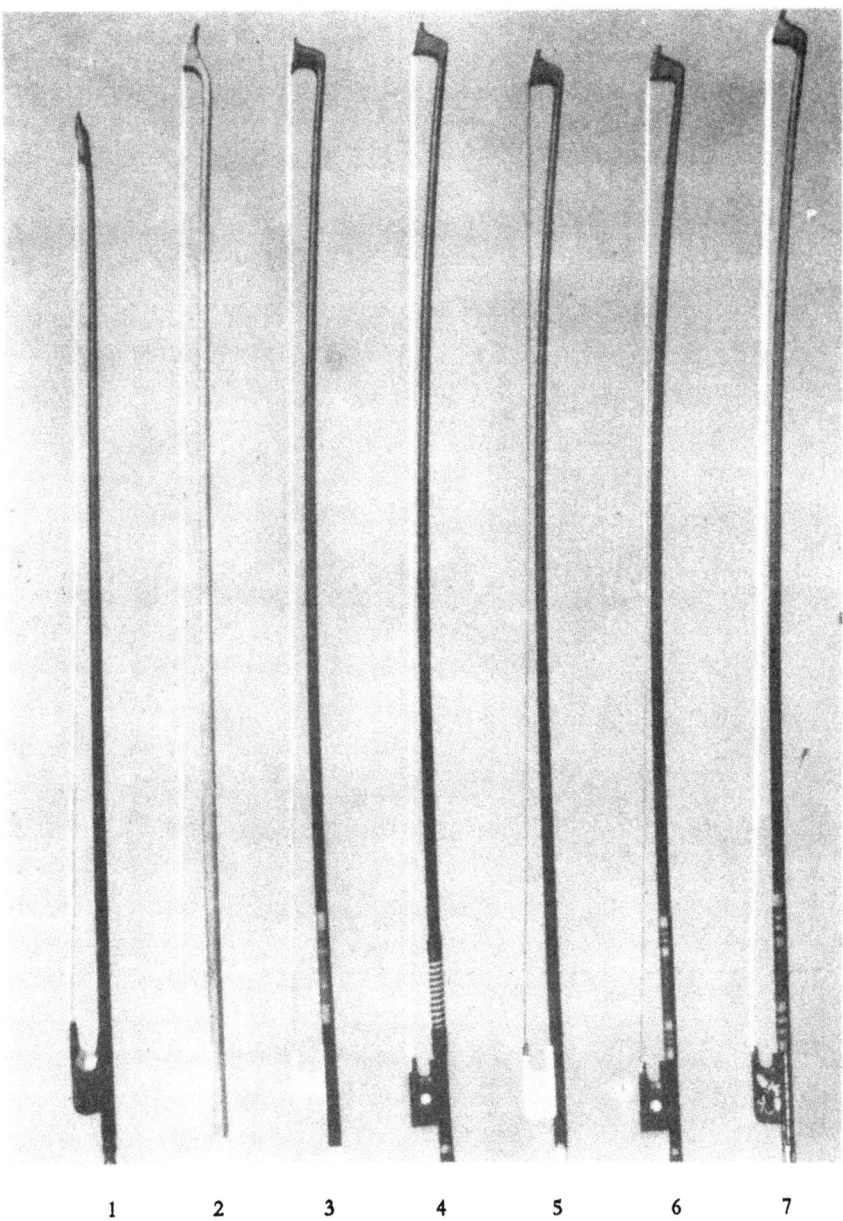

FAMOUS BOWS

The first bow is an early English specimen dating from 1694; the second, also an English bow, bears the name of Thos. Smith of Piccadilly, who made many instruments (mid. 18th century); the third is by Tourte ainé, and is one of his earliest experiments; the fourth, an example after perfection by Tourte le jeune; the fifth is by John Dodd; the sixth by Panormo; and the seventh is an early specimen of German work dating from the beginning of the XIX century: it is interesting because, though modern in form, it is adorned with ornamentation one associates with the previous century.

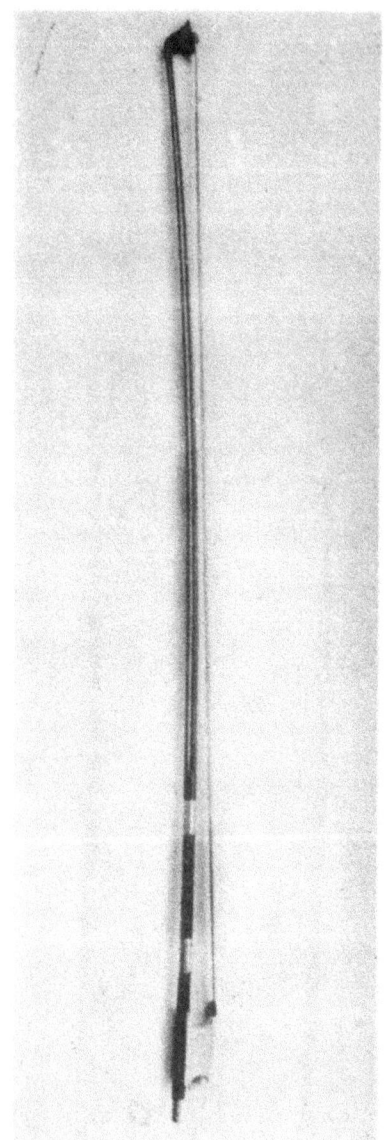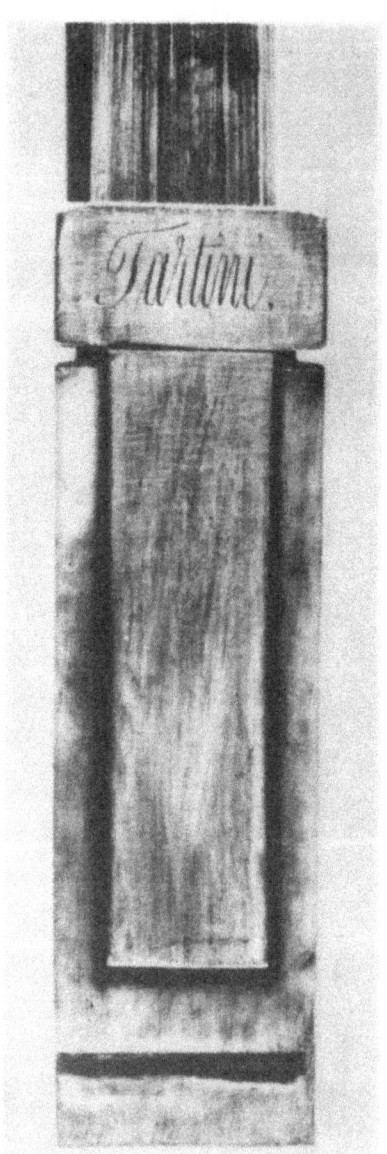

Bow by the elder Tourte, said to have been used by, and belonged to, Gius. Tartini, by kind permission of the owner, W. Howard-Head, Esq.

Introduction of the Bow

born 1752 at Sheffield, who died at Richmond, Surrey, in 1839, who is sometimes called the English Tourte, conceived the same idea of the slide and ferrule as the latter, yet with the strained relations between England and France, which existed at that time, the consequently restricted intercourse between the two countries, and the violent prejudice against all things French, especially in a man who, apart from his genius as a bowmaker, was quite uneducated, precludes the probability of his knowledge of Tourte's invention until many years after he had applied the same device to his own bows. Another curious coincidence in the lives of these two artists is that both were engaged in different trades before taking up bow-making. Tourte was for eight years a clockmaker, and Dodd, in his early years, was a gun-lock fitter, and afterwards a money-scale maker before he started bow-making.

Although Dodd produced bows which are still very highly valued, he was surpassed by Tourte in several particulars, especially in the inimitable grace of the outline.

In the earliest bows strands of silk were used instead of horsehair. Mersenne mentions that one might use it for that purpose, but horsehair was used already at an early time, and in Hugo von Trimberg's "Renner," mid-13th century, a man plays on a fiddle "with the hair of a horse's tail."

While Mersenne tells us that 80 to 100 hairs were used for hairing a bow, nowadays it requires from 150 to 200.

The nut of 17th-century bows was mostly of boxwood, but ivory was also used in special cases in the 17th and 18th centuries. In the latter century ebony was more generally employed for the nut, as it is still in our time.

We have only given those of the 19th-century makers who show any marked individual features in their workmanship, although many others have produced bows of great excellence, and a list of most of these is in H. Saint-George's "The Bow, its History, Manufacture and Use." Mr. Alfred E. Hill has kindly supplied the photograph (*see* Plate), of a representative selection from their unique collection of bows, showing their evolution from late in the 17th to the 20th century. Although among the leading bow-makers of the present time they have too modestly refrained from adding a specimen of their own make.

CHAPTER 4

The Viols

AN exceptionally interesting instrument is an Italian fiddle of ca. 1500 in the Museum of Ancient Musical Instruments in Vienna. It (Fig. 25) formed part of a set of five "geigen" (fiddles), 1 bass, 2 tenors and 2 trebles, which belonged to Archduke Karl of Steiermark, who gave this tenor to the Archduke Ferdinand before 1596, according to an entry in the inventory at Graz of that date.

FIG. 25.—Italian Fidel: c. 1500.

The fiddle or viol has the circular lower bouts, while the somewhat elongated upper bouts show an elliptical form. The middle bouts, corners and soundholes are those of the perfect viol. The head is surmounted by a heavy, clumsy scroll strongly resembling that of the treble gamba (see fig. 32, p. 42) by Francesco Linarol, whose work it recalls. The table shows the, for that time not usual, feature of neatly purfled edges. The ribs are concave (grooved) like those of the lyra. Whether the pegbox itself has undergone any alteration or not we cannot say, as we have only seen the beautiful heliogravure in Julius Schlösser's sumptuous catalogue, which, though giving all the markings of the wood, does not show enough of the pegbox to judge of any possible modification in more recent times. It is therefore impossible to say if the present number of four strings is the original number, although this appears very probable, though the tailpiece, fingerboard and bridge are modern. It is in all probability the oldest and most

The Viols

interesting instrument of its kind which is still in existence.

From about the middle of the 15th century the older viol form began to evolve from the guitar-fiddle, and in Bartolomeo Ramis de Pareia's "De Musica Tractatus" (Bologna, 1482), we find already a perfect instrument of this kind (Fig. 26), which is moreover remarkable in that it gives *the first representation of a perfect scroll*, a feature which was afterwards, except in Italy, almost exclusively reserved for the mem-

FIG. 26.—Pareia's Viol: 1482.
Note holes and pegs for six strings.

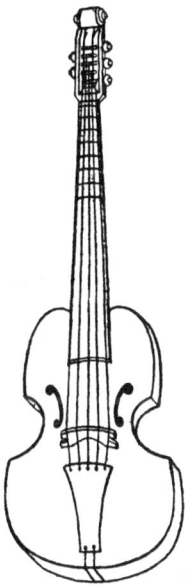

FIG. 27.—Viol of 1542.

bers of the violin family. It has also the sharp corners of the deepened middle bouts, and six strings, whereas the viols in the first edition of Ganassi dal Fontego's "Regola Rubertina" (1542), have only five strings; they approach, however, more closely the shape of the perfect viol, from which they differ only by the incurvation of the upper bouts at the neck (Fig. 27).

The first appearance of the perfect ff's is probably in a treble viol da gamba (Fig. 32, p. 42) by Francesco Linarol, Venice, ca. 1540, therefore a few years older than the Regola Rubertina. It is a unique specimen of this master, no other instrument of his being known, and it is moreover in all probability the oldest real viol da gamba still in existence. Moreover it is, apart from some modern repairs, entirely in its original condition, of carefully chosen wood, finest workmanship, and covered with a beautiful reddish-yellow varnish. Apart from the fact that the *ff*'s are placed somewhat low, which makes the upper bouts appear rather long although the deepest part is exactly in the middle of the sound-body, not reckoning the slope of the shoulders, we have here the earliest specimen of a perfect viol. The guitar-like incurvations, in place of the middle bouts with sharp corners, are an heritage from the guitar-fiddles, which appears also in an interesting viol da gamba by Hans Vohar, owned by Mr. Arnold Dolmetsch, probably ca. 1550, and in later instruments, so for instance in the bass and alto of a set of three gambas, of ca. 1600, by Antonio Ciciliano, another Venice maker. The head of Linarolo's gamba is a scroll without a centre rib, like that of the above-mentioned fiddle, but more elegant. The instrument has the orthodox number of six strings tuned

and the neck is fretted with seven frets.

The dimensions are: Total length, 86 cm.; length of body, 48 cm.; width of upper bouts, 22·5 cm., lower bouts, 26·5 cm.; height of ribs, 8·5 cm.

The bass instrument of these older viols was tuned, according to Mersenne,

and the treble naturally an octave higher, thus recalling the tuning of Albinus' fiddle (*see* p. 15). Prætorius ("Organographia") gives the tuning for the lowest string as F.

About the middle of the 15th century, the perfect viol (Fig. 28) came into existence; it was constructed in four sizes, tuned as follows:

Bass   Tenor and Alto   Treble

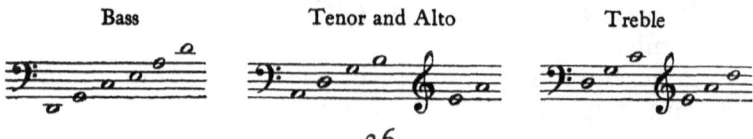

The Viols

The tenor and alto were sometimes tuned one note lower, viz. G, c, f, a, d', g', and the French tuned their alto (Haute contre) only one note lower than the treble (dessus), viz. c, f, b flat, d', g', c''.

It must be clearly understood that the viols were not the parents of the violin family, but they were cousins who came into existence about the same time, both being descendants of the guitar-fiddle.

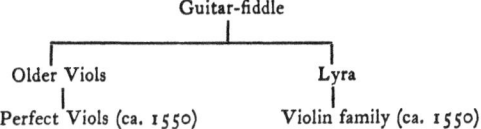

The alto and treble viols were originally arm-viols (held against the collar-bone, like the guitar-fiddle), but being rather weak in tone, they had been superseded towards the end of the 16th century by the knee-viols (viols da gamba), which were deeper in the ribs. These too were in the course of the 17th century superseded by the violin and the viola. In France, however, the "*Pardessus de Viole*," a smaller form of the treble viol, about the size of an ordinary violin, remained in use to the end of the 18th century. It had only five strings, tuned like the first five strings of the treble viol, the sixth or d string being omitted. L'Abbé Fils, in his "Principes de Violon" (Paris, 1772–81), states that "this work may also be used for the study of the Pardessus de Viole." Louis Guersan (Paris, ca. 1710– ca. 1780) was famous as a maker of these instruments, quite a number of which are still in existence. They are very decorative, the backs, and sometimes also the ribs, being made of alternate strips of cedar (very light) and sycamore (brownish), the pegbox surmounted by a beautifully carved head, and the tail-piece fitted with an ivory nut, while the fingerboard and tail-piece are sometimes edged with strips of ivory.

FIG. 28.—Tenor Viol da Gamba: 1699. ("The Perfect Viol.")

The History of the Violin

The treble, alto, and tenor viols da gamba, which were held on the knee, were used especially in England and France, down to the end of the 17th century, when many were converted into violas. The bass viol da gamba, however, was cultivated much longer, and its last virtuoso, C. F. Abel, died in London, 1787.

CHAPTER 5

The Lyra

THE name, taken from the Roman lyra, was at first transferred to the mediæval instrument of the rebec type, as recorded on pp. 6 and 7, and afterwards to a guitar-fiddle with one or two bourdons, as well as to the primitive hurdy-gurdy, called lira Teutonica, or lira rustica, which was but a guitar-fiddle provided with a clavier, and a bourdon on either side of the neck. It is only the former that interests us here, as it became the direct parent of the violin. In Fra Angelico's "Coronation of the Virgin" (15th century) in the Louvre, there is a beautiful figure of an angel playing on a three-stringed guitar-fiddle with one bourdon. It was the immediate precursor of the lyra, which was merely a viol with two bourdons. Fra Angelico's instrument has a curious kind of oval pegbox into the sides of which the pegs are fixed in the same way as in modern instruments, but the table runs into the neck and serves as fingerboard, no separate fingerboard being visible.

The frontispiece of "Epithome Plutarchi" (Ferrara, 1501) (Heyer cat.) shows another guitar-shaped lyra, which has already the five strings running over the fingerboard and two bourdons, which henceforward became the standard number for this instrument. The *c*-shaped soundholes are placed rather high, no bridge is indicated, but as a fingerboard is clearly indicated this is an evident omission on the part of the artist, as otherwise the strings would have been lying flat on the fingerboard. The pegs are set in a heart-shaped block, similar to that most common on the guitar-fiddle, which became the standard form for all lyra heads. From this drawing an instrument was made in the workshop of the Wm. Heyer Museum at Cologne, under the supervision of Dr. Kinsky, which still forms part of the collection, and being in playable condition, gives a

The History of the Violin

good idea of the nature of the lyra. An important advance is noticeable in the lyra da braccio, played by an angel in a picture "The Enthroned Madonna," by Giovanni Bellini (1505). This instrument (Fig. 29) is already a distinct viol, with well-defined though shallow middle bouts, low ribs, and rather wide in proportion to its length. It is evidently an instrument of large size, resting on the left shoulder, the lower end of the table has a slight incurvation which becomes more pronounced in later lyras, and forms one of their characteristics. Another lyra (Fig. 30) in the hands of an angel, from a picture of the

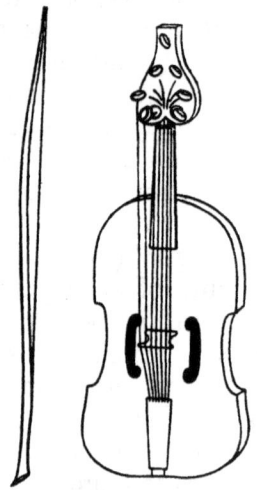

FIG. 29.—Lyra da Braccio and Bow: 1505.

FIG. 30.—Lyra da Braccio and Bow: 1499.

"Madonna," by Bartolomeo Montagnana, though a little earlier (1499) than either of the two preceding ones, shows an even greater approach to the model of the violin, in spite of the long *c* holes and the absence of an upper corner for the middle bouts, yet the proportions of the upper and lower bouts, the arching of the table, the grooving towards the edges are a close approach to the violin shape, and the lower half of the instrument is quite like that of the violin, but for the curiously grooved ribs which became a characteristic feature of the lyras, as did also the projecting edges of the table, which were absent in all fiddles and viols, but here clearly visible. From this painting, also, a lyra was made in the Heyer Museum work-

The Lyra

shop, which forms part of the collection, now in possession of the Leipzig University.

In a picture by Tintoretto of women singing and playing (ca. 1550), from the Dresden Gallery, we see, lying in the foreground a lyra (Fig. 31) which has the complete contour of the violin model. The soundholes have the imperfect f-shape ∫ sometimes to be met with in instruments of this time and even later.

A lyra da braccio, formerly in the possession of Alexander Haidecki, who was the first, in his monograph "Die italienische Lira da braccio," etc. (Mostar, 1892), to point out the importance of that instrument as the parent of the modern violin, is the work of a Brescian maker, Giovan Maria (dalla Corona ?—*see* Plate), who settled at Venice, where he made this instrument ca. 1540. It is now in the possession of Messrs. W. E. Hill & Sons, the well-known firm of instrument-makers of London, who kindly supplied us with the photograph for our illustration. This has also the primitive *ff*'s, and all the characteristics of the instrument depicted by Tintoretto, and is therefore the earliest perfect lyra still in existence. The head is painted with gold arabesques in the Venetian Renaissance style. The dimensions are: Length of body, 38·7 cm.; width, 23·5 cm.; which, compared with the respective average dimensions of the violin, viz. 36·4 and 21·2 cm., shows but a difference of 2·3 cm.

Fig. 31.—Lyra da Braccio: 1550.

Venice looms conspicuously in the foreground in the history of the violin, for although Andreas Amati and Gasparo da Salo are generally credited with being the first to produce violins similar to those in use at the present time, yet it was in Venice that most of the still existing lyras were made, and the family of Linarol appears to have taken an important part in their production. The most interesting member of the family is Ventura Linarol, the son of Francesco, whose exquisite workmanship is exemplified in three beautiful instruments in the Vienna Museum of Old Instruments. The one of these

The History of the Violin

which concerns us in this place is a lyra da braccio which, apart from the slight incurvation at the bottom, characteristic of the lyras, shows the complete violin model with *ff*'s, which are however without the nicks. The back is of beautifully flamed sycamore, ornamented by parallel lines of purfling, running alongside the back. The varnish is of a lustrous golden-yellow colour. In the place of a label is written in ink: "Ventura di Fran^{co} Linarol in Venetia, 1580." The ribs are not hollowed out, as usual in lyras, but flat, as in the violin. The total length is 70 cm.; length of body, 47.5 cm.; width of upper bouts, 22.5 cm., lower bouts, 26.5 cm.; height of ribs, 4 cm. Both back and table are slightly arched. The instrument has unfortunately at some time or other been turned into a viola, the head, neck, fingerboard, bridge and tailpiece having been replaced to suit that purpose.

The two other instruments by Linarol in the Vienna Museum are a violin, to be discussed later on, and a seven-stringed violone (Contrabass Viol) which has the characteristic shape of the scroll and *f*-holes seen already in his father's gamba. The written label in the latter reads: "1585, Ventura di Fran^{co} Linarol in Padova f." He had removed to Padua ca. 1580/81.

In the Heyer collection there is a "lirone," or large-arm lyra, by the same maker, which shows the same fine workmanship and varnish, but, for some reason impossible to conjecture, the two sycamore slabs of the back have been inverted so that the flames do not meet in the middle as they evidently would have done otherwise. The instrument had been used as a violoncello up to 1896 in a Silesian nobleman's family, but has been restored to its original condition. The neatly written label reads: "Ventura di Francesco Linarolo in Venetia. 1577." The total length is 92 cm.; length of body (to centre of incurvation), 59 cm.; width of upper bouts, $31\frac{1}{2}$ cm., middle bouts, 23 cm., lower bouts, 40 cm.; length of fingerboard, 31 cm.; length of neck, 16 cm.; width of ribs, 5.8 cm. The instrument was held in two ways, either resting with the lower end on the left shoulder, or holding it, sitting, across the chest, with the lower end resting on the right thigh, somewhat like a guitar. This instrument has also the perfect violin model except for the bottom incurvation, with Linarol's characteristic *f* holes. It has the usual seven strings of the lyra, two of which are bourdons, and Dr. Kinsky is no doubt justified in thinking that considering its size, which stands in a ratio of 4 : 5 as compared with the ordinary lyra, the lirone was tuned a third lower than the former.

The tuning of the ordinary lyra da braccio was:

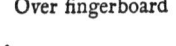

Or as in Prætorius with the usual seven strings:

With the progress of instrumental music, the bourdons, as well as the g' string, were found to be superfluous, the latter in particular, as it prevented a systematic fingering of scales and running passages. This resulted in their omission, a consequent improvement of various features in the model of the body, and the substitution of a pegbox surmounted by a scroll, instead of the flat rhomboid head. The outcome of these alterations was an instrument corresponding to our modern viola. They were no doubt due to more than one instrument-maker, and Venice unquestionably had its share in that evolution, being an important centre of lute and viol makers, and the home of Giov. Maria dalla Corona, whom Dr. G. Kinsky thinks to be identical with Giov. Maria, the maker of that beautiful early 16th-century lyra, in perfect preservation, now in possession of Messrs. W. E. Hill and Sons, which led A. Haidecki to point out the connexion between the lyra and the violin. Venice was, moreover, as already stated, for several generations the seat of the Linarols, a viol-makers' family, one at least of whose members made both lyras and violins.

Before the lyra da braccio had come to the highest state of development, towards the middle of the 16th century, which led to the birth of the violin, we find many evolutionary and tentative forms. One of the most interesting being that discovered by Dr. G. Kinsky on the title page of a very rare book: "Symphonia Platonis cum Aristotele: et Galeni cum Hippocrate," by Symphorianus Champerius (Paris, 1516), reproduced in his Heyer Catalogue, ii, 505, representing the above-named four sages playing on stringed instruments, three of which are held between the knees, the fourth like a violin. Of two, the front is fully visible, foreshadowing distinctly the outlines of the violin. They have four strings, but the large-circular soundholes, and the absence of a bridge, are reminiscent of the "Grosse Geigen." The pegboxes end in a backward curve. Transition forms also occur in Woeriot's portrait of Duiffoprugcar. Ca. 1600 we find at least one eminent musician who was both lyra player and violinist, viz. Alessandro Striggio, who appeared in that capacity at festival performances at Florence (E. Vogel, Bibliotek, ii, p. 384), and who was at the Court of Mantua in 1607.

CHAPTER 6

The Violin

THE first treatise which gives a description of the violin is Philibert Jambe-de-Fer's "Epitome Musical," published at Lyons in 1556 (*see* p. 36). At that time the famous lute and viol maker, Gaspard Duiffoprugcar (real name Kaspar Tieffenbrucker, of Füssen, Bavaria; *see* E. v. d. Str., "Hist. of the v'cello"), had already been living at Lyons for ca. five or six years, and must have known the treatise, as well as the violins, which were made there, and by Italian makers who constantly sent instruments to the Lyons Fair. It is held by most authorities that Duiffoprugcar never made a violin, because none is known to exist, those that passed as such having proved clever imitations of his style by Vuilleaume; and even of the violin which Aug. Wilhelny's father acquired as a battered old instrument at Geisenheim on the Rhine, and which the great violinist told the writer he considered an absolutely genuine Duiffoprugcar, we do not know that it was what he believed it to be, yet it seems very strange that the great artist, who made all kinds of stringed instruments, should not have made at least some violins. In Woeriot's portrait of Duiffoprugcar, dated 1562, there is, however, one four-stringed instrument which, in spite of the incurvation of the upper bouts at the neck and the *c*-shaped soundholes, is to all intents and purposes a violin, and in the shadow of the left-hand rim there is part of another instrument, which appears to be a violin in its perfect form. The picture shows also another instrument which Pougin calls a violin; it has the projecting corners, shape of the middle bouts, and *ff*'s of the violin, but the elongated upper bouts slope elliptically towards the neck, and it is mounted with five strings. This is of particular interest, as Pougin asserts (on what authority he does not state), that Baltazarini and his violinists used five-stringed violins tuned: a, d', g', c", f", which, he says, were then in use in Italy. If he is right, they would most likely have been of a pattern like, or similar to, that shown in Woeriot's picture, which in itself proves beyond doubt that such instruments existed, and that Duiffoprugcar, among others, made them. The instruments from the Gilling Castle pictures of 1583, kindly sent to me by the Rev. Canon F. W. Galpin, are no doubt of this kind. They evidently belonged to the transition forms which retained still some of the viol features. That the four-stringed violin tuned in fifths was then already in existence is obvious from the above-mentioned: "Epitome musical de tons, sons et accordz is voix humaines, fleustes d'Alleman, fleustes à 9 trous, violes et violons," etc. Towards the end of the little book it speaks of the French five-stringed viol tuned in fourths, and the violin which has four strings tuned in fifths, and further on it says:

"On appelle violes celles desquels les gentilhommes marchands et autres gens de vertu passent leur temps. Le violon est celui duquel on use en danserie communément, et a bonne cause; car il est plus facile à accorder, la quinte étant plus douce à ouïr que la quarte. Il est aussi plus facile a porter, qui est chose fort nécessaire, en conduisant quelque noce ou momerie."

The author of the book (pub. Lyons 1556) is Philibert Jambe-de-Fer.

H. J. Moser ("Geschichte des Violinspiels"), who found Weckerlin's account of the Epitome musical not very reliable, examined the original, and gives the additional information:

"The violin, Jambe-de-Fer says, is diametrically opposed to the viol; firstly it has only four strings, tuned in fifths, ... it is flatter (?) and smaller in the body, much sharper in tone, and has no frets ... Philibert recognizes the advantage of adopting the number of four strings for the alto, tenor, and bass instruments, which was then still unknown in Italy and Germany. He gives the tuning for the treble as g, d', a', e"; middle parts, c, g, d', a'; bass, BB flat, F, c, g. This bass ('cello) tuning is still given by Mersenne in 1636/7, and even by Dan. Merck ("Compendium Musicæ") in 1695."

Although the standard tuning of the violin is given by Jambe-de-Fer there were, if we can believe Pougin's statement about Baltazarini's violins, which from the nature of the music of the Balet Comique appears quite probable, still other tunings used in the early times of the violin.

G. Beckmann ("Das Violinspiel") speaks of an instrument

The Violin

(violin?) mentioned in the appendix to Aristotel's "Morals" of 1576 (in Paris Conservatoire library), tuned g, d' g', d", for which a tablature is given. He also states that two kinds of tablature existed in the early times, viz. the German, in which the top line stood for the G string and the bottom line for the e", numbers indicating the fingers to be used, and the Italian tablature in which the order was reversed, the bottom line standing for the G string and the top line for the e", letters being used instead of numbers, "a" standing for the open string, as in the English viol tablature. He gives two examples from MSS. in the Nuremberg town library, the German example being a "Danntz" (dance): "Bei mir mein hertz" (with me my heart), by Wolf Gerhard, and an Italian piece evidently written for the violin tuned g, d' g', d". In the German piece the numbers are on the respective lines, but they contradict his above statement about the order of the strings in the German tablature, for they are only in accordance with the translation given by him, if read with the G string at the bottom.

We subjoin here both examples. The Italian piece he gives evidently only partly, and as he left some of it untranslated after the first six notes, we have supplied the missing part:

Danntz: Bei mir mein hertz   Wolf Gerhard

The superscription of the MS. 14976 in the Nuremberg library is: "Johann Wolff Gerhard bin ich genannt zu Nürnberg ist mein Vatterlandt Papier ist mein Acker Darmit

schreib ich wacker." At the back of page: "Deus Fortunet angefangen den 26 September a. 1613."

Gasparo Zanetti in his "Method showing the Way to Play the Violin," etc., published at Milan, 1645, uses still the tablature, and in Playford's "Skill of Music," of which nineteen numbered and five or six unnumbered editions appeared between 1654 and 1730, and which contained primitive "Instructions and Lessons for the Treble, Tenor, and Bass Viols, and also for the Treble Violin," it is likewise explained, and he even recommends the use of frets (*see* fuller account in E. v. d. Str., "The Romance of the Fiddle," pp. 68–78), but explains in the "Conclusion" that both frets and tablature should merely serve "as a guide to young practitioners" who afterwards should "practice by notes only." On p. 117 he gives the tune of "Maiden Fair," both in tablature and staff notation (reproduction in the "Romance of the Fiddle," facing p. 69.

To avoid ledger lines, Playford uses the alto clef for all notes below d'. Mersenne, who in his "Harmonie Universelle" book iv (pub. Paris, 1636), deals more extensively with all the members of the violin family, likewise speaks of, and explains, the tablature, but adds: ". . . the notes are preferable, as they mark better the actual sound, time, bars, etc., and are more generally employed in Europe." By his remark that one can play on the violin "all kinds of diatonic and chromatic scales . . . because it is not hampered by frets," he shows that they were not used in France. A more extensive account of Mersenne's chapter on the violin may be found in "The Romance of the Fiddle," pp. 39–59, which shows that he had already a very clear idea of the fundamental principles of violin playing. To show the compass and function of the various members of the violin family in concerted music, he adds a "Fantaisie à 5," by Henri Le Jeune, one part of which in condensed score, as well as a diminution are given in the above-named work, pp. 55–7. As this *Fantaisie* was undoubtedly chosen as representing the average standard of the violin technique of that time in France, it is evident that this could in no way compare with that of the contemporary or even earlier Italian violinists.

The "violette da arco senza tasti" mentioned by Lanfranco ("Scintille di Musica," Brescia, 1533) and by Sylvestro

The Violin

Ganassi ("Lettione Seconda," Venice, 1543) were instruments of the gigue or rebec type with a pear-shaped body, which became practically obsolete in the second half of the 16th century and did not belong to the violin family. Count Luigi Francesco Valdrighi, in his "Nomocheliurgographia," mentions Sebastiano Scotto of Verona, 1511, as maker of viols and violins but without giving his authority. It is safe to assume the statement to be erroneous so far as violins are concerned. There was still a great deal of confusion even in the latter part of the 16th century in the naming of musical instruments, thus Vincenzo Galilei in his "Dialogo . . . et della Musica Moderna" (Florence, 1581), p. 147, speaks of the "Viola da braccio which not many years ago was called lira"; Zacconi ("Prattica di Musica," Venice, 1596), however, says the violas da braccio . . . are tuned in the order of the violin, and that is tuned in fifths. The dimensions of the lira da braccio were those of the viola, apart from slightly larger bouts, and it appears therefore that the viola was the first instrument of the violin family, but being distinctly an alto instrument the treble and bass followed very soon. A viola, described as by Peregrino Zanetto of Brescia, ca. 1550, belonging to Col. T. Myles Sandys, M.P., figures in the Catalogue (p. 158) of the Music Loan Exhibition at Fishmongers' Hall, 1904. If the description is correct, this is probably the oldest instrument of the violin family, and seems to confirm the belief that the viola preceded the violin, whereof Messrs. Hills' Amati violin of 1564 is probably one of the first specimens. The reasons that no violins of the earliest time have been preserved are: (1) that it was in its beginning only used for dances and at fairs, and in most countries, apart from Italy, it remained a more or less despised instrument, the cinderella of the strings, for quite a century, and the early instruments, which moreover often showed transition forms that were discarded as soon as the perfect model appeared, were not treated with the same care as the beloved viol; (2) there are scarcely any viols left of the early 16th century, apart from the unique guitar-fiedel of 1500 in the Estense collection in the late Imperial Palace at Vienna, the equally unique treble viol by Francesco Linarol of ca. 1540 and the beautiful lira da braccio by Giovanni d'Andrea, of Verona, of 1511, both in the same collection. The pointed lower

The History of the Violin

corners of the middle bouts, and projecting edges of the upper and lower table are shown in a lira da braccio in a painting of "The Madonna with Saints and Angels," by Montagna, 1499 (Palazzo Brera, Milan), and a pen-and-ink sketch of a lyra by Raffael, ca. 1510 (both reproduced in Kinsky's Heyer catalogue, vol. ii).

The first reproduction of a perfect, though rather wide, scroll, which we have been able to find, surmounts a viol depicted in "De Musica tractata," by Bartolomeo Ramis de Pareia (Bologna, 1482, fig. 26). This is very curious, as there is little doubt that it is the earliest representation of a real scroll, and on an instrument on which it was rarely used except in Italy, while the violin of which it became eventually an integral part did not come into existence until some seventy years later.

Of the *f*-shaped soundhole, however, we discover no trace until ca. 1540, when it occurs in a primitive form, without the nick, in a treble viol by Francesco Linarol mentioned above, and likewise in the Haidecki lyra by "Giovan Maria," of about the same date, if not earlier (*see* Ch. 5). After that time we see it in all lyras and even in the Italian viols da gamba, so for instance in the treble viol by Gasparo da Salo of 1580 in the Vienna Museum, while the tenor viol of the same set shows a nick in the outer line of the *f* } and the bass has nicks on both sides; all are of the same date. A set of three gambas by Antonio Ciciliano (Venice, 1600), has *ff*'s without the nicks. These as well as the de Salo viols have scrolls.

There occurred, however, in the 16th century occasional reversions to older types of soundholes, as, for instance, in a violin by Giovanno Marco del Busseto, Cremona, the reputed master of Gasparo da Salo, dated 1570, with elongated corners, and high vaulted back, mentioned by Sandys and Forster ("Hist. of the Violin," p. 201), said to have had, like all his violins (?) *s*-shaped soundholes with rather large openings. We do not know whether this instrument is still in existence.

Perhaps the oldest violin in existence is a "violino piccolo," by Andreas Amati, dated 1564, now the property of Messrs. W. E. Hill and Sons. It is said to have formed part of the instruments made by Andreas Amati for Charles IX of France, viz. 12 large and 12 small violins, 6 tenors and 8 basses. It

Front   Back

Lyra da braccio 1540, by Giovan Maria of Brescia, in the possession of Messrs.
W. E. Hill & Sons, who kindly permitted its reproduction in this book.

Treble Violin and Pandora player.

Viola and lute player.

Bass (or tenor?) violin and Cittern player.

Violinists from panels in the Hall of Gilling Castle, Yorkshire, painted between 1575-80, by permission of the trustees, kindly obtained for the author by the Rev. Canon F. W. Galpin. (See Vol. 1, p. 58.)

bears the initials w. c. which have been attributed to William Corbett (*see* p. 69). Most of the aforementioned instruments were kept in the Chapel Royal, Versailles, until Oct. 1790, when they disappeared. J. B. Cartier succeeded in recovering two of them many years later. The *Strad*, Mar., 1922, says:

"'Musique et Instruments' states that an American has purchased one of the violins made for Charles IX. The instrument which bears the Arms of the Kings of France is said to have been painted by Rubens (?? Rubens, b. 1577) and is moreover studded with diamonds. Mozart is reported to have played on it before Marie Antoinette at Versailles."

Messrs. Hill, who have made a close study of the Amatis and their work, give little credence to these accounts.—A violoncello from that set belonged to Sir William Curtis (E. v. d. Str., "History of the V'cello," p. 126). George Hart (*The Violin*, p. 101), writing about Andreas Amati, says:

"His early works are so Brescian in character as to cause them to be numbered with the productions of that school. . . . The work is carefully executed. The model is high, and, in consequence, lacks power of tone; but the violins possess a charming sweetness. The soundhole is inelegant, has not the decision of Gasparo da Salò, although belonging to his style, and is usually broad. His varnish may be described as deep golden, of good quality."

Several violins by A. Amati, in the possession of Messrs. W. E. Hill and Sons, do not quite bear out Hart's judgment, as they are of the most perfect workmanship and elegance of form as may be seen from the specimen, which their courtesy has enabled us to reproduce in a photogravure plate.

The viola by Andreas Amati, dated 1551, mentioned by Sandys and Forster as having belonged to Baron Bagge in Paris ca. 1789 is described by Fétis as a "viola moyenne, appelée par les Italiens Viola bastarda" (a middle size viol called by the Italians a viola bastarda) which proves that it was a viol and did not belong to the violin family.

Gasparo da Salò, A. Amati's contemporary, is credited with having laid the foundation of the Italian style of violin-making. He was essentially a maker of viols and the number of his violins is small. The earlier ones are of a deep model but later on he adopted a flatter one. All are still of a primitive form, with broad soundholes, the workmanship is bold, and not highly finished. Ole Bull possessed a fine example of his work with an inlaid fingerboard and a finely carved and painted head. The third outstanding Brescian master of that time, Giovanni Paolo Maggini (b. Botticini, Aug. 25,

The History of the Violin

1580; d. Brescia, 1640), is believed to have been a pupil of Gasparo, but there exists no positive evidence with regard to this. His instruments are flat, the varnish brown or yellow. Many show double purfling and sometimes ornamental designs in purfling on the back, and these have led to many forgeries.

In some respects his work marks an advance on that of Gasparo, although it is considered to lack the classic symmetry of the latter. Both de Beriot and Léonard played on fine specimens of Maggini violins, which increased the demand for them and enhanced their price. Full details about the two great Brescian makers may be found in the beautifully illustrated monographs by Messrs. Hill, London.

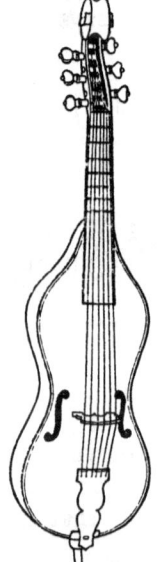

FIG. 32.—Viol da Gamba: 1540.

About the same time as the above Brescian masters there lived and worked at Venice, Francesco and his son Ventura Linarolo (q.v.). Francesco was born at Bergamo ca. 1520; he was a viol-maker who worked for a number of years at Padua, where his son Ventura was born ca. 1550.

There is a treble viol (Fig. 32) by Francesco in the Estense collection in Vienna, of ca. 1540, which is probably the oldest still existing *perfect* viol, and is moreover the first stringed instrument the writer has been able to discover with soundholes in the shape of the ƒ without, however, the middle line, a not unfrequent occurrence in viols as well as violins of the 16th and early 17th century, as stated above. The treble viol of Francesco has a scroll which is grooved but without a middle rib, and this is also a characteristic of his son Ventura's scrolls. The latter made, apart from other instruments, both lyras and violins. A beautiful lyra da braccio by Ventura, in the Estense Collection, of 1580, has been altered into a tenor violin and provided with a neck, fingerboard and scroll suitable for that purpose. The back of the instrument is of beautifully flamed sycamore with longitudinal lines of black purfling; the ƒƒ's are of the primitive form without middle line. The length of the body is 47.3, while the body of the

The Violin

lirone in the Heyer Collection is 59 cm. long. In the Estense Collection there are, moreover, a violin by Ventura dated 1581, which has the scroll characteristic of his work, but the *ff*'s have the middle line and are of a more advanced form; the total length is 55·5 cm.; the body, 34·5 cm.; and a violin dated 1622, by his son Giovanni, who worked also in Venice. The total length is 59·5 cm.; length of body, 36 cm. His workmanship is greatly inferior to that of his father; the very primitive *ff*'s are without the middle line. Ventura apparently returned to Padua, as the Estense Collection contains a beautiful six-stringed violone by "Ventura Linarol, Padua, 1585."

The violin by him is one of the earliest larger violins still in existence, although ca. 1 cm. shorter in the body than the standard model. There is, however, an earlier violin in the Bach-house at Eisenach, apparently of Bohemian origin, of the year 1575 (Kinsky: Heyer Cat., ii, 511, footnote 2).

Violins for the courts of kings and princes were made in sets (like the chests of viols), and Julius Schlösser, in his "Alte Musikinstrumente," which contains excellent illustrations of the above-mentioned Linarolo instruments, mentions a chest which figured in a catalogue of the Graz Collection (Kunst Kammer = art treasure room) of 1577, containing a bass-, 3 tenors-, and one discant Geig (violin), also "an old set of *Geigen*," viz. 1 bass, 2 tenors, 2 discant (trebles). The latter being described as "old," makes it doubtful whether they were violins or viols as the word Geige was used for both, just as the word *violino* originally was used as the diminutive of viola (viz. for a small viol), and in the rare chap book published at Brescia ca. 1550, or perhaps a little earlier, in the possession of Mr. E. Heron-Allen, and described with illustration in E. v. d. Str.,"The Romance of the Fiddle," p. 4, we find the name "*La violina*" applied to an instrument which, although the number of the strings cannot be ascertained with certainty from the crude woodcut, appears to be a "lyra da braccio."

In France the term "*joueur de violon*" occurs in a document of the duchy of Lorraine in 1490, eight *joueurs de vyolons et d'instruments* are mentioned among the musicians of Francis I of France (1515–47), and violinists are mentioned in connexion with the wedding festivities at Rouen in 1550 at the marriage of Henry II with Catherine of Medici. It is beyond doubt that the word *violon* must in these cases be identified with the Italian word *violone*. Fétis, from a MS. of 1559 in the National Library, Paris, mentions Hondré Castelan as a chamber violinist of Henry II in 1555; no doubt he was not the only one, but he is the only one of whom we know. Charles IX, for whom A. Amati made the above-mentioned set of violins, sent Dolinet, flautist and violinist, one of his musicians, to Italy, in Oct. 1572, to buy a Cremona violin for which he paid 50 Tournay livres, ca. £10, a large sum at that time, which may, however, have included incidental expenses, as suggested by Sandys and Forster, who also tell us (from the "Archives Curieuses de l'Histoire de France") that, on Nov. 7, 1572, Baptiste Delphinon, *violon ordinaire de la chambre*, of the King, received 75 Tournay livres to go to Milan to engage musicians for the King's pleasure. They also mention Pierre de la Haye as violinist, appearing in the register of the performances of the ancient drama (mystery plays?) at Bethune in 1550. As Jambe-de-Fer's Epitome appeared in 1556, it is at all events *possible* that this was really a violinist and not a violist. There are several other references to the early use of the violin, in the above-mentioned book, among which one is of particular interest. It is taken from the memoirs of Marguerite de Valois who, in giving an account of a fête at Bayonne in 1565, on the occasion of an interview of the notorious Catherine de Medici with her son Charles IX, when provincial dances were performed, accompanied by the appropriate instruments which for the "Bourguignones" and "Champenoises" were: small oboes, *dessus de violin*, and village tambourîns. These "*dessus de violin*" were no doubt the small, high treble violins like the twelve made by A. Amati about that time for the same King, and which are called *violini piccoli* in Monteverdi's "Orfeo."

In 1577 Marshal de Brissac, then governor of Piedmont, sent from Turin to Catherine de Medici, no doubt at her request, Baltazarini, a balletmaster and violinist, with a band of 10 violinists. Baltazarini gained favour at the French Court, where he received the name of Baltazar de Beaujoyeux. On the occasion of the marriage of his favourite, the Duc de Joyeuse with his sister-in-law Marguerite of Lorraine, Princesse de Vaudemont, Henry III instituted brilliant festivities, and on Oct. 15, 1581, the grand "Balet Comique de la Royne" was performed in the Salle de Petit-Bourbon in the Louvre, upon which he lavished the fabulous sum of 3,600,000 francs (equal to at least four times that amount at present values). The work was really a ballet-opera, as it contained songs and choruses, as well as dances. Baltazarini had conceived the subject (the story of Circe), scenery, action and dances, while the King's Almoner, Le Chesnaye, had written the book, the court painter, Jaques Patin, had designed the costumes and decorations, while Lambert de Beaulieu and the violinist Salmon, two of the King's most distinguished musicians, had composed the music, which was written for lutes, viols, harps, brass and reed, and various wind instruments, etc., while the violins were reserved for the dances. The contrast of their brilliance with the softer, more veiled tone of the viols, particularly in the "air de la clochette," which accompanies Circe coming out of the wood, aroused great enthusiasm.

It is in connexion with this description of this ballet that Pougin says Baltazarini's players used five-stringed violins tuned in fourth, as described above. If this is correct the treble part, probably for a violino piccolo, could be played entirely in the first position, as the highest note, C''', would then naturally come under the fourth finger. The air, which is in five parts, has been given in short score in E. v. d. Str., "The Romance of the Fiddle," in its original form, and it also was published in an arrangement by Ghys as "Air de Louis XIII," which is still very popular. Unfortunately, the edition of the "Balet Comique," published by le Roy, Ballard and Pattison, Paris, 1582, giving pictures of all the scenes, has none showing a violinist, although the picture of the "Fountain" depicts Baltazarini playing the bass viol and his wife playing the lute, both in gorgeous and costly costumes. Baltazarini's violinists formed the first band of the "violons du roy," which was afterwards enlarged to the number of twenty-four.

CHAPTER 7

The Evolution of Violin Playing

THE Viols, which during the greater part of the 16th century found their literature still in the contrapuntal forms of vocal music, began towards the end of that century to free themselves from their fetters, and develop a figuration and forms which were more in their nature, and which culminated in the "In Nomine," the "Fantasia," and the various dance forms, wherein the English school from the Elizabethan to the end of the Stuart times, stood far above those of all other countries. The viols were then the dominating instruments, while, during the first fifty years of its existence, the violin had been the Cinderella among the stringed instruments, as we know from Jambe-de-Fer's account. It was only used by tavern- and dance-musicians, except in Italy, where we find it used already in serious music at an early period. Michel de Montaigne, the famous essayist, and descendant of an originally English family, writes from Verona, Oct., 1580: "There were organs and violins accompanying the singers at the Mass" (transl. from the French).

The first Italian violinist whose name has come down to posterity was GIOVAN BATTISTA DEL VIOLINO (real name, Jacomelli), a singer in the Papal Chapel 1582–5. He is mentioned in the Preface of the "Intermedii for the Wedding of Ferdinand de Medici," and in the Preface of Peri's "Euridice" (*Rivista Mus.*, May 30, 1914, Cametti "Orazio Michi").

The neck of the violin was, in the first stages of the instrument, still broad, short, and clumsy, reminiscent of the viol neck, and continued thus until the early part of the 17th century, when it was adapted to the needs of an advancing technique by a more suitable form. Until the beginning of

The Evolution of Violin Playing

the 17th century the first position only was used on the violin, and the use of the G string was avoided by all the early composers, probably on account of the manner of holding the instrument at that period. An instrumental piece was called "suonata" (sonata), as distinct from "cantata" (a vocal piece), "Canzona," of indeterminate form, or "Concerto." These terms were used indiscriminately for one and the same kind of composition, and in some cases we find even the title: "Sonate ôver Canzoni," as, for instance, in the case of Uccellini's sonatas of 1649. The word Concerto, also used sometimes instead of sonata, denoted originally the singing or playing or both, together of two or more people, in the same sense as the word "consort" was used in the English language.

All three forms had their origin in the "Madrigal," which was often described as apt for voices and instruments of sundry kinds, or "apt for voices and viols" even down to nearly the middle of the 17th century.

The first work, to our knowledge, in which the instruments to be used are distinctly specified, is "Concerti di Andrea e Giovanni Gabrieli . . . per voci e stromenti musicali " (Venice, 1587). Some of these concerti or sonatas are based on Gabrieli's vocal style, others are purely instrumental. In a sonata of the former kind the instruments are divided into two choirs, one formed of a cornet and three trombones, the second of a violin and three trombones, which choirs were used antiphonally. In this, the violin part differs very little from that of the cornetto. Those of the latter kind are sonatas or canzoni for three violins with a bass. They are in a more complicated, fugal style which is distinctly instrumental; containing as they do the germs of modern instrumentation, they mark an epoch in the history of music. The Royal library of Berlin contains a sonata by Giovanni Gabrieli for three violins and bass, reproduced in E. v. d. Str.'s "The Romance of the Fiddle." The date given there, 1615, is evidently too late; Gabrieli died 1612 or 1613, and probably refers to the time when the copy was made. It is quite in the nature of the violin, in contrapuntal style, and never exceeds the first position, in which the highest note, C''', can be played by the extension of the fourth finger, and entirely avoids the use of the G string.

The History of the Violin

GIOVANNI GABRIELI, b. Venice, 1557; d. there Aug. 12, 1612 or 1613, was the first composer who indicated the instruments for which he wrote sonatas, and who fixed the rudiments of sonata form. "He was the first to find the principles of composition for the orchestra which Mich. Prätorius took consciously over from him. He and his uncle Andrea were the first to develop the sonata (Canzoni da sonar) for an *ensemble* of instruments, and to write for distinctly specified instruments, while before them, and by many even after them, the choice of instrument or instruments for the performance of their ricecare or canzone was left to the executants. His sonata for 3 violins and bass served as model for about half a century" (Riemann).

CHAPTER 8

The Violin in Italy from 1600 to circa 1650

THE first sonata for violin solo and bass of which we have any knowledge is by Giovanni Paolo Cima, organist at Milan, whose "Concerti Ecclesiastici," published there in 1610, comprise one sonata for cornetto and trombone, or violin and violone, and one expressly for violin and violone. The latter forms part of a number of 17th-century sonatas, advertised as in course of republication in G. Beckmann's "Das Violinspiel," but we have not yet been able to see it.

The first violinist composer after Cima, whose name has come down to us, is:

BIAGIO MARINI (*see* p. 125). Early in the 17th century he was employed as violinist at Venice, when he published his "Affetti musicali . . . symfonie, canzone, sonate . . . a 1, 2, 3" (for violins, cornets and other instruments), containing a violin solo sonata, and employing, according to Schering ("Geschichte des Jnstrum. Konzerts"), for the first time the tremolo for artistic purposes. This was followed in 1618 by "Madrigali et symfonie, Op. 2." In 1620 he wrote "Arie, madrigali et correnti a, 1, 2, 3, op. 3," published in Venice. He was then director of music at Sant' Eufemia, Brescia. This work contains a Romanesca for violin solo with bass ad lib. (reproduced in E. v. d. Str., "The Romance of the Fiddle"); it shows a great advance in several respects. Firstly, it approaches the form of the suite, as it consists of an abstract movement followed by a Gagliarda and a Corrente. The first movement is in four parts, the first and second, which have the same bass, are each in two repeated sections. The third part "in ALTUS (altro?) MODO" has a sustained bass and running quaver figures, the fourth part has a running bass and sustained upper part; neither of these have a middle section. The Gagliarda is in two parts, both with two repeated sections. The Corrente has two repeated sections. In the first movement there are a number of shakes, of which there is no trace in Gabrieli's sonata, and some of these, on a' and e", point to the use of the third position, although none of the movements, all in g minor, exceeds b" flat. In the Romanesca he has entirely abandoned the contrapuntal style, and follows melodic lines. Marini wrote in all twenty-two works of vocal and instrumental music, a list of which appears in "Grove's Dictionary," op. 22 being "Per ogni sorte d'istrumento musicale diversi generi di'sonate da chiesa e da camera, a 2–4" (Venice, 1655). Here then we find the distinct separation of the church- from the chamber-sonata.

FRANCESCO TURINI, b. Prague, ca. 1590; d. Brescia, 1656; composed "Madrigali à una, due, tre voci, con alcune sonate à 2 e 3, libro primo e secondo" (Venice, Bartolomeo Magni, 1624). Wasielewski describes the three sonatas contained in the work, from the copy in the Breslau town library, as written for 2 violins and bass, in fluent counterpoint but showing neither in respect of the violin technique, nor the form of the sonatas any advance upon those by Gabrieli.

MASSIMILIANO NERI was appointed first organist at St. Mark's, Venice, Dec. 18, 1644, where he remained till 1664, when he became court organist to the Elector of Cologne. In 1651 the Emperor Ferdinand II raised him to the rank of nobility. For his instrumental compositions "Op. 1 and op. 2" *see* Eitner and W'ki. Among his sonatas there is one of seven movements in different time and tempo. He, as well as Legrenzi, did much to advance the sonata from the formal side. He must not be confounded with Filippo (San Filippo) Neri, the founder of the *"Congregazione dell' Oratorio"* in Rome.

CARLO FARINA, b. Mantua, towards the end of the 16th century; from 1625 to ca. 1632, violinist at the Saxon Court at Dresden; 1636–7 in the band of the town council of Danzig; returned afterwards to Italy, according to Nerici. That is all we know about one of the most important figures in the early history of the violin. Fortunately a complete set of all his works was discovered during the latter part of last century in the Grand-Ducal library at Casse; Wasielewski ("Die Violine,"

The Violin in Italy from 1600 to circa 1650

etc., pp. 60-2) gives the lengthy titles in full; we give them here only in so far as they have direct bearing upon our subject.

The first is "Libro delle Pavane, Gagliarde ... Sonate, Canzone à 2, 3, 4 voci con il Basso per sonare, di Carlo Farina Mantovano, sonatore di violino" ... Dresdæ ... 1626; dedicated to the Elector Joh. Georg I. The dance movements were mostly in four parts, while three sonatas were in three parts, and two sonatas and a canzona are in only two parts. The sonatas and the canzona have fancy titles: "La Polaca, la Capriola," etc., as was the custom of the time, followed by the French violists and clavecinists for their suite movements right into the 18th century.

The second book: "Ander Teil Newer Gagliarden, Couranten," etc. (transl.: "Second part of new Galliards, Courants, French Arias, besides a merry Quodlibet, of all manner of curious inventions, the like of which has never been seen in print before, with some German dances, all to be played gracefully on viols (Violen); in four parts"), by Carlo Farina of Mantua, violist to the Elector of Saxony ... 1627. The dedication to the Electress Sibylla ... is dated Jan. 1, 1627. Although viols are mentioned in the title, and Farina calls himself *violist*, violins are clearly indicated in the text, and he was *violinist*, as he calls himself in the title of op. 1. In the Italian titles he mentions no instruments, while in the German titles (op. 2 and op. 5) he says: *auf Violen* (on Viols) although violins are evidently meant.

The third book, dedicated to the Landgrave of Hesse, Mar. 25, 1627, contains, apart from a number of dance movements, in 3 and 4 parts, six three-part *symphonies*, which the writer has been unable to see so far. The name at that period applied, however, to single instrumental movements for three or more instruments.

The fourth book, dedicated to the Elector of Saxony, Mar. 1, 1628, contains, besides the usual dance movements, two sonatas in 3 parts, one sonata in 2 parts and one canzona in 2 parts.

The fifth book, "Fünfter Teil Newer Paduanen," etc., dedicated to Baron von Schwanberg, Dresden, Apr. 20, 1628, says again in the title, "to be played on viols," and Farina calls himself violist; here also violins are meant (*see* above).

The confusion in the naming of the instruments which existed in the 16th century (*see* p. 43), thus continued right into the 17th century.

This book, apart from the dance movements, contains one sonata in 3, and one in 2 parts.

Farina was no master of polyphonic writing, and contented himself with four parts at most. In his sonatas he follows Gabrieli's precedent of a three-movement form: a movement in triple time standing between two movements in common time, the first being developed to larger proportions, the latter of shorter dimensions, often merely a short postlude. The movements are, as in Gabrieli's sonatas, built up of a number of sentences, each having a distinctive motive treated in imitative counterpoint. The sentences, sometimes connected by a short link, show no particular inner connexion. His style testifies to ease and fluency in his productive talent, though it is not free from the faulty progressions, impure harmonies, and unsymmetrical periods, frequently met with in the works of that time. For all these natural shortcomings, Farina's works form important links in the evolution of instrumental music. His sonatas show that his technique as an executant was in advance not only of his contemporaries but even of later players. His figuration was varied, and he already introduces rapid passages, double stopping, and the occasional use of the G string, which still was generally avoided by most violinist composers. The "Kurtzweiliges Quodlibet" (merry quodlibet), better known as the "Capriccio stravagante," has been severely criticized by some writers as a proof that Farina was a mere charlatan, but one must not forget that in the early stages of the art of violin playing, many eminent virtuosi tried to find out the possibilities of the violin in all directions, and naturally the sounds of nature were drawn into the scheme, and could not fail to entertain, especially as the possibility of expressing the inner life had not yet come under serious consideration. Even if we may smile at his imitation of the mewing and spitting of cats, barking of a dog, cocks and hens, the drum, the trumpet and many others which do not belong to the domain of music, and for the production of which he gives minute instructions at the end of the capriccio in all seriousness, we must not forget that they led him to the discovery of the use of harmonics, staccato, pizzicato, tremolo, col legno, which more than a hundred years later found their place in the legitimate art of violin playing. The full titles of the books, and specification of the pieces therein, are given in Wasielewski, "Die Violine."

In order to follow the customary sequence, the Biographies of Violinists are grouped into countries, and these countries are arranged in alphabetical order and not in regard to their relative importance in respect to the evolution of the Violin: the various introductory paragraphs will reveal this latter status.

VIOLINISTS FROM C. 1550 TO 1700

CHAPTER 9

England

THE time at which the violin made its first appearance in England remains a matter of conjecture, chiefly on account of the indifferent use of the words viol and violin. From 1532 Italian viol players began to come to the English Court, and in 1559 the names of seven Italians are given as "violetts" in the King's Musick (Nagel, "Annalen der englischen Hofmusik"). On Oct. 31, 1563, we find an entry: "Francesco de Venetia one of our vyolons for a sett of vyalls (viols) by him sold to us the some of 15 powndes." Here we have distinctly the two different words used for one and the same instrument, when the violin had only quite recently appeared in Italy and France. Until 1570 we find again and again 7 Italians as "vyolons," but in the latter year, for the first time, we find the name of an Englishman, "Thomas Browne," among their number. In 1581 the "Vyolins" (7) mentioned in the list are all Italians, although Browne must have still been there, for in 1582 under "The Violine" we find him as well as the Italian vyolins. Nagel uses the word "Violine" here, and as he appears to follow strictly the spelling of the records, and the word occurs again in 1586, this is significant, although we find "8 Viollists" mentioned in the lists of 1588, etc., and in 1597 we even find once more the older spelling, viz. "8 Vialls"; but we know how keen Elizabeth was to keep her music quite up to date, and it is certain that she must have heard all about Baltazarini and his band of violinists, sent to the French Court by Marshal Brissac from Piedmont, and although the viols were, and remained still for a century after, the favourite instruments of the English, it would seem strange if Elizabeth had not secured the services of players of the new instrument, even were it but to comply with the

The History of the Violin

fashion. No actual proof for this, however, existed until the Rev. Canon F. W. Galpin discovered lately at Gilling Castle, Yorks., a frieze, painted on wood between 1575 and 1580, when the Great Hall was decorated by Sir William Fayrefax.

This frieze has three panels with illustrations of a stringed consort; the first representing a man playing a treble violin, accompanied by a lady on the Pandora; in the second the man plays a large viola, the lady a lute; and in the third picture in similar hands are a bass (tenor?) violin and a cittern. These instruments belong quite distinctly to the new Violin family, in spite of the incurvations of the upper bouts, which, it might be objected, did not belong to the violin nor to the lyra da braccio from which it descended; but the 16th century, like its predecessor, was most prolific in the creation of new forms, and many artists and craftsmen would have despised themselves, had they not added something original to the already existing forms.

There is, moreover, a lyra da gamba in the music-historical museum in Vienna, by W. Tieffenbrucker of Padua, dated 1590, therefore of the same period, which shows *exactly* the same outline. The pictures are here reproduced by kind permission of the Trustees of Gilling Castle and by Canon Galpin, who kindly supplied us with copies of the photographs which he had taken for the third edition of his beautiful book, "Old Instruments of Music" (Methuen). From these it will be seen that they have five strings, like the contemporary instruments used by Baltazarini (q.v.), instead of the orthodox four strings. They all have a scroll like the violin, but the peg-box appears to have a sharp backward bend in its upper part, near the scroll, into which the uppermost of the three pegs of the right side is set. The soundholes of treble and bass are f-shaped, the former very clumsy, with a peculiar indication of the middle line. The viola, or Mean, however, has crescent-shaped soundholes, the curve running parallel to that of the middle bouts. All three instruments have well defined corners. The bow is held by each of the players with the fingers on the top of the stick, very near the end (in the case of the viola the little finger appears to be held under the end-button), the thumb holds the stick just in front of the nut, between the hair and the stick.

A picture by Hoefnagel in the possession of the Marquess

England

of Salisbury, at Hatfield, represents a wedding at Horselydown in 1590, in which two violinists and a piper appear on one side of a group of dancers, and two more violinists on the other side of the group (*see* Plate). Two of the players are too much in the background to see any detail of their instruments, but of each pair one plays a violin, the other a viola. They are four-stringed instruments with distinct *f* holes. The bouts of the violin are rather elongated, and in the viola, the lower bouts of which have a more normal form, and which has also quite pronounced corners, we find once more incurvations in the upper bouts, though less marked than in the Gilling violins. The Hoefnagel violin, if any, has very blunt corners between lower and middle bouts, which run straight into the upper bouts, as in the guitar, and in the old chanot model. The upper bouts of the instruments are sloping towards the neck as in the instrument on the right side of Woeriot's portrait of Duiffoprugcar (E. v. d. Str., "History of the Violoncello," vol. i), but the soundholes are elongated *ff*'s. The instruments, of the size of the ordinary violin, are held against the collar-bone, with the chin over the right side from the tailpiece.

As it was customary for viol players to play not only all the members of that family, but also the lute, and frequently the virginals and the organ, it is only natural to suppose that they were also the first to take up the violin, and we must attribute it to this circumstance, that we do not find any players singled out as violinists in those early times, although, as stated above, the string players are referred to sometimes as "vialls," and sometimes as "vyolons."

On Nov. 26, 1607, a warrant was issued to pay Daniel Farrant, one of the King's musicians for the violin, £46, as this was the inventor of two instruments strung with wire, viz. the stump and the polyphant, on the latter of which "Queen Elizabeth did often recreate herself" (*see* Introduction to Playford's "Skill of Musick"). Pulver (Biog. Dict.) very reasonably suggests that this must have been the *father* of the Dan. Farrant who on June 23, 1619, received a warrant "for allowance of a yearly livery," as he was appointed "a Viall, in the place of Thomas Browne (*see* p. 57), deceased." It was the latter Farrant who, with Ferrabosco and Coperario, was one of the first to compose for the Lyra-viol. In 1608 there is, on Mar. 22, a grant to Alex. Clesham as violinist, and on July 4 one to Alex. Thessam (Nagel thinks they might be identical). In a list of musicians of Charles I, to whom the payment of the subsidies was remitted, we find a clear distinction between the "Mus. for the Violins": Cæsar Galliardetto, Thos. Lupo, Ant. Coney (Comy, Conti), Alex. Chisham (Clesham?), Thos. Warren, Horatio Lupo, Harding, Leon. Mell (mentioned also as a "tenor violin," see Pulver, Ib.), Hopper, Adrian Valet, Thos. Lupo (composer—not the above); followed by the lutenists (6), and the "Mus. for the Violls:" Alph. Ferrabosco, Dan. Farrant (see above), Roger Mayer, J. Friend. On Nov. 29, 1628, Stephen Naw and John Woodington were appointed violinists, and Jan. 5, 1639, Simon Naw (son of Stephen N.?) succeeded John Hayden as violinist in the Royal Musick.

In 1595 Edmondo Schertz (Schütz?) is mentioned as "Maker, repayrer and Tunor of her Ma$^{te.}$ musycall Instruments" as receiving £50 annually. This is one of the earliest names of an instrument-maker in England whose name however appears to be German.

JOHN JENKINS, b. Maidstone, Kent, 1592, d. Kimberly, Norfolk, Oct. 27, 1678, one of the greatest viol and lute players of his time, and highly gifted, most prolific composer, was probably also an executant on the violin, as apart from a "Sute in D-sol-re" from "New Lessons for Viols or Violins," 1678, he is credited by Hawkins with having composed "Twelve Sonatas for Two Violins and Bass" (published in 1660, reprinted in Amsterdam, 1664—W. H. H. in Grove), which formed the first essay towards the introduction of the Sonata into England." They remain, however, a mystery, as nobody seems to have ever seen a copy of this work, and Pulver, in his Biographical Dictionary, etc., suggests that the origin of the story lay in the manuscript set of sonatas in the Bodleian Library. In any case, they would not be the first, as Wm. Young's sonatas were pub. in 1653. Jenkins composed, however, "New Lessons for Viols or Violins," 1678.

DAVIS (DAVIES, also DAVID) MELL, b. Wilton, Nov. 15, 1604; d. London in 1662 or 63. Nagel ("Annalen," etc.) mentions a Warrant, of May 3, 1662, for a grant as violinist

England

for John Banister in the place of David Mell, deceased, but J. Pulver quotes an entry from the Lord Chamberlain's Records according to which John Banister was admitted to the place of "Daniel" (an obvious clerical error) Mell on Mar. 20, 1662–3. From other documents relating to Banister (q.v.) it appears evident that the date of his appointment was May 3, 1663, and that we must place the death of Mell about the end of April of that year, in spite of the Lord Chamberlain's Record. Mell's father was in the service of the third Earl of Pembroke, and Davis was apprenticed to a clockmaker, but soon devoted himself entirely to the study of music, and in 1625 he appears as one of the musicians for violin at the funeral of James I. On Jan. 22, 1628–9, he received 20 Marks to buy a treble violin for use in the Royal Musick, and in April, 1633, as well as on Mar. 6, 1635–6, he received payments for providing music books "for the violins."

The musicians' lot during the Commonwealth was a sad one, especially in the early times, those who were not imprisoned as Royalists, were not allowed to go beyond a certain distance of their dwelling-places. Some died of starvation, others eked out a scanty living by teaching, and one of these was Mell. Eventually the Government relented somewhat and set up a "Committee of the Councel for Advancement of Musicke," and on Feb. 19, 1656, John Hingston, Davis Mell, Wm. Howse, Rich. Hudson and Wm. Gregory petitioned to this Committee for permission to found in London a College of Music, but in this they met with no success.

From all accounts Mell was a violinist of outstanding talent. Evelyn speaks of him in his diary as a "rare musician" (Aug. 1, 1652), and on Mar. 4, 1656, when he visited Roger L'Estrange, "to hear the incomparable Lubicer" (Thos. Baltzar of Lübeck), he says: "There were at that time as excellent in their profession as any were thought to be in Europ, Paul Wheeler, Mr. Mell, and others, till this prodigie appeared." A. Wood, who heard Mell at Oxford in 1657–8, tells us that "the company did look upon Mr. Mell to have a prodigious hand on the violin, and they thought that no person, as all in London did, could goe beyond him ... (he) played farr sweeter than Baltzar, yet Baltzar's hand was more quick"; and again he says that Mell "was accounted hithertoo the best for the violin in England, . . . but after Baltzar came unto England, and shew'd his most wonderful parts on that instrument, Mell was not so admired, yet he played sweeter, was a well-bred gentleman, and not given to excessive drinking as Baltzar was." In a petition to Cromwell, Mell styles himself "Gentleman of His Highness' Musique," and when the Protector died, he followed in the funeral procession. At the Restoration Mell was reappointed as member of the "broken Consort" and together with George Hudson as master of the band of violins at a salary of £110. There is some confusion between the annals and lists of the King's Musick, as published by Nagel (Ib.), and the Lord Chamberlain's Records, according to which William Yowckney succeeded Mell, deceased, on Aug. 30, 1662, but the annals appear more reliable, and in these there is no mention of a Wm. Yowckney, while John Yowkeney was appointed violinist on Dec. 12, 1661, and a Walter Yowckney is to be found among the "Musicians in ordinary" in 1663. As usual under Charles II, after the death of Mell some of his livery allowance was still owing and in 1667 his executors applied for his salary due for 1661. Some pieces of his for the violin, including a set of variations on the favourite tune "John, come kiss me now," may be found in Playford's "Division Violin" (1685), "Court Ayres" (1655), "Courtly Masking Ayres" (1662, Roy. Coll. Mus.), as well as in Add. 15118 in the British Museum (*see also* J. Pulver, Biographical Dictionary of Engl. Mus.).

PAUL WHEELER, mentioned by Evelyn, Mar. 4, 1656, as a violinist as excellent as any in Europe, an estimation in which somewhat exaggerated nationalism may have borne its part, appears in Playford's "The Division Violin" (Ed. 1685), and in "The Virgin's Pattern" to which he contributed some not very remarkable pieces, as Paulwheel and Powlwheel. J. Pulver suggests that the latter may have been his real name, of which Evelyn's version was a corruption, and that he was probably of Cornish origin. Although he was held in high esteem during the Commonwealth, and in Charles II's time, no particulars of his life are obtainable apart from a few short references by writers of the late 17th and early 18th centuries.

One of the most remarkable of the families of Italian

England

musicians who settled in England in Henry VIII's time is that of the Lupos. Very early in the 16th century several composers of the name of Lupus, or Lupi, appear in Italy, Germany and France, and in 1540 Alexander, Ambroso and Romano da Milano, are mentioned among the newly appointed "Vialls." Ambrose de Lupo appears among the Violetts of Elizabeth in 1559 and the same players are enumerated as Vyolons in 1570 and in later years, in 1586, he is mentioned as Ambrose de Millane, alias Lupo, as one of the violins together with Jos. and Petro Lupo. Ambrose died 1594. The name of Thomas Lupo appears as composer of Madrigals as well as of Consorts for viols, which are all of outstanding merit, but as there were three Thomas Lupos, an uncle and two nephews, who were all good composers, it is difficult to apportion the authorship of any particular work. The Lupos exercised a great influence on the development of violin- as well as viol-playing. After a period of over a hundred years, during which their name appears in the lists of the Court musicians, they disappear during the Commonwealth. A more detailed account of the Lupo family is given in J. Pulver's Biographical Dictionary of English Music. Charles II's twenty-four violins, in imitation of the "violons du roy" at the French Court, Purcell's decided predilection for the violin family, and the advent of Matteis, did much to bring the violin into favour, although the sympathy of music lovers remained largely with the viols throughout the century.

JOHN JENKINS (*see* p. 60).

DAVIS MELL (*see* p. 60).

LEONARD MELL appears in the list of Charles I "musicians for the violins" of 1625 (Nagel, "Annalen," etc., p. 40). Pulver (Ib., p. 326) says that he is given as a "Tenor violin."

THOMAS MELL was appointed as flautist in 1612 and appears in lists of 1634–5 and 1670. It cannot be ascertained whether or how these two were related to Davis Mell.

JOHN ADSON. Author of "Courtly Masking Ayres," for violins, consorts and cornets, 1611; later ed. 1621 (Brit. Mus.). Under Charles I (1625) he was a Member of the Royal Chapel; from 1634 to the end of 1640 he received

£46 per annum. On Jan. 7, 1634, he was appointed teacher, with a grant of twenty pence a day for life. (*See* Eitner.)

JOHN HARDING. Became violinist in the King's band, London, Dec. 20, 1625; sworn in as gentleman of the Chapel Royal on Lady Day (Mar. 25), 1683, and died Nov. 7, 1684 (Nagel, i, 52, 54).

VALENTIN FLOOD. An English violinist, 1627, at the Court in Berlin (Schneider, 37).

ROBERT TOMKINS. He is mentioned by Eitner as violinist, but was undoubtedly a violist, 1635 and onwards, in the Royal private band. The word "vyollins" or "vyallins" was often used for viols (not necessarily, *see* Holborne).

PAUL WHEELER (*see* p. 62).

JOHN BANISTER, I, b. London, 1630; d. there, Oct. 3, 1679. His father was one of the waits of St. Giles' in the Fields. We first hear of him in connexion with the performance of Sir William Davenant's "Siege of Rhodes" in 1656, when he played as violinist in the orchestra with Thomas Baltzar and Christopher Gibbons. On the ascension of Charles II he became one of the King's musicians, and in December of that year he was sent to France "on special service and to return with expedition." The object of that mission has been variously given (*see* J. Pulver, Dict. of Eng. Music; E. v. d. Str., "Romance of the Fiddle," p. 91). On May 3, 1663, he was installed as one of the "violins in Ordinary for the King's Private Musick," in succession of Davis Mell, at £110 a year, and was ordered to instruct and direct twelve players chosen from the band of twenty-four Violins as a special band, for which he received £600 to be divided amongst them. There were continual troubles about the musicians' salaries, which were always in arrears, and in 1666 Banister was accused of having appropriated payments intended for them. It is also reported that he said within the King's hearing that the English violinists were superior to the French; either by this or the former he incurred the King's displeasure, and the privy seal for the band of violins passed from him to Grabu in Aug., 1666, but he remained in the band. At the end of 1672 he instituted the first public concerts in London at his house in White

Front. Back

Violin by Andreas Amati, in the possession of Messrs. W. E. Hill & Sons. It formed part of Wm. Corbett's collection bequeathed to Gresham College, but refused.

Photographs by Donald Macbeth.

Violinists from the above picture showing detail of the instruments.

A Marriage Fête, by Joris Hoefnagel, 1590.
Reproduced by kind permission of the Right Honourable Marquess of Salisbury, from the painting at Hatfield House. Hoefnagel, who was a painter at the English Court, is seen standing (without hat) against the tree on the right. (See Vol. 1, p. 59.)

England

Friars. The room was surrounded with seats and small tables "alehouse fashion, and there was a large raised box for the musicians, whose modesty required curtains." More particulars about these concerts are given in E. v. d. Str., "The Romance of the Fiddle." In 1674 they were removed to Chandos Street, St. Martin's Lane, and in 1676 to Little Lincoln's Inn Fields. In 1678 he had removed his Academy to Essex Street, Strand. In the following year he died and was buried in the cloisters of Westminster Abbey. There are several references to him in Pepys' Diary, which show that the author thought highly of him as a player as well as a composer. He wrote a number of pieces for violin as well as for viol; of those contained in Playford's "The Division Violin," it is not certain whether some are not the work of his son (q.v.). Others are contained in various collective works, and a few of his compositions, mostly for viols in manuscript, are in the libraries of the Brit. Mus., Oxford Music School and Christ Church, Oxford. He also composed vocal music and pieces for flageolet, on which he was a master executant. A detailed account of his life and works may be found in J. Pulver's Dict. of Eng. Musicians.

JOHN BANISTER, II, b. London, ca. 1652–5; d. there, 1735; son and pupil of John Banister, 1 (q.v.). There is a reference in the wages book of the Duke of York, for 1677, to a Mr. John Banister as music master to the Lady Ann which J. Pulver thinks, with good reason, to indicate the younger Banister. In 1679 he succeeded his father as musician in ordinary and he was also appointed to the "Private Musick in Ordinary" in the succeeding reigns. He was leader at the first Italian Opera in London; a member of Thomas Britton's Music Club, and the first to bring over Corelli's op. V from Italy in 1700, copies of which he sold from his house in Brownlow Street, where he died in 1735. For more particulars about the above facts, *see* E. v. d. Str., "The Romance of the Fiddle," which has for its frontispiece a fine reproduction of J. Smith's mezzotint portrait of the younger Banister. He wrote two instruction books, viz. "The Complete Tutor to the Violin" and "The Gentlemen's Tutor for the Violin." Unfortunately no copies of either of these have been discovered so far, nor are any other tutors of that time extant, so that we know very little about the method of their violin teaching except for a few remarks on Lenton's Tutor in Hawkins' "History of Music." The younger Banister's compositions for violin consist only of a "Set of Ayres in four parts" which appeared as an appendix to Gottfried Finger's "Ayres, Chacones," etc., unless we must attribute to him some pieces in "The Division Violin" and a few MS. pieces.

RICHARD DORNEY. In 1634–68 a violinist in the King's band in London, except of course during the time of the Commonwealth.

GEORGE HUDSON. On Jan. 18, 1642, there is record that he was sworn as musician for the lutes and voices, to date from Dec. 3, 1641. In Playford's "Musical Banquet" he is mentioned as one of London's eminent teachers for "Voyce or Viol." May 31, 1661, he is appointed as superintendent for the practices of the King's band. July 10, 1665, he becomes one of John Banister's band of 24 violins. He died in 1772. In that year his signature appears still in the minutes of the corporation of music. He was also a distinguished composer. (*See* Pulver, p. 426; Nagel, i.)

WILLIAM YOUNG. Very little is known as to the life of this remarkable artist. About the middle of the 17th century he left England for the Netherlands, where he took service with the Archduke Ferdinand Charles of Austria, who resided in Tyrol, but was then Governor of the Netherlands. He returned with Charles II in 1660 as violinist and flautist in the Royal private band. W. Nagel ("Annalen der englischen Hofmusik") mentions him in the lists of violinists of 1661 as newly appointed, again in 1663, and in 1667 when, in Sept., he petitions, together with Isaac Staggins, for payment of arrears of salary—generally a fruitless task, of common occurrence among the musicians of Charles II. Young appears again in the lists of 1668. J. Pulver (Biog. Dict. of Old English Music) states that he was still active in 1670, but is given as "deceased" in the Lord Chamberlain's Record of 1671. Dr. T. L. Southgate in the Preface to the MS. copy of Young's Sonatas of 1653, presented by him to the Brit. Mus., mentions 1672 as the year of his death. He was an excellent violist, violinist, and, according to Pulver, also flautist; but his greatest importance lies in the fact that he wrote instrumental sonatas of a very advanced form and

England

instrumental technique, with all the characteristics of the church Sonata. He is, moreover, a distinct melodist and frees himself from the shackles of the severe counterpoint by which his predecessors and most of his contemporaries were still fettered. The most important of his still existing works is: Sonate à 3, 4 e 5, con alcune Allemand [sic] Correnti e Balletti à 3, di Guglielmo Young Inglese, Dedicate al Sermo. Arciduca Ferdinando Carlo D'Austria. In Inspruch appresso Michael Wagner, 1653. It is worth noting that in Feb. of that year Corelli was born, whose first book of Sonatas did not appear until 1681, twenty-eight years after those by Young. The work of the latter comprises: 11 Sonate da Chiesa Nos. 1–3 à 3; 4–10 à 4; 11 à 5; for 2 to 4 violins, viola, violoncello and basso continuo; 19 Dances (Allemands, Courants, etc.), and four Dance-suites of from four to six pieces, Nos. 1, 2 in d min., 3 in g min., and 4 in B maj. Sir Frederick Bridge had one of the Sonatas performed at one of his Gresham Lectures where it was found very interesting. Sonata 11 was performed at the Haslemere Festival of 1929, arranged for 4 violins, viola da gamba, violone, and harpsichord, by Arnold Dolmetsch, and met with great success. It begins with a fine, melodic Grave for 2 violins, followed by an Allegro, a "Resposte" and a "Canzona" both in 5-part imitative counterpoint, which in the Resposte appears over a pedal bass. The only existing copy of the original edition is in the University Library of Upsala. The Brit. Mus. copy of the Sonatas is preceded by 6 viol da gamba pieces by Young. The Sonatas have been erroneously referred to as viol sonatas, perhaps owing to the fact that in the Brit. Mus. copy the parts of the first Sonata appear as 1st viol and 2nd viol; but in the 2nd Sonata the parts are marked for 2 violins and viola and the printed parts are headed "Violino primo," etc. According to Eitner the Music College at Groningen, Holland, was at one time in the possession of Sonate à 3 viol, by "Guilleaume Joungh" (a spelling of Wm. Young's name probably adopted during his sojourn in Holland). A. à Wood mentions 3-part Fantasies by Young which Playford advertised in 1669, but it appears doubtful whether they were ever published; they may conceivably have been identical with the aforementioned Sonatas. Pieces by him appear in Playford's "A Musical Banquet, 1651" (Part I), "Musick's Recreation on the Viol,

Lyra-way" (1669 and 1682), and in Ayres (1661). A number of his MS. compositions are in the Oxford Music School Library.

GERVACE LITTLETON, alias WESTCOT, ca. 1655; violinist at Oxford (Burney, vi, 425).

JOHN LENTON, b. 1656 (Riemann). In Aug. 2, 1681, he was appointed musician for the violin in the Royal band. Nov. 10, 1685, sworn as gentleman of the Chapel Royal, London; violinist, flautist, composer. He appears in the lists till 1710, but is not mentioned as missing in following lists. In 1719 a John Lenton is mentioned as deceased who was groom of the vestry since 1708, thus probably not the same (Rimbault, 224; Nagel, i, 65, 66; Viertelj, viii, 515; Grove; Pulver; "Romance of the Fiddle"). He wrote "The Gentleman's Diversion, or the Violin Explained" (1693), which contained some pieces of his own at the end. Lenton cautions the learner against holding the violin so low as the girdle "as some do in imitation of the Italians." Where he received this idea is puzzling, as we know from "La Violina con la sua Risposta" that as far back as 1550 they held even the lyra under the chin. A second edition, with an appendix but without the pieces, appeared in 1702 as "The Useful Instructor of the Violin," which contains interesting remarks about the holding of the instrument (Playford, i). "The Division Violin" contains some pieces by him. He was a prolific composer of operatic and chamber music and songs. He also revised the second book of Playford's "The Dancing Master" (1713). More particulars in Pulver, Biog. Dic.

HENRY BROCKWELL. Appointed violinist in the Royal Chapel, London, Oct. 25, 1660; was there still in 1668 (Nagel, 51).

SIMON HOOPER. In Mar., 1661, Simon Hooper, "violinist to H.M. practice of dancing," petitions successfully for the grant of a sum of money and for appointment in the Private Musick, and he appears in the lists until 1668 as violinist in the King's band, London. (Hawkins, iv, 371.) The statement that he resigned Nov. 24, 1663, must therefore be erroneous. The violinist Hopper (Christian name not given) which appears in the list of 1625 (Nagel, i, 40) cannot be the same as the above.

England

THEOPHILUS FITZ. Appointed Aug. 20, 1661, as violinist in the King's Private Musick, London, where he appears in the lists up to 1700. In the Viertelj, viii, 515, he is mentioned as member of the King's band in 1710.

HENRY HAWES. On Jan. 21, 1662, succeeded Robert Tompkins in the King's band, London, as violinist (Nagel, i, 52).

ISAAC STAGGINS. Violinist in the English Royal Private Musick, 1661–8 (Nagel, i, 51 ff.). According to Pulver (Biog. Dict., 438) he played also the tenor oboe in that orchestra.

HENRY COMER. Violinist in the Royal private band, London, from 1663 to 1668 (Nagel, 54 and 60).

NICHOLAS STAGGINS, son of Isaac; d. 1700. He gained the personal favour of Charles II, and to this rather than to his ability he owed his preferment in the Royal Musick. On Dec. 21, 1671, he was appointed musician in ordinary for the violin in the place of William Young, deceased. Pulver (Biog. Dict., 438) says that according to official documents, he became a violinist in the Royal Musick soon after the Restoration, probably "a violin extraordinary without fee." In 1674 he became Master of His Majesty's Violins in the place of Grabu, and, soon after, also of the Royal Chamber Musick. In 1682 the King procured for him the degree of Mus.D. from the University of Cambridge, the usual exercise being waived. As dissatisfaction made itself heard at this proceeding, Staggins produced an exercise which was performed in July, 1684, whereupon he was appointed professor of Music, the first to hold that office. He continued as Master of the Royal Musick, composing music for various events at the Court until 1700, when on June 30, according to the Lord Chamberlain's Records, John Eccles was appointed Master of the Musick in the place of Dr. Staggins, deceased. He composed apparently nothing for violins.

WILLIAM CORBETT, b. ca. 1668; d. London, Mar. 7, 1748. About 1700 he was first violinist in the Royal Chapel and in 1705 leader at the first Italian Opera at the Haymarket Theatre. In 1710 he went to Rome with the King's permission, returning in 1724. After giving some concerts in

London he went again to Rome and only returned in 1741 (according to Mendel). It is said on good authority that he was there as a political agent of the English Government to watch the movements of the Pretender. This enabled him to collect a number of valuable pictures as well as fine Cremona violins, including instruments which formerly belonged to Corelli, Cosimi, Torelli, and to Gobbo (probably C. A. Lunati, called il Gobbo [the limping]). These instruments he left to Gresham College, London, together with a sum of money to cover the expense of their protection and preservation. Nevertheless they were afterwards sold. He composed 2 sets of sonatas for 2 violins and bass, op. I, London, 1705, and op. IV (12), Ib., 1713; 2 sets of sonatas for 2 flutes and B.C. op. 2 and 3; VI sonatas for oboe, etc.; 12 concertos for all Instruments; XXXV concertos or Universal Bizzaries in 7 parts, in 3 books, op. 5 (Mendel, op. 8). In the preface to these he explains that they are intended to illustrate the respective styles appertaining to various countries, and to the principal towns and provinces of Italy. Gerber says that they awakened no interest and were shelved by the music sellers. He also wrote incidental music to various plays and songs. The violin sonatas are more or less respectable imitations of Corelli with some quite pretty movements.

RICHARD HUDSON. One of the violinists of Banister's band, and Keeper of the King's instruments. He died before Mar. 27, 1668, when Thomas Fitz takes his place. He was one of the five musicians who in 1656 approached the Council with a proposal that a College of Music be founded, which however proved fruitless. (Pulver.)

THOMAS DEAN, MUS.DOC., b. ca. 1670. Violinist and organist at Warwick and at Coventry at the beginning of the 18th century. He is said to be the first who played in public in England, in 1709, a sonata by Corelli. He received the degree of Mus.Doc. of Oxford University in 1731. Some pieces by him are in "The Division Violin."

ECCLES (also EAGLES). A remarkable family of English musicians of the 17th and early 18th centuries.

SOLOMON ECCLES, descendant of musical ancestors, was a popular and prosperous teacher of the virginals and viols during the Commonwealth. He was a religious fanatic who

England

joined the Society of Friends, and in a religious frenzy burnt his instruments and music books on Tower Hill and became a cobbler. He died Feb. 11, 1683. His three sons:

JOHN ECCLES (Eagles), the eldest, d. Kingston-on-Thames, Jan. 12, 1735, violinist and composer, became Musician in Ordinary without fee on Mar. 28, 1695, and succeeded Thomas Tollett in 1696 with a salary of £40. In 1700 he became Master of the King's Musick in succession of Dr. Staggins at a salary of £200 a year. He was a very popular composer for the stage, and as such collaborated with Purcell in the third part of "Don Quixote." He also wrote odes for Court festivities, a St. Cecilia ode and many songs.

HENRY ECCLES (Eagles), date of birth unknown; Mendel ("Lexikon") states that he died in Paris in 1742 as violinist in the Royal Chapel. He was a violinist of distinct merit, and as such a member of the King's Private Musick from 1674 to 1710. In 1690–1 he accompanied King William on the latter's journey to Holland, but eventually finding himself neglected, went to Paris where he was greatly admired, and appointed one of the Twenty-four Violins of Louis XIV. Composed: "Premier Livre de Sonates a violon seul et la Basse" (Paris, 1720), and "Second Livre de Sonates a violon ... avec Deux Sonates pour la Flûte Traversière" (Paris, 1723). One of the Sonatas (in D min.) has been edited by Alfred Moffat with pianoforte accompaniment (1906). Hawkins, in his "Hist. of Music," praises Henry as a composer. The first book of the sonatas contains adoptions from G. Valentini's Alletamenti, op. 8 (Barclay Squire, in Mus. Times, Nov., 1923).

THOMAS ECCLES, the youngest of the three brothers, was the pupil of Henry, whom he accompanied to Paris. He was a violinist of great talent, who in 1733 returned to London and became a member of Handel's Orchestra, but abandoning himself to a life of idleness and dissipation, he was dismissed and eked out a precarious livelihood by playing in city taverns (*see* E. v. d. Str., "The Romance of the Fiddle"). Grove's Dict. mentions another HENRY ECCLES, violinist in the King's Mask, etc., in 1674 and later, who in 1685 is mentioned as a "base," and in 1689 was appointed member of the King's Musick. He was probably an uncle of the above. Pulver (Dict. of Old Eng. Mus.), in an interesting account of the

The History of the Violin

Eccles family, mentions another SOLOMON ECCLES, who was Musician in Ordinary in 1685, appointed member of the King's Private Musick in 1689, where he was still after 1700. Probable author of some string trios in Brit. Mus. and composer of vocal music.

HENRY NEEDLER, b. London, 1685; d. there Aug., 1760. Needler was a co-founder of the Academy of Ancient Music and composed Anthems, etc. He was a higher officer in the Excise office and an excellent amateur violinist. He was considered one of the best performers of Corelli's music and he led the first performance of Corelli's Concerti Grossi, op. VI, on their arrival in London, at Loeillet's house. He was also one of the original members of Tom Britton's music club, and a frequent performer at the weekly concerts at the houses of various noblemen (*see* "The Romance of the Fiddle," E. v. d. Str.).

FRECKNOLD. English violinist, represented in Playford's "Division Violin," 1685.

JOHN GAMBLE, d. 1687. A cornet and violin player in the Royal band. He composed vocal music (Pulver, pp. 195–6); pupil of Ambrose Beyland. Airs and songs with Theorbo and bass appeared in 2 books, London, 1657, 1659. The first book contains his portrait, engraved by T. Cross.

JOHN ERNEST GALLIARD, b. ca. 1687 at Celle; d. London, 1748; oboist and flautist. Composed 6 solos for violin, comprised in "12 Solos by Caporale," pub. 1746, and 1 solo MS. in R.C.

WILLIAM HALL. From 1692 to his death, at Richmond, in 1700 violinist of the Royal private band. Some airs of his in "Tripla Concordia" (Hawkins, v, 19); a "Courante for Clavier" by Hall in Collective vol., 1673, by Locke (Eitner).

EDMUND TANNER. Violinist in the English Royal Chapel ca. 1668.

EDWARD (EDMUND?) FLOWER, ca. 1694, violin player in the Royal band, where he was still in 1700 (Nagel, i) and in 1710 (Viertelj, viii, 515).

DANIEL BOON, d. 1700; English violinist and painter. The only record is a portrait representing him playing the violin (Gerber, ii).

England

WILLIAM BABELL, b. London, ca. 1690; d. there 1723. He was the son of a bassoon player. He is recorded as Organist of All Hallows', Bread Street, and said to have been a pupil of Handel. He composed "12 solos for a Violin or Hautboy with a Bass figur'd for the Harpischord," Part I of the posthumous works, London (Walsh); "12 solos for a Violin, Hautboy or Germ. Flute, with B. fig. for the Harpischord," London; a sonata arranged by A. Moffatt (Novello); Allegro from Sonata No 8 by the same in "Courtly Ayres and Dances"; 1 concerto grosso, 3 books of harpischord music and vocal music. His well written sonatas prove him a composer of outstanding talent.

TALBOT YOUNG, b. London towards the end of the 17th century; d. there in Mar., 1758. He was the son of John Young (q.v.), music seller and instrument maker at the Dolphin and Crown at the west end of St. Paul's Churchyard and at the corner of London House Yard. There Talbot with his co-student Maurice Greene (afterwards Dr. Greene) established weekly music practices which were joined by gentlemen performers, and when, soon, the available room proved inadequate, the Talbots moved to the Queen's Head Tavern in Paternoster Row, where the painter Woolaston, a good amateur violinist and flute player, his friends and a number of other efficient players also joined the society. The growing prosperity of the society enabled the members to engage in addition professional performers, and in 1724 the Youngs moved into the still more commodious Castle Tavern, where Talbot was leader of the orchestra until his declining health compelled him to retire. His portrait, painted by Woolaston, adorned the room; unfortunately it appears to be unknown what became of this portrait. The Castle Concerts increased in popularity, especially under the leadership of Prospero Castrucci and other eminent violinists (see E. v. d. Str., "The Romance of the Fiddle," pp. 81, 133, etc.). On Aug. 8, 1719, Talbot Young became a violinist in the King's band. In the "Vierteljahrsschrift für Musikwissenschaft," viii, 516 and 527, he is also mentioned as singer in the Chapel Royal in 1718, as newly appointed (?) in 1723, and also in 1743.

Dr. Caesar wrote a clever catch on the two Talbots which was published in the Second book of "The Pleasant Musical

Companion," by Henry Playford.   It is generally quoted from the edition of 1726:

A CATCH UPON MR. YOUNG AND HIS SON (DR. CAESAR)

You scrapers that want a good fiddle well strung
You should go to the man that is old while he's Young,
But if this same fiddle you fain wou'd play bold,
You must go to his son, who'll be Young when he's old.
There's old Young and young Young, both men of renown,
Old sells, and young plays the best fiddle in town.
Young and old live together, and may they live long,
Young to play an old fiddle; Old to sell a new song.

CHAPTER 10

France

SEVERAL writers have claimed for France the honour of being the country in which the violin came first to light; a fruitless contention, as we have seen already that it was the outcome of a gradual process of evolution from the lyra, in which no doubt many eminent *luthiers* had their part, including Gaspard Duiffoprugcar (the Bavarian Tieffenbrucker), in whose work the claim for France has been based, which we have discussed already in Chapter 6. That the violin became known in France almost contemporaneously with its first appearance in Italy we have seen already from the facts stated in Chapter 6, and it was fostered by the music-loving French kings, especially by the formation of the famous band of the "Twenty-four Violins of the King," created under Louis XIII. Marin Mersenne, in his "Harmonie Universelle" (Paris, 1636), speaks, in his loquacious manner, with enthusiasm of this band:

"... *Et ceux qui ont entendu les* 24 *violons du Roy, aduoiient qu'ils n'ont jamais rien ouy de plus ravissant ou de plus puissant; de là vient que cet instrument est le plus propre de tous faire danser, comme l'on experimente dans les balets, et par tout ailleurs. Or les beautez et les gentilesses que l'on pratique dessus, sont en si grand nombre, que l'on le peut preferer à tous les autres instruments, car les coups de son archet sont par fois si ravissans que l'on n'a point de plus grand mescontentement que d'en entendre le fin, particulierement lorsqu'ils sont meslez des tremblement et des flattements de la main gauche, qui contraignent les Auditeurs de confesser que le Violon est le Roy des instruments* . . ."

The combination of the band he gives as: 6 trebles, 6 basses, 4 altos (hautes-contre), 4 tenors (tailles), and 4 *quintes* (quinte or cinquième), and their combined compass as seven Fifths, or four octaves, with a tuning for the violoncello (*basse*) as "BB flat, F, c, g." In the "Fantaisie à 5" by Henri Le Jeune (*see* Ch. 6), of whom nothing is known apart from this piece, which Mersenne uses as showing the compass of the various instruments, the tuning of the violoncello is however the orthodox one: "C, G, d, a." The shape of the violin illustrated in the "Harmonie Universelle," Livre iv, p. 45 ("Romance of the Fiddle," p. 52), makes one suspect that the tentative forms had not yet entirely disappeared. He also gives a full explanation of the Tablature, which was sometimes used in violin music. The tuning he gives as that still in use, but states that also other tunings, fifths and fourths, etc. (*see* Baltazarini), were sometimes used, which made possible the playing of chords by pressing down two or three strings with one finger; but the bridge must be flatter for this purpose, like the bridge of the Lyra, thus showing that this precursor of the violin was still known and in use. The fingering for the first string of the violin he gives as:

for c''' and d''' he gives no fingering, but as the art of shifting into positions was as yet unknown they must have been played by the extension of the fourth finger. He simply says, after giving the fourth finger for b'': "If one advances still farther towards the bridge one obtains C and still farther up D, so that the complete compass of the violin is a nineteenth."

The effect of the mute was already known, as appears from his remark: "The violin loses a great deal of its tone if a key or similar object is fixed to the bridge." There are many more interesting remarks on technical details; but for these we must refer the reader to "The Romance of the Fiddle," pp. 39–60. In his remark, "I shall now speak of the *concert* which can be played on five hundred violins (!) although twenty-four are sufficient . . .", etc., thus anticipating Berlioz's, and the Handel Festivals' monster orchestras.

The band of Twenty-four Violins of the King received their final organization from Lully in Louis XIV's time, when it was composed of 6 violins, 4 violas (hautes-contre), 4 tenor violins (tailles), 3 quintes de violons (alto violin), 5 basses, and 2 grosses basses (contrabasses). The members, who received 365 livres annually, enjoyed many privileges, freedom from taxation, free board as "*officiers domestiques et commesaux*" (officials of the household who received free board). They were under the direct governance of the King, and wore the

France

most costly uniforms of any of the officials of that extravagant Court (for a detailed account of these *see* Pougin, "Le Violon," p. 143). For the performance of Lully's operas, ballets, court festivities and other occasions, Louis XIV created a special band of violins called *"les petits violons de Lully,"* which was under the sole direction of the latter, and consisted of: 6 dessus de violon (ordinary violins), 2 hautes-contre, 3 tailles, 2 quintes, 4 basses, 2 treble cromornes, and 2 bassoons. According to Fétis ("La Revue Musicale," 1830), they played at all court entertainments, such as serenades, balls, ballets, operas in the palace, private concerts, water and garden festivals, coronations, on entering a town, at weddings, funerals and other solemnities. Besides these two bands there was still a third, the "Musique de la grande Escurie," which had its own particular sphere of activity.

Mersenne, in explanation of the instruments for the middle parts, says: "With regard to the middle parts, viz. the *Taille*, the *Cinquième partie*, and the *Haute-contre*, it should be noted that they are of different size although they are all in unison." On p. 129 he says:

"What the Twenty-four Violins of the King call the *Quinte* or *Cinquième partie* (Fifth part), is called by the ordinary musicians *Haute-contre*, and what they call *Taille* is what we call *Haute-contre*, so that our *Haute-contre* is their *Taille*, that is why I observed their order in the Latin edition (of the 'Harmonie Universelle'). The '*Cinquième partie*' of the preceding notes is in compass (quant a l'aigu) nearest to the treble (dessus), therefore it must be between the dessu (treble) and the *Haute-contre* (alto), consequently it must be the smallest violin of the three which are in unison: from that it comes that the violinists call this part the Haute-contre, the Haute-contre Taille, and the Taille Cinquième partie."

It is difficult to follow the logic of his deduction in this last sentence, nor is it less so to see how all the middle parts could have been tuned in unison, which all modern writers have taken to be that of the viola, viz.: c, g, d', a'. Although it would be *possible* to play any of the middle parts of the *Fantaisie*, which he gives as an example, on an instrument of that tuning, as their combined compass does not exceed c–e'', it does not strike one as convincing that this should have been the case.

The name Cinquième appears to indicate an instrument somewhat different from the violin, but does it refer to any particular instrument at all? It was evidently used by some for a high middle part, by others for a low middle part (taille). If we look at the full name thereof, which is Quinte ou cinquième partie, we find it corresponds to "Quintus pars" in the scores of the old vocal composers, also called "the Wanderer," as it might appear in any middle part, where however it would remain throughout any one particular composition, and some of the old violinists placed it in the second, while others placed it in the fourth part, but it did not change the character of the instrument, it simply was the "Quintus pars." Now if we examine the part of the Cinquième, which significantly appears at the bottom of the page, underneath all the other parts, in Mersenne's book, we shall find that its compass is between c' and e" with the bulk between f' and c", which is evidently far more suitable for a violin than for a viola. Lully in his Ballets and Operas uses the same clefs as appear in the above Fantasie, but unfortunately he does not name the instruments in his scores except in a few of his works, like "Amadis" (1684), where in a few numbers only the word violons appears under the first line. In the "Ballet des Saisons" (1700), by Colasse, with additional numbers from Lully's works, most of the numbers are for violins (one or two, in G clef on first line) and bass only. In the Scene 2, "Plainte de Zephire," he uses two recorders (flûtes douce, in G clef on the first line) with a "violon" in the alto clef, thus evidently a Taille, alternating with two violins (in G clef on first line) and bass. In the "Temple de la Paix," by Lully (1685), p. 74, we find a Prélude with a "Choeur des Ameriquains, in which the following passage for the first violin occurs:

This shows:
(1) How anxiously the old composers avoided ledger lines either above or below the stave. Had the Cinquième of Mersenne, or the Twenty-four Violins been a viola, tuned c to a', all the notes of its lower octave would have necessitated ledger lines if written in the C clef on the first line.

(2) The use of both G and C clef for the first violin shows that the Violin and Cinquième did not necessarily indicate different instruments.

France

Taking all these circumstances into consideration we may safely conclude that the Cinquième part here was played not on a viola but on a violin, perhaps of a large pattern, as a difference in size is insisted upon by Mersenne. Niccolo Amati and others made violins of a small as well as of a large pattern. As regards the Taille, Mersenne's statement that it was tuned like the Haute-contre, c, g, d', a', is surprising, although that part in the Fantaisie, which, he says, shows the whole extent of its compass, does not go below c', yet at all events later in the 17th century it was tuned a fourth or a fifth lower than the viola (*see* article E. v. d. Str., "The Violin Family," in Grove's Dict.).

Technically, the French violinists were far behind their Italian and German contemporaries, and although Lully did a great deal to raise the status of the instrument, yet the nature of his music was not suited to further its technical development. This was hampered furthermore by the institutions of the band of the Twenty-four Violins and the Musicians' Guild, the "Confrérie de St. Julien" (for details, *see* L. Grillet, "Les Ancêtres du violon"), who kept out all foreign artists, especially those who endangered their reputation, and even J. B. Anet, as pupil of Corelli, and the great J. M. Leclair, as a pupil of Somis, had to suffer from their maleficent influence. When we hear that the test-piece for membership in the band of the Twenty-four Violons du roy was a simple little air from Lully's "Songe d'Atys" (republished in F. Hermann's arrangement by Augener, Ltd), we can well believe that J. Banister's assertion that the English violinists surpassed the French (in Charles II's time) contained a large modicum of truth.

JEAN CHARMILLON, King of the minstrels. He is the first minstrel king known to history; b. in the Champagne about the middle of the 13th century. He was elected King of the minstrels of the town of Troyes in 1295 in the reign of Philip le Bel. In the 18th century the title was altered to "Roy des Violons." A. Pougin ("Le Violon," etc.), however, thinks the office existed long before that time.

CLAUDE LEJEUNE (called CLAUDIN). A Belgian, b. Valenciennes ca. 1530; d. Paris between 1598 and 1603. Although his fame rests chiefly on his compositions (he was chamber composer to Henry III and Henry IV), he is mentioned by Pacquot in his "Mémoires littéraires" as "an excellent violiniste of the 16th century."

MAZUEL, a dynasty of French violinists which covers nearly one and a half centuries. All were "violons ordinaires" of the band of Twenty-four Violins of the King. The first was GUILLAUME MAZUEL, b. ca. 1540, who was succeeded by his son JEAN MAZUEL, b. 1568, d. 1616; his two sons were JEAN MAZUEL II, b. 1593, d. 1663, and PIERRE MAZUEL, b. 1605. The last and most important was MICHEL MAZUEL, whose date of birth is unknown but who died in Oct., 1676. His compositions attracted the attention of Louis XIV who, in recognition of his artistic merit, appointed him in May, 1654, by letters patent as composer for the band of Twenty-four Violins (Em. Thoinan, "Un Bisaïeul de Molière, Recherche sur les Mazuels," Paris, 1878). Apart from his compositions for this band, which are lost, he contributed to the music for the Court ballets in which the King himself danced. Ecorcheville has published a selection from "Vingt suites d'orchestre du XVII siècle" (Mss. in the Cassel library) containing two pieces by Mazuel, which Pougin describes as of an "amiable rhythm and good sense of melody."

CLAUDE GERVAISE. A 16th-century violist and violinist in the chamber music of Francis I; composed "Livres de danseries à 4 et 5 parties," published by Atteignant (4 in 1550, 5 in 1550, 6 in 1555, 3 in 1556), also chansons in 4 parts in collected works, 1542–53 (Eitner, i). Fétis says that his pieces are remarkable for their workmanship (facture).

HONDRÉ CASTELAN. The first French violinist whose name has been preserved. He was chamber violinist to Henry II of France ca. 1555 according to a MS. bill of 1559 in the Bibliothèque Nationale (Fétis, *Revue Musicale*, 1832, 6me année, p. 257).

PHILIBERT JAMBE DE FER, b. at Lyons, where he appeared as teacher of the Protestant (Reformed) religion. It is uncertain whether he died before or was murdered on St. Bartholomew's night, like Goudimel, Aug., 27/28, 1572. Apparently he lived some time at Poitiers and Paris. He published, together with Pierre Coussonel and Martin la Roche, the 150 Psalms of David in Clement Marot and Th. de Bèze metrical

France

translation which he set to music in 4 and 5 parts (Lyons, 1564).

His "Epitome Musical," pub. 1556, is the first printed account we have of the violin. Pougin gives an extract from the original copy in the Paris Conservatoire library, which follows here in translation: After explaining that the French viols have only 5 strings, while those of the Italians have 6, and that they are tuned in fourth from the highest string to the lowest, and that the violin has 4 strings, tuned in fifths, he says: "One calls viols those (instruments) which the gentlemen merchants and other people of quality use for their pastime. The violin is that (instrument) which one commonly uses for dances, and with good reason, for it is much easier to tune, the fifth being sweeter for the ear than the fourth. It is also easier to carry, a thing which is very necessary in conducting (playing at) a wedding or mummery" (*see also* p. 36).

CLAUDE GUILLAUME NYON (called LAFONT or LE FOUNDY), b. Paris ca. 1567; d. there 1641. Studied music from early boyhood and devoted himself chiefly to the violin, on which he became an excellent executant. His father, CLAUDE NYON, violin in ordinary to the King, became King of the minstrels in 1590 and distinguished himself so much that he was allowed in 1600 to retire in favour of his son, who followed him on Feb. 8, 1600, as "King of the violinists and Master of players of instruments, both high and low." On Aug. 21, 1608, he became also "violon ordinaire de la chambre du roi." After his death he was succeeded by Gaillard Taillason, called Mathelin. A Sarabande by him is contained in the Philidor collection.

PIERRE ROUSSEL. Chamber violinist of Charles IX and "Roy des joueurs d'instruments du Royaume de France" (King of the minstrels) from 1572; (he is thus styled in a document *re* the birth of his son Jehan).

JACQUES SALMON. Late 16th century, violinist, chamber valet, chamber musician and composer at the Court of Henry III of France. Together with Beaulieu, he composed the music to Baltazarini's "Ballet Comique de la Royne." In 1575 he received at the *concours* at Évereux, the prize of a silver lyre, for a four-part song.

The History of the Violin

BOCAN (JACQUES CORDIER), b. in Lorraine ca. 1580; d. Paris, Sept., 1653 (*see* Lionel de la Laurencie and Pougin). Of unknown, low origin, small stature, misshapen, of ugly features, without the slightest education of any kind, unable to read or write, ignorant even of musical notation, yet praised by Mersenne and other notable contemporaries as an eminent violinist, rebec player and composer. Amorous, conceited, knock-kneed and gouty, this grotesque oddity was the most famous dancing master of his time, who counted among his pupils the Queens of England, France, Denmark, Poland, some of the kings and the members of the nobility. The tunes and airs which he composed were pleasing and became very popular, and in spite of his grotesque appearance he must have possessed a fascinating personality, for Charles I of England often invited him to dine at the Royal table and overwhelmed him with presents. He invented a new dance which was called La Bocane and remained in fashion for a long time. His praises were sung by eminent writers in prose and poetry. In 1621 he married Radegonde de Chedeville, a member of the famous family of musicians, and a French Duke and Duchess were the god-parents of his first child. (For a longer account of this curious man, *see* Pougin, "Le Violon," etc.)

GAILLARD TAILLASSON (called MATHALIN or MATHELIN), b. Toulouse ca. 1580; d. Toulouse (?) 1647. A good violinist who was by the King of violinists, Nyon, given the legal right to bring under his direction all the minstrels of Toulouse (Paris, Aug. 21, 1608). When they objected, the matter came before Parliament, which confirmed the edict in 1609. After the death of Claude Guillaume Nyon in 1641, Taillasson was nominated as Roy des Violons, and confirmed by Louis XIII. Fétis gives part of the legal warrant and enumerates dialogues and airs of which he says some are still sung by the people. Fétis: He had under him a band of violinists. In 1639 he was paid 30 livres by the government of the province (état de la province) for himself and his band for playing in the processions. He had a rival named Poucet, who also had a band and both strove with each other in the processions and public ceremonies for supremacy. Anger Gaillard sang their praises in the provincial language (dialect), and in his "Dialogué sur l'abus que se coumet à las dansos" he intro-

France

duces Mathelin as interlocutor. After the death of Nyon he succeeded by letters patent of Louis XIII to the burlesque dignity of Roy des Violons, which he occupied till he died. He composed the chansons of his friend, the celebrated Languedoc poet Godelin or Goudelin, which became so popular, that some survive even to present times in Toulouse and Languedoc.

LOUIS CONSTANTIN, b. ca. 1585; d. Paris (?) during the last days of Oct., 1657. In 1619 he was one of the band of Twenty-four Violins of the King of France, and succeeded Fr. Richomme as "Roy et Maistre des Ménétriers" in 1624. Mersenne in his "Harmonie Universelle" says that "many who have heard the violin on which Bocan, Constantin, Lazarin and others play all kinds of chansons, admit that the part they play surpasses all manner of concerts, and that they would willingly dispense with all compositions for several voices to hear these, although they never play more than one part." About Constantin's life and musical education nothing is known. Fétis says "he composed pieces in 5 and 6 parts for violin, viol and bass, which are not without merit." One of these, "La Pacifique," became exceedingly popular (for detailed description *see* Wasielewski, "Violine," p. 326); a copy thereof with the date 1636 is contained in vol. i of the famous "Collection Philidor" in the Paris Conservatoire library, and Paulus Matthys "Cabinet" (1646). A collection of 20 French orchestral suites in the Cassel library contains (according to Pougin) likewise pieces by Constantin. In his "Dernier Musiciana," Weckerlin gives the facsimile of a diploma granted by Constantin to François Chouallié (?) in the year 1656.

FRANÇOIS CHEVALIER. In the 16th and 17th centuries, a chamber musician of Henry IV and Louis XIII of France, played the violin and the "viole bâtarde appelée quinte" (quinton?—Fétis). In a catalogue of the Court ballets, in four and five parts, by Michel Henry (MS. de la Valliere, Paris library), one of the "grande bande" of the Twenty-four Violins of Louis XIII, one finds the following entry: "seven airs played on the night of St. Julian, in 1587, by us Chevalier, Lore, Henry the elder, Lamotte, Richaine, and others on lutes, spinets, manduras, violins, flutes with nine holes, etc.; the whole well

The History of the Violin

together, playing and walking through the town; Henry performed most of the trebles (dessus); there were not more than five parts then. Planton played the *quinte* then, and afterwards Chevalier played the *quinte* also." The catalogue also mentions Chevalier as the composer of the ballet of St. Julian to which the above refers. He appears to have been one of the best composers of his time in France for instrumental music, and especially for the ballet. According to Pougin he composed 35 ballets, some only in part, between 1595 and 1616.

NICOLAS GUESTON, b. Châteaudun, ca. 1614. A French violin virtuoso whose compositions were held in high esteem among his contemporaries.

GUILLAUME DUMANOIR, b. Paris, Jan. 16, 1615; d. there (?) towards the end of the century. The son of a violinist, he became violinist at the Court of Louis XIV; succeeded Louis Constantin as Roy des Violons, Nov. 20, 1657, after being leader of the Twenty-four Violins from 1655. In 1658 the King issued an ordinance that dancing-masters as well as musicians should take out a license from the King of the minstrels. This lead to long and violent quarrels (described at length by L. Grillet, "Les Ancêtres du Violon," Pougin, La Laurencie, and others, "Hist. du Théatre de l'académie Roy, de la Musique") which caused Dumanoir to attack the dancing-masters in a rather coarse pamphlet: "Le Mariage de la Musique avec la Dance" (Paris, 1664). He left some compositions, but it is generally considered doubtful which of them are by him and which are by his son except perhaps of the "Charivaris," 3 airs in 5 parts, dated 1646, which would be too early for the son. (More particulars in Riemann, 11th ed.)

MICHEL LEJEUNE, HENRI MICHEL. Both belonged to the Twenty-four Violins du Roy, ca. 1587.

HENRI LEJEUNE, ca. 1600. A violinist-composer, who, among others, wrote a "Fantaisie a cinq parts" for members of the violin family, which is contained in Mersenne's "Harmonie Universelle"; one movement in E. v. d. Str., "The Romance of the Fiddle."

France

FRANÇOIS RICHOMME, d. Paris (or Versailles?), Dec., 1624. Violinist in Chapels of Henry IV and Louis XIII of France; succeeded Claude Guillaume Nyon as Roy des Violons and Violon Ordinaire du Roy. He instituted proceedings in court against 4 musicians of the Royal Chapel for refusing to follow the Court on its journeys and for wanting to give dancing lessons without his permission. The verdict was given in his favour.

LAZARIN, d. probably at the beginning of 1653, when Lully succeeded him. He was violinist and Court composer in Louis XIII and XIV's chapels and is already mentioned by Mersenne in his "Harmonie Universelle" (1636) as one of the greatest French violinists. Some pieces by him are contained in the "Vingt Suites d'orchestre" in the Cassel library.

LÉGER. Was one of the Twenty-four Violins of the King of France and is mentioned by Mersenne in his "Harmonie Universelle" (1636) as an eminent French violinist who was also leader of the Court dances (dance orchestra).

JEAN FRANÇOIS LALOUETTE, b. Paris, 1651; d. Versailles, Sept. 1, 1728. He received his first music lessons at the *maîtrise* of Saint Eustache, and studied the violin under Guy Le Clerc, violinist in the "grande bande du roi." Lully, who taught him composition, took him into his orchestra as violinist while he was at the head of the opera. Lalouette, who passed for one of the best violinists of his time, was afterwards conductor of the opera for nine years, at the end of which in 1677 he was replaced in that position by Colasse, at the instigation of Lully (who had made him his secretary), because he had boasted that he was the composer of some of the finest airs in operas of Lully who had merely employed him to fill in some parts of the recitatives. Later on, however, he became master of the chapel of Saint-Germain l'Auxerrois, and after that of the church of Notre-Dame in Paris (Pougin). He composed operatic and church music, but apparently nothing for the violin.

GUILLAUME DU MANOIR, I. A son of a Paris minstrel; "Roy des Violons" et maître des ménestriers, Nov. 20, 1657. He is manifestly the Guillaume Dumanoir referred to on p. 84.

GUILLAUME DU MANOIR, II, d. Paris, 1697. Followed his father Guillaume Du Manoir, I, as Roy des Ménétriers in 1668 and held this office till 1693 (?). The differences with the various bodies of musicians continued, and in 1672 he embarked in a bitter quarrel with Lully, who had obtained a privilege for the opera and the training of musicians, but he lost in both cases. The quarrels with the dancing-masters, however, continued, and on Dec. 31, 1685, he resigned all material privileges, merely retaining his title; but other difficulties arose which made his position become still more distasteful, and, embittered at the treatment meted out to him, he resigned fully and finally in 1693. It was intended to indemnify him for his reduced income by making him a lifelong examiner for the certificate of Mastership in music, but he never made use of this privilege. When he died, the office of Roi des Ménétriers or Roi des Violons was suppressed and only revived passingly in favour of J. P. Guignon some time during the 18th century. (*See* Grillet, Pougin, etc.)

JEAN BAPTISTE VOLUMIER (WOULMYER), b. in Spain, 1677 (Riemann says he was really born much earlier); d. Dresden, Oct. 7, 1728. He became violin and dancing-master at the Royal Chapel and the "Princes and Ritter-Academie" in Berlin on Nov. 22, 1692. In 1706 he entered the Electoral Chapel at Dresden, where he became concertmeister June 28, 1709, at a salary of 1,200 thaler. He is said to have studied the violin in France, and contemporaries describe him as an excellent violinist in the French style. He composed numerous ballets which were burnt at the bombardment of Dresden by Frederic II (Schneider 50, 2; Hauptwerk, 25; Fürstenau, i, 114, 129; iib, 64 ff.).

JEAN FERRY (FEREY, FERREY) REBEL (LE PÈRE) (*see* Pougin), b. Paris, between 1660 and 1670; d. there (buried Jan. 3) 1747. He was a pupil of Lully, and became one of the Twenty-four Violons du Roy and chamber composer in Paris. In 1699 he entered the opera orchestra as 1st violinist; 1707 he became (1st violin and) conductor; 1718 Royal chamber composer; 1734 elected director of concert spirituel (Brenet); 1737 he received 1,200 lires as conductor at the opera. From

France

1751 his name disappears from the lists. His elder sister married Lalande. Composed "Pièces pour le violon," etc. (title, *see* Eitner), Paris, 1705; sonates (12) a violon seul mêlées de plusieurs récits pour la viola; Recueil de 12 sonates à 2 et 3 voix, Paris, 1712, etc., etc. (*see* Eitner). His opera (tragédie lyrique) "Ulysse," performed 1703, had little success. According to Pougin:—Rebel was the son of an obscure singer in the Royal Chapel. He became a pupil of Lully for violin and composition at a very early age, and was placed in the orchestra for the Court operas at Saint Germain en Laye. One day at a final rehearsal before members of the Court Lully noticed a big roll of paper sticking out of the boy's pocket. He took it and found that it contained the orchestral parts of an act of an opera composed by the boy. Curious to hear such a precocious production, he asked the audience to remain, told the boy to put out the parts, mounted him on a table in front of the orchestra; little Rebel then conducted his work, which proved quite a success. His only opera of later years, "Ulysse," as noted above, was not a great success. His chief importance as a composer lies in the fact that he and F. du Val were the first to introduce the Italian violin sonata into France. A more detailed account of his three books of sonatas is given by Pougin "Le Violon," etc., p. 165. An air, "Le Caprice," for violin solo, the only thing that survived from his opera, remained for years a test-piece for *ballerinas*.

JACQUES HUGUENET. Entered the service of Louis XIV in 1661 and was still living in 1699. He was the son of Pierre Huguenet, tenor viol player in the Royal Chapel. He received his first lessons from his father, and afterwards studied the violin under Jean Noël Marchand, chamber violinist of the King. He became a member of the select band, called the "petits violons." He composed solo and trio sonatas for violin, pub. in Paris, without date. Both he and his father played at the performance of Molière and Corneille's "Psyche," at the Court, Jan. 17, 1670.

PIERRE HUGUENET. Entered the Royal Chapel at Versailles 1661 as tenor violist and afterwards became a member of the Twenty-four Violins of the King, but retired in 1687. He took the 3rd violin, and his son, Jacques, 7th violin at

The History of the Violin

the performance of Molière and Corneille's "Psyche," at the Court, on Jan. 17, 1671.

LEWIS (LOUIS) GRABU (GRABUE, GRABUS, GRABUT). A French violinist who came to London before 1665 and was appointed in the Royal band, 1666; 1668 leader of the band, succeeded John Banister as master of the Twenty-four Violins Nov. 12, 1666. Dryden praised him above English composers, and he composed Dryden's "Albion and Albanius," which proved a failure at the Dorset Garden Theatre, owing to the excitement over the Monmouth rebellion. There was strong opposition to his appointment, as appears from a MS. poem discovered at the Guildhall, London. One of the verses runs thus:

> "Each actor on the stage his luck bewailing,
>   Finds that his loss is infallibly true,
> Smith, Nokes, and Leigh in a feverish railing,
>   Curse Poet, Painter, and Monsieur Grabue."

He was succeeded on Jan. 29, 1675, by N. Staggins as master of the English chamber music; but continued to reside in London as composer until 1694 (*see* Riemann, *also* Pulver). Compositions in Eitner, including Aires for the Violin MS. in Christ Church, Oxford.

SEBASTIAN LE CAMUS, d. Paris, Apr., 1677. Master of the "Grande bande des violons" of Louis XIV. In 1665 he is Master of the music of the Queen of France, with a salary of 1,800 francs (M. f. M., 21, 128). (*Mercure galant*, Avril, 1677, p. 18.) He composed airs for 1 and 2 parts with Bc., published through the care of his son Charles (Paris, Chr. Ballard, 1678). He was also a player on the pardessus de viole, on which according to Mersenne he had no rival, and Jean Rousseau says "the memory of the beauty and tenderness of his playing effaces anything one has heard on that instrument up to the present time." CHARLES LE CAMUS, son of Sebastian, was also a violinist in the King's Musick.

JEAN CLAUDE GILLIER, b. ca. 1667 in Paris; d. there 1737. A violinist at Comédie Française. Composer of numerous operettas which were very melodious, and popular during ca. 1740, also in England. (List in Eitner.)

France

MICHEL PIGNOLET DE MONTECLAIR, b. Andclot, Dec. 4, 1667; d. Saint Denis, near Paris, Mar. 24, 1737. First double-bass player at the Grand Opera, and a fertile composer. He wrote "Methode pour apprendre a jouer du violon" (1712, 2nd ed., 1736), one of the first tutors for the violin; 6 trios or sonatas for 2 violins, and bass, 1728. His first work was "*Serenade au concert*," divided into 3 suites of pieces for violins, flutes and oboes, consisting of airs de fanfare, airs tendres, and airs champêtres proper for dancing (Paris, Ballard, 1697). He was highly esteemed as a teacher of the violin. His real name was Pignolet, the additional appellation Monteclair he adopted from the ruined fortress of that name which dominates Andelot and fascinated his youthful imagination (E. Voillard, "Essay sur Monteclair," quoted by Pougin).

PIERRE JOUBERT. One of the best pupils of Lully, was violinist at the Grand Opera, Paris, in 1690; Royal chamber musician in 1677 and apparently then already a member of the opera orchestra.

AUGUSTE LEPEINTRE. A violinist in the Chapel of Louis XIV with 912 livres in 1677 (Castil Blaze, 146); Richelet (Dict. Franc., 1679, under Violon) says: "Lepeintre, one of the best violinists in Paris, earns more than Corneille, one of our most famous French poets." Some pieces of his were in one of the unfortunately lost volumes of the "Collection Philidor."

JACQUES, AUBERT, "LE VIEUX," b. 1678; d. Belleville, near Paris, May 19, 1753. Chamber violinist of the King, and Concert Spirituel; entered the Royal Academy of Music in 1727; leader of first violins 1748; and about the same time superintendent of the Music of the Duc de Bourbon. He retired from the opera in 1752. He composed three books of sonatas, pub. Paris (Riemann). In 1730 appeared his "Concerts de symphonies," the preface to which is *very* important (*see* text in footnote, Schering, p. 166); he also wrote divertissements, ballets, etc., for the opera and a cantata, "Le ballet de Chantilly" (Fétis and Wki.).

PIERRE JAVARY. Violinist in the Dresden Court Chapel before 1678. He is probably the "petit violon" who received a salary of 250 thaler. The archives refer to him as a French musician who in 1678 received a present of 14 thaler from the Elector (Fürstenau, iia, 201, who wrongly calls him Janary).

ANTOINE MUTAN, 1679, violinist, probably "petit violon" in the Dresden Court Chapel, at 250 thaler (Fürstenau, iia, 201).

GENSIEN GROSMIER, ca. 1679, violinist, probably for the "petit violon" at the Dresden Court Chapel (Fürstenau, iia, 201).

JEAN BAPTISTE, SÉNALLIÉ LE FILS, generally called Sénallié (on the titles of his Sonatas he calls himself Sénallié le Fils); b. in the parish of Saint-Germain l'Auxerrois, Paris, Nov. 23, 1687; d. Paris, Apr. 29, 1730 (others give the date as Oct. 8, 15, or 25). Son of one of the Twenty-four Violins of Louis XIV; violin pupil of Queversin, then of de Bonnefons, one of the Twenty-four Violins, and finally pupil of Bapt. Anet. In 1713 he succeeded his father as member of the Twenty-four Violins of the King, according to Castil-Blaze, as "haute-contre" (viola), and from that time he calls himself "Ordinaire de la musique du roi." Fétis seems responsible for the statement repeated by later biographers, that he was for some time assistant of one Bonnefons, a dancing-master, which Pougin declares to be without foundation. Certain is that about this time the desire to make the acquaintance of some of the great violinists, whose praises were sung by his master Anet, a pupil of Corelli, decided him to visit Italy. He arrived at Modena in May at the time of the Fair, and made so great an impression by his playing that the composer of the opera which was then being performed, asked him to join his orchestra, and as a mark of distinction gave him a chair which was higher than those of the other musicians. After the opera he played some of his own sonatas, which greatly pleased the Duke and all the members of his Court. On his return to Paris in 1719 he was engaged by the Duke of Orleans, Regent of France, for his private music, at the recommendation of the duke's daughter, the Duchess of Modena. He became a very popular teacher, and his sonatas, on account of their pleasing melodious style, as well as the rich and varied figuration of the bass parts, which attracted the bass-viol players (they were written mostly for the bass-viol), found a ready market and provided him with ample means. Violin-playing in France was still in its

France

infancy, and Sénallié, who had been trained in the school of the great Italian masters, handed on their art to his pupils, and the best of these, Guillemain and Guignon, transmitted it to a following generation. He composed 5 books of sonatas for violin solo and bass, published in 1710, 1712, 1716, 1721, 1727. A selection of 13 of these sonatas adapted for musettes and vielles was published in M. Pincherle's collection, Paris. His 9th sonata was republished in Alard's "Maîtres classiques" (Schott & Co.) and by Gust. Jensen (Augener). A sarabande and allemande and a sonata in G has been re-edited by Alfred Moffat (Simrock). A composition by Sénaillé appears in "Pieces Diverses Choisies" by E. M. E. Deldevez (Paris, Richault, 1858). There are also some numbers by Sénallié in Maupetit's Menuets.

MICHEL MATHIEU, b. Paris, Oct. 28, 1689; d. there Apr. 9, 1768. In 1728 he was appointed as violin in the Royal Chapel and afterwards Master of the Chapel. In MS. No. 1809 of the Brussels Royal library he calls himself Maître de chapelle à St. Louis de Versailles. He was pensioned in 1761, when his son Julien succeeded him. His wife, Jacqueline Françoise Barbier, was an eminent singer at the Court of the Queen.

MICHEL CORRETTE, b. St. Germain, France, ca. 1690; d. Paris, ca. 1783. His great and real merit lies in the excellence of his teaching and the part he had in the general advancement of musical life in Paris. His real name (*see* Riemann, who says he merely edited Zipoli's works in 1739) apparently was Zipoli, as he calls himself thus on his Method for the Transverse Flute (Paris, 1710), and his numerous following works up to 1729. He wrote a number of tutors for various instruments for his school of music which he opened in Paris. In his "*Le maître de clavecin pour l'accompagnement,*" etc. (advice for playing from figured bass), Paris, 1753, he says that when Corelli's sonatas arrived in Paris there was not a single violinist who could play them. Only after practising day and night for several years three managed to do so. This statement, which no doubt was true, and tallies with John Banister's opinion as well as what we know from other sources, called down the wrath of the Paris musicians upon his head, who in revenge, with more wit than fairness, called his pupils "*les anachorètes*" (*Anes à Corette*). He was an enthusiastic admirer of Lully and of Campra, whose works besides his own he had performed at his house.

A list of his numerous compositions is given in Riemann (11th ed.). In the second half of the 18th century he was organist at the Jesuit college, and of the Duke of Angoulême, also Knight of the Order of Christ. Among his numerous vocal and instrumental compositions of the most varied kind are some violin concertos, and two instruction books for the violin. The first of these is "L'Ecole d' Orphée an easy method for the study of the violin in the French and Italian manner, with the elements of music and numerous lessons for one and two violins ... op. 18, Paris, 1738, at the author's." In this book, which is not above the average standard of the time, he speaks still of various tunings for the violin, viz. g d' a' e'', g d' a' d'', and f c' a' e''. The second work: "L'Art de se perfectionner dans le violin [*sic!*] ("The arts of perfecting oneself on the violin"), in which are given studies for all four strings of the violin, and the various kinds of bowing ... forms the sequel to *L'École d'Orphée* ... Paris, Castagneri, 1738, "and contains a number of pieces by various composers, mostly Italian (names in E. v. d. Str., "Romance of the Fiddle"), many of which have come down to us in this work only.

CHARLES ROSIER. Late 17th-century violinist and afterwards vice-capellmeister at the Court of the Elector of Cologne at Bonn. He composed 12 sonatas à 6 (2 dessus, haute-contre, bass, B.c. and trumpet) and a book of "Pièces choisies a la manière italienne" (3-part instrumental pieces, 1691), also motets, and a guitar tutor.

ANTOINE DORNEL, b. 1695; d. Paris, 1765. Composer, and distinguished organist; composed three books of Trios for 2 violins and bass; Sonates à violin seule, op. 2. Paris, 1711 (*see* E. v. d. Str., "Eighteenth Century Violin Sonatas").

GILLIER, LE JEUNE, b. end of 17th century; son of Jean Claude. He appears to have lived for some time in London, where his 8 sonatas for 2 violins and violoncello as well as harps. pieces were pub. (B. Wagner). L'Hymenée royal. Divertiss. présenté à la reine des romains (German Empress?) Paris, Chri. Ballard, 1699. This must be Jean Claude's.

France

ANTOINE BOILEAU. Succeeded Charles Lecomte as teacher of the violin of Louis XIII of France, who also played the lute.

BELLEVILLE. One of the Twenty-four Violins of Louis XIII and XIV. Some pieces of his are contained in the Collection Philidor and in 20 French orchestral suites in the Cassel library.

QUEVERSIN. An early 17th-century violinist in the band of Twenty-four Violins of Louis XIII and Louis XIV; he was the first teacher of Sénallié.

N. BAUDY. Violinist under Louis XIV at a salary of 912 livres and provisions (Castil-Blaze, 146).

CHARLES GOUPY. Violinist of the Royal Chapel of Louis XIV, at 912 livres, 10 sous extra and provisions (bread, wine, etc.) (Castil-Blaze, 146).

BELASIUS. Known only by a sonata in Alard's "Maîtres classiques."

CHAPTER 11

Germany: to 1650

LIKE France, Germany had its Musical Fraternities and Guilds from the early 13th century, and they as well as the "Stadtpfeifer" (town musicians, waits) and the wandering minstrels had an important share in the evolution of instrumental music; while the numerous Courts attracted musicians, chiefly from England and Italy, and through this free intercourse between the various nations the German players, in contradistinction to the French, benefited by the art of the former, which, like the English, they transmuted, by imbuing it with the spirit of the people. The Courts, on the other hand, in spite of their predilection for the Italians, for which they had every reason at that early period, gave their native musicians fullest encouragement, when they showed themselves worthy of it, and thereby contributed largely to the advancement of instrumental playing and of music in general. The Lombardian towns, who witnessed the birth of the violin, were in some way or other connected with the German Empire from the times of Charlemagne, and it is but natural that anything important in music, or any other art, that happened in either country, should within the shortest time become known also in the other. It is therefore not impossible that Knöbel of Goldberg in Silesia, who is said to have been the teacher of the eminent blind musician Krumbhorn (q.v.), for composition, clavier, flute and violin about the middle of the 16th century, was really a violin (probably as well as viol) player; and he was followed by several others even before 1600, as will be seen in the following pages. The most important event in the evolution of violin-playing in Germany was the arrival of Carlo Farina. The unspeakable horrors of the Thirty Years War, which laid waste more or less the whole of Germany, naturally arrested the progress of musical art, yet in spite of that it was kept alive by a few, as will be seen from the notes on Bleyer and Schop, and Baltzar must have been a product of the latter part of that time.

KASPAR KRUMBHORN, called the "blind musicus Stimmler." A 16th-century violinist, b. Liegnitz, Oct. 28, 1542; d. there June 11, 1621. He was so excellent a player on the violin, the flute and the clavier, that the Elector August of Saxony, after he had played before him, wanted to take him into his service, but he returned to Liegnitz as organist at St. Peter and St. Paul, acting also as teacher and conductor (Hawkins, iii, 202, gives the inscription on his tombstone at Liegnitz (Gerber, ii; Fürstenau, i, 31).

ANT. ANDRIEL. A Welsch, i.e. Italian, violinist (?), 1569, in Weimar Court Chapel (M.f.M., xxix, 138). It remains doubtful whether this really refers to a violinist or to a violist, as the terms were used indifferently.

GEORG KETTERLE. From June 1, 1595, to Mar. 21, 1602, the time of his death, he was violinist in the Court Chapel, Vienna, at a salary of 15 florins per month (Köchel, i).

NICOLAS BLEYER, b. 1590; d. Lübeck, May 3, 1658. He had the reputation of being an excellent violinist, as well as a cornet-player; he was a town musician at Leipzig, where he published, in 1624: Pavans, Galliards, Canzonas and symphonies; he went afterwards to Lübeck.

ADAM. "Der Pohlnische Violist" (violinist ?, Eitner), 1612, at the Berlin Court, his salary being 400 thaler = £60 per annum (Schneider, 28).

BERNHARDIN. Violinist and lute-player in Berlin, 1612–18, his salary being 480 thaler (ca. £74).

PAUL RIVANDER, lived at Nürnberg in the early 17th century and wrote: "Neue lustige Couranten auf Instrumenten und Geigen (violins) lieblich zu gebrauchen mit 4 Stimmen" (Quoltzbach, 1614). Also part songs pub. Nürnberg, 1614 and 1621.

WALTER ROWE, JUNIOR. Appears in the accounts (pay lists) of the Court Chapel of Berlin on Oct. 4, 1621, as *violinist*. He was apparently the son of the famous English gambist of that name who came from Hamburg to Berlin and was appointed in the Court Chapel on St. John's Day, 1614. The history of these artists awaits further elucidation. One Rowe died in 1671, probably the younger.

JONAS GÜNTHER. Of him it was said: "Ein sehr guter cornettist (a very good cornet player) also violinist (Diskantgeige): in 1614 with the Elector of Mayence, is now in service at Dresden, has been highly praised by all Dresden musicians." Prætorius (Chrysander, i, 155).

JOHANN SCHOPP (SCHOP, SCHOOPE), b. Hamburg at the beginning of the 17th century. Violin (Diskantgeige), lute, trombone, and cornet player; appointed Feb. 27, 1615, in the Court Chapel at Wolfenbüttel, being paid 220 thaler per annum (Chrysander, i, 55). In 1618 he was at the Danish Court as violinist and enjoyed a high reputation, so that pupils came to him from all parts. Viertelj, ix, 76, gives his sojourn in Danemark from Nov. 1, 1615, to Mar. 7, 1619 (*see* Mattheson), "Niederrh. Musikzeitung" (iii, 365). In 1621 he became director of the *Ratsmusik* at Hamburg with 800 marks, and in 1649 he was organist at St. Jacob, Hamburg. In Johann Risten's "Himmlische Lieder," 1644, he is called capellmeister of the town of Hamburg, and went afterwards to Lüneburg. Georg Neumark praises him exuberantly after hearing him at a Court concert together with Scheidemann. Sittard, i, 19, says he received a donation of 100 thaler. He died 1664 or 1665. Appreciation of his compositions, *see* Allgem. deutsche Biogr.; according to Eitner only 3 violin pieces of his are known so far, of which he gives no particulars, but a great many songs and vocal compositions, also organ pieces in tabulature. Fétis, "Neue Paduanen, Galliarden, Allemanden, Balletten, Couranten und Canzonen mit 3, 4, 5 u. 6 Stimmen, etc.," 1st part, Hamburg, 1633 and 1644; 2nd part, 1635 and 1640. His other works are all vocal, mostly sacred music, several of which were pub. at Lüneburg between 1644–58; Cantique de Salomon at Amsterdam, 1657. Others at Hamburg (songs) (1651 and 1655).

KASPAR FÖRSTER, b. 1617, Danzig; d. at the monastery of Oliva, near Danzig, Mar. 1, 1673. A highly gifted capellmeister and composer whose adventurous life is given by Mattheson, "Ehrenpforte," pp. 73–6. Wrote among his numerous compositions, 6 sonatas à tre: 2 violins, viola, and

Germany: to 1650

bass for viola da gamba or harpsichord which Matheson praises as very beautiful. (Copy in Upsala—Eitner.)

AMBROSIUS GÖTZE. A 17th-century violinist in the Dresden Court Chapel. The Elector sent him to Copenhagen in 1618 for further studies under Joh. Schop. Previously he was at Wolfenbüttel. (Saxon. State Archives.—Eitner.)

AMBROSIUS SCHERLE (SCHERL). Ca. 1621, chamber-musician (violinist) in the Court Chapel, Berlin, with 300 thaler; ordered by Elector in 1651 to come to Cleve (Schneider, 35, 42). On Apr. 20, 1666, he entered the service of the Duke of Brunswick. In 1661 he had been called from Celle as assistant, must therefore have been engaged in Celle between 1651–61 (Chrysander, i, 182, 183).

MICHAEL RAUCH (RUCH, RUECK), b. ca. 1627; Oct. 1, 1664, to Oct. 1, 1711 (pensioned). Violinist in Vienna Court Chapel; d. July 4, 1715, aged 88; received 30 florins per month (Köchel, No. 607, 712).

CONSTANTIN CHRISTIAN DEDEKIND, b. probably Apr. 2, 1628, at Reinsdorf, Anhalt-Köthen; d. Dresden (?). In 1697 he was still living (Mendel). He often added the letters K.R.P. (Poet ?) or K.S.M. (Royal Saxon Musician). In 1654 he became bass singer in the Royal Chapel, Dresden, with 150 florins per annum. He was also an excellent violinist, and in 1666 the post of concertmeister was specially created and he became the first to occupy it with a salary of 400 thaler. In 1676 his name disappears from the list of the Electoral Chapel, and he had been given a tax collector's post. He was also a poet laureate, and composed his own poems and sacred plays, pub. at Dresden in 1670 and 1676. For the solo violin he left no published compositions—if any, although he wrote a large quantity of vocal music with introductions and postludes for violins.

JOHANN JACOB LÖWE (L. VON EISENACH), b. Vienna, 1628 ; d. Lüneburg, Sept., 1703; son of the resident of the Elector of Saxony, Joh. von Eisenach; 1652 pupil of Heinr. Schütz at Dresden; 1655 capellmeister at the Court of Brunswick, then in residence at Wolfenbüttel. In 1663, on Schütz's recommendation, he was appointed Court capellmeister at Zeitz; 1682 finds him organist at Lüneburg. One of the first composers of German songs for a single voice. He wrote the oldest still existing German suites (G. R. Ahle's and M. Rubert's, both, 1650, have not yet been found) with introductory sinfonies: "Synfonien, Galliarden, Arien, Ballette, Couranten, Sarabanden mit 3 oder 5 Stimmen" (Bremen, 1658, 11 suites à 4–6 with introductory symphony, and one single symphony at the end); sonatas, canzonas and caprices à 2 (Jena 1664). 12 "neue geistliche Concerten," for 1, 2, 3 voices and 2 violins with B.c. for the organ (Wolfenbüttel, 1660).

GRÜNSCHNEIDER. "Discant Geiger" (violinist) in the service of the Grand Duchess of Toscana. In 1629, he was in Venice, whence he was engaged for the Court Chapel at Dresden. Schütz was against his appointment, saying that he was more a fiddler for dances than a perfect musician. From the Dresden State Archives it appears that a Tobias Grünschneider was sent to Italy by the Elector in 1617 for further tuition. Eitner points out that this could be no other than the above.

JOHANN DAVID. Musician of Hamburg; appointed violinist at the Electoral Court Chapel, Berlin (Schneider, 38), in 1629.

DANIEL EBERLIN, b. Nuremberg, 1630; d. Cassel, 1692. He was the father-in-law of Teleman, who described him as an excellent violinist and contrapuntist. He composed trio sonatas for violins and bass. "Trium variantium fidium concordia hoc est moduli musici quas sonatas vocant, ternis partibus conflatur," Nuremberg, 1675. He also calculated that there are 2,000 different tunings possible for the violin. Fétis has given an account of the adventurous career of this very talented and learned man, and his roving life, being at one time fighting the Turcs, as a captain in the Papal army, then in succession, capellmeister at Cassel, private secretary and capellmeister of the Duke of Eisenach, regent of the Westerwald, banker at Hamburg, and finally captain of the Militia at Cassel. A cantata for tenor and violin obbligato and a chorale in MS. still exist.

THOMAS BALTZAR (BALTAZAR, BALTZER [this is no doubt the correct spelling]), b. Lübeck, ca. 1630 (Riemann); d. London, July 24, 1663. Chamber violinist of Queen Christina of Sweden in 1653; was the first virtuoso on the violin that was heard in England. He arrived early in 1656 according to Evelyn's Diary Mar. 4, 1656 (*see* "Romance of the Fiddle,"

WILLIAM CORBETT

JEAN FERRY REBEL
From a Crayon Portrait by Watteau.
By courtesy of K. Parker, Esq., of the British Museum.

ADALBERT GYROWETZ

THOMAS PINTO

JOHN BANISTER THE YOUN[G]
From a contemporary engraving
British Museum.

MICHEL CORRETTE
From a contemporary engraving.

Toy qui du pouvoir harmonique,
Veux faire on jour sentir les merveilleux effets
D'une docte et simple practique
Puise icy les premiers secrets

p. 66), and lived for two years at the house of Sir Anthony Cope of Hanwell, Oxfordshire. There he made the acquaintance of Anthony A. Wood, who tells us in his diary of a visit to Baltzar at the house of Will Ellis, on July 24, 1658: "Mr. Davis Mell was accounted hitherto the best for the violin in England . . . but after Baltzar came to England and showed his most wonderful parts on that instrument, Mell was not admired, yet he played sweeter, was a well-bred gentleman, and not given to excessive drinking as Baltzar was. . . ." He saw him run up his fingers to the end of the fingerboard (which was very short at that time [Ed.] and in his compositions he does not exceed the "d") of the violin, and run them back again insensibly, and all with alacrity and very good time, which he (Wood) nor any in England saw the like before." Dr. Wilson, who accompanied Wood, in his humorous way stooped down "to see if he had a huffe (hoof)." Roger North in his memoirs says that Baltzar's hand "was accounted hard and rough, though he made amends for that by using often a lyre tuning (the scordatura which was very popular especially with German composers right into the 18th century.—E. v. d. Str.), and comfortable lessons which were very harmonious." Wood says: "about the same time (1658) he commenced bachelor of Musick at Cambridge" . . . but "being much admired by all lovers of Musick, his company was desired: and company, especially musical company delighting in drinking, made him drink more than ordinary, which brought him to his grave." Hawkins, Burney and others state that he was appointed as Master of the King's Twenty-four Violins under Charles II, but W. Nagel ("Annalen der englischen Hofmusik") proves that the only ascertainable fact is that he was appointed to the King's Musick on Nov. 30, 1661, and in his "Geschichte der Musik in England" he says that through Baltzar a greater interest in the violin was awakened in England. A few pieces by him were published in Playford's "The Division Violin," and of these an Allemande, edited by Wehrle, has been republished by Breitkopf and Härtel. Burney possessed a manuscript collection of Baltzar's solos, presented to him by the Rev. Montague North, and "A set of sonatas by Baltzar for a *lyra* violin, treble violin, and bass" formed Lot 55 of the sale catalogue of Thomas Britton's musical property. Burney considered these compositions technically the most difficult of their time, which is only relatively true. Baltzar astounded the English by his chord playing, which at that time was largely cultivated in Germany (Strungk, JJ. Walther, Biber). Baltzar was buried in the cloisters of Westminster Abbey, July 27, 1663.

JOHANN HEINRICH SCHMELZER AB EHRENRUEFF, b. ca. 1630; d. Vienna, June 30, 1680. Chamber musician in the Imperial Court Chapel, Oct. 1, 1649–70; vice-capellmeister Jan. 1, 1671; capellmeister, Oct. 1, 1679; succeeding Felix Sances as the first German to fill this post at the Austrian Court. The Emperor Ferdinand III bestowed upon him the title and rank of a baron. He composed "Sacro-profanus concentus musicus, fidium aliquorumque instrumentorum" (Nüremberg, 1662, fol.), consisting of 13 sonatas for violin with viola and trombone; 12 sonatas for violin solo (ib., 1663); 6 sonate unarum fidium (for violin solo) (ib., 1664); Duodena selectarum sonatarum, 12 sonatas for 2 violins and B.C. or violin, gamba and B.C. (Nuremberg, 1669); many MSS. compositions in Vienna, Kremsier, Upsala. Some of his works have been republished by Riemann. He also wrote the trumpet fanfares for Bertali's festival play "La contesa da' numi," etc. (pub. as "Arie per il baletto a cavallonello," etc., 1667).

CLEMENS THIEME (TIEME, TIME, THIME), b. Gross-Dietmansdorf, near Dresden, Sept. 7, 1631; d. Zeitz, Mar. 27, 1668. He went to school at Rodeburg, then studied music under Ph. Stolle, Dresden; in 1642 he became choir boy in the Court Chapel, Copenhagen. He returned in 1646 to Dresden and was at the Elector's expense instructed in playing various instruments. In 1651 he was appointed as instrumentalist in the Court Chapel. Christopher Bernhard was his teacher in composition. In 1657, when the chapel had no service on account of Court mourning, he travelled to perfect himself, and in 1659 he married the apothecary's daughter Emilie Jockaworts. In 1663 he took his congé and went to Hamburg, but finding no appointment, he went to Zeitz at the recommendation of H. Schütz, first as head- (chief) instrumentalist (Oberinstrumentist), then as concertmeister and finally as capelldirector (Obit. Sermon M. f. M. 3, 38). He wrote 2 books of sonatas for 2 violins, op. 10 and 11, sonatas for 2 violins, bassoon or violone, and Bc. (MS. in Upsala library); sonatas

Germany: to 1650

for 2 violins, 4 violas and Bc.; 2 sonatas for 5 viols (violins ?), see Todeschini: 4 viole, cioë (that is), 2 violini, viola e basso (Eitner) (MS. Cassel); sonata 2 violins, 2 trumpets, 4 viole da braccio, Bc. (MS. Upsala), besides Masses and other sacred vocal compositions.

JOHANN HUBNER, b. Nuremberg, 1631. Is mentioned by Choron and Fayolle (Dictionnaire des Musiciens) as a blind violinist of such exceptional talent that his portrait was engraved at Nuremberg.

NATHAN SCHNITTELBACH (SNITTELBACH), b. Danzig, June 16, 1633; d. Lübeck, Nov. 16, 1667. He was violinist and council (Rats-) musician, son-in-law and pupil of Nicolas Bleyer, and teacher of Strunck. Præludium, allemande, courante, sarabande à 4 violins (Upsala), Magnificat à 7, 2 violins and 5 voices in G (Mattheson, i, 353; Fürstenau iia, 299; Stiehl Lex). Gerber calls him the greatest violinist of the 17th century (see Wki.; Strungk). Pougin, who says that he was looked upon as a master from 1660, gives his works as: 2 suites for 4 violins, and sacred music in which he introduced instruments, including a Magnificat in G major for 5 voices and 2 violins.

JOHANN WILHELM FURCHHEIM (FORCHHEIM), b. Dresden (?), ca. 1635; d. Nov. 22, 1682. In 1651 he figures as an orchestral pupil in the Court Institute, Dresden; 1655 violinist in the Court Chapel; 1666 Court organist and head instrumentist (Oberinstrumentist) to the Elector Johann Georg II; 1680 German concertmeister, and 1681 vice-capellmeister to Johann Georg III at the Court of Dresden. From 1667 to 1676 he was the director of the church music and the table music (at dinner, etc.). He wrote: "Auserlesenes Violinen Exercitium" (selected violin exercises), consisting of various sonatas, with their airs, ballads, allemands, courants, sarabands, and gigues, in five parts, Dresden, 1687; and "Musikalische Tafelbedienung" (musical table service) of Instruments, viz. 2 violins, 2 viols, 1 violone with the thorough bass, Dresden, 1674 (Mendel says: of 8 instruments, viz. 2 violins, 5 viols, 1 violon, etc.). Five sonatas, 3–7 parts, MS. in Upsala; and a sonata for 2 violins and bass.

JOACHIM WAGENHUEBER, ca. 1635; violin pupil of Fr. Piber at Munich (Kreisarchiv).

The History of the Violin

JOHANN JACOB STÖSZ, ca. 1638. Violinist at the Court of Düsseldorf (*see* Jos. Stösz in Eitner—also M. f. M. 28, 94 ?).

NICOLAUS ADAM STRUNGK, b. Brunswick, bapt. Nov. 15, 1640; son of Delphin Strungk, Court organist of Duke of Brunswick-Lüneburg at Zelle. In his twelfth year he was organist at St. Martin's Church (Riemann), Brunswick, went to school and then studied at the University Helmstädt. In holidays he studied violin under N. Schnittelbach at Lübeck, and acquired unusual technique. In 1660 he became 1st violin at Wolfenbüttel, soon after, 1661–5, at Celle with 200 thaler. With the permission of the Prince (of Celle) he went to Vienna, where he played before the Emperor, who rewarded him with a golden chain with a medal showing his effigy. He returned in 1665 and after the death of the Prince he entered the service of the Elector of Hanover. In 1678 he was called to Hamburg as director of the Municipal Orchestra (Ratsmusik) and as such he conducted at the theatre, for which he wrote eight operas up to 1682. In the latter year the Elector Frederic William visited Hamburg and requested Strungk's release from the town council, to engage him as capellmeister, but the Duke Ernst August of Hanover claimed him as vassal, and to indemnify him for any possible loss, he made him organist of his chamber music and later on also titular Canon of the Stift Beata Virgina at Einbeck with 460 thaler (Dr. Fischer's "Musik in Hanover," 1902, extract in M. f. M., 1903). He also took him with him to Italy where he met Corelli at Rome. *See* anecdote of their meeting in "Corelli." After a sojourn in Italy of several years he returned via Vienna, where he played again before the Emperor, this time on the harpsichord, and was again presented with a golden chain.

Jan. 26, 1688 (Docum. of appointment, M. f. M., xiii, 4) finds him vice-capellmeister at Dresden with 500 thaler; next to Pallavicini and Chr. Bernhard, after the death of the latter, 1693 capellmeister with 1,000 thaler. In 1694 he does not appear in lists, but reappears 1697; 1698, pensioned with 300 thaler; 1691 he applied to the Elector for the privilege of building a German opera at Leipzig, and built a wooden theatre in the Brühl for 10,000 thaler, which he opened May 8, 1693, with his opera "Alcesta" (M. f. M., xxi, 89). As he could only have performances on Fair (Messe) days he retained his position at Dresden, but ruined himself financially (J. O. Opel,

Germany: to 1650

Die ersten Jahrzehnte D. Oper zu Leipzig; also other sources, *see* Eitner). He was haughty and ambitious, quarrelled with colleagues and the Elector had to intervene frequently as peacemaker. For biographies, *see* Eitner. He composed Sonatas à 3 and ditto à 6 in Upsala. "Mus. Uebung auf der Violin," Exercises for Violin or viola da gamba consisting of sonatas, chaconnes, etc., with 2 violins and B.C. (Dresden, 1691, fol.). Fétis says among his pieces for clavecin are: Ricercare on the death of his mother, composed Venice, Dec. 20, 1685.

BURKHARD KUGHLER, Jan. 1, 1640, to Mar. 30, 1683, violinist in the Court Chapel, Vienna, with 30 florins per month. In 1657 he became 1st violinist. According to Buccelini's Germ., he was a native of Vienna, but was never vice-capellmeister. Perhaps he conducted the chamber music (Köchel, i, 110, and Walther).

PETRUS ELERT. Ca. 1643. Violinist, singer and typographer at the Polish Court; also undertook political missions; secretary to King Vladislav IV. Scachi in his scribrum, p. 222, gives a canon by him.

HEINRICH IGNAZ FRANZ BIBER, b. Wartenburg, on the Bohemian frontier, Aug. 12, 1644 (Riemann: Wartenburg in Bohemia); d. Salzburg, May 3, 1704. Son of a gamekeeper (Flurschütz). It is not known where or with whom he studied music. Until 1670 or 1673 he was at Kremsier in the chapel of the archbishop, which was one of the best of its time. In 1673 or 1676 he entered the Salzburg chapel to which he belonged till he died. In the dedicatory epistle of his sonatas published in 1676 he calls himself "musician and chamber valet" to the Archbishop Maximilian Gandolph, Count Khuenburg, to whom he also dedicated the 8 sonatas published in 1681. From 1677 he is teacher of the choir boys of the cathedral (Dom), and in that year Emperor Leopold I presented him with a golden chain. By 1684 he is prefect of the chapel institute. It is curious to note that he had not to teach the violin. At the beginning of 1679 he became vice-capellmeister and his fame began to spread far and wide. In May, 1681, he applied unsuccessfully for a patent of nobility. He repeated his request in 1690, emphasizing the fact that he was now well known at many courts of Europe as he had been touring in Germany, France, and Italy. This time he was successful and raised to the rank of nobility under the title of "Biber von Biebern." On Mar. 6, 1684, he was made archiepiscopal capellmeister and high steward. One of his sons, Karl Heinrich von Biebern, was afterwards capellmeister at Salzburg. Gerber says that Heinrich Biber stood also in high esteem at the Bavarian Court, where both the Elector Ferdinand Maria as well as his successor presented him with a golden chain, so that he possessed three in all. Compositions in Wki. and E. v. d. Str., "Eighteenth Century Sonatas." Mendel: 2 works printed at Nürnberg: Fidicinum sacro profanum twelve 4 and 5-part sonatas, and Harmonia artificiosa-Ariosa in septem partes vel paritas distributa à 3 instrumentis. In "Denkmäler der Tonkunst in Oestreich," which republished the former, another work by Biber, consisting of 15 sonatas with bass and a 16th for violin solo was pub. in 1905. The solo sonata is really a Passacaglia, remarkable for the boldness and variety of his treatment of the four-note subject, making considerable demands upon the technical ability of the executant, especially in double stops and chord playing. He made extensive use of the Scordatura. Some of the sonatas contain movements of great beauty. The C minor sonata, pub. in "Die hohe Schule," etc., has undergone so many changes from the original text at the hands of Ferd. David, that it is advisable to refer to the original form in the "Denkmäler." Biber is one of the outstanding figures in the history of the violin, who, technically at all events, far surpassed his Italian contemporaries.

AMBROS SCHIELE. In 1644 a violinist and chamber musician in the Court Chapel, Berlin; in 1646 his salary is raised to 150 thaler per annum. (Schneider, 41.)

DIETRICH BECKER (BEKKER), d. Hamburg, May 12, 1679. Organist at Ohrenburg, Holstein; afterwards violinist and composer to the Senate of Hamburg ca. 1644; composed: "Sonaten für 1 Violin, 1 Viol di gamba und den General-Bass über Chorallieder"; "Die Musikalischen Frühlingsfrüchte Bestehend in 3, 4 und fünfstimmiger instrumental-harmonie, nebst dem B.c."; both pub. Hamburg, 1668; also some sacred and secular songs preserved in MS.; One Sonata in A major is repub. in A. Einstein's "Zur deutschen Literatur der Viola da gamba" (1905). The sonatas on chorales he composed

Germany: to 1650

especially for evening concerts which he gave at Hamburg churches. (*See* Walther.)

JOHANN CHRISTOPH II BACH, b. Erfurt, Feb. 22, 1645; d. Arnstadt, Aug. 25, 1693. Uncle of Joh. Seb. Bach; violinist and Court musician to Count Günther of Schwarzburg-Arnstadt, with 30 florins and provisions (Naturalien). On Jan. 7, 1681, the Count dissolved his chapel and Bach was without employment until the young Count appointed him again as Court and town musician in 1682. (Spitta, i, 154, etc., 169.)

RUPERT IGNAZ MAYR, b. Schärding, Upper Austria, 1646; d. Freising, Feb. 7, 1712 (Mendel, 1716). Violinist in Freising in 1670 (Mendel, 1666), Court musician at the episcopal court of Eichstädt ca. 1678; 1685–1706 (latest entry in list of chapel) violinist in the Court Chapel at Munich; afterwards prefect of music to the bishop of Freising. He composed: Arion sacer, 4 voc. col. B.c. (1678—bass part only at Eichstätt); Pythagorische Schmieds-Fünklein, 7 suites of dances, most of which show evidences of the order of the movements as fixed by Frohberger, viz. Allemande, Courante, sarabande, gigue, while on the other hand the French influence is noticeable already in the use of an overture, sonatine, sinfonia or prelude as first or introductory movement. He also wrote according to Mendel: Palestra musica, 13 sonatas in 2, 3 and 4 parts; a Lamento in 5 parts (Augsburg, 1674); church music for voices with violins, trombones (or violins) and B.c., some with violins, viols or trombones, and B.c., etc. (*see* Mendel, vol. xii, p. 269).

JOHANN FISCHER, b. Augsburg, Sept. 25, 1646, as son of the town musician; d. Schwedt, 1721. He received his first musical training from capellmeister Sam. Capricornus at Stuttgart. While still very young, he went to Paris as copyist of Lully, whose style of composition he studied and adopted. After that he toured as violinist and in 1681 he was engaged at the church of the Barefooted Friars at Augsburg, where his "Musikalische Mayenlust," 50 French airs for 2 violins and B.c., were pub. in quartets (apparently lost). Not long after, he started touring again, and in 1686 he was at the Court of Anspach, where he wrote songs and Madrigals for one voice and instruments (pub. at Nuremberg) and other compositions.

Some time after he was capellmeister to the Duke of Courland at Mitau, where honour and reward were liberally bestowed upon him; but he spent his money as quickly as he received it; yet he was never in want, as his fertile pen was continually producing new works which brought him in a rich harvest. While he was at Mitau the Great Merchant's Guild of Riga paid him an annuity for supplying weekly a new composition for their "Collegium Musicum" and he often went there to supervise the performances thereof. In 1701 he left Mitau to become concertmeister, with the title of capellmeister, at the Court of Mecklenburg-Schwerin. There appear to have been frequent differences between Fischer and the other musicians, and he went to Copenhagen, where he took the part of Friedr. Erh. Niedt, who fought for a higher standard and better conditions of music, but both had to suffer from intrigues and persecutions of the majority, and Fischer returned first to Mecklenburg, then to Stralsund, and went finally via Stettin to Stockholm, where he found music still in a rather primitive state, and the exercise of his art was restricted to a few select private circles. His sojourn there was not of long duration. He returned once more to Germany and was appointed by the Margrave of Schwedt as capellmeister at his Court, where he remained, greatly honoured, to the time of his death at the age of 70 years. Mattheson, who had only heard him play as an old man, said that even then his tone and technique were such, that one could well understand the reputation he had in his younger years of being one of the greatest virtuosi of his time. He made, like Biber, frequent use of the scordatura in his solos. The viola was one of his favourite instruments, and he wrote not only independent parts for it in his numerous orchestral works, but also solo and obbligato passages. Of his solos for violin and viola, his overtures, suites, etc., which show the influence of Lully, only a small fraction has been preserved, including a partita for the flute douce (recorder) and some overtures and suites for viols, oboes, or recorders. A set of minuets for the latter instrument seems to have been lost as well as apparently all his violin solos (*see* Eitner, "Quellenlexikon"). (Full biography in Mattheson's "Ehrenpforte," pp. 61–5).

ELIAS GMEINER. Ca. 1648. Violinist at Kremsmünster; received for 3 quarters, 28 florins 30 kreutzers (Huemer, 23) (Eitner).

Germany: to 1650

JOHANN HAKE. Violinist and town musician at Stade about the middle of the 17th century; composed: Pavans, ballets, courants, and sarabands for 2 violins and bass, 1st part, Hamburg, 1648, 4to; Pavans, ballets, etc., 2nd part, for 2, 3, 4, 5, and 8 instruments, Stade, 1654, 4to.

GREGOR ZUBER. Town musician and violinist at Lübeck in the middle of the 17th century. He wrote: "Paduanen, Gaillarden, Balleten, Couranten, Sarabanden, etc., von 5 Stimmen," Lübeck, 1649, 4to; a second part, containing instrumental pieces in 2 to 4 parts with basso continuo was pub. at Frankfort-on-the-Main, 1659, 4to. Stiehl's Lexikon adds: "he was forbidden to further occupy his post as musician," but gives no date for this.

JOHANN JAKOB WALTHER, b. Witterda, near Erfurt, 1650. Was in early youth valet to a Polish nobleman, and learned to play the violin by hearing and seeing his master play. In that manner he acquired a high degree of efficiency, and in 1674 he became 1st violinist and chamber musician in the chapel of the Elector of Saxony at a salary of 600 thaler which rose to the at that time considerable amount of 700 thaler in 1680. It is not known where he studied composition, but it would not be surprising to learn that he spent some time in Italy and that there he familiarized himself sufficiently with the Italian language to enable him to become Italian secretary to the Elector of Mayence in 1680. He was not only the greatest virtuoso of his time, as Fétis justly remarks; one finds in his work ("Hortulus chelicus") all that others believed to have discovered long after him with regard to the various features of violin technics of a virtuoso character, and the best violinists of the 19th century have not surpassed his use of double stops to the same extent that he surpassed his contemporaries, except Biber, and they would have to practise the fugal duet for one violin No. 17 for a long time before they could fully master it. Walther is the inventor of playing a sustained melody with the bow accompanied by left-hand pizzicato. This has afterwards been imitated by others, but not to the same extent and in less difficult compositions. The last piece of the work is "Serenata," for a number of various instruments, imitated on the solo violin. Walther has been severely criticized by most of his biographers for his attempts of naturalistic effects, such as the above, as well as imitation of bird calls, etc., reminiscent of Farina's capriccio stravagante, which led to the discovery of some of the most valuable features in the art of violin playing, nor are they justified in judging the average artistic standard of his work from these experiments. Fétis is juster when he says that "apart from these his work is interesting from the point of composition and the harmony is elegant (varied) and pure." This is amply borne out, for instance, in his sonata in D major which was played at the Haslemere Festival of old music 1926, and proved a delightful work. It is fairly simple from the violinistic side and shows none of the virtuoso features which caused Fétis to call him the Paganini of his century. In saying this he must, however, have forgotten Biber, who was technically almost, if not quite, his equal, while he stood as composer far above him. Walther composed: "Scherzi di violino solo," etc., dedicated to the Elector of Saxony, Prague, 1676 and "Hortulus chelicus," etc., Mayence, 1688 and 1694. In the latter he calls himself: Elector Moguntiae Secretarius italianus.

ZACHARIAS MADRA. He received his musical education at the expense of the Elector of Brandenburg, and became violinist and chamber musician in the Court Chapel at Berlin in 1650 (Schneider, 42).

STEPHAN HAU (HAW). In the first part of the 17th century he was violinist and "Dancing master of the Princess at Heidelberg," as he is described in the MS. 114, No. 47, of the town library, Breslau, a "Fantasia for violin."

GÄRTER. Lived during the first half of 17th century. On a toccata for violin, MS. 114, No. 15, in the Breslau town library, he is called organist and violinist at Nuremberg (Eitner).

CHAPTER 12

Germany: to 1700

SCARCELY had the roar of the cannons ceased, and the country been freed of the murderous bands of freebooters and soldiers of fortune, who during the thirty years of war had terrorized the people, when the Germans turned their thoughts to arts of peace and in particular to that of music. Violin-playing made rapid progress and surpassed technically all other countries.

The virtuosity of Walther, Biber, Baltzar, Schmelzer and others surpasses that of the Italians by about fifty years, for even if Uccellini, as the only one, equalled Walther by going into the 6th position, neither he nor any of his compatriots approached either of the above-named German composers in their variety of bowings and of figuration, nor their use of double stops and chords. Their musical form was not yet clarified and crystallized like that of the Italians, especially of Corelli, yet their musical conceptions and especially their melodic invention were often far ahead of the former. Walther's Sonatas were treated far too cavalierly by Wasielewski, and as they were almost inaccessible until within recent years, his judgment has unfortunately been accepted too readily by violinists, in spite of Fétis' praise of them. At Dolmetsch's Haslemere Festivals the sonata in D major was performed on two occasions and proved a great success. The Sonatas by Biber too, although not all of equal value, deserve to be better known.

The compass used by most of the German violinist-composers, like that of their Italian contemporaries, does not exceed the third position, but they had not attained to the systematic co-ordination of the technical features of the violin, nor of the structural features in composition, which the Italians were able to develop under the aegis of art-loving

Princes, undisturbed by the turbulent times which hampered and retarded their progress in Germany.

BALTHASAR RODERIG. Ca. 1651. A violinist and cornetist in the private chapel of the Electoral Prince at Dresden (Fürstenau, i, 70).

SIMON BERNHARDT. Boy in the Dresden Chapel for violin and trumpet, 1651. In 1680 he became Court Musician for the same instruments, receiving 250 thaler (Fürstenau, i, 70, 98).

PAUL ALBER, b. 1652; d. Nov. (Oct.?) 30, 1732, aged 80. June, 1701–32 (Eitner), a violinist in the Imperial Chapel, Vienna. From 1712 he received 810 florins.

JOHANN ALBER, b. 1673; d. May 28, 1745, aged 72. From 1706 to 1740 (Eitner) a violinist in the Imperial Chapel in Vienna (from 1712 he received 540 florins); also at St. Stephen in Vienna.

JOHANN CHRISTOPH ROTHE, b. Rosswein, district of Leipzig, 1653; d. Sondershausen, 1720. He was pupil of his father, a cantor at Rosswein, and was then appointed falsetto singer and violinist at the Court of Coburg, and became, 1693, valet and violinist at the Court of Sondershausen. Johann Christopher is the head of a numerous family of musicians who served the Prince of Sondershausen (Gerber, i).

ANDREAS ANTON SCHMELZER (SCHMELTZER) AB EHRENRUEFF, b. Vienna, Nov. 26, 1653; d. there, Oct. 13, 1701; son of Joh. Heinrich. He was violinist in the Imperial Chapel, Vienna, Jan. 1, 1671–1700, with 45 florins per month. As his father, he composed ballet music for operas performed at the Court theatre, especially from 1681, for the operas by Draghi (Köchel, i and ii). Much of his music is in the National Library, Vienna.

PETER CLEMENS SCHMELZER, Aug. 1, 1692–June 30. In 1740 a violinist in the Imperial Chapel, Vienna; probably a son of the above.

CHRISTIAN HEINRICH ASCHENBRENNER, b. Alt. Stettin, Dec. 29, 1654; d. Jena, Dec. 13, 1732. His father, a musician in Stettin (town-musician) and former capellmeister at Wolfenbüttel, was his first music teacher. At fourteen he received lessons in composition from J. Schütz. When his father died soon after, Schütz took his place and sent him to Vienna in 1676 to perfect himself on the violin and in composition under Capellmeister Andreas, Anton Schmelzer. In 1677 he entered the chapel of the Duke of Zeitz, who died in 1681, when the chapel was dissolved. He went to Wolffenbüttel, where he gained the good graces of Rosenmüller, who asked him to join the Duke's chapel, but he had scarcely returned to Zeitz to fetch his family, when he learned that Rosenmüller had died, and that the Duke had decided not to make any further appointments. For two years he remained at Zeitz before he received, in 1683, a post as 1st violinist to the Duke of Merseburg, and the following years appear to have been the happiest of his life. In 1692 he paid a second visit to Vienna, where he played before the Emperor, to whom he dedicated 6 sonatas, which so pleased the former that he presented him with a golden chain and a large sum of money. But about this time the Duke of Merseburg died and the chapel was dismissed, whereby his existence became precarious, and he found at times a great difficulty in maintaining his family. In 1695 he returned to Zeitz as director of music and retained this post until his third visit to Vienna in 1703. He lived at Zeitz until 1713, when he was appointed capellmeister to the Duke of Merseburg. In 1719, however, he was obliged to retire to Jena, at the age of 65, where he lived the rest of his life on a small pension. It is not known whether the sonatas dedicated to the Emperor were published, but one book known to be by him is: "Gast und hochzeit freude, bestehend in Sonaten, Praeludien, Allemanden, Curanten, Baletten, Arien, Sarabanden, mit drei, vier, und fünf Stimmen, nebst dem Basso Continuo," Leipzig, 1673. Corneille à Benghem (Bibl. Math., p. 300) mentions a 2nd ed., Leipzig, 1675. A 3rd appeared at Innsbruck, 1676.

JOHANN PAUL VON WESTHOFF, b. Dresden, 1656; d. Weimar, Apr., 1705; son and pupil of Friedrich von Westhoff, b. 1611 at Lübeck, captain in a Swedish cavalry regiment under Gustav Adolph who, on returning from a campaign, had been robbed by marauders of all his belongings, went to Dresden, where as a good amateur violinist he was appointed in the Court chapel and gave his son an excellent education. The latter, apart from showing a great musical talent, evinced as well a linguistic ability. He became chamber musician for violin in the Electoral Chapel, and teacher of languages of the Saxon Princes. An outbreak of the plague in 1679 drove him to Sweden, whence he went in the same year to Hungary and took part as ensign-bearer in a campaign against the Turcs. At the end of this he was recalled to Dresden to resume his functions at the Court; but soon after, he went on tour as a violin virtuoso and was well received by the Grand Duke of Tuscany at Florence. He then went to Paris, where he arrived in December, 1682, and played a sonata and a suite of his composition before the King, who was greatly pleased with his works as well as with his playing, and named one of the movements of his sonatas "La Guerre." His success became the talk of the town and the *Mercure* published the two works mentioned above, one in its Dec. number of 1682, the other in that of Jan., 1683. Pougin describes them as well written both as regards form and harmony, and very difficult in style, rhythm and his use of double stopping and chords, which in the suite, of six movements, he employs throughout, although he does not go beyond the neck positions. After leaving Paris he went to England, the Netherlands, Germany, and Austria, where he played before the Emperor in Vienna, who was so charmed by his talent that he presented him with a gold medal and chain. After that he returned to Dresden, where six of his violin sonatas, with bass, were published in 1694. In 1700 he became professor of languages at the University of Wittenberg, and in 1704 chamber musician and secretary at the Court of Weimar. A sonata of his in d minor and a solo suite in A major (apparently the one he played at the French Court) were re-edited by G. Beckmann, 1921 (the latter also by Karl Gerhartz, 1921).

PHILIP HEINRICH ERLEBACH. Violinist-composer, b. Esen, Ostfriesland, July 25, 1657; d. Rudostadt, Apr. 17, 1714. He went to Paris in his youth and lived there for some years, studying Lully's style of composition. In 1683 he was appointed as Court capellmeister at Rudolstadt, where he remained for the rest of his life. He composed 6 sonate a due violini, viola da gamba e continno, Nuremberg, 1694 (No. 2 republished in Einstein, "Zur deutschen Litteratur der Va da Gamba"): Overtures à 5 parties; 2 books of arias

Germany: to 1700

with 2 violins and bass, cantatas with viols and organ (MS.), etc. List of numerous vocal compositions in Eitner.

PAUL GLEITSMANN (GLEITZMANN), b. Weissenfels, ca. 1660; d. there?, Nov. 11, 1710. He was the son of the town musician, and pupil of Joh. Beer. In 1690 he became chamber valet and capellmeister at the court of Count Schwarzburgh Arnstadt, being esteemed an excellent violin-, lute-, and gamba player. In 1707 he became capellmeister in the place of Drese. (Walther; Spitta i, 166, 169.) Composed church music with instrumental accompaniment; also "Concentus harmonicus, or 20 pieces for 2 violins and cont.," Nuremberg, 1703.

GOTTFRIED (GODFREY) FINGER, b. Olmütz, Moravia, ca. 1660 (Pougin); the place and date of his death are unknown. 1685 (Riemann) (Eitner: 1688) he became master of the private band of James II and composed musical plays and operas, also 12 sonatas for 1, 2 and 3 violins, Gamba and Bc. He composed the opera "The Rival Queens" and a set (Pougin: 6 sonatas or solos with B.c., 3 for violin and 3 for flute, 1690) of sonatas for flute and a bass together with Daniel Purcell. Becoming offended at not receiving the prize in a competition for setting to music the book of an opera, "The Judgment of Paris," in 1700 he returned to Germany as chamber musician to the Count Palatine at Breslau. (Riemann: 1702 he went to Berlin as capellmeister to Queen Sophie Charlotte.) In 1706 he was called to Berlin to take part with Stricker and Volumier in the composition of an opera for the nuptials of the Crown Prince. Schneider (p. 23, etc.), who gives this information, says he was Royal capellmeister there until 1708. During 1717–23 he was concertmeister at the Court of the Prince Palatine at Neuburg a/D., where he received the title of Court Councillor. There he composed several operas. He appears still as concertmeister in a list after 1723 (Walter 77, 78, 369; Gerber ii; Pohl i, 14, gives a different account). (Riemann: 1717 he became capellmeister at Gotha. Mendel says: at the Court of Anhalt.) As a violinist he is said to have belonged to the school of Torelli and Bassani (Mason Clarke).

JOSEPH FRANCK, b. ca. 1660; d. July 5, 1713; aged 53. A violinist in the Vienna Court chapel at 30 florins per month from Jan. 1, 1702, to his death (Köchel, l).

GEORG BLEYER, b. Saalfeld. Probably a relative of Nicholas. In 1660 he was secretary to the Count of Schwarzburg-Rudolstadt; composed "Lustmusik" consisting in 4 part pieces, Leipzig, 1670; "Zodiacus Musicus," 12 sonatas for 1, 2, and 3 violins, violetta, viola and bass, Antwerp 1683, which show a charming freshness in their melodic invention. He also composed sacred vocal music.

JACOB BALTHASAR SCHÜTZ, b. Nuremberg, Jan. 5, 1661; d. there, Jan. 22, 1700, of consumption. He was the son of the council (Rats) musician Gabriel Schütz, master of J. P. Krieger, and began to study music in early childhood. At the age of 10 he had already performed on the violin with his brother Johann Jacob, aged 11, before the Prince at Anspach. After that he developed a fine voice which he trained under Hinrich Schwemmer, and was appointed as town soprano, and as such was called again to the Court at Anspach to sing in an opera. When he lost his soprano voice he devoted himself entirely to the violin, and was looked upon as an excellent player, even by the Imperial virtuosi of the Austrian Court. He was also a very clever performer on the viol da gamba. For the violin he composed several solos and partitas. (Mattheson, "Ehrenpforte.")

JACOB BERNHARD. Ca. 1661; was recommended as violinist from the Saxon Court at Dresden to the Elector of Brandenburg in 1661.

SAMUEL PETER VON SIDON. Mattheson ("Ehrenpforte," p. 75) calls him a famous violinist; Caspar Förster stayed with him at Hamburg on his return from Denmark, in 1661. Mattheson says (Ib.), "I should like to put him (Sidon) in the 'Ehrenpforte,' but I am lacking the necessary material so far."

KONRAD STENEKEN, b. Bremen. A literary man and musical amateur. He composed "Hortulus musicus," German courants and songs for 2 violins, viola and B.c., Bremen, 1662.

BELWISCH. Ca. 1663. Violinist at Plesse. W. C. Printz mentions him in his autobiography (Mattheson, i, "Ehrenpforte," 270) as one with whom he became on friendly terms at the Court of Count von Promnitz at Plesse.

JOHANN GOHL, b. Berlin. He studied music at the expense of the Elector and was appointed as chamber musician (violin?)

in 1663 (Schneider, 46). On Nov. 11, 1690, Peter Gohl is mentioned as having died (Ib., 49), but Schneider is not always reliable.

NIKOLAUS BRUHNS, b. Schwabstädt, Schleswig, 1665; d. Husum, 1697. Pupil of his uncle, Peter Bruhns, and of Buxtehude at Lübeck; excellent violinist, gambist, clavecinist, organist and composer. On the recommendation of Buxtehude he became organist at Copenhagen but afterwards town organist at Husum. He had a remarkable technique in double-stopping on the violin, and he used to astonish his hearers by his two part improvisations on that instrument to which he played the bass with his feet on the organ pedal. He was a remarkable composer, but chiefly for the organ. A complete edition of his works by the University of Kiel has been recently pub., but apparently he wrote nothing for the violin.

ELIAS BRUNMÜLLER (BRÖNNEMÜLLER), b. in Germany, 1666; d. Amsterdam, Sept. 17, 1762. A pupil of Corelli, C. Lunati and Scarlatti, and teacher of music (violinist and harpsichord-player). His first work, consisting of violin solos and trios for 2 violins and bass, appeared at Amsterdam, 1709. In 1710 at Amsterdam, was published his "Fasciculus musicus" containing toccatas for pianoforte, solos for oboe, violin and flute, and Italian and German airs dedicated to the Queen of England. He also wrote 6 sonatas for violin and 6 for oboe with thorough bass and a "Suite for viol," Amsterdam; "Augustissimæ Annæ reg. Magnæ Britanniæ hæc modorum ac consentum musicorum varii generis tabulæ notis consignatas," Amst., 1710, probably same as "Fasciculus." In the library at Leyden are: Sonatas for 2 violins and cello, with organ, op. 1; Simon von Beaumont, op. 2; Toccata Fugen, etc., for clavier and organ, op. 3; the 12 solos and "Fasciculus musicus" and "Rechter Grund der Composition" (Correct Foundation of Composition) (Apr. 30., 1710, given to F. Halma to be his property). He appeared as virtuoso with great success at many European Courts, including London and Paris.

JOHANN PEZEL. A native of Austria, canon of the Augustinian Order, who went over to the Protestant religion and became music-master at the school of St. Thomas, Leipzig. He composed 15 works of instrumental music, pub. 1669–89, among which the most outstanding were "Deliciæ Musicales, etc." (1678), in 5 parts for 2 violins; 2 viols and B.c. and "Opus Musicum" (1686), composed of a suite of sonatas of 2 violins, 3 viols, bassoon and B.c., which Pougin describes as very beautiful.

JOHANN MICHEL NICOLAI. Active during the second half of the 17th century as composer and Court Musician at Stuttgart. Wrote: "Erster Theil geistlicher Harmonien von drei Vocalstimmen und zwei Violinen" (Frankfurt, 1669); "12 Sonaten für zwei Violinen und ein Viola di Gamba oder ein Fagott" (i, Theil, Augsburg, 1675, obl. fol.); "24 caprici für 4 Violinen und Bass" (i, Theil, Augsburg, 1675; ii, Theil, Ib., iii, Theil, Ib., 1682).

JOSEPH HOFFER. Violinist in Vienna Court chapel from Apr. 1, 1687, with 30 florins per month from 1695 as composer; by 1706 he disappears from the lists (Köchel, i). According to Köchel, ii, he is still in office in 1729, but Fux describes him as unfit for service on account of illness; Köchel, however, thinks that he means Johann Jakob as to this. In "Beilagen" (Appendix), vi, p. 424, he confirms that it is Joseph. He wrote incidental music and numerous ballets for operas which are in the Imperial Court library, Vienna, under the name of Johann Joseph Hoffer, which seems to exclude Eitner's assumption that they are by Johann Jakob. They date, moreover, from 1695 to 1703, which would be too early for the latter.

JOHANN JAKOB HOFFER, b. ca. 1673; d. Vienna, Aug. 14, 1737, aged 64. Violinist in Vienna Court chapel. From 1725 he filled for 2 years the "Officianten-Amt" (post of civil officer?). His salary in latter years was 900 florins (Köchel, i. and ii, 170).

IGNAZ LEOPOLD KUGHLER. A violinist in the Vienna chapel from 1674–86, at 40 thaler per month (Köchel, i).

STEPHAN RINGK (RINCK). Musician in 1677 to the Saxon Court at Merseburg (Abel's "Musikalische Blumenlese"); entered the Dresden Court chapel in 1681, became first violinist there in 1697 with a salary of 350 thaler (Fürstenau, i, 110; iia, 262).

Germany: to 1700

JOSEPH ERNST. Violinist at the Salzburg Court chapel and teacher at the Institute of the chapel 1677–87 (Peregrinus, 169).

AYMÉ BERTHLEIN. A player on the French violin (petit violon) ca. 1679 at Dresden (Eitner).

JOSEPH KARL DENK (DENKH, DENCK), b. ca. 1683; d. Vienna, Mar. 4, 1761, at the age of 78. Violinist in the Court chapel, Vienna, from July 1, 1713, to the time of his death, at 700 florins per annum.

JOHANN HERMANN KÖHLER, b. Anspach, 1686. He studied in Italy under Torelli, by whose advice he visited Venice, Rome, and Naples, and on his return became 1st violinist in the Court chapel at Anspach (Mattheson, i, 52; Gerber, ii). Joh. Mattheson ("Grundlage einer Ehrenpforte," p. 52) calls him "a famous violinist."

JOHANN ADAM BIRCKENSTOCK, b. Alsfeld, Hesse-Darmstadt, Feb. 19, 1687; d. Eisenach, Feb. 26, 1733. In 1700 his father went to Cassel as an architect, and here the Landgrave noticed the boy's talent and placed him under his capellmeister, Ruggiero Fedeli, who taught him for five years, after which the Landgrave sent him for a further year to Volumier in Berlin, then another year to Fiorelli (not Fiorillo) at Bayreuth, and finally to Paris, where for 18 months he studied under François du Val. He was appointed 1709 in the Ducal chapel at Cassel, where in 1721 he became first solo violin. In the following year he went on tour and stayed for some months at Amsterdam, where his 12 sonatas for violin and bass, op. 1, were published. During that time a competition took place at that town for the post of concertmeister at the Court of Portugal in which Birckenstock took part and was offered the post, but would not forsake his patron, to whom he owed his education. He therefore returned to Cassel and in recognition was made Court concertmeister in 1725. When the Landgrave died in 1730 he was elected director of the Ducal chapel at Eisenach, where he remained to his death. He published 12 concertos and 2 books of sonatas, which show the influence of Corelli and are the first German works in the Italian sonata form, but with distinct individuality with regard to thematic material and treatment. A. Moffat arranged one of the sonatas for violoncello.

AUGUST GALLI, b. 1687, violinist; d. Munich, Apr. 8, 1738; aged 96. Violinist in Court chapel, pensioned 1778. Buried in the "Frauenkirche," where, in the church register, he is described as singer in the Electoral chapel.

JOHANN GROSS, b. near Nuremberg, ca. 1688; d. Rudolstadt (?), 1735. He was at first the bandmaster of a Hungarian regiment; then violinist in the chapel of the Prince-bishop of Bamberg, and finally capellmeister at the Court of Schwarzburg Rudolstadt. Composed for the violin 6 sonatas and 6 solos. Pougin describes him as a clever violinist.

JOHANN ALBERT FRANKH. May 1, 1690, to Jan. 18, 1733, when he died, aged 67, Violinist in the Court chapel, Vienna, at 30 florins per month, afterwards 720 florins per annum.

GEORG GOTTFRIED BACKSTROH. Known in 1691 as third violinist in the Dresden Court chapel, at a salary of 300 thaler (Fürsteman, i, 110); 1697 he became concertmeister and inspector of instruments there, and had to play at the church. 1703 he sent in a claim for arrears of salary (Ib., 113, etc.).

DANIEL MERCK. Town musician at Augsburg late in the 17th century. Wrote "Compendium Musicæ Instrumentalis Chelicæ," Augsburg, 1695 (*see* Brit. Mus.), which is the first German tutor for violin, viola, gamba and bass.

AUGUST FRIEDRICH ROTH (ROTHE), b. Sondershausen, Feb. 4, 1696; d. there, July 4, 1784. Was a pupil of his father, Joh. Christ. Rothe; entered the Bayreuth Court chapel in 1723, and afterwards went to Sondershausen as secretary (Kanzellist), chamber musician and leader (Vorspieler). With advancing age he ceded this position to Concertmeister Abel (Gerber, i).

PRINCE JOHANN ERNST (?)—JOHANN ERNST OF SAXE-WEIMAR, b. Weimar, Dec. 29, 1696; d. Frankfort a/M., Aug. 1, 1715. He studied the violin under his chamber-valet, G. Christoph Eylenstein, and became one of the best violinists of his time. He also studied the harpsichord and composition under J. G. Walther, the famous lexicographer, and after nine months' tuition he composed 19 works, including 6 harpsichord concertos, which were published. He died while travelling for the purpose of further study.

Germany: to 1700

JOHANN GEORG LINIKA (LINICKA, LINIGKA). Became a violinist chamber musician in the Electoral chapel, Berlin, in 1696, and studied composition under Joh. Theile, who esteemed him highly, and when prevented from conducting, chose him as his deputy. When, on the accession of King Frederic William I in 1713, the chapel was dismissed, Linika was called to the Court at Weissenfels whence he obtained leave from the Duke to go to England. There he remained for three years giving concerts (and teaching) which brought him both fame and wealth, with which he returned to Weissenfels. In 1725 he was appointed leader and conductor at the Hamburg opera, for which he composed a prologue, a festival play, and the recitatives to Handel's "Julius Cæsar"; he also wrote 6 symphonies and 2 sonatas.

JOHANN CHRISTIAN HERTEL, b. Oettingen, Suabia, 1699; d. Oct., 1754, at Strelitz (Mecklenburg). Although his excellent playing of one of Corelli's violin sonatas gained for him the consent of his father to embark upon a musical career, and although he became first violinist in the Court chapel at Eisenach in 1719 and succeeded Birkenstock there in 1732 as concertmeister and capellmeister, he was chiefly a gambist and his more detailed biography may be found in E. v. d. Str., "History of the Violoncello, the Viola da Gamba," etc., p. 78, et seq; also Marpurg, iii, 46 (same in Gerber, ii).

CHRISTOPH WOLFGANG DRUCKENMÜLLER. A 17th-century violinist mentioned by Pougin as having composed "Musikalisches Tafel Konzert" consisting of pieces for violins, violas, and gambas.

DEYFFEL. A 17th-century violinist. There is a manuscript Fantasia (often only two parts) in B Br. (*see* Eitner).

HENRICO ALBICASTRO (HEINRICH WEISSENBURG), b. in Switzerland in the second half of the 17th century. He was a captain of horse in the allied army and died during the last of the Spanish succession wars. He was an excellent violinist and composer, and Schering, "Geschichte d. instrum. Konzerts," speaks highly of his XII Concerti a quattro, op. 7, Amsterdam, Rogers, ca. 1703. He is probably identical with Heinrich Weysenbergh, who appears in the registers of Leyden University, on Apr., 1686, as Musicus Academiæ, as well as "Rittmeister Henricus Albicastro." He was of German origin, and lived in the Netherlands about 1700. Eight works of solo and trio sonatas for violin as well as his concerti, op. 7, enjoyed a European reputation. Some of his compositions pub. by Rogers, Amsterdam, are signed only "D. H. W. Cavaliere"; they show melodious invention (*see* E. v. d. Str., "Eighteenth-Century Violin Sonatas," *The Strad*). Some MS. violin sonatas (Autogr.?) are in the Brit. Mus., and one MS. sonata for violin solo and organ is in the Dresden Library.

CHAPTER 13

Italy: to 1650

THE introductory remarks to this period are sufficiently covered in Chapter 8.

FLORENTIO MASCHERA (MASCARA), b. 1540 or 1541; d. Brescia, ca. 1580 or 1584. For a short time Maschera was a pupil of Cl. Merulo. From 1557 he was organist at Brescia. An excellent violinist and one of the first composers of instrumental canzonas (2 numbers in Wasielewski: "Die Jnstr. Mus. im 17ten Jahrhundert"), also some in Woltz' "Tabulatura," 1617, Rauerji, 1608, Terzi, 1599, and B. Schmid, jun., 1607.

MATTEO BESUZIO. Violinist, ca. 1555, in the Dresden Court chapel with 180 florins, went to Munich in 1568 at a salary of 150, afterwards 180, florins. In the lists he appears at first as Matheisn, Mathias, etc., der Geiger. In 1590 he appears also as "Silberdiener," with 360 florins allowance. He was there still in 1595 (Eitner).

ZERBONIO BESUZIO, d. Munich, ca. middle of 1579; brother of Matteo. He was engaged as violinist in the Dresden Court chapel with 228 florins (Fürstenau, ii, 173; MfM, ix, 238); went to Munich Court chapel with Mateo, 1568, at 150 florins. Composed motets.

AMBROSE DE MYLLAN (AMBR. LUPO). A native of Milan; violinist in the King's band, London, 1559, till his death, 1594.

THOMAS LUPO, SEN. Violinist, at the English Court, 1593, and composer, 1626. Died shortly before 1627.

THOMAS LUPO, JUN. Violinist, at the English Court, Nov. 17, 1599; d. 1637. (*See* Davey, Grove, etc.)

HORATIO LUPO. Appointed for lifetime, at the English Court, Feb. 6, 1612, at £40 per annum. Still mentioned in 1625.

The History of the Violin

ADRIANO BANCHIERI, b. Bologna, ca. 1567; d. 1634. Olivetan Monk, organist, and afterwards titular abbot of S. Michael in Bosco. Eminent composer, who wrote sonatas for 2 violins and trombone on an Aria of the Grand Duke (Eitner gives more particulars); also church compositions and didactic works. They are among the earliest violin sonatas.

GIOVANNI BATTISTA GIACOMETTI (DEL VIOLINO), b. Brescia, lived at Rome from ca. 1571. Haberl ("Jahrbuch," 1891, pp. 86, 391) mentions him as singer in the Papal chapel. In 1586 he was in treaty with the Duke of Mantua, but demanded an appointment for life, at which the Duke demurred, but on June 15 of that year he was appointed as director of the chapel in the place of Soriano at 100 ducats per annum with board (Naturalverpflegung) for 3 persons, a servant, and his old father (Canal, 46, 47; Haberl, "Jahrb.," 1806–45). Eitner calls him an excellent violinist (violist?).

BALTAZARINI. (Mendel says the correct name is Baltagerini.) Known in France as Beaujoyeux, foremost violinist of his time, introduced by the Marshal de Brissac with his band of violinists to the Court of Catherine de Medici in Paris (see pp. 44–5), where he became intendant of music and valet of the chamber under the name of de Beaujoyeux. Henry III charged him with the arrangement of the Court Festivals, for which he conceived the "Ballet Comique de la Royne," the music being written by Beaulieu and Salmond, chamber musician of the King. (More particulars in E. v. d. Str., "Romance of the Fiddle.") Mendel says he came to Paris about the middle of the 16th century as a distinguished violinist, to arrange Italian dances for Catherine de Medici. To improve these dances through his own talent and make them musically more effective, he associated himself with talented chamber musicians like Beulieu and Maltre, who wrote the music according to his indications. The Ballet Comique was published in 1582, after his death, which took place ca. 1576. After the death of the King he had left the Court and lived in Paris as private teacher and composer. According to other sources, the Ballet was only performed in 1582, in which case his death must have occurred much later.

GIOVANNI COLTELLINI (surnamed DEL VIOLINO). A member of the town chapel of Bologna during the second half of the 16th

Italy: to 1650

century. Fétis enumerates 3 books of madrigals by him dated respectively 1579, 1582, 1586 (pub. Ferrara, Vitt. Baldini), but no compositions for violin.

ALESSANDRO OROLOGIO. A violinist in 1580 in the chapel of the Emperor Rudolph II at Prague at 15 florins per month. From Apr. 1, 1603, he was vice-capellmeister, for 30 florins per month; in 1613, on the accession of the Emperor Mathias, he retired from office. Köchel (i, 112) says that he lived at Prague till 1630 and figured in the annals (Akten) as Court composer. Köchel (i, 126) says that apart from his salary he received annually 20 florins for a suit of clothes (? ein Kleid), 30 florins New Year's money, and 70 florins for house rent. According to Fétis, he was musician at the Court of Hesse-Cassel in the latter part of the 16th century; went from there to Venice, then to the Court of Helmstadt, and finally to Vienna. Composed Canzonets, for 3 voices, pub. Venice, book 1 in 1590, book 2 1594; Intradas in 5 parts, Helmstadt, 1597, and Motets, Venice, 1627; which makes it probable that he revisited that town towards the latter part of his life.

GIOVANNI BATTISTA JACOMELLI (surnamed DEL VIOLINO), b. probably at Brescia. According to the Prefaces to the "Intermedi," for the wedding of Ferdinand de Medici (1591), and Peri's "Euridice" he excelled in all branches of music and *almost exchanged his name with that of the violin on which he is admirable*. During 1582–5 he was also a singer in the Papal chapel at Rome, but was dismissed in the latter year, probably for want of assiduity.

CAMILLO CORTELLINI (detto IL VIOLINO), of Bologna. From ca. 1583 member of the municipal chapel. "Musico della Illustrissima Signoria di Bologna" as he calls himself on his works. He was a pupil of Alfonso Ganassi. In 1613 he was conductor of the chapel. His numerous compositions consist of church works and madrigals.

RICCARDO ROGNONE. A late 16th-century violinist and composer living at Milan; wrote "Canzonetti alla Napolitana a tre e quattro voci" (Venice 1586); "Libro di passagi per voci ed instromenti" (Ib., 1592); "Pavane et balli con due canzoni e diversa sorte di brandi per suonare e quattro e cinque" (Milan, 1603).

FRANCESCO ROGNONE, second son of Riccardo, concertmeister of the Duke of Milan ca. 1620; composed "Correnti e Gagliarde a 4 con la quinta parte ad arbitrio per suonare ou varii stromenti" (Milan, 1624); "Aggiunta della scolare di violino ed altri stromenti col basso continuo per l'organo" (Milan, 1614).

TAEGO FRANCESCO ROGNONE, son of Riccardo R. F. (Riemann). "Sonatore di diversi stromenti di corda et fiato." In Joh. Andr. Herbst's "Musica Pratica" (1642), "Musical examples on violins and cornettos in unison"; in the same author's "Musica Moderna" (1653), example on page 20. "Correnti e Gagliarde" (1624); "Aggiunta dello scolare di violino" (1614); "Selva di varii passagi secondo l'uso moderno" (1620); "Manners of Embellishment, etc., for Singers and Players."

TAEGO RICCARDO ROGNONE. A 16th-century violinist at Milan; composed "Canzonette alla Napolitana," 3–4 parts (1586); "Passagi . . . nel diminuir" (1592) and "Pavane e balli . . . canzone . . . brandi," 4–6 parts (1603).

SALOMONE ROSSI (called EBREO), b. Mantua, of an ancient and distinguished Jewish family. 1587 he was already, with his sister, musician and singer at the Court of Vincenzo I of Mantua. In 1622 he was still in that chapel as violinist with 383 lire per annum. Instrumentalist; composed sonatas till 1623 for viols, then for violin; 1 sonata for 4 violins and 2 chittarones. (*See* important particulars in Eitner.) Apparently he died 1628. So highly was he esteemed at the Court that he was exempted from wearing the yellow badge of the Jew at his hat or cap when walking about. In a letter to his councillor (agent?), Annibale Chioppio, of Sept. 29, 1612, the Prince orders the latter to invite Rossi and his company to his Court (Ed. Birnbaum, "Jüd. Mus. am Hofe von Mantua," Vienna, 1893; also Bertolotti, 68, 87).

SCIPIONE BARGAGLIA. Neapolitan violinist, or rather violist, of the second half of the 16th century mentioned by Ceretto, who wrote "Trattenimenti ossia divertimenti da suonare" (Venice, 1587), in which, according to Fétis, the word "Concerto" is used for the first time.

ALESSANDRO (ALESSANDRINO) STRIGGIO. Famous violinist and lyra player, son of Alessandro Striggio, called Alessandrino

Italy: to 1650

in the account of the Festivities at Florence of May 15, 1589 (E. Vogel, Bibl., ii, p. 384). In 1607 he was at the Court of Mantua. Striggio wrote the libretto of Monteverde's "Orfeo"; in 1596-7 he published books 3-5 of his father's 5 part Madrigals, and composed himself madrigals and other vocal music but no compositions by him are known for violin or lyra, of which he is the only virtuoso whose name as such has been handed down to history.

BERGEMENA BOVIS. Italian (?) violinist, ca. 1590, at the Saxon Court at Dresden, in Rogier Michael's time, at 228 florins 12 grosschen per annum.

PELLEGRINI MUZZOLI. In 1591 an instrumentalist (violino) at S. Petronio, Bologna (Gaspari, i, 8), with L1.10 salary.

AGOSTINO TESSARO. A violinist, ca. 1594, at S. Antoniana (Tebaldini, 17).

BIAGIO MARINI, b. Brescia before 1597; d. Venice, 1665. He is mentioned as musician at St. Mark's in 1615; in 1618 as violinist in the town chapel (?segnoria), Venice. In 1620 he went to Brescia as capellmeister at S. Eufemia and the academy Erranti, and in 1622 he was in the service of Ferdinand Gonzaga at Parma. By 1626 he calls himself "Accademico occulto gentilhuomo e Maestro della musica," and in Oct., 1626, addressing the Palgrave Wolfgang Wilhelm of Neuburg, Duke of Bavaria, he calls himself "maestro della musica," and states that he played quite recently at Brussels, being awarded with honours and presents. He then became capellmeister, ca. 1640, of the Prince Palatine at Düsseldorf (MfM, xviii, 108-9), who, in 1634, bestowed upon him the title of "gentil'huomo e cavaliere." 1653 finds him capellmeister at the Academia della morte, Ferrara, and 1654 capellmeister at S. Maria della Scala, Milan. He was a prolific composer of instrumental and vocal music (see i, p. 49). Eitner gives his still existing works. Wasielewski says he wrote the first solo piece for the violin, a piece without title, in his first work "Affetti Musicali," Venice, 1617. This was followed by a "Romanesca" for violin solo with bass ad lib. pub. in "Arie, madrigali, e correnti a 1, 2 e 3 voci," Venice, 1620. It is dedicated to Signor Gian Battista Magni, "a most promising young violinist," and evidently an occasional composition for a comparative beginner which does not exceed the first position, and is in many ways inferior to his "Sonate, Canzoni, Passamezzi," etc., in 1 to 6 parts, Venice, Bartolomeo Magni, 1655. The Romanesca which has been reproduced and described in E. v. d. Str., "Romance of the Fiddle," p. 14, etc., is moreover noteworthy by the fact that it shows the first-known application of the trill in instrumental music, as well as an embellishment called "in the Lombardian manner" (in Part I, bar 4, and Part III, bar 19) which consists in shortening the harmony note by the length of the auxiliary note (see p. 156).

MORARI. Four musicians of this name were "Geiger" (violins?) in the chapel of the Elector of Bavaria in the latter part of the 16th century (*see* Eitner).

PAOLO QUAGLIATI, b. Rome?; organist, 16th–17th century, harpischord player and violinist. He wrote "La Sfera armoniosa," 2- and 3-part vocal pieces, followed by pieces for violin solo with Theorbo including a Toccata, which gives only the necessary outlines, intended to be ornamented and embellished by the executant according to the custom of the time, a device which was gradually curtailed, as the thematic or subject-matter assumed greater importance. The embellishment of a slow movement, however, continued right into the 18th century; and was even taught as a special art.

BARTOLOMEO MONTALBANO, b. Bologna, ca. 1600. Capellmeister at S. Francesco at Palermo, composed symphonies for 1 to 4 violins with organ and two with additional trombone, Palermo, 1626. According to Torchi they show attempts at characteristic effects as well as the rudiments of an instrumental style. In some, the violin shows brilliant figuration and they are perhaps the first which contain marks of expression and slurs.

MARTINO PESENTI, b. Venice ca. 1600; d. there before 1648; blind from birth. Composed dance movements, pub. 1630–45, which excel for their spontaneous melodic invention and clearness. He did much for the inner evolution and consolidation of the melody (Wki., 72). He was probably a pupil of Monteverde, in whose style he writes; the dances are for spinet or harpsichord; he composed 7 books of concerted Madrigals. Wasielewski says he wrote symphonies for 1–4 violins with organ (two also with trombone), pub. Palermo,

Italy: to 1650

1629, where he was capellmeister at the church of S. Francesco (see Torchi).

ANTONIO BERTALI, b. Verona, 1605; d. Vienna, Apr. 1, 1669. Violinist; entered the Imperial Chapel, Vienna, as instrumentalist on Apr. 1, 1637, and became capellmeister Oct. 1, 1649, at 1,200 florins. He was a favourite at Court as a composer. In 1652 he was sent with a message to Dresden, and in 1653 the Emperor had his opera "L'Inganuo d'amore" performed at the Reichstag at Ratisbon. He composed chiefly church music (see Eitner).

OCTAVIO MARIA GRANDI. Violinist, a pupil of Alfonso Pagani. In 1610, organist at Reggio (see letter in Banchieri's "Armoniche," p. 40). On the title page of his only known printed work he calls himself organist at the cathedral and the church of Miracolosissima Madonna de Servi at Reggio and professor (teacher) of the violin: Sonate per ogni sorte di stromenti 1, 2, 3, 4, and 6 con il basso per l'organo del ... op. 2, Ven., 1628, Magni, 5 part books, fol. mentioned are violins and trombones, 22 pieces. Some also for voices, Brit. Mus. Sopr. II, B. Br.; there also in MS. III, 9 sonatas for 3 to 5 parts.

GIOVANNI BATTISTA MUTI. In Radesca's 2 lib. delle Canzonette, Venetia, 1616, p. 18, he calls himself "violino di S.A.S. et musico di camera dell'Eccell. sig. D. Amadeo di Savoia." Radesca gives a corrente of Muti's for instruments.

MICHEL ANGELO ROSSI, b. Rome, end of 16th century; lived there from 1620 to ca. 1660; pupil of Frescobaldi. In 1625 his opera "Erminia sul Giordano" was performed before a company of music lovers. In this he took himself the rôle of Apollo. The work was published in 1627 (Riemann, 1637) at Rome, and in the Preface it says that *the tones which Rossi evokes from his violin* are worthy of an Apollo, etc. He composed chiefly organ pieces.

MAURIZIO CAZZATI, b. Guastalla, ca. 1620. He was a priest and violinist who came to Bologna in 1657 when he produced some of his sacred music at the church of S. Salvatore which created such a sensation that he was appointed capellmeister at the church of S. Petronio from 1657 to 1671, and a member of the Academia Filarmonica. He opened a school of music there which proved very successful and counted among its

The History of the Violin

pupils Giov. Bat. Vitali. Apart from numerous works for the church he composed: Sonatas for 2 violins and bass; Sonate a uno, duo, tre, quattro, cinque, con alcune per tromba (1–5 parts with some for trumpet), one book Concerti et Balletti, and one book "Trattenimenti per camera, d'arie, concerti e balletti" for 2 violins with violin ad lib. including passacaglia, ciacona and a capriccio on 12 notes. "Sonate a 3 Anversa," 1659; do., op. 22, 1660; do., op. 30, 1662, Bologna: "Sonate a 3," op. 50, 1669; do., op. 55, 1670; "Concerti e balletti a 5 alla francese et all'Italina a 5–8 voci," op. 15 (all at Bologna).

CARLO VARINO, of Mantua, violinist (Eitner?). Receives a letter of recommendation from the Elector of Saxony in 1621 (State Archives).

TARQUINIO MERULA, b. Cremona, of a noble family (cavaliere). In 1623 he was capellmeister at Santa Maria Maggiore, Bergamo, and in 1624 organist at the church and Court at Warsaw; 1628 organist at the church of Ss. Agatha (Pougin, "Le Violon, etc.," calls him solo violinist there, as often the case, he may have played both) and at the Cathedral of Cremona. In 1639 he occupied again his former position at Bergamo. In 1640 he calls himself "Acad. filomuso of Bologna"; he was also a knight of the golden spur, as well as organist at Bergamo Cathedral, where he was still in 1642, and in 1652 he was once more at the Cathedral of Cremona. Lucchini (p. 19), who also mentions Cremona, says that he was capellmeister at the Court of Florence between 1622 and 1680. His importance with regard to the history of the violin lies in: "Il 1º libro delle canzoni a 4 voci per stromenti," Venice, Magni, 1615; "Canzoni overe sonate concertate per chiesa e camera a 2 et a 3, lib. 3 (?), op. 12," Venice, 1637; "Il 2do libro delle canzoni da suonare a 3, due violini e Basso, op. 9," Venice, 1639; "Canzoni da suonare a 2–3, lib. 4, op. 17," Venice, 1651. They show a transition from the vocal style, still noticeable in Gabrieli's works, to that which is more in the nature of instruments. In one canzona, "La Cancelleria," he has already sequences of octaves moving from the first to the third position, as well as some quick passages with fairly complicated changes of position, which is quite new for that time. The form of his canzonas, moreover, shows already

NICOLA COSIMI
a painting by Sir Godfrey Kneller.
a contemporary mezzotint by
ith in the British Museum.

JEAN BAPTISTE LULLY

GIUSEPPE TORELLI

TOMMASO ANTONIO VITALI

From original portraits in the L
Musicale, published for the first time f
photographs kindly supplied by F.
Arnold, Esq., M.A., Cantab.

the development which led to the sonata form, and it was not uncommon about that time to find instrumental compositions described as "Sonate ôver Canzoni" (sonatas or canzonas—*see* Uccellini). His latest work, however, Merula describes as "Sonate concertate per chiesa e camera," 1651. Specimen from his works for violin in Riemann's "Alte Kirchenmusik," 3-part canzona "La Pedrina," Musikgeschichte in Beispielen (Id.), No. 90, and 2 canzonas are to be seen in Wasielewski, "Zur Geschichte der Instrumental Musik."

GIOVANNI LEGRENZI, b. Clusone, near Bergamo, ca. 1625; d. Venice, July 26, 1690. Composer. A pupil of Giov. Rovetto and C. Pallavicino. "Sonate per chiesa," Venice, 1655; "Sonate da chiesa e da camera," Ib., 1656; "Una muta di suonata," 1664; "Suonate a due violini e violone con il basso continuo per l'organo op. ottava," Ib., 1667; "Le Cetra consegrata al nome immortale della Cesarea R.M. di Leopoldo I in sonate a 2, 3, 4 stromenti, op. 10," Ib., 1673; "Suonate a 2 violini," Ib., 1677; "Sonate da chiesa e da camera a 2, 3, 4, 5, 6, 7, stromenti con trombe e senza ovvero flauti libro sesto, op. 17," Ib., 1693, 4to. His importance lies in his work in connexion with the development of the instrumental sonata. He paid more attention to euphony between the different parts, key relationship and modulation, more varied rhythm and the symmetry of the periods. In 1685 he became capellmeister at S. Mark's at Venice, where he augmented and reorganized the orchestra, introducing violins. He arranged the orchestra in the following manner: 8 violins, 11 small viols or violettas, 2 viols da braccio, 3 big viols da gamba and violone (double bass viol), 4 theorbos, 2 cornettos, 1 bassoon and 3 trombones.

GIOVANNI BATTISTA BUONAMENTE. In 1626–9 he was Imperial Court musician and in 1636 capellmeister at the concert of St. Francis of Assisi. He is among the earliest composers for the violin, his works consisting of 7 books of sonatas, symphonies and dance pieces published by Alessandro Vincenti at Venice. The sonatas in books 4 and 5, 1626 and 1629, are for 2 violins and bass, in book 6 (1636) (*see* in Wki., pp. 68–9), in book 7 (1637) for 2 violins. Copies of these are in the Breslau library and book 6 also in the Cassel library. Sonata a 3, 2 V. et B.c. (MS. Upsala), 1636. Sonate et Canzoni a due, tre, quattro, cinque et sei voci ... con il suo Basso continuo, dedicate, etc., etc., lib. vi. They are in advance of their time; indeed, they show the construction of the Sonata da camera. Musically they are distinguished by nobility of conception and simple grandeur.

GIUSEPPE SCARANI. A Carmelite monk who, in 1630, was organist and "musico" of the Venice Republic. By 1641 he is Court organist at Mantua. Composed "Sonate concertante a 2 e 3 stromenti, lib. 1, op. 1," Ven., B. Magni, 1630; 9 sonatas (violins?) (B. Br., Bologna); "Concerti ecclesiastici a 2, 3, 4, 5, voci con il B.c., lib. 1, op. 2," Venice, B. Magni, 1641; 21 vocal pieces.

SIMONE ARIETTO, b. Vercelli at the beginning of the 17th century. After having been for a time in the service of the Duke of Mantua, he returned to his native town and in 1630 entered the Court chapel of the Duke of Savoy. His name is mentioned by Fétis erroneously as that of the first virtuoso on the Violin (*see* G. B. Jacomelli). His sons FRANCIS and SIMON were both clever violinists, but they did not equal their father.

GIOVANNI BATTISTA FONTANA, b. Brescia; d. Padua, 1630, of the plague. One of the foremost violinists of his time. He lived alternately at Venice, Rome, Padua. He wrote violin sonatas, published after his death, 1641: "Sonate a 1, 2, 3, per il violino o cornetto, Fagotto, Chitarone, Violoncino o simile altro instrumento. Del gia Mto Illre sig, . . ." Venezia, 1641, Magni. (18 sonatas: 6 for violin and bass, 1 for 3 violins; others consist of movements for 1 and 2 violins with and without bassoon.) The violin sonatas are essentially similar to those by Farina, although the latter are, musically as well as with regard to the violin technique, superior to Fontanas. These, on the other hand, possess a special interest in so far that although written still in the one movement form, they show already the germ of the cyclic form in contrasting sections finishing on full cadences which differ in rhythm and time. According to G. B. Reghino, the editor of his sonatas, Fontana exercised a distinct influence upon the art of violin playing in his time.

GIULIO CESARE LISARDO. Violinist in the Court chapel, Madrid, 1633 (Str., viii, 424).

Italy: to 1650

ESTAFANO LIMIDO. In 1633 a violinist in the Court chapel, Madrid (Str., viii, 424). Composed 3-part motets, in Lucino's collection of 1608; other vocal compositions, *see* Eitner.

JEAN BAPTISTE LULLY, b. Florence, ca. 1633; d. Paris, Mar. 22, 1687. He came, through the Duke of Guise, into the service of Mme de Monpensier as kitchen boy; studied musical theory with the organist Métra, became violinist in the Royal chapel. Thereafter, he soon became master of the chapel and formed the band of 16 violins called "Les petits violons." On Mar. 16, 1653, he was made Court composer, and on May 16, 1661, intendant of the Court music and Court library. He raised the status of the violin in France and trained some good pupils, including the German violinists, J. Fischer and Muffat, but he is chiefly to be considered as an opera composer.

GIUSEPPE COLOMBI, b. Modena, 1635; d. there Sept. 27, 1694. He was "suonatore," i.e. instrumental player in the Ducal chapel in 1673, under Francesco II, being called "Capo degl' instrumentisti" (head of the instrument players). He was also leader of the violins and director of the instrumental chapel (Court orchestra). From Dec. 1, 1674, he received 96 lire per month. From 1676 he added to his former title that of vice-capellmeister, and in 1678 he succeeded (according to Fétis) Giov. Maria Bononcini as capellmeister at the cathedral in Modena. In 1689 he uses the latter title on the front page of one of his printed works (sonatas for 2 violins and violone or harps., op. 5, 1689) as well as that of violin teacher of the Duke. Numerous works of his, printed and in MS., are in the Estense library in Modena, including sonatas and books of: Balletti, Gighe, Correnti, Sarabande, etc., mostly for 2 violins and bass, but also for 1 violin and bass (*see* list in Eitner). Sonate a 3, op. 1, Bologna, 1668; sonate a 3, op. 5, Ib., 1689 (both in Bologna library).

GIOVANNI MARIA BONONCINI, b. Modena, 1640; d. there Nov. 19, 1678. For some time he was violinist (Pougin) in the Ducal chapel, afterwards church capellmeister at Modena and at Bologna. Composed sonatas for 2 violins with spinet or violone; Ariette, Correnti, Gighe, etc., for violin solo with 2 viols; and Primi Frutti del Giardino Musicale for 2 violins.

BARTOLOMEO GIROLAMO (GERONIMO) LAURENTI, b. Bologna, ca. 1644; d. there Jan. 18, 1726. 1st violinist at S. Petronio, and one of the first members of the Academy dei Filarmonici after its foundation in 1666. Composed Sonate per camera a violin e violoncello, op. 3 (Fétis, op. 1), Bologna, 1691, Bologna, Monti; Sei Concerti a 3 cioè violin violoncello ed organo, Bologna, 1720 (Eitner, i) (E. v. d. Str., "Eighteenth-Century Sonatas"), 1 sonata con violino violoncello and B.c. in collected vol. 1700, by Buffagnotti.

GIOVANNI BATTISTA VITALI, b. Cremona ca. 1644; d. Modena, Oct. 12, 1692. As it says in the Cod. in the B. Estense "at an advanced age," he must have been born earlier than 1644. After being a pupil of Maur. Cazzati he commenced his career as "sonatore di violino da brazzo" at S. Petronio and afterwards at the chapel of the Rosary, Bologna, as he calls himself on his first published works, 1666-8. On Dec. 1, 1674, he entered the service of the Duke Francesco I of Modena, and calls himself, 1677, vice-capellmeister and member of the Academia Filaschese. He was a fertile composer. Sonatas and Balletti, etc., for solo violin, 2 violini e Bass, and greater number of strings, also vocal compositions, all in the Estense library. He plays an important part in the evolution of the sonata before Corelli.

NICOLAUS KEMPIS, b. Florence (? calls himself Fiorentino). A 17th-century organist at St. Gudule, Brussels. Wrote: 2 symphoniae 1–5 instrumentorum, adjunctae 4 instrumental et 2 vocal (2 books 1647 and 1649, Antwerp); 11 symphoniae 1, 2, 3 violinum (Antwerp, 1644). In the latter sonatas he develops to a considerable extent the cantabile style (cantilena). One sonata in A republished in Riemann's "Alte Kammermusik" (Schott).

PIETRO DEGLI ANTONII, b. Bologna ca. 1645. Composed, Sonate op. 4, Bologna, 1676; do., op. 5, Ib., 1686; do., op. 3, Ib., 1688. In 1680 he was capellmeister at S. Maria Maggiore and Member of Acad. fil., and in 1676 and 1718 principe of the academy. By 1686 he was at S. Stefano, and in 1697 at S. Giovanni, Bologna. (*See also* Wki.)

GASPARO ZANETTI. Il Scolaro per imparare a suonare di violino ed altri stromenti, etc., Milano, 1645 (Becker, i, 360, gives the full long title).

Italy: to 1650

GIROLAMO ZANETTI. Musico di violino of Milan; wrote a theoretical treatise published Milan, 1680; also some motets in F. Vigoni's "Nuova Raccolta," 1681.

D. MARCO UCCELLINI. On the title pages of his op. 5, published in 1649, he calls himself "head of the music of the Duke of Modena." His latest composition is the opera "Giove de Elide fulminanto," dated 1677. As a violin virtuoso he seems to have been far ahead of all his contemporaries; not only did he make use of 6 positions but his passages were more varied both with regard to fingering and to bowing than any of his contemporaries. Wasielewski speaks of his violin sonatas as possessing no artistic value. We have unfortunately not been able to see any of them, but Wasielewski is also unjustly harsh in his condemnation of J. J. Walther's works. His sinfonie boscarrecie, op. 8 (1677), for violin and bass with 2 additional violins ad lib. resemble in form the French suites, consisting of short pieces with fancy titles connected only by key relationship. A pretty Adagio and Allegro are reproduced in Wasielewski's "Die Violine im 17ten Jahrhundert." Even the battle-piece, beloved from the times of the old Netherlands and the English virginal composers, is represented by "La gran battaglia." Wasielewski mentions: 33 sonatas for 1 and 2 violins with bass, op. 4, pub. 1645; Sonate over canzoni da farsi a Violino solo e Basso continuo, opera quinta di D. Marco Uccellini. Capo di Musica del Serenissimo Signore Duca di Modena. In Venetia apresco Alessandro Vincenti, 1649. This work comprises 13 sonatas for violin and bass as well as a piece entitled "Trombetta sordina per sonare con un violino solo." A copy of this is in the library (Landesbibliothek) at Cassel. The title of the work shows that "canzona" and "sonata" were still synonymous terms. The letter D(ominus) in front of his name indicates that the author was a monk or priest. Wasielewski mentions a third work, consisting of 20 correntes and 10 arias for violin solo with a second violin ad lib., but gives no further particulars. Fétis mentions: Sonate, sinfonie e correnti a 2, 3, e 4 stromenti, lib. 1 and 2; sonate a 2, e 3 violini o altri stromenti, lib. 3; sonate, correnti ad arie a 1, 2, e 3 stromenti, lib. 4. He says they were written between 1650–60 which is evidently an error, especially if any of the above belong to the works preceding op. 4.

MICHAEL FARINELLI, b. Grenoble, May 23, 1649. (Uncle of Carlo Broschi?) Farinelli appeared as solo violinist at Lisbon, 1668; was in Paris in 1672, and in 1675–9 he was engaged at the English (Hanover?) Court. He is the composer of the "Folies d'Espagne," which appeared in Playford's "Division Violin," 1685, as Farinel's Ground, and was used afterwards by many composers, including Corelli, whose beautiful variations "La Folia" from his op. V are still a favourite concert piece. Marin Marais wrote 32 variations on the theme for the viol da gamba.

ANDREA FALCONIERI. His first compositions were published at Rome in 1610; and "the first book of" Canzoni, Sinfonie, Fantasie, Caprici, Brandi, etc., for violins and viols or other instruments in 1, 2, and 3 parts with B.c. at Naples in 1650, as in the same year were his Sonate a 3, at Venice (Bol.).

ROBERTO SABBATINO. Of Rome, was touring in 1650 and appeared also at Liège. Giles Heine calls him an excellent virtuoso (M.f.M., xxviii, 113).

FRANCESCO TODESCHINI. A 17th-century violinist, and violinist to Carlo II, Duke of Mantua. Composed "Delle correnti, Gagliarde, Balletti et Arie, a 4 da sonare con 4 viole cioè 2 violini, viola e Basso, e si possono sonare à 3, à 2, lasciando fuori le parti di mezzo, op. 1 di ... Musico, and Sonatore di Violino e di Violone del Serenissimo...." Ven., 1650, Aless. Vincenti (B. Br.).

GIOVANNI ANTONIO LEONI. A 17th-century violinist, as he calls himself in the Preface of his "Sonate di Violino à voce sola di ..., Lib. 1, op. 3, Roma, 1652, Vitale Mascardi ... ad istanza di Ant. Poggioli," 2 partbooks in 4 (V.º and score 12½ and 23½ fols.) 31 sonat. of the 1–6 and 8 mode (B. Br., Breslau). In Sammaruco's "Sacri Affetti," 1625, the motet "Domina, Dominus noster a C. e B." (copy in Breslau town library).

ERCOLE GAIBARA (called DEL VIOLINO). Early 17th-century violinist at Bologna, where he had a school of music and violin-playing which produced a number of excellent virtuosi, especially Giovanni Benvenuti and Leonardo Brugnoli, the teachers of Corelli. About Gaibara's life no dates or particulars are available.

Italy: to 1650

MICHEL ANGELO VEROVIO (called MICHELANGELO DEL VIOLINO). Lived in the first half of the 17th century. An excellent violinist. Pietra della Valle, G. B. Doni and Arteaga give particulars about him, and the latter also of his playing; extracts in Fétis. Arteaga says (in "Le Revolusioni," etc.) that Verovio was one of the first who introduced the new embellishments, viz. the shake, mordent, tremolo.

GIOVANNI ANTONIO PANDOLFI MEALLI. In the middle of the 17th century he was in the chapel of the Archduke Ferdinand Karl of Austria.

CHAPTER 14

Italy: to 1700

THE second half of the 17th century was a very important period in the evolution of the Sonata; apart from its final severance from the contrapuntal vocal forms, which commenced at the beginning of the century, a clear distinction was established between the Church sonata (Sonata da chiesa) and the Chamber sonata (Sonata da camera), in the development of which M. Neri and G. Legrenzi played a considerable part, although only with regard to sonata-form, while Bassani not only clarified the form and rounded it off but also advanced the technique of the violin. In both capacities Torelli went still farther, not only by the greater variety and boldness of his passage work but also by the use of double stopping and chords. He also was the first to write sonatas in several parts with one or more obbligato instruments to which he gave the name of Concerti. He also wrote a *Concertino* for violin and violoncello, and his famous Concerti grossi, op. 8, published after his death—which led to the futile discussions as to whether he or Corelli was the inventor of that form—to which also, according to Wasielewski ("Die Violine," 1920, p. 80), Lorenzo Gregori, a composer of the lesser order, contributed a set of Concerti grossi in 1698, and Alessandro Scarlatti's fine Concerti grossi were published by Benj. Cooke early in the 18th century.

Giov. Bat. Vitali was one of the first to introduce abstract movements from the church sonata into the chamber sonata, which he perfected also by his skilful treatment of the usual dance forms. In this respect he had a worthy successor in his son Antonio, whose justly famous Ciaconna figures still in the repertories of modern violinists, unfortunately only in the edition by F. David, who, as usual, took great liberties with the original.

Italy: to 1700

The bow had undergone many changes during the 17th century, and towards the latter part was gradually approaching its modern form, but before this was reached it passed through many tentative stages, which existed side by side; it cannot be said that the bow in 1650 was of such and such a form; in, say, 1680 it was so and so. The devices of tightening the hair by means of the nut were various: one was the *crémaillère*, consisting of a number of metal teeth to which the nut was fixed by means of a metal hook; another was to fix the hair into the stick at both ends, and slip the detached nut into a slot with a snap, where it is held in place by the pressure of the hair. It is uncertain when the screw regulating the position of the nut came into use, but apparently it was already applied to some bows towards the end of the 17th century. The straightening-out of the bow-stick, from the strongly outward arched form of the early bows, had commenced already in the 16th century, and in the 17th it continued while the bow gradually developed more elegant forms, although it retained, in some cases to about 1700, a sudden downward slope in the upper part which ended in the long pointed head characteristic of the viol bows. This is also still noticeable in the 17th-century bow, described and illustrated in H. Saint-George's excellent little book "The Bow, its History," etc. (Strad Library), pp. 35–6, which has already a well-defined *cambre*, as well as a perfect screw-nut. These achievements, however, did not become general until much later (*see* Ch. 3).

The violin itself was reaching the height of perfection during the latter part of the 17th century through those great Cremonese artists, the Amatis, Giuseppe Guarneri del Gesù, and the greatest of all, Antonio Stradivari (*see* the sumptuous works on these, containing many new discoveries relating to their persons and their work by A. F. and A. E. Hill).

ARCANGELO CORELLI, b. Fusignano, Feb. 19, 1653; d. Rome, Jan. 8, 1713. He was the youngest of five sons, and was born six days after the death of his father. Quite young, he was sent to relatives at Faënza, where he commenced his musical studies under a priest, continuing under an unknown master at Luogo. In 1666 or 1667 he went to Bologna for his further education, which in the first instance was directed towards different ends, but it is said that after hearing the violin he became so enamoured of its tone that he decided to devote himself entirely to the study of that instrument. His first master was Giovanni Benvenuti, solo violinist at the church of San Petronio and member of the Philharmonic Academy, but later on he became a pupil of Leonardo Brugnoli, whose playing had roused him to enthusiasm and admiration. Brugnoli, a native of Venice, belonged to the same institutions as Benvenuti; he was a remarkable violinist of distinct individuality. Of his life nothing is known, but of Benvenuti it is known that in 1710 he entered the hospice of St. Joseph, a retreat for aged people, where he died Feb. 11, 1715. In 1671 Corelli went to Rome to complete his studies in theory and composition under Matteo Simonelli, chaplain chanter of the Pontifical chapel, and maestro di capella at several Roman churches, who was called the Palestrina of the 17th century. His sojourn at Paris in 1672, and the anecdotes told in connexion therewith, appear to be apocryphal. He had already gained a great reputation at Rome, when on Jan. 6, 1679, Bernardo Pasquini entrusted him with the leadership of the orchestra on the occasion of the first performance of his opera "Dove è amor e pieta" at the Capranica Theatre, Pasquini presiding at the harpsichord. This shows the confidence which the older master reposed in Corelli. In the second half of 1679 he went, however, to Munich (Printz also met him at Anspach), where he was engaged in the chapel of the Elector of Bavaria until the beginning of 1881, when he returned to Rome, where his trio sonatas, op. I, were published in that year by Mutii. The dedication of that work to Queen Christina of Sweden is dated Apr. 30, 1681.

Chrysander states that between 1680 and 1685 Corelli spent some time with his friend Farinelli at Hanover. This could only have been during the time that he was at Munich, but, taking into account the time which the journey alone would have entailed, this appears at least very doubtful. It is certain that in the early eighties he formed many friendships not only with the famous composers and musicians, but also with eminent painters, especially with Trevisani, Lignani, and Maratte, who assisted him in forming a remarkable collection of pictures of considerable value. The circle of his friends also included the sculptor Angelo Rossi as well as poets and

Italy: to 1700

literary men. The comprehensive nature of his genius, his amiable, modest and unassuming personality attracted towards him also the benevolent attention and patronage of persons of the highest rank, such as the ex-Queen Christina of Sweden mentioned above, and Cardinal Benedetto Panfili, who invited him to live in his palace on the Corso, and conduct his private music at a salary of 10 piastres Florentine per month, which position he held for two or three years. During this time he was visited by Nic. Adam Strungk, whose remarkable technique, use of the scordatura, and art of improvisation elicited from him the exclamation: "I am called Arcangelo, but you one might justly call Archidiavolo" (*see* Hawkins, ii, 676; *also* Strungk). In 1685 he dedicated to Cardinal Panfili his second book of trio sonatas, while the third book, published in 1689, was dedicated to Francesco II, Duke of Modena, at whose Court he is said to have stayed in 1689–90. From a document mentioned by Valdrighi, 12, 20, p. 72, stating that Arcangelo, detto il Bolognese (meant for Corelli), travelled through Modena to Rome in 1687, it would appear that he either was there earlier, or at least on two occasions. These works soon spread his fame far and wide. In the latter part of that year Cardinal Ottoboni ascended the Papal throne as Alexander VIII, and a few days after, on Nov. 7, 1689, he appointed his nephew Pietro Ottoboni Cardinal of San Lorenzo in Damaso and Vice-Chancellor of the church. The latter was a man of great culture, and devoted to all arts, especially to music, who had a princely establishment, where he entertained lavishly and on a grand scale. One of his first cares was to secure the services of Corelli, to whom he allotted apartments in his palace, appointing him director of his private music. Ottoboni instituted there the Academy of the Arcadians. Every Monday and on feast days he gave concerts under the direction of Corelli, which were attended by great church dignitaries, ambassadors, princes, members of the aristocracy, etc. Cresimbeni tells us that he was the first who formed at Rome an orchestra on a large scale, comprising a variety of instruments, and that Corelli's fame as violinist was equalled if not surpassed by that as conductor. As a violinist, however, he was fully deserving of the title "Maestro dei Maestri," bestowed upon him by his contemporaries. He was not so much an innovator as a consolidator who synthesized the most valuable achievements of his predecessors and, guided by his unfailing artistic instinct, perfected, and formed them into an organic and well articulated structure which remained the basis of all further development not only of violin playing, but also of the sonata. His outwardly simple and uneventful life was wholly dedicated to the pursuit of his ideals, and his untiring work to attain that which is noblest and most beautiful in art, is traceable in his compositions. His Sonatas, op. I, are still based on the work of his predecessors, and they do not show any marked originality in the conception of their thematic material, although they already exhibit that clearness and terseness of expression which is characteristic of Corelli. They are church sonatas, generally of four movements: adagio, allegro, adagio, allegro. Occasionally, however, we find him still experimenting with regard to form by altering the order of the movements. The 12 Sonatas, op. II, are chamber sonatas, beginning with a prelude (adagio or largo), followed by three dance movements. Sometimes, however, he substitutes an abstract movement for one of the latter, as we find already in Tommaso Vitali's sonatas, but with Corelli this leads to fresh experiments in the combination of movements of various character. His op. III consists again of 12 church sonatas, while op. IV is another set of 12 chamber sonatas. They correspond in their general outline to op. I and op. II, but the movements show a great advance in their development, and purity of writing. The dance forms in particular lose their primitiveness, and grow to wider proportions, taking a first step towards higher instrumental forms. Especially the allemande grew in time to considerable proportions and eventually developed into the first movement of the modern sonata. Whereas the first four works consisted of trio sonatas for 2 violins and violone, with archlute or harpsichord, op. V comprised 12 sonatas for violin and violone or harpsichord; and while in the former all three instruments were of equal importance, the violin in op. V became a solo instrument accompanied by a figured bass. The first six of these are church sonatas, the remainder are chamber sonatas, the twelfth being the famous "La Folia," with 23 variations. This work, therefore, more than the others, reveals to us the state of Corelli's violin technique. We notice here in the first instance the total absence of virtuoso display, which

Italy: to 1700

accounts to a great extent for the fact that he very rarely exceeds the third position. In op. V, No. 6, in the second movement are about three bars in the 4th position and in "La Folia," No. 20 (19th var.), he goes once up to e''' in a broken chord.

His greatest care was bestowed upon the production of a beautiful tone, variety and elegance in bowing, great expression in slow movements, and a well-developed technique of the left hand in the lower positions. To the higher technique of the German violinists he remained a stranger, and this accounts for his astonishment at Strungk's playing, and his failure to master a passage in the 7th position which occurs in Handel's "Trionfo del Tempo," told by Hawkins in his "History of Music." Handel had written the orchestral part of this work in a more brilliant and complicated style than that with which the Italians were familiar, and which accounted for its comparative failure when produced at Ottoboni's palace, and when he became irritated at Corelli's inability to master the passage, after he had explained and finally shown him how it should be played, Corelli quietly answered, "But my dear Saxon, this is in the French style which I do not understand." This happened in 1708. Shortly before this, on Easter Sunday, Apr. 8, 1708, Handel's "Resurrezione" was performed with brilliant success at the Palazzo Ruspoli, and Corelli had engaged the orchestra of which he was the leader. About this time a quarrel arose between the State and the Pope, Rome was threatened with a siege, and Handel with Scarlatti, father and son, went to Naples (see N. Flower, "Handel," pp. 73–5). As to whether Corelli accompanied them we do not know, but he went there about the same time, and took with him two violinists and a violoncellist to make sure of a good accompaniment. After his arrival, however, some of his works were performed there in such a perfect manner that he exclaimed: "Si suono a Napoli"—they can play at Naples. Soon after, however, adversities dogged his footsteps. At the Court he played one of his sonatas from op. 5, when the King suddenly left the room in the middle of his performance, a tactlessness in keeping with the ruthless despotism of that Court. On another occasion he was leading a performance of a work by Scarlatti, when he made a noticeable mistake in a certain passage which the Neapolitan leader, to whom it was familiar, played with ease. Disconcerted, and agitated by this mishap, he next led off a piece in C major instead of C minor. "Ricominciamo" (let us begin again), politely remarked Scarlatti, but, nervous and absentminded he started again in C major, and Scarlatti was obliged to point out his mistake. Mortified by these humiliating experiences, he left Naples, but he had lost confidence in his own powers, and when on his return to Rome he found that Valentini, a young Florentine violinist, had won the favour of the public, he felt himself slighted and neglected and fell a prey to melancholy, which hastened his decline. During his last years, however, he produced one of his greatest works, the 12 Concerti grossi, op. 6, which were published by Roger and Lecène at Amsterdam in 1713 (second ed., 1714). They were dedicated to his patron and admirer the Elector Palatine, who had bestowed upon him the title of Marchese de Ladenburg; the dedication is dated Dec. 3, 1712. They consist of eight church and four chamber concertos, and remained the standard models for all succeeding concerti grossi. There has been a great deal of controversy as to whether the originator of this form was Corelli or Torelli, whose Concerti grossi, also works of sterling merit, appeared as early as 1709. As Georg Muffat relates that he heard concerti grossi by Corelli in 1682, and includes some in a collection of such concertos published at Passau, in 1701, it is evident that it is not easy to decide the question. Neither can have been really the originator, as concerti grossi were extant written by Stradella, Lorenzo Allegri and others between ca. 1675 and 1685 (*see* Schering, p. 42, etc., and Wasielewski, "Die Violine," p. 80, etc.). Corelli's concertos in any case soon became universal favourites and are still so to this day. His achievements as a violinist, which formed the foundation upon which the modern art of violin playing was built up step by step, were handed down to posterity by his numerous pupils, the foremost of whom were: Geminiani, Somis, Locatelli, Baptiste Anet, Castrucci, Carbonelli, and Mossi.

Corelli died Jan. 8, 1713. He was interred in the Pantheon on the left of the entrance, where a marble tablet in his memory was fixed on the wall by order of his admirer the Elector Palatine, Joh. Wilhelm (text in Wasielewski, p. 84). A bust of him was erected at the Vatican with the inscription: "Corelli, Princeps Musicorum." To clarify the various exaggerated accounts about the disposal of his earthly possessions, we subjoin from Pougin an exact translation of his will which was discovered some years ago and published in the Roman periodical "Musica":

To Sigr. Cardinal Ottoboni patron I leave a picture according to his choice, and beg of him to have me interred wherever it may please him best. To Sigr. Mateo Fornari I leave all my violins, and all my papers, as well as the plates of my opus V, and moreover I leave to him my sixth work (and also any benefit that may accrue from it). To the most Eminent Cardinal Colonna I leave a picture by Brugolo "in tella da testo." To Pippo my servant I leave double his month (wages), and to his sister Olimpia I leave the four testoni per month for her lifetime. My universal heirs are my brothers, my testamentary executors Sigr. D. Giuseppe Mondini, and Sigr. Girolamo Sorboli, and these my executors shall charge themselves with my burial and have five hundert masses said for me.
This I give the 5th of January, 1713.

I, ARCANGELO CORELLI,
Mano propria.

Handel has left us a graphic account of Corelli's personality. He says that his favourite pastime was to look at pictures which cost him nothing. Saving was an obsession with him; his wardrobe was almost ostentatiously shabby. Generally he was dressed in black and wore a blue mantle. He always walked to wherever he had to go, and made the most ludicrous excuses whenever we tried to persuade him to take a carriage. He was most abstemious throughout his life. According to Mr. Arthur Hill's investigations he played preferably on a violin by Stainer, also on one by Mathias Albani. Wm. Corbett acquired the latter, as Mr. Hill found it mentioned as an Albani violin, which belonged to Corelli, and it is no doubt this instrument which afterwards was in the possession of Salomon. Giardini is said to have also acquired one of Corelli's violins.

It is worth while to record a violent controversy which arose in connexion with a series of alleged consecutive 5ths in bars 3-5 of the "Allemanda" in Sonata III of Corelli's op. 2. The work was performed at the house of Giovan Paolo Colonna, whose attention was called by the players to the questionable passage. Padre Matteo Zani was deputed to write to Corelli, and ask for an explanation of the license. Corelli's reply was bitter and contemptuous in the extreme. Others were drawn into the controversy, including Antimo

Liberati (a former pupil of Gregorio Allegri), G. B. Vitali, and Giacomo Ant. Perti, all of whom supported Corelli. There was an amusing sequel to this affair when, some time later, Colonna received anonymously from Rome a copy of his own latest work *with all the mistakes marked*. For a full account of the controversy *see* Vatielli, *Arte e vita musicale a Bologna*, pp. 184–9, and Nestore Morini, "Notizie di Arcangelo Corelli," Bologna, 1913.

GIOVANNI BATTISTA BASSANI, b. at Padua ca. 1657; d. Ferrara, 1716. A pupil of the Franciscan priest Castrovillari at Venice, he was at first organist and music-master of the religious order "della morte" at Modena. By 1680 he was director at S. Petronio, Bologna, and from 1685 capellmeister at Ferrara. He was a member of the Academia Filarmonica, Bologna, and the Academia della Morte, Ferrara. The statement that he was the teacher of Corelli has been disposed of by Pougin from authentic documents. There is, however, no question that he was one of the outstanding violinists of his time. His chief claim to be remembered lies in the fact that in his sonatas we find the first attempts of thematic development and organic co-ordination of detail within the movements, in which he far surpassed his predecessors, although he adhered still to the prevailing form of the church and the chamber sonatas. According to Fétis he composed: Sonate de camera, cioè balletti, correnti, gighe e sarabande a violono e violone ovvera spinetta, con il secondo violino a beneplacito, opera prima, Bologna, 1693 (reprint); Dodici sonate a due violini e basso, op. 5, an excellent work; the style is lofty and noble, the writing pure and elegant. Completori correnti a 4 voci concertati con violini rip. a beneplacite, op. 25, Bologna, 1701. He composed a large amount of vocal music.

CARLO GROSSI. A composer of Vicenza; composed "Concerti Ecclesiastici con alcune suonate a 2 e 3 di . . ." Venice, 1657, Franc. Magni 8 voc. pieces 2 Suonate; "Il divertimento di grandi; musiche da camera 6 per servizio di tavola . . . a 2 e 3 violins con un dialogo amoroso and uno in idioma Ebraico a 4," lib. 2, op. 9, Venice, 1681. Sala 4º (Brit. Mus., Paris Nat.).

DOMENICO GABRIELLI, b. 1659; d. 1690. Cellist and composer (*see* E. v. d. Str., "History of Violoncello"). Sonate a

Italy: to 1700

3, op. 1, Bologna, 1684 (Bol.). Gighe, correnti e Sarabande a due violini e violoncello con Basso continuo, Bologna, 1703.

GIUSEPPE TORELLI, b. Verona, ca. 1660 (Pougin); d. Feb. 8, 1709, at Bologna. In Sept., 1686, he became violetta player at S. Petronio. In 1687 he calls himself "Musico sonatore nella perinsigne collegiata d. S. Petronio di Bologna." From 1689 he played the tenor viola and violin there. Early in 1695 he appears still in documents of S. Petronio, but not after Dec. 31, as then he went to Vienna. Later on he went to Anspach as concertmeister to the Court, and was there in 1698, but on Feb. 17, 1700, he wrote to Perti from Vienna, about the forthcoming performance of an Oratorio of his composition; apparently this never took place, and for want of success he returned Mar. 31, 1701, to Bologna where, Nov. 30, 1707, he appears for the last time in the lists of S. Petronio. As the master of Pisendel he was of importance to the development of violin playing in Germany. As to his superiority over his predecessors, and his importance for the art of violin playing and the evolution of the concerto, *see* Wki., pp. 79 ff. The greater number of Torelli's works are in MSS., many being in the archives of S. Petronio, Bologna; others at Dresden. Among the latter is a fine "Sonata per violino, violoncello obbligato e cembalo" in D major, reprinted by Wasielewski in his "Instrumentalsätze." Except for a few stray works included in collections, only the following works were printed: Op. 1. Sonate a tre stromenti con il Basso continuo, Bologna, Micheletti, 1686. Op. 2. Concerto da Camera a due violini e Basso, 1686. Op. 3. Sinfonie a 2, 3 e 4 Istrumenti, Bologna, 1687. Op. 4. Concertino per Camera a Violino e Violoncello, Bologna, Silvani, n.d. Op. 5. Sei Sinfonie a tre e sei Concerti a quattro, etc., Bologna, Micheletti, 1692. Op. 6. Concerti musicali, Augsburg, 1698. Op. 7. Capricci musicali per camera a violino e viola, ovvero arciliuto, Amsterdam, fol., n.d. Op 8. Concerti grossi con una Pastorale per il Santissimo Natale, Bologna, Silvani, 1709.

Torelli forms a link between the dignified style of the 17th century and the freer and more melodious style of the 18th century. He combined both with consummate mastery. An interesting analysis of his works is given by A. Schering, in his "Geschichte des Instrumental Konzerts," where he says that if the works were better known, and more easily accessible, one would soon find them in concert programmes by the side of the great orchestral concertos by Bach. According to Vatielli, there are in the library of S. Petronio about 20 (Schering says 22) symphonies (concerti grossi—Schering) with wind instruments in MS., some of considerable dimensions.

GIULIO TAGLIETTI, b. Brescia, ca. 1660. Maestro at the Collegio de Nobili di S. Antonio. Evidently a violinist, as he wrote 6 or more sets of sonatas for 2 violins or violone and cemb. and at least 10 sonate for violin solo "per camera col suo B.c." (1715), apart from Concerti a quattro. Some he calls concerti a 3, others sinfonie a 3 (see more complete list in Mendel-Reissmann).

LUIGI TAGLIETTI. Lived also at Brescia in the late 17th century, probably a brother or relative of Giulio. He composed "Sonate per violino e violoncello con B.c.," op. 4 (Venice); "Sonate a violino e basso," op. 7 (Ib.); "Sonate da camera a tre, 2 violini, violoncello, violone o clavecino," op. 9; "Pensieri da camera a tre, 2 violini e basso," op. 12 (Ib.); concertos and symphonies for 3, 4 and 5 instruments; arias with violin, violoncello and violone or "clavecino," op. 10 (Ib.) (see Mendel-Reissmann).

GIOVANNI BIANCHI, b. Ferrara, ca. 1660; was living in Milan, 1710. He composed 12 sonate a 3, 2 violins and organ, op. 1, Modena, Rosati, 1697; 6 trio sonatas, op. 3, and 6 church concertos for 4 instruments, op. 2. 12 sonate a 3 in MS. (Berlin, Hausbibliothek).

NICOLA COSIMI, b. Rome, 1660; d. there 1724. He came to London, ca. 1702, where he was greatly admired as a virtuoso. Later, he returned to Italy, where he died. His violin, which had attracted the admiration of London artists, was sold after his death to Corbett, one of his London admirers (see Burney). The engraving by J. Smith of his portrait by Kneller is dated 1706, at which time he was probably still in London. His 12 "Sonate da camera a violino e violone o cembalo," op. 1, dedicated to the Duke of Bedford, were published in London in 1702, and by Roger in Amsterdam. They have been fully described in the author's "Eighteenth-Century Violin Sonatas" (*The Strad*).

Italy: to 1700

TAGLIAFERRI LIBERATI IL CONTE GERMANO. 1st violinist and conductor in the Ducal Philharmonic Society of Parma; composed oratorios and other church music; there are some vocal duets by him in MS. in Vienna Hofburg. Fétis says: His first master in the first half of the 17th century was Gregorio Allegri, and after the death of that famous master he studied with Orazio Benevoli. After being in the chapel of the Emperor Ferdinand III and afterwards of Leopold, he became organist in several churches in Rome, including the college of lay chaplains of the Holy See from 1661, and still lived there in 1685.

CARLO FRANCESCO CESARINI (surnamed DEL VIOLINO), b. Rome, 1664. An excellent violinist. He was attached as musician to the church De la Pieta in 1700, and afterwards became capellmeister of the Jesuit Church in Rome. Of his compositions, only oratorios and church music are known, and an opera which he wrote in conjunction with Caldara and A. Scarlatti.

TOMMASO ANTONIO VITALI, b. Bologna, ca. 1665; d. Modena, after 1747 (?). Son of Giov. Batt. He was at first engaged at S. Petronio, Bologna, from 1677 to ca. 1747, director of instrumental music at the Court of Modena. He is said to have trained many pupils (Valdrighi, 12, 20, 73). On his "Sonate 12 da chiesa a 2 violini e violoncello," op. 1, Modena, 1693, he calls himself Bolognese and "servitore attuale dell' A. S. di Modena." His sonate a doi violini, col basso, p. l'org., op. 2, ded. "Princip. di Parma" were pub. Modena, 1693, and also his concerto di sonate a violino, violoncello e cemb., op. 4, in 1701. Riemann says: In 1706 he was a member of the Philharmonic Academy of Bologna. A ciacona by him was pub. by David in "Die hohe Schule," etc. Among his best pupils was G. N. Laurenti.

PARIS FRANC. ALGHISI, b. Brescia, June 19, 1666; d. 1733. A violinist-composer. Sonate à 3, 2 violins and bass.

GIOVANNI BENVENUTI. An eminent violinist of the second half of the 17th century, and member of the Philharmonic Academy at Bologna from the time of its foundation in 1686; from ca. 1666, for some time, teacher of Corelli. He was solo violinist at the church of S. Petronio, and was also attached to the "Concert Palatin" (Pougin).

GIORGIO GENTILI, b. Venice, ca. 1668. In 1708 1st violinist in the Ducal chapel, Venice, with a salary of 40 ducats per annum (Fétis). In 1714 still in office (Caffi, ii, 61). Composed 12 concertos, violino principale with string quartet and harps, Venice, 1716; 12 sonatas for 2 violins and violoncello with bass for organ, op. 1, Amsterdam; 12 concerti da camera, 2 violins and cemb.; dedicated to Leopold I, MS. Hofb., Vienna. Mendel mentions 12 sonatas for violin and B.c. as well as the above works, and places the dates of publication of his works in Venice between 1701 and 1708. Sonate a 3, op. 5, Venice, 1707.

FRANCESCO GASPARINI, b. Camajore, near Lucca, 1668; d. Rome, Apr., 1737. A pupil of Corelli and Pasquini, and a prolific vocal composer; for violin (doubtful if by Francesco) a collection of several overtures to which is added that [*sic*.] sonata for a flute, a violin and a bass (London, ca. 1710—Brit. Mus.); Sinfonia a 2 violini concertini, 2 violins rip. tenor and B.c. (MS. Berl. Th.); Sinfonia del opera seconda di S. Cassano a 3 et 4 del Sigr ... ex F. (MS. Berlin Church Institute); 6 Trii p. 2 violins e violoncello, London, Johnson without Christian name (Brit. Mus.). He was, in ca. 1700, philharmonic academician and maestro di coro at the Conservatoire della Pieta, Venice. In 1735 he became capellmeister at St. John Lateran, but had to resign in 1726 on account of ill-health. He was one of the best Italian composers of his time. His most famous pupil was Benedetto Marcello. A Method of thorough-bass playing, "L'Armonico pratico al cimbalo ..." Venice, Borzoli, 1708; 7th ed., 1802, was his chief work.

BERNARDO TONINI, Verona (according to Fétis), b. ca. 1668. Instrumental pieces of his were pub. between 1693–7: of these are known: "Sonate a violino e B.c.," op. 1, Venice, 1693; "Sonate da chiesa a tre, due violini et organo con violoncello ad lib.," op. 2, Venice, 1595; 2nd ed., Amsterdam, Roger, no date; "Balletti da camera a violino, spinetta o violone," op. 3, score in 4to obl., Venice, 1697; 2nd ed., Amsterdam; "Sonate a due violini, violoncello e continuo," op. 4.

GIOVANNI BATTISTA PASCUCI (PASCUCCI). Violinist in the Dresden Court chapel. He received his congé and a ring

Italy: to 1700

worth 50 thaler on Apr. 13, 1669, and went to Italy. He seems to have returned to Dresden, as he appears in Fürstenau iib, 19, for the first time at the end of 1697.

MICHELE ANGELO BESSEGHI, b. Bologna, 1670; d. Paris, 1744. An excellent violinist and composer whose fame spread throughout many countries. He went to Paris ca. 1684, where he was greatly admired as virtuoso, and eventually became Director of Music to de Fagon, superintendent of finance, who accorded him an ample pension when he broke his arm and was no longer able to play. His instrumental works found great favour and brought him considerable gain. He composed 12 chamber sonatas and a "Suite de pièces" for harpsichord, pub. Amsterdam.

LEONARDO BRUGNOLI, b. Venice, 16 . . . Violinist at S. Petronio and one of the original members of the Philharmonic Academy at Bologna. He is highly praised as a violinist of distinct originality, and was the master of Corelli for some years before 1671 after having awakened the greatest admiration for his genius in Corelli.

CARLO ANTONIO AMBROGIO MARINO (MARINI) (in Brit. Mus. catal. CARLO ANTONIO), b. Bergamo, ca. 1671. In 1687 violinist at S. Maria Maggiore there. In the dedication of his "Sonate da camera a 3 stromenti" (2 violins, violone and spinetta), op. 1, Bologna, Monti, 1687, he gives his age as 16; this was followed by 5 more books of sonatas, including the "Suonate," Ven., 1692, Gius. Sala, mentioned by Alessandri (p. 149); one book Baletti a tre, Correnti, Gighe e Menuetti for 2 violins and violoncello or spinet, op. 2, and cantate a voce sola, op. 4. Fétis, who calls him "Charles Antoine" Marini, mentions: 12 sonatas, op. 3, 8 being for 2 violins and bass and 4 for 6 instruments, Venice, 1696; Balletti alla Francesi a 3, op. 5, Ib., 1699; 12 sonatas, 6 being op. 6 for 2 violins, violoncello, and B.c. and 6 op. 7 for 2 violins, viola, violoncello and B.c.; 12 sonatas for solo violin and B.c., op. 8. *See also* Brit. Mus. (g. 1009): sonate a tre, 1730.

NICOLA MATTEIS. The dates, places of birth and death, and master, of this distinguished Italian violinist are unknown. He was the first Italian violinist of note who came to England; he settled in London ca. 1672, and the first notice

The History of the Violin

of him we receive is from Evelyn's Diary, in an entry of Nov. 19, 1674: "I heard that stupendous violin Signor Nicholao (with other rare musicians), whom I have never heard mortal man exceed on that instrument. He had a stroke so sweet, and made it speak like the voice of a man, and when he pleased like a concert of several instruments. He did wonders upon a note, and was an excellent composer. Here was also that rare lutanist, Dr. Wallgrave, but nothing approached the violin in Nicholao's hand. He played such ravishing things as astonished us all." Roger North in his Memoirs says that although many musical amateurs had heard him play his solos, and observed his style, yet none would attempt "to do the like, for none could command that fulness, grace and truth of which he was master. So that in his own time his compositions were thought impracticable from their difficulty.... His staccatos, tremolos, divisions, and indeed his whole manner was surprising, and every stroke was a mouthfull." He was very poor when he came to England but stood upon his dignity, which was resented by the aristocracy of his time, and North tells us that he "behaved himself *fastously*; no person must whisper while he played, which sort of attention had not been the fashion at court." Other amusing incidents concerning him are told by North (*see* E. v. d. Str., "The Romance of the Fiddle"), also that Sir Roger L'Estrange and Bridgman persuaded him, in his own interest, to conform to English manners and ways, and he soon found that his conversion thereto was auriferous. He had some of his compositions engraved on copper plates, printed in oblong octavos and well bound, which he presented to his pupils and to musical amateurs, who in return gave him from three to five guineas each. In Dec., 1676, his "Ayres of all sortes, fitted for all Hands and capacities," in two parts (for violin) cut at the desire and charge of certain wellwishers to the work, were advertised in the *London Gazette* for sale by John Carr ..., Thomas Fisher ..., and the Author, who was then living at an apothecary's, over against Essex Street in Catherine Street. Three more books of a similar nature appeared in 1685, 1687, and 1688. He also wrote a capriccio in the French style which he took to Paris to publish it in the same manner, but failed in his object, for, as Roger North says, "he soon found that pistolls (French gold coin) did not walk so fast as ginneys." A Solo for violin of his was published at Hamburg. His Ode for St. Cecilia's day was performed at York Buildings, Jan. 7, 1696, and on May 30, 1698, he gave a concert, there, for vocal and instrumental music. He also wrote a book on thorough Bass for the guitar, on which he was an excellent virtuoso, a book of songs, and "Symphonies for two flutes." Many of his concertos and solos remained in MS. and were mostly, if not all, lost. He amassed a fortune, and, as North tells us: "took a great hous, and after the manner of his country lived luxuriously, which brought diseases upon him of which he died."

NICHOLAS MATTEIS, son and pupil of Nicola, d. Shrewsbury, 1749; was also an excellent violinist who went to Vienna, where he was a 1st violinist in the Imperial Chapel from 1717 to 1724, when he went to Prague, and there wrote the ballet music to an opera by Fux for the coronation festivities of Charles VII. In 1737 he went to Shrewsbury where Burney studied French and the violin under him. He speaks highly of him both as artist and as man, and says that he was an excellent executant of Corelli's sonatas, which he provided with new embellishments. He composed "Arie cantabile a violino solo e violoncello con B.c.," pub. at Amsterdam.

AGOSTINO GUERRIERI. Known by his sonate a 3, op. 1, Venice, 1673 (Bol.).

GIOVANNI BATTISTA MAZZAFERRATA, b. Como, second half of 17th century. Capellmeister at the Academia della Morte at Ferrara, composed 12 sonatas for 2 violins with a bassetto, viola ad lib. (1674) (repub. 1678). One of these has been republished by Wasielewski. Mazzaferrata advanced the form of the sonata and stands also from the point of his musical invention in the front rank of his contemporaries. Pougin enumerates him among Italian violinists. His other compositions consist of psalms, madrigals, and cantatas.

TOMMASO ALBINONI, b. Venice, 1674; d. there 1745; "Dillettante Veneto" e "Musico di Violino," as he calls himself on his 12 sonatas for 2 violins and bass, op. 1. He wrote his first opera together with Gasparini in 1690; this was followed by a large number till 1741. For his instrumental compositions, *see* Schering, Grove, and Eitner, including "Zusätze." He composed 43 sonatas, 36 concertos, 6 symphonies and 12 cantatas. His "12 Sonate da camera o Balletti a tre," op. 3, and "6 Sonate a violino solo con B.c." were generally valued and admired. He was rich in melodious invention but lacking in power to develop his ideas.

EVARISTO FELICE DALL' ABACO, b. Verona, July 12, 1675; d. Munich, July 12, 1742. At Modena during 1696–1701; then at Munich in Feb., 1704; was on Apr. 1 appointed as Court musician at a salary of 700 florins per annum and 100 florins for the expenses of his journey. After the battle of Höchstädt he had difficulty in obtaining his salary and in Jan., 1705, applied for his discharge from Munich but followed the elector Max Emanuel into exile to Brussels where he was appointed nominally, and in 1714, after the return of the Court to Munich definitely, as concertmeister, which position he retained to his death. Apart from being an eminent violinist he was one of the most important instrumental composers of the early 18th century. He doubtless experienced the influence of Torelli, who was at Verona till ca. 1685. In 1696 Abaco went to Modena and played at the church and the opera without a fixed appointment. He remained there till 1701. He composed: 12 violin sonatas with bass, op. 1; 10 four-part church concerts, op. 2; 6 church and 6 chamber sonatas à tre, op. 3; 12 violin sonatas with bass, op. 4; 6 concertos in 7 parts, op. 5; and concerts for several instruments, op. 6. A. Sandberger, who has his complete works, published 4 concertos in "Denkmäler der Tonkunst in Bayern" (vol. i, 1900) with monograph of Abaco. A triosonata arranged by Riemann is published by Augener, and a violin sonata arranged by A. Moffatt, pub. Simrock.

GIOVANNI BATTISTA SOMIS, b. Piedmont, 1676; d. Turin, Aug. 14, 1763; likewise called Ardij by his contemporaries, which name was apparently also used by his father. In early youth he became a pupil of Corelli, and afterwards he studied under Vivaldi at Venice. From the combined teaching of the two great masters he formed a style of his own, which marked a forward step in the art of violin playing, and which he handed on to his numerous pupils, among whom were: Chabran, his nephew, Leclair, Guillemain, Giardini, Friz and Pugnani, the master of Viotti, who is the father of modern

Giovanni Battista Somis, from the original portrait by his brother Ignazio Somis in the Liceo Musicale, Bologna. Published for the first time, from a photograph kindly supplied by F. T. Arnold, Esq., M.A., Cantab.

ANTONIO VIVALDI

FRANCESCO MARIA VERACINI

PIETRO NARDINI

P. SPAGNOLETTI

violin playing. Somis is therefore the link between the old school and the new. Pougin ("Le Violon," p. 91) quotes from a letter by de Brosses who heard him at Turin, and speaks of him as merely a good violinist but inferior to Tartini, Veracini, etc.; but de Brosses was often prejudiced. Hubert le Blanc, who heard him in Paris, is full of admiration. In his "Défense de la Viole" (quoted also in Baillot's "Method") he states that Somis has the most beautiful stroke of the bow in Europe and that he can play a whole note in one bow that it takes one's breath away when one thinks of it; he considers it the great achievement (le grand œuvre) on the violin. The *Mercure* of Apr., 1733, in a notice of Somis's appearance at the Concert Spirituel praises his brilliant technique and perfect intonation, adding that owing to his success he was in great demand during his sojourn in Paris. After the conclusion of his studies he had been appointed solo violinist and conductor of the Court chapel at Turin, which he raised to a state of great perfection. Fétis states that his "Opera prima di sonate a violino e violoncello o cembalo" was published at Rome, 1722; Pougin, however, thinks that these are attributable to his brother Lorenzo. P. David (Grove's Dict., p. 808) mentions as Giambattista's also, a set of sonatas, op. 4, Paris, 1726; 12 sonatas, op. 6, 1734, an edition of some of his works published at Amsterdam and a MS. concerto in the Dresden State library. Among the Aylesford collection now in the library of Mr. Newman Flower, there are two MS. concertos, one "Concerto à 4 con Ripieni," del Sigr. Somis a Turin (*sic.*, added in the Earl of Aylesford's writing), this concerto in G maj. appears to be by Giambattista S., while the other, "Giov. Batta. Ardij, concerto con violino Io obl. in A maj.," is undoubtedly by him, Ardij being a name used by the family. We do not know whether the concerto at Dresden is identical with one of these two; one, in any case, has been hitherto unknown. His daughter, the beautiful wife of the court painter Carl Andr. Vanloo, was a famous prima donna of the Paris and Brussels operas.

GIOV. BATT. ARDIJ (SOMIS). In Dresden Museum is MS. Concerto a violoncello concert., with string quartet F maj. score.

LORENZO, SOMIS. Younger (?) brother of Giambattista, of whom but little is known. He was for some time a member of the Turin Court chapel, and afterwards lived in Paris. According to his compositions, which surpass those of his brother in musical interest, he was technically fully his equal. Published are: 8 chamber sonatas for violin and bass, op. 2, Paris, 1740 (No. 6 arranged by A. Moffatt). In the Aylesford collection, now in the possession of Mr. Newman Flower, there is a MS. "Concerto à 4 con stromenti," Lorenzo Somis (apparently autograph, the name added in the Earl of Aylesford's (?) hand), in B maj., and another "Concerto di Lorenzo Somis," in A maj., MS. 18th-century copy. The existence of these concertos has been unknown hitherto. It appears questionable whether some of the eminent violinists described as "pupils of Somis," which was generally accepted to refer to Giambattista, were not really pupils of Lorenzo. Fétis, for instance, mixes up both under the name of the latter. A third brother, Ignazio, painted in 1765 a portrait of both, which is now in the Licee Musicale at Bologna.

LORENZO ARDIJ (SOMIS) of Turin. In Dresden Museum is MS. of 2 concerti a violoncello concert., with string quartet, F and G maj., score.

GIUS COLONNA. Composed Sonate a 3, op. 4, Bologna, 1676 (Bol.).

ANTONIO CALDARA, b. Venice, 1678; d. there Aug. 28, 1763. A prolific opera and instrumental composer, who wrote 2 books of Sonatas for 2 violins and B.c. (1700 and 1701). Two movements of a sonata by Caldara have been republished by L. Torchi in Boosey's collection.

FRANCESCO ANTONIO BONPORTI, b. Trient, 1678; d. there (?) 1740. According to Riemann, Bonporti was in the private chapel of Joseph I, ca. 1700, and 1715–21 at Trient. An Imperial Austrian Councillor and distinguished amateur composer of violin concertos; sonatas for 2 violins and bass (E. v. d. Str., "Eighteenth-Century Violin Sonatas"), 100 minuets for violin and bass; solos for violin and B.c.; and motets for soprano solo and 2 violins. Up to 1714 he had published 10 works for violin, the concerti a quattro form op. 2, and Concerti e Seranati, op. 12. These two works are very favourably discussed at some length in Schering's "Geschichte des Instrumental Konzerts" (History of the Instrumental Concerts), in which he points out their formal excellence as well as melodious invention, which the writer also praised with regard to the sonatas in the above-mentioned work. From the fact that he was almost exclusively a composer for the violin it appears certain that he must also have been a good executant thereon, but nothing certain about this is known, nor anything more about his life. On op. 10 and op. 12 he calls himself: "Nobile dilettante e familiare aulico di sua Maj. Cesare," which shows that he was in some minor position at the Court though not, as Eitner thinks, that he was in the Imperial Chapel. 5 Dedicatory Letters to the Dukes Karl and Leopold of Schwerin (with instrumental compositions) are dated from Trient, 1736–Mar. 30, 1783. FRANCESCO BONPORTI. Sonate a V. e B., 1696 (Bologna). F. A. BONPORTI. Sonate a 3, op. 10, Bol., 1713 (Bol.); Concerto a quattro, op. 2, Trento s.a. (ca. 1714, Bol.). All by the above.

ANDREA GROSSI, b. Mantua, end of 17th century. Violinist, 1725, in the service of the Duke of Mantua; composed sonatas, Bologna, 1696 (Gerber, ii). Gerber, Fétis: 12 sonate a 2, 3, 4, e 5 stromenti, op. 3; sonate da camera a 3 stromenti, op. 5, Bologna, 1696. Balletti, corrente, sarabande, etc., for 2 violins and bass; sonatas for 2, 3, 4, and 5 instruments, composed between 1679 and 1685 (3 works, discovered by Torchi). Sonate a 3, Bologna, 1679 (Bol.).

STEFANO PASINO. Composer of sonate à 3 e 4 stromenti, 1679 (Wasielewski, 66, only mentioned).

GIAMBATTISTA VIVALDI, ca. 1708. Violinist at S. Mark's, Venice, with a salary of 25 ducats (Caffi, ii, 61). He was the father and teacher of Antonio Vivaldi.

ANTONIO VIVALDI, b. Venice, ca. 1680; d. there, ca. 1743; son and pupil of Giambattista Vivaldi. One of the most remarkable figures not only in the history of the violin but also of music in general. He surpassed all his contemporaries in the wealth of the varied figuration for the violin; it was brilliant and sometimes difficult even from a modern point of view, but always effective. It may be said here that the great violinists of that time had a remarkable technique of the bow, especially in the playing of arpeggios entirely in detached notes. At least of equal, if not greater, importance was his evolutionary progress with regard to form. He broke the fetters of the severe church sonata and extended the limits of the allegro movements, preserving a clear and symmetrical articulation, and imbuing it with a more modern spirit; he brought the sonata a considerable step farther on the road towards Haydn and Mozart. He raised the Italian instrumental concerto to such a state of perfection, that for 30 years or more his concertos served as models for all other composers: Quantz, Benda, and even J. S. Bach. Vivaldi also began to mix wind instruments with strings in a manner which shows the beginnings of true art of orchestration, and in his programme music, in which he delighted, he shows a fine sense of characterization, even if we cannot defend this as the highest form of art. In any case we must look upon him as a father of the modern symphony. If his merit with regard to form stands very high, yet he was no mere formalist, as some have been at pains to assert; and all who have heard the beautiful concerto for viol d'amour, lute and strings played by the Dolmetsch family, or Mr. Anthony Bernard's excellent performances of the charming concertino for 2 violins with string orchestra, will readily admit the fact. A more extensive analysis and appreciation of Vivaldi's work may be found in A. Schering, "Geschichte des Instrumental Konzerts." In his concertos he made frequent use of the *tempo rubato* and of the syncopation ♪♩., called the "Lombardian manner" and became the fashion all over Italy. Vivaldi's influence in music was international, and many young musicians from various countries went to him to study the violin or composition or both. Pisendel was one of his most eminent pupils. Vivaldi was called "il preto rosso" (the red priest) on account of his red hair, and it is said that he was so bigoted that he always had a rosary in his hand except when he played, or took up his pen to compose. His priestly duties evidently sat lightly upon his shoulders, for when he was celebrating the Mass one day and some musical idea suddenly entered his head, he left the altar, went into the vestry to write it down and then returned to finish the Mass. This would have met with severe punishment but for the intercession of friends who attributed this lapse to mental aberration; he was however permanently suspended from officiating at the altar. In 1707 he became capellmeister of the Prince of Hesse-Darmstadt, a great lover of music who was then

Italy: to 1700

Governor of Mantua, where he maintained a private orchestra. In 1713 he returned to Venice, where in 1714 he became leader of the orchestra at S. Mark's and director of music at the Ospidale della Pietà, where he was also cembalo and singing master. The great Faustina was one of his pupils. Schering, from the superscription of two of his concertos, one written for St. Anthony, the other for St. Laurence at Padua, thinks that in 1712 he sojourned at that town. After 1713 he apparently left Venice only once in 1735, when he went to Rome for the performance of one of his operas. Bach, in order to familiarize himself with the form of Vivaldi's concertos, arranged 16 of these for the harpsichord and 4 for the organ; Bach's concerto for 4 claviers in A minor is adapted from Vivaldi's concerto for 4 violins in B minor. Fétis says that he had the MSS. of 2 concertos from the "Estro armonico" arranged by Bach for string quartet, but their present whereabout is unknown. Vivaldi composed for the violin: 12 trios for 2 violins and bass, op. 1, Paris, 1737; 12 sonatas for violin solo and bass, op. 2; Estro armonico, op. 3, consisting of 4 concertos for violin solo, 3 concertos for 2 violins, 1 with cello obl. and 4 for 4 violins, including 3 with cello obbligato. La Stravaganza, op. 4, 12 concertos for solo violin with 2 violins, viola and organ; 6 sonatas for the same; Le quattro staggione, ovvero il cimento dell armonia, etc., in 4 and 5 parts, 12 concerti grosso. Four of these are headed by sonnets descriptive of the four seasons, depicted in the respective concertos. They were immensely popular and "The Spring Concerto" was adapted by Mich. Corrette as a motet to the words of the 148th psalm; La Cètra, op. 9, 6 concerti grosso a 4 and 5 parts; 6 concertos for flute, violin, viola, cello and organ, op. 10; 12 concertos for solo violin, 2 concertante violins, viola, cello and organ, op. 11 and op. 12; Schering discovered in the Munich library: "Il pastor fido, sonates pour la Musette, Flûte, Hautbois, Violon avec La Basse continue" (Paris, Boivin). Apart from these published works he wrote a large number which remained in MS., among which are the 2 concertos for Padua mentioned above, 5 concertos written for Pisendel, and 3 concertos dedicated to the Elector Friedrich Christian of Saxony on his visit to Venice in 1740, including one for "2 Flauti, 2 Teorbe, 2 Mandolini, 2 Salmò (?), 2 violini in Tromba Marina et un violoncello and the concerto for viol d'amour, lute and muted strings, mentioned above. These with some 70 more MS. concertos are in the Dresden Library, and Schering says that those who do not know them, know only one-third of Vivaldi's genius. There are still more of Vivaldi's MS. works in various Continental and English libraries. (5 MS. concertos in 18th-century copies from the Aylesford collection, as well as some original printed editions in the library of Mr. Newman Flower.) The Cuckoo concerto was a favourite of 18th-century and early 19th-century English as well as Continental violinists.

FRANCESCO GEMINIANI, b. Lucca, 1680 (Grove, 1667); d. Dublin, Sept. 17, 1762. He commenced the study of the violin under Carlo Ambrogio Lunati, surnamed "il Gobbo" (the hunchback), at Milan. Afterwards he became a pupil of Corelli at Rome, and from Aug. 27, 1707, to 1710, he was violinist in the band of the Signoria at Lucca, with 2.45 scudi per month. In 1711 he was appointed concertmeister at Naples, where at the same time he studied composition under Alessandro Scarlatti. Although he had acquired a brilliant technique both of the left hand and the bow, his manner of playing was very erratic, and he made a constant use of the *Tempo rubato*, which threw the orchestra into confusion, and he had to exchange his position for that of a viola player. It is said that he toured for some time as a soloist in Italy, but in 1714 he went to London, where he was greatly admired as an eminent virtuoso. He was invited to play at Court, but only consented on condition that Handel should accompany him, declaring that nobody else in London was capable of doing this. He rarely appeared in public, but occupied most of his time in composing, and in writing theoretical works, of but mediocre value. He had a passion for dealing in pictures which was greater than his knowledge of the subject, and caused losses which brought him into prison, from which he was only extricated by his pupil and patron, Lord Essex. The latter procured for him the post as master and composer of the State Music in Ireland in 1727, but this was objected to on account of his being a Roman Catholic, and the appointment was eventually given to his pupil Dubourg. Geminiani, however, paid prolonged visits to Dublin, where in 1733 he even acquired a house with a concert-room in which he gave private concerts, devoting part of his time to teaching. In 1741 he was back in London, gave a benefit concert at the Little Theatre in the Haymarket, and published his Concertos, op. 6. In 1749 he conducted Lenten Concerts at Drury Lane, and at the beginning of 1750 he went to Paris, where he remained till 1755, and wrote the music to a spectacular pantomime, "La Forêt enchantée" (subject, from Tasso's "Gierusalemme liberata"), performed Apr. 10, 1754, at the Tuileries. He had a new edition of his solo sonatas published there, and a number of his works were performed at the Concert Spirituel during that time, but apparently he never played there in public himself. In 1755 he returned to London, in the spring of 1759 he revisited Ireland, and 1760 he went to his former pupil Dubourg, when, it is said, grief over the theft of a MS. treatise on music from his rooms in College Green hastened his death. Together with Veracini he was mainly responsible for the advance in the art of violin playing in England, where till then it had remained in a very primitive condition. In 1740 appeared his tutor, "The Art of Playing on the Violin," op. IX, which epitomized the essence of Corelli's teaching, and was one of the earliest, and certainly the best instruction books of its time. A German edition of it was published in Vienna in 1785, twenty-nine years after the appearance of Mozart's tutor, and J. A. Hiller, in his tutor, which appeared in 1793, speaks of it still as a useful instruction book. In 24 chapters, each with a separate exercise, he deals with the principal items of violin technics, and what he says holds good to this day, although it requires a great deal of supplementing before it can be considered adequate for the training of a violinist. Moreover, he wastes much space and time in explaining how one turn or shake can express gaiety, another tender passion, etc., etc. (*see* E. v. d. Str., "The Romance of the Fiddle," 213–15). The 12 exercises at the end, though good in themselves, lack systematic progression, which the very paucity of their number precludes. Geminiani habitually held the violin on the left side of the tailpiece, while L. Mozart and most of the German masters held it on the right side of the tailpiece. The frontispiece of Geminiani's tutor (*see* fig., p. 213 *ib.*) shows him using a bow of elegant proportions, with a long straight stick, which he holds, however, several inches above the nut, as was then the custom. Mozart, on the other hand, uses a bow of a far more primitive shape, though apparently of equal length, but he holds it by the nut like the modern players (fig., pp. 234 and 238, *ib.*). From the portraits in his tutor it is evident that he is using his beloved Stainer violin of a deep model, while Geminiani is playing on an Italian instrument of a flat model. The latter was undoubtedly one of the greatest, if not *the* greatest, violinist of his time, who had enlarged in many ways the resources of the instrument, as his concertos and sonatas clearly show. He also extended the sonata form, which is more developed and freer in form, even if that often lacks the clearness and beautiful symmetry of the work of his master Corelli. Burney and many great musicians have pointed out his want of originality and weakness in his harmonic treatment, but those who have the courage to judge for themselves will find many beautiful melodies in his slow movements and most delightful dance movements, while some of his allegros are likewise attractive, and he was a master of the instrumental fugue. He composed 18 concertos for violin, 6 concertos in 7 parts, and 6 do. in 8 parts, 3 sets of 12 violin sonatas each, 6 solos for violoncello, arranged by Geminiani also for violin; one set of 12 trios, and one set of 6 trios, arranged from his solos, op. 1, besides harpsichord pieces and an arrangement of Corelli's sonatas, op. V, as concerti grossi. He also wrote a number of theoretical works. (Complete list in Grove.)

GIUSEPPE VALENTINI. Data about the life of this artist vary widely. Some biographers mention Florence as his birthplace and the year as ca. 1680. Riemann says: "The latter date is impossible, as his op. 1 appeared in 1701 at Amsterdam and Rome, in the dedicatory letter of which he describes himself as a youth of scarcely 20 years." 1681 is therefore undoubtedly correct. The date of his death is also unknown. In 1710 he was probably at Bologna, where his concerti grossi, op. 7, were then published. In 1712 he was at Rome, and his growing fame there so mortified Corelli, that it contributed to his death soon after. Of Valentini's subsequent life nothing appears to be known except that he was in the service of the Grand Duke of Tuscany in 1735. His concerti grossi have been discussed by Torchi and by A. Schering ("Zur Geschichte des Instrumental Konzerts"), and his sonatas, etc., by E. v. d. Str. ("Eighteenth-Century Violin Sonatas," *The Strad*, May and June, 1918). He composed: "12 sinfonie a 2 violini e violoncello," op. 1, Amsterdam, Roger, 1701; "Bizzarie a 2 violini e violone o Cembalo," op. 2, Ib.; "12 Fantasie a 2 violini e violoncello," op. 4, Ib.; "12 sonate a 2 violini e violoncello," op. 5; "Concerti a 4 violini, alto viola, violoncello e B.c.," op. 7, lib. 1 and 2, Ib., 1710. "Alletamenti per camera a violino e violoncello," op. 8, Ib., 1714; "Concerti," op. 9, Ib. Fétis describes the "Alletamenti" as sonate a violoncello solo e B.c. Valentini's solo sonatas show an advanced technique and originality in the passage work. A sonata in D major for 2 violins and B.c. has been re-edited by Alfred Moffat (Simrock, 1913). An Adagio in Cartier's "L'art de violon."

ROBERTO VALENTINI (Robert Valentine, an Englishman), contemporary with the above, was a flautist, living in Rome, who composed: 12 sonatas for 2 violins and bass with a thorough bass for harpsichord or arch lute (Walsh & Hare); 6 sonatas for 2 violins and a bass, op. 6 (London); 6 sonatas for 2 violins, op. 7 (Ib.) and several books of flute sonatas, etc.

CARLO MANNELLI, b. Pistoja. He calls himself "violino Romano oriundo di Pistoja" on his op. 2, Rome, 1682. In the dedication he says that his father, D. Camillo, had already appointed him among the musicians of his chapel and that he made a special study of the violin. His first work he calls "Sinfonie," a violino solo. In the B.B. are his sonate a 3, 2 violini e leuto, o violone con il B. per l'org., op. 2, Roma, 1682, Mutij; 14 sonatas of 4 movements each. The Brit. Mus. has only violin 1 and Organ (?), but also some songs in MS. under Manelli del violino. Torchi's criticism of Mannelli's work is rather surprising. He calls him a "compositore technico" whose merit consists in his careful notation of marks of expression, slurs, etc. The writer, who has given a fairly full analysis of his sonatas (E. v. d. Str., "Eighteenth-Century Violin Sonatas," *The Strad*, Oct., Nov., 1916), found that while lacking in that perfection of form which we admire in Corelli, he "has a wealth of beautiful melody of a very advanced nature, in which he surpasses, perhaps, all his contemporaries."

COUNT PIRRO CAPACELLI ALBERGATI. Of an ancient noble family of Bologna: late 17th and early 18th centuries. Composed Balletti, correnti, sarabande e gighe a violino e violone con el secondo vno. a beneplacito, op. 1, Bologna, 1682, republished 1685; Sonate a due violini col basso cont. per l'org⁰. ed un altro per benplacito per tiorbo e vcl⁰., op. 2, Bologna, 1683; Sonate a trè, op. 3, Bologna, 1683; Plettro armonico composto di dieci sonate da camera a due violoni e B.c. con violoncello obbligato, op. 5, Ib., 1687; Concerti varii a tre, quattro e cinque, op. 9, Modena, 1702; also operas, cantatas, oratorio, church music, etc. (*See also* Mme Parravicini Albergati.)

GASPARO GASPARDINI, ca. 1683. Capellmeister at Verona Cathedral; composed sonate (12) a 3, 2 violini e violoncino con il B. per l'organo, op. 1, Bologna, 1683, Gios. Micheletti (Modena, printed copy and MS.); sonate a 3, op. 2, Amsterdam, Roger (Paris, Nat.—Eitner).

ALESSANDRO MARCELLO, b. Venice, ca. 1684; d. there, 1750; elder brother of the famous Benedetto Marcello. Allessandro was an accomplished amateur and art patron. He composed 12 solos for violin, Augsburg (Joh. Christ. Leopold?), 1737, also 6 concertos for 2 flutes or violins with strings and harpsichord, Ib. 1738. He gave weekly concerts at his house, where chiefly his own compositions were performed.

SALVADORE GANDINI, composed sonate a 3, op. 1, Bologna, 1684 (Bol.)

DOMENICO MANINI, b. 1684. From 1705 till the time of his death, Sept. 7, 1708, at the age of 24, he was violinist in the Court chapel, Vienna. He composed an oratorio, "La constanza trionfante nel Martirio di S. Canuto Ré di Danimarca," 2 parts, 1708 (MS. in Hofburg, Vienna).

GUIS. MATTEO ALBERTI, b. Bologna, ca. 1685; d. there, Feb. 18, 1750. Violinist at S. Petronio, Academico Filarm.; composed 10 concerti a sei, op. 1, 1713; 12 solos with Th.B. for harpsich. or bass violin, op. 3, Walsh, 1720?; 12 sinfonie a quattro, 2 violins, viola, violoncello ed organo (Mendel). He was a pupil of Carlo Manzolini and Pietro Minelli, and in counterpoint of Floriano Aresti. He was a member of the Philharmonic Academy of Bologna, as appears from the title pages of his works; and Principe in 1721, '24, '28, '33, '40 and '46.

Fétis mentions also a JEAN MATHIEU ALBERTI, early 18th-

LORENZO SOMIS
From the portrait by his brother Ignazio which is in the Liceo Musicale, Bologna, published for the first time from a photograph kindly supplied by F. T. Arnold, M.A., Cantab.

FRANCESCO GEMINIANI
From a contemporary engraving by Thos. Jenkins.

Violin by Antonius Stradivari 1721, which the present owners, Messrs. W. E. Hill & Sons (by whose kind permission it is here reproduced for the first time) declare to be as fine as the "Messie." Formerly it belonged to Lady Ann Blunt, a descendant of Lord Byron, and violin pupil of Leopold Jansa, who knew all the leading musicians of her time.

Italy: to 1700

century Italian violinist, whose "concerti a cinque per chiesa e per camera" were pub. Amsterdam, 1713. *Apparently identical with the above op. 1?*

GIO PIETRO FRANCHI, b. Pistoja. A mid-17th-century concertmeister of the Duke of Rospigliosi de Zagarolo. He composed: Sonate a tre, op. 1, 2 violins and bass? Bologna, 1687; Duetti da camera, op. 2, Bologna, 1689. (*See* Fétis.)

CARLO ANDREA MAZZOLINI (MAZOLINI). Second half of 17th century and early 18th century, violinist at Bologna, composed a book of chamber sonatas for 2 violins and harpsichord or theorbo, op. 1, Bologna, (?) 1687. One sonata by him is contained in the sumptuously produced collection of violin sonatas published by Carlo Buffagnotti at Bologna, (?) ca. 1690, of which one volume containing the violin parts is in the King's library B.M. (E. v. d. Str., "Eighteenth-Century Violin Sonatas," *The Strad*, Jan., 1917). Pougin mentions Carlo Manzolini, a violinist of Bologna, as the teacher of Guis. Alberti (ca. 1700), who is evidently identical with Mazzolini.

GIOVAN BATTISTA BORRI, b. Bologna. Composed 12 symphonies for 2 violins, with cello and organ, 1687, and a similar work dedicated to the Duke Francis II of Modena, grandnephew of Cardinal Mazarin, 1688.

FRANCESCO MANFREDINI (called "IL BOLOGNESE"), b. Pistoja, 1688. Violinist: studied counterpoint under Giac. Ant. Perti at Bologna, and went to Ferrara as 1st violin at the church of Spirito Santo. Afterwards he held that position at S. Petronio, Bologna, where he became a member of the Philharmonic Academy in 1704. In 1711 he is noted as capellmeister in the Court chapel of Monaco, then at the cathedral at Pistoja, finally returning again to S. Petronio. He composed 6 sonatas for 2 violins and thorough bass for the harpsichord, London, Chs. and Sam. Thompson (another ed. "for 2 violins and violoncello with a thorough bass"). 12 sinfonie da chiesa a 2 violini (violoncello) col B. per l'organo e una viola a beneplacitoc on uno pastorale per il Sant^{mo}. Natale, op. 2, Bologna; Silvani republished as "quartetti a due vi., va. e, B.c." by Roger, Amsterdam. Concerti grossi, Bologna, Silvani, 1718; 1 son. a 3 in Corona di 12 fiori, Bologna, 1706. Wrote also several Oratorios, performed between 1709–26. (Biog. in "Catalogo Masseangeli"; Fétis appears to be wrong.) His son VICENZO MANFREDINI was Imperial capellmeister at the Russian Court.

LUC'ANTONIO PREDIERI, b. Bologna, Sept. 13, 1688; d. Naples, 1769 or 1770. A violin pupil of Vitali, and studied counterpoint under Giacomo Cesare Predieri. From 1706 member, and from 1723 president, of the Academia Filarmonica, Bologna. In 1739 vice-capellmeister and from Sept. 1, 1764, first capellmeister of the Vienna Court chapel; pensioned 1751. Composed church music, operas, etc.

DOMENICO BRASOLIN. In 1688 1st violin of the Accademia della Morte, Florence. Fétis, who calls him Brassolini, states that an opera of his was performed at Modena in 1707; no other compositions by him are known.

GIOVANNI LORENZO GREGORI. From Apr. 13, 1688, to 1742, a violinist in the municipal band of Lucca; d. there in 1743; Nerici, 210, 314, 331, describes him as capellmeister, violinist and poet. Composed Concerti grossi a piu stromenti, 2 violini con i ripieni, se piace, a Arcileuto o Violoncello con il basso per l'organo, op. 2, Lucca, 1698, G. Gregori (Brit. Mus., Bologna); also oratorios, cantatas, etc., and theoretical works. He is therefore the first who published concerti grossi under that name, though Torelli and Corelli may have anticipated him in the composition thereof. (Schering, ib., p. 43, 44.)

NICOLA ORIO. Inventor of a 6-string violin. In 1689 appointed to the Ducal chapel, Venice (Caffi, ii, 57), by 1691 he became a member of the Court chapel at Berlin with a salary of 400 thaler (Schneider, 49), but is not mentioned again at any later date.

GIOVANNI BATTISTA GIGHI (called TEDESCHINO). Composer to the Grand Duke of Tuscani towards the end of the 17th century: Sonate da chiesa e da camera a tre stromenti, col basso continuo per l'organo, Bologna, 1690. Sonate a 3, op. 1, Bologna, 1689 (Bol.).

IGNAZIO ALBERTINI. A musician of Milan, who composed 12 violin sonatas dedicated to the Emperor Leopold I, pub. Vienna, 1690. (Pougin, 57.)

ALFONSO DEL VIOLINO. Late 17th century; is mentioned in Angelo Berardi's "Arcani Musicali," 1690, with a fragment of a Sinfonia. (*See* Eitner.)

Italy: to 1700

A. L. BALDASSINI. Sonate a tre, op. 1, Roma, 1691; sonate a 3, Roma, 1699 (both in Bologna library).

ANTONIO FEDELI. 1692, violinist at the Ducal chapel at Venice (Caffi, ii, 57).

FEDELE—*see* TREU (Index), b. 1695.

GIORGIO BUONI, b. Bologna. An Italian violinist who appeared successfully at Lucca, Cremona and Milan. Composed Allettamenti per camera a due violini e basso, and sonate a due violini e violoncello col basso per l'organo, Bologna, 1693.

PIETRO BETTINOZZI. A pupil of Torelli (Vatielli, "Arte e vita musicale a Bologna"); violinist at the Court of the Margrave of Anspach in 1695, and possibly instrumental in securing for his master, Torelli, the position of capellmeister to the Margrave in 1698. There are two "concerti a violino concertante" with string quartet, 18th-century MS. score, by GIOVANNI BETTINOZZI in the Dresden Museum; this may possibly have been a relative of the above.

ANTONIO VERACINI, of Florence, ca. middle of 17th century. Violinist in the service of the Grand Duchess of Tuscany (E. v. d. Str., "Eighteenth-Century Violin Sonatas"); his sonate à 3, 2 violins and violone o arcileuto col B. p. l'org., op. 1, were pub. Firenze, 1692, Ant. Navesi alla Condotta. Sonate da chiese a vno. e vcl. ò B.c., op. 2, Amst., Roger; sonate (10) da camera a violino e violone o arcileuto col B. per il cemb., op. 3, Modena, Fortuniano Rosati (1696, R.C. Mus.). Wasielewski: In his sonatas he proves himself a man of talent and learning. His style is noble and select, not only in his allegros but also in his slow movements, which before him show rarely any real melodic interest or clearly defined periodical construction. His chamber sonatas, like those of Torelli, are written in the manner of church sonatas, and with regard to them he belongs to the few composers of his time who strove for higher ideals and serious thought in secular music. Gust. Jensen edited 1 sonata each from op. 1 and op. 2 in "Classical Violin Music" (London, Augener).

FRANCESCO MARIA VERACINI, b. Florence, 1685; d. near Pisa, 1750; nephew and pupil of Antonio Veracini. During the early part of his career he is said to have toured extensively, and stayed for a long time in Poland. Nothing definite is known about him before his return to Italy, when he was appointed as 1st violinist at S. Mark's, Venice, in 1714 (or more probably late in 1713). It was then that both he and Tartini were invited to an artistic contest at an academy given in the palace of Donna Pisana Mocenigo in honour of the hereditary Prince of Saxony. When Tartini had heard Veracini's new and bold manner of playing he withdrew from the contest and retired to Ancona for renewed study. Soon after, Veracini went to London, where he made his début at the King's Theatre on Saturday, Jan. 23, 1714, as leader of the orchestra, playing "Symphonies" (solos and concertos) between the acts, and this position he occupied for about two years. On Mar. 17, 1714, he played at a benefit concert of the famous singer who was known only as "The Baroness," and on Apr. 22 he gave his own benefit concert at Hickford's room near Panton Street, Haymarket, where he produced vocal and instrumental compositions of his own, including "several solos for violin never performed before."

In 1716 he returned to Venice where the Crown Prince of Saxony invited him to Dresden. He went there in 1717, presented the Prince with three violin sonatas and was appointed chamber musician and composer. Mattheson ("Critica Musica"), from contemporary news he received, says that in a fit of insanity, on Aug. 13, 1722, Veracini threw himself out of a second-floor window, breaking his hip and his foot. He adds that the cause of his mental aberration was too close application to his musical studies, and the reading of chymical (alchymical? Ed.) books. According to Fétis, he had by his arrogance and haughty manner incurred the enmity of the German musicians, and Pisendel, to humiliate him, asked him in the presence of the Court to play a concerto of his from sight, and afterwards made a violinist from the orchestra repeat it. As the latter had been secretly coached in it by Pisendel, he gained the greater applause, which so mortified Veracini that it drove him to commit the above desperate act. Whichever version be the right one (and Mattheson's is from direct contemporary communication), it is certain that in 1723, after being cured, he went to Prague, where he was for several years in the chapel of Count Kinsky, which Tartini also joined in the same year, and thence he returned to Italy.

Italy: to 1700

In 1735 he went to London and shared with Festing the leadership at the King's Theatre, Haymarket, where his opera "Adriano" was performed on Nov. 25, by His Majesty's command, and given 17 times during the season.

The complaint of the Dresden musicians about Veracini's vanity and arrogance finds its justification in an anecdote from the early time of his career. According to general custom he had gone to Lucca to take part in the celebrations of the Feast of the cross, on the 14th of Sept. He announced his intention to play at the church, and on entering the musicians' gallery he marched straight up to the leader's desk, which he found already occupied by Father Girolamo Laurenti (q.v.), who asked him what he desired. "The place of the first violin," Veracini replied. "That I have already taken as usual," replied Laurenti, "but if you are to play a concerto at Vespers or at High Mass, no doubt a place will be found for you." Veracini turned with disdain and seated himself right at the back. While Laurenti played his concerto, Veracini did not play a note in the orchestra, but listened attentively. When he was asked to play he refused to play a concerto, but said he would play a solo on condition that the violoncellist Lanzetti of Turin should accompany him. This request being granted, he stepped right to the front, using all his virtuoso devices to arouse the enthusiasm of the audience which gave vent to their feelings by shouting "Evviva!" unmindful of the occasion. When he came to the cadenza, he turned to Laurenti and said aloud: "Thus plays the first violin."

Handel is said to have admired Veracini's playing, and when he gave his Oratorio performances at the Haymarket Theatre, the latter often took part in them, and his beautiful, powerful tone penetrated the whole orchestra; but the performances came to an end in Apr., 1745. Dr. Burney, who heard him lead the band in Hickford's room in that year, was greatly impressed with his bold style; but he had passed the zenith of his fame and Geminiani's rising popularity overshadowed him, and about the middle of 1745 he left England. On the journey he was shipwrecked, and though saved himself, he lost all his belongings, including his beautiful pair of Stainer violins, which he had named Peter and Paul. He returned to Italy, where he died in comparative poverty.

The History of the Violin

As a virtuoso, Veracini received the fullest recognition in his lifetime. He was praised and admired by all who heard him throughout the whole of Europe. His left-hand technique was brilliant and facile, and he was particularly strong in the execution of shakes, arpeggios and double stops, and in the art of bowing he surpassed his contemporaries by the introduction of many new devices, especially of the graceful and airy kind, without sacrificing the power and beautiful quality of his tone. It was this art that caused Tartini to take him for his model. As a composer he was too far in advance of his time to be understood by his contemporaries, who looked upon his work as capricious and bizarre. His bold modulations, the wealth of his delicately worked-out harmonies, his originality in expressing his conceptions, differed too widely from anything that had been heard before, with the result that for over a century his compositions were entirely neglected. Only since the second half of last century, violinists and the musical public have become aware of their rare beauty. In form they show a progress over his predecessors, but it is especially in his thematic material, its bold harmonic treatment, and the characteristic chromatic passages, that he appears quite modern. Some of his slow movements are truly enchanting, while his allegros often fascinate by their brightness and natural flowing form. He composed: 12 sonatas for violin solo and B.c., op. 1 (Dresden and Amsterdam, 1721); 12 sonate Academiche for do. do., op. 2, dedicated to the Elector of Saxony (London and Florence, 1744). An engraved portrait of Veracini faces the title page of op. 2. Several of the sonatas have been edited by Alfred Moffat (Simrock, Schott), Ferd. David (Breitkopf and Härtel) and von Wasielewski (Senff, Simrock). A set of Veracini's sonatas for violin and flute were pub. at Venice, 1716. In the first movements of his sonatas he makes an important step forward towards the final sonata-form, which, curiously, as Schering ("Geschichte d. Instr. Konzerts," pp. 106–7) points out, is not present in his concertos and symphonies, etc., which remained in manuscript, some in libraries of Florence and Bologna.

FRANCESCO VENTURINI. Married the daughter of his colleague Ennuy at Hanover, Jan. 13, 1697. In the Roman Catholic register he is described as "Gallus." He was a pupil of Jean

Italy: to 1700

Bapt. Farinelli and became a member of the Hanoverian Court chapel in 1698. On Farinelli's resignation in 1713 Venturini succeeded him as director of the instrumental music. Afterwards he became capellmeister and died Apr. 18, 1745. (Dr. Fischer, "Musik in Hanover"). Mattheson met him in Hanover on June 5, 1706. Venturini composed several violin concertos, with orchestra; concerti grossi, some dedicated to Duke George Ludwig of Brunswick Lüneburg (Wolfenbüttel).

BARTOLOMEO BERNARDI, b. Bologna. Violinist, and in riper years capellmeister and member of the Philharmonic Academy at Copenhagen, where he died 1730 (Riemann: 1732). Characteristic in Scheibe's "Krit. Musik," p. 759, in 2nd ed. of 1745. His MS. compositions are said to have perished in the great fire at Copenhagen, 1794. A considerable number of sonatas and trios (2 violins and bass) and some concertos and vocal compositions in various libraries (*see* Eitner). 12 sonatas for 2 violins and bass, op. 1 (Bologna), 1692; 10 sonatas, do., op. 2 (Ib., 1696); 12 sonatas for violin and B.c. (Amsterdam). In Dresden Mus. is a MS. Solo with Bass, without Christian name, but probably by the same. He also wrote two operas.

G. A. BERNABEI, Sonate a 3, Bologna, 1698 (Bol.).

GASPARO VISCONTI, b. Cremona, second half of the 17th century; violinist. Lived in London at the beginning of the 18th century (Gerber, ii); composed 6 sonate a violino e violone o cemb., op. 1, dedicated to the Duke of Devonshire (2nd ed., Amsterdam, Roger, 1703); 3 concerti with string quartet in score MS., 5 soli a violino e Basso, MS. in Dresden Mus.; and 1 sonata a violino solo e Basso, C min., MS. in Schwerin (Eitner). Tartini held him in such high regard that he dedicated to him a book of his sonatas (Pougin).

CARLO AMBROGIO LUNATI (called "IL GOBBO"). A celebrated violinist who lived at Milan during the latter part of the 17th century. He was the teacher of Geminiani. Composed 12 sonate a violino solo col B., Milan, 1701; 1 sonata do. do., MS., Modena; operas, cantatas, ariettas, etc.

GAETANO MARIA SCHIASSI, of Bologna; in the latter years of the 17th century calls himself violinist and member of the Philharmonic Academy at Bologna on the title page of his

12 concerti a 1 vo. princ., 2 violini, alto o viola, violoncello, e cemb., op. 1, lib, 1, 2, Amst., Mich. C. Le Cene (6 concertos in each book). 3 concertos a violino con violino, viola e Basso, MS. Cx. 855/58, Dresden Mus. He also wrote operas, arias, and "Pastorale per il S^{smo}. Natale etc., a 4": 2 violini, viola, violoncello, MS. (Upsala; operas dated 1732, 1735).

FRANCESCO MONTANARI, b. Padua towards the end of the 17th century; d. Rome, 1730. A pupil of Corelli who was apparently for some time at Bologna, where his sonatas for violin or flute, op. 1, were pub. According to Wasielewski, they are poor in invention and workmanship, but were reprinted at Amsterdam. In 1717 he went to Rome as violinist in the chapel of S. Peter's, where he remained to the time of his death. Burney says that he was accounted the finest performer of his time. Pisendel went to study under him for a time when he had already acquired the reputation of an excellent violinist. When Burney tells us that when Bini was accorded the palm in 1730 it broke Montanari's heart and caused his death, he must of course have been mistaken, as Bini was only born in 1720. Schering says that according to 4 concertos for 1 and 2 violins in the Dresden Library, he must have been a composer of a strong individuality and a temperamental player and gives the description of some movements to prove this. Hawkins, Gerber (ii), and Fürstenau call him ANTONIO. 8 concertos for 2 violins and accompaniment, as well as 6 sonate a violino e violoncello, op. 1 (part of a set of 12), also arranged for flute (*see* above), in the library of the Musikfreunde, Vienna, are catalogued under the latter name, while a "Sonata a tre" for 2 violins and bass, 18th century, MS. in the library of Mr. Newman Flower (Aylesford Collection), a feeble work, bears the name of ANDREA MONTANARI. This makes it appear as if there had been several violinist composers of that name of whom we have no accurate knowledge so far.

CARLO DEL VIOLINO. A 17th-century violinist-composer who lived in Rome. 2 songs. He is identical with CARLO CAPRIOLI or CAPROLI.

MARTINO (MARTINELLO) BITTI. A late 17th- and early 18th-century violinist and composer in the service of the Grand Duke of Toscana at Florence, where he was living in 1714,

Italy: to 1700

when the famous Stoelzel visited him. He composed 12 sonatas for 2 violins and bass (Walsh, 1712?; E. d. v. Str. "Eighteenth-Century Violin Sonatas," *The Strad*, Nov., 1917). Solos for flute and thorough-bass and sonatas for oboe and B.c. (the latter in Fétis are probably the same as the flute sonatas). A sonata for 2 violins and bass, and 3 sonatas for violin solo and bass (in score), all in MS., are in the Dresden Mus.

GIROLAMO NICOLO LAURENTI, b. Bologna; d. there, Dec. 26, 1752. Son of Bartolomeo; pupil of Torelli and Vitali; violinist at S. Petronio and other churches; member of the Academy; composed 6 concerti a 3 violini, viola, violoncello ed org., Amst., Roger; 6 concerti per violoncello con 2 violini, viola e Basso, op. 1, only signed Laurenti in "Musikfreunde." In Mich. Corrette, "L'Art de V.," one piece signed only Laurenti.

PIER PAOLO LAURENTI, his brother, b. Bologna, 1674/5; d. there, Mar. 25, 1719; was 2nd violinist and afterwards violist at S. Petronio (Busi, i, 128, more details); composed operas, oratorios; also instrumental pieces for 3 instruments, Bologna, 1706.

GIACOMO DETTO SCATOLA, of Bassano. Is mentioned as a violinist at Vicenza (Gasparella).

GIUSEPPE ANTONIO VINCENZO ALDROVANDINI. 1702, president of the Academia Filarmonica, Bologna; d. there, Feb. 8, 1707. Concerti a 2 violini e violoncello, op. 1, Bologna, 1704. Sonata a tre (ditto?), op. 5, Ib., 1706. (Eitner.)

CARLO PASSIONEI. Violinist to the Duke of Ferrara, contemporary of Corelli. Composed, in the style of the latter, 12 sonatas for "basse de violon" (violoncello) with basso continuo for harpsichord (Amsterdam, Roger, 1710). Pougin mentions them as "sonates pour violon seul," etc.

CHRISTOFORO CARELIO (Mendel: Antonio), b. Messina, Sicily, 16... Violinist. Composed sonatas in 3 parts (2 violins and bass?), pub. Amsterdam, 1710. Pougin calls him ANTONIO CORELIS.

CHAPTER 15

Netherlands

APART from F. Massi, mentioned by E. van der Str. ("La Musique aux Pays-Bas") as a violinist in the band of Charles V at Brussels, ca. 1550, who most probably was not a violinist but a viol player, we meet with no names of violinists in the Netherlands before the early 17th century, when we find Peter van Laar (q.v.) mentioned as the first eminent native violinist, although the instrument must have been well known from about the middle of the 16th century, when Pietro Lupo lived as musical instrument-maker at Antwerp. In 1559 he sold to a musician of the Utrecht Magistrate (Town Council) 5 violins in their cases ("cinq violons renfermés dans leurs étuis") for the sum of 72 Livres (Dr. Kinsky's "Heyer Catalogue," ii, 511). This is the earliest record of a sale of violins. Lupo was evidently an Italian who settled in Antwerp, and brought with him the then new art of violin-making from his native country. He was probably related to the Lupos at the English Court.

FRANÇOIS MASSI. Violinist (?) in the chapel of Charles V; a Fleming who lived at Brussels in 1550 (Document in Str., iii, 177).

PETER VAN LAAR, surnamed BOMBOCCIO, b. Laren, near Naarden, Holland, ca. 1613; d. Harlem, ca. 1674. A painter and musician who acquired what was, for his time, an exceptionally high degree of technique as a violinist. After receiving his first education in art and general knowledge at home, he went to Rome at the age of 16 for further studies in both his arts. There he came into contact with the greatest musicians and painters of that time and not only benefited thereby himself but also exercised a beneficial and stimulating influence upon the Italian artists. He received the nickname

Netherlands

of Bamboccio (cripple) on account of his curious figure. After his return to Holland he resided first in Amsterdam, then in Harlem, where he committed suicide in a fit of melancholy.

WILLEBROD VROESEN. Nederlandish violinist and advocate, ca. 1666. A poem about him by P. Elzevier is in Gregoir Panth., v, 85.

DAVID PETERSEN. A Dutch violinist of the latter part of the 17th century, who composed sonatas for violin and bass, or theorbo and viola da gamba, entitled "Speel Stukken," Amsterdam, 1683. Fétis describes them as of "very good style."

JOHANNES QUICKELENBERGH, b. Hague, ca. 1686; lived 1715 as distinguished violinist and composer at Rotterdam (Bouwst., i, 32, Aktenst.-Gregoir Panth., v, 14, has panegyric of his masterly playing).

WILLEM DE FESCH, b. Amsterdam, late 17th century; d. 1760 (Bouwst., ii, 185). Violoncellist and composer of violin sonatas; 6 sonate a 2 violini (Amsterdam); 10 sonate a 2 violini o Flauto e basso cont. (Ib.); 6 flute and violin solos with bass, op. 8, liv. 1. One of the sonatas has been re-published in A. Moffat's "Alte Meister"? *(see* Mus. Cat.).

C. VAN SHMETT. Has one piece in Playford's "Division Violin," 1685.

CHAPTER 16

Poland and Scandinavia

Poland

SOME writers have claimed for Poland the honour of being the native country of the violin, for the reason that they took the "Polnische Geiglein" as the immediate ancestors of the former. They were however of the Gigue family, and as such, as we have seen in the introductory chapters, could have no part in the evolution of the violin.

Although the Poles are a musical nation, they produced no violinist of note before Hübner, at the end of the 17th century.

JOHANN HÜBNER, b. Warsaw, Mar. 1696, went to Vienna in 1714 to study the violin under Rosetti, with whom he went to Russia, where he was engaged by Count Kinsky. He afterwards became concertmeister in the Private chapel of the Empress Anna (Dlabacz).

Scandinavia

In the Scandinavian countries music was chiefly cultivated at the Courts, who engaged foreign artists, and perhaps the earliest native violinist was the Norwegian Baron L. von Holberg (q.v.), to whose existence we owe Grieg's beautiful well-known Suite. English musicians were in great favour at Copenhagen and Upsala from Elizabethan times, but they were lute- and viol-players. Their native "Fele," the *Hardanger Fiedel*, which was cultivated to a high degree of perfection by the Norwegian fiddlers, the folk musicians, was first constructed by the schoolmaster, Lars Klark of Østersjœ, in 1670, and perfected by his pupil, Isak Nielson Botnen; it has sympathetic strings like the viole d'amour, but is restricted to popular use, and beloved by the people (more particulars in G. Kinsky's "Heyer Catalogue," ii, 533).

BARON LUDWIG VON HOLBERG, b. Bergen, Norway, Nov. 6, 1684; d. Copenhagen, Jan. 27, 1754. He was an excellent violin virtuoso and musician, whose greater claim to fame is based on his being the father of modern Danish literature. He studied theology, and by teaching gained the means to visit Holland, France, Germany, and England, where he appeared also with success as a violinist. In 1718 he settled as professor in Copenhagen, where he devoted himself chiefly and most successfully to literary work. He was created a baron in 1747. In memory of him, Grieg wrote his beautiful Suite "From Holberg's Time."

PART II
HISTORY OF THE VIOLIN FROM 1700 TO 1800

CHAPTER 17

History of the Violin from 1700 to 1800

THE 18th century marks the most important evolutionary period in the art of violin playing. The instrument had already reached its final form under the brothers Antonio and Girolamo, and Nicolo Amati, and was brought to its highest perfection by the greatest of all violin makers Antonio Stradivari. The bow, however, had as yet to undergo many changes before it could respond to all the demands made upon it by the exigencies of the modern school. At the end of the 17th century it had still a very primitive form, while Corelli's bow, ca. 1700, although still short, had a straight stick, and a more modern nut. Geminiani's bow, as shown in the frontispiece of his tutor (French ed. 1740(?), has also a straight stick, but of the average length of a modern bow, with a head and nut of a very advanced pattern. A bow said to have belonged to Tartini, whose name is engraved on the silver slide of the nut, now in the possession of Mr. Howard-Head, London, and presumed to be the work of the elder Tourte, shows the characteristics of the modern bow, except that the stick, which has a slight cambre, is fluted in the upper part, a feature not infrequent in 18th-century bows; it possessed a far greater elasticity than the older bows, and this may have borne its part in the freer and bolder use which Tartini made of it in his compositions. Towards the end of the century the bow was brought to its highest perfection by François Tourte, the Stradivari of bowmakers, who has never been surpassed, although a few 19th-century makers approached him, as Guarnerius, Bergonzi, and a few others approached Stradivari, more or less closely, in violin making. It is said that Tourte was assisted by Viotti in his investigations, calculations, and experiments which resulted in the perfect balance and elasticity of the stick. Tourte has also been credited with the invention of the slide, and the ferrule, the little metal band which keeps the hair flat, when it has been fixed in the nut; they appear, however, to have existed before his time, and certainly were used by his English contemporary, John Dodd, whose bows were of high excellence, and who for various reasons is not likely to have copied Tourte in these devices (*see* H. Saint-George, "The Bow," pp. 37, etc).

The evolution of the sonata remained during the first half of the 18th century still bound up with that of violin-playing. The ever richer figuration in the technique of the violin was reflected in the more varied passage work of the sonata. The structural element, and harmonic progressions became more ordered with regard to key relationship, repetition of subject and cadences, but no fixed or settled form had so far appeared. Everything was still in its experimental stages. The place of the free fantasia was taken by a long section generally beginning with the subject in the relative major or minor or a nearly related key. These movements, which approached the strict sonata form, appeared generally as last, and not, as in modern sonatas, as first movements, and as such they may be found in some of the sonatas by Geminiani, Locatelli, Tartini, etc. The rules which distinguished church from chamber sonata were gradually relaxed, and we find abstract movements followed, and intermixed with dance movements, while the allemanda, gradually assuming larger proportion, became transformed into the first allegro. The last great violin composer who wrote sonatas based on the style of Bach and the masters of the early 18th century was F. W. Rust, whose last sonata, written on his deathbed, anticipates and even surpasses Paganini, as it is written for the E string, with the recommendation to practise it, in transposition, on each of the other strings.

About the middle of the 18th century violin playing began to divide into two divergent directions, one which continued in the tradition of Corelli and the great masters, and which culminated at the end of the century in Viotti, the father of modern violin playing. The followers of the other direction cultivated the virtuoso element to gain the admiration of the multitude by dazzling them with their fireworks, and pander to sensuous emotionalism. Locatelli who, in his caprices, already aimed at the acquisition of transcendental technique,

History of the Violin from 1700 to 1800

was however still a composer of a high order; while Lolli, Giornovichi, Woldemar, Boucher, and others were essentially violinistic acrobats, though it cannot be denied that they played their part in the general advance of the technique of violin playing.

In Germany the chief centres for violin playing during the 18th century were: Dresden, Berlin, Prague, Mannheim and Vienna. The Dresden Court had employed Italian violinists throughout the 17th century, and these had formed a number of pupils which gradually consolidated in a native school, and found its chief representative in Pisendel, who also studied under Torelli, Vivaldi and Montanari. He transmitted his art to J. G. Graun, who, together with Franz Benda, became a leading master of his instrument in Berlin, and Benda's pupil, F. W. Rust, became one of the greatest violin virtuosi of the century at the Court of Dessau. Prague, Mannheim, Munich, and Vienna became so closely allied in their musical life, that it is almost impossible entirely to separate their schools of violin playing. Stamitz, the founder of the very important Mannheim School, was born in Bohemia, while his contemporary Cannabich was a native of Mannheim; their pupil Wm. Cramer transmitted their art to London. Both Fränzl father and son, who also were of Bohemian descent, though natives of Mannheim, and Eck father and son, brought the art of the Mannheim school to Munich, and Franz Eck became the master of Spohr.

In the Prague school, and in Vienna lived the direct traditions of Tartini, who for three years was in Count Kinsky's service, and in Munich those of Felice d'all Abaco, so that both had absorbed the principles of the best Italian masters. Dittersdorf and Anton Wranitzky may be looked upon as the founders of the Viennese school of violin playing, and both were offsprings of the Italian school; the former (q.v.) by direct tuition from Ferrari's pupil Trani, the latter, a pupil of his elder brother Paul, was trained chiefly on the works of Corelli and Tartini. Of almost equal importance, both as players and teachers, were Gyrowetz and Krommer. They were all in the service of the nobility, the members of which kept private bands or at least quartets; while the Imperial Court, being chiefly interested in vocal music, took but little notice of instrumental art and artists.

The History of the Violin

At the beginning of the 18th century in France, the violin —as well as the sonata—met with unqualified hostility in many quarters. J. J. Rousseau, who regarded instrumental music as entirely subordinate to vocal, attacks it vigorously in his "Dictionnaire de Musique," as exemplifying the bad taste of those who want to introduce contemporary Italian music. In spite of all this it soon asserted itself. Du Val was the first to raise the status of the violin in France by introducing and playing Corelli's sonatas; he also composed pieces for the instrument, while Joseph Marchand, a pupil of Lully, and Charles La Ferté, one of the "Twenty-four Violins," each published a book of violin sonatas in 1707. Even later, however, the violin is mentioned in an apologetic tone, as being now in the hands of respectable musicians, and as having gained admittance in the best houses. In Hubert Le Blanc's quaint little book "Defence de la Viole," etc., 1740, the violin and the violoncello are roundly abused as vulgar intruders.

In England too, the violin was long regarded with mixed feelings. Evelyn, who in an entry in his Diary of March 4, 1656, sings the praises of Baltzar, the violinist, "the incomparable Lubicer," as he calls him, writes on Dec. 21, 1662: . . . "One of His Majesty's chaplains preached, after which, instead of ye ancient grave and solemn wind musick accompanying ye organ, was introduc'd a concert of twenty-four violins between every pause, after ye French fantastical light way, better suiting a tavern or playhouse than a church. . . ." Purcell, however, disliked the viols, and only wrote for the members of the violin family, and with the advent of Handel, the Castruccis and Geminiani the violin rapidly gained the ascendancy.

VIOLINISTS OF THE PERIOD

CHAPTER 18

Austria

FRANZ KARL PERNEMBER, b. ca. 1697, son of an Imperial trumpeter. From Nov. 25, 1727, till his death on June 2, 1754, at the age of 57, he was violinist in the Court chapel, Vienna. Fux, in a report concerning his appointment in 1726, says that Pernember was worthy to rank with the greatest violinists (Köchel, i, and ii, 407).

GOTTFRIED MUFFAT. Violinist at the Vienna Court chapel, at 45 florins per month from July 1, 1701, to the time of his death.

JOHANN MUFFAT. Violinist in the chapel of St. Stephen's Cathedral in Vienna before 1740 (Pohl, iii, 47). It would be interesting to know whether and how Gottfried and Johann and the following Muffats were related to the famous organists and composers Georg and his son Gottlieb, and to one another. The Muffats came of a Scottish family who emigrated to Germany and the Savoy to escape religious persecution.

JOHANN ERNST MUFFAT was violinist in the chapel of Joseph II in Vienna. He was dismissed on the reduction of the chapel, but in 1728 he appealed for re-institution which was granted on Dec. 1, 1730, with a salary of 500 florins per annum. He died at the age of 48 on June 25, 1746 (Köchel, i, and ii, 420).

JOSEPH MUFFAT, a son of Gottlieb, b. Vienna, 1721, was a Court scholar of the Imperial Chapel from 1734 to his death in 1756; but apparently did not give satisfaction, as he was never appointed (Köchel ii, 231).

ANDREAS FREITIG (FREYDIG). From Oct. 1, 1701, to Oct. 15, 1718, when he died, Freitig was violinist in the Court chapel, Vienna, at a salary of 500 florins per annum (Köchel, i).

FERDINAND GROSSAUER, b. ca. 1704; d. Vienna, Sept. 14, 1763, aged 59. He was appointed on May 10, 1732, violinist in the Court chapel, Vienna, at 400 florins. Fux praises him as an excellent violinist (Köchel i, and ii, 433).

FRANZ REINHART, the elder. From June 15, 1706, to his death, Sept. 27, 1727, violinist in Vienna Court chapel with at first a salary of 45 florins monthly, then from 1712, at 900 florins per annum. Fux, in a report to the Court, calls him "a distinguished virtuoso" (Köchel i, and ii, 394). Whether the sonata a 2 violini, tromba, violoncello e organo (Musikfr.) is by him or the son, requires investigation. His son:

FRANZ REINHART, the younger, was Court scholar for the violin, 1725–31 (Köchel, ii, 230); in 1740 he was violinist at St. Stephen's Cathedral.

JOHANN FRANZ REINHART, b. ca. 1714; d. Vienna, Apr. 22, 1761, aged 47. Violinist in Vienna Court chapel from Dec. 1, 1730, till the time of death, with 460 florins per annum (Köchel).

JOHANN ALBRECHT HAIN. From Dec. 1, 1706, to his death on Nov. 24, 1727, at the age of 50, a violinist in the Imperial Chapel, Vienna, where he received, finally, 360 florins, which would imply that he was a good artist (Köchel, i).

KARL HOECKH, b. Ebersdorf, near Vienna, Jan. 22, 1707; d. Anhalt-Zerbst, 1772. He received his first violin lessons from his father, and was sent at the age of 15 to Pruck to receive his complete musical education from the town musician of that place. At the end of his studies he passed two years (Mendel says four years) as oboist in a regiment in Hungary and Transylvania, afterwards going to Vienna. There he met Franz Benda, who took a great interest in him, and when Benda left Vienna, Hoeckh was allowed to accompany him to Warsaw, where the Starost Suchaczewski engaged Benda as capellmeister and Hoeckh as a member of his chapel. After the death of the Starost they both were in the Electoral Chapel of August the Strong until the latter also died in 1733, when through Benda's recommendation Hoeckh became concertmeister at the Court of Anhalt-Zerbst. There he succeeded Fasch as capellmeister in 175? and remained greatly honoured to the time of his death. He counted

Austria

F. W. Rust among his many pupils, and was not only a distinguished violinist but also a composer of merit. Fétis mentions as his compositions: 7 "Parthien" (suites of pieces) for 2 violins and bass, Berlin, 1761, and as remaining in MS. 12 violin concertos, 12 solos, and 6 symphonies. His autobiography appears in Marpurg iii, 129.

KARL HARTMANN was violinist in the Vienna Court chapel from Oct. 1, 1708, to Aug. 1, 1730, when he died, aged 66. His salary was 45 florins per month.

JOS. ADAM, b. ca. 1710; d. Vienna, Apr. 29, 1787. A violinist in the Imperial Chapel, 1772, 1st violin (Köchel), also, at St. Stephen's (Pohl, iii, 47).

MATTHÄUS TEYBER, b. 1711; d. Vienna, Sept. 6, 1785. Violinist and Court capellmeister. (C. F. Pohl's "Denkschrift der Tonkünstler Societät," Wien, 1871, 125, No. 80.)

JOS. FASCHING. Violinist at the Court chapel, Vienna, at a salary of 360 florins from 1712 to his death, Feb. 6, 1732 (Köchel, i).

GEORG HÄMETTER. Violinist in the band of the Empress Eleonora of Austria. After four years' service he applied, in 1715, for a place in the Imperial Court chapel, but was not appointed in spite of his good testimonial by Fux. He was also harpsichord player. (Köchel, ii, 378.)

JOSEPH PIRLINGER, b. ca. 1726; d. Vienna, June 17, 1793. Violinist in Vienna Court chapel from 1789 to the time of his death at the age of 69. He composed string quartets, trios (2 violins and bass), duets, etc., and prepared a new ed. of L. Mozart's tutor (Vienna, 1800). Fétis says: "He visited Paris ca. 1786, where 6 string quartets and 6 symphonies in 8 parts of his were pub. about that time." Several compositions were pub. by Steiner, Vienna, 1802.

JOSEPH STARZER, b. Vienna (?), 1726; d. there, Apr. 22, 1787 (Mendel). He was concertmeister in the Vienna Court chapel until 1760, when he went to St. Petersburg as concertmeister and Court composer, but was in Vienna again in 1770 at the theatre conducted by Noverre (*see* Fétis). Hanslick says he led the concert performances at Baron van Swieten's to the time of his death. He wrote Singspiele (ballad operas) and ballets, which enjoyed great popularity. Composed also a concerto in F for violin and quartet, string trios for violin, viola, violoncello, and divertimenti for string quartet, some symphonies and an oratorio. Fétis says that his immense corporation prevented him in latter years from playing and conducting.

KARLJOSEPH DENK. During 1731–7, he was a Court scholar for the violin in Vienna, and from May 9, 1737, to 1770, he was violinist in the Court chapel there, with a salary of 430 florins per annum. In an ordinance of July 4, 1769, he is mentioned as deceased, and his salary of 400 florins is given as additional stipend to Kapellmeister Reutter. The Friends of Music in Vienna have 3 trios for 2 violins and bass by Karl Denk.

LEOPOLD REINHARD, b. ca. 1740; d. Vienna, Jan. 24, 1806, aged 66. Violinist in Vienna Court chapel, 1795, till time of death (Köchel). The "Wiener Diarium" mentions JOH. GEORG RAINHARD(T), b. 1677; d. Nov. 6, 1742; and his son MATHIAS KARL, b. ca. 1711; d. Feb. 1, 1767; pensioned 1762; both Court organists. It is not clear whether they were related to the above.

JOSEPH ZIEGLER. A violinist in Vienna, ca. 1750, teacher of Dittersdorf. Of his compositions are known—a violin concerto in A with violin, viola e bass; and a sonata per violino e basso (score—Musikfr.). Masses, motets, etc., in Klosterneuburg and Göttweih.

ERNST FUX. After 1750 organist and teacher of music in Vienna. Sonata in G per violino e basso, time unknown (Musikfr.). Trios per 2 violini e basso, MS. 3 part books, one in C maj. and one in E flat maj. In Traeg's catalogue, Vienna, 1799: 3 sonatas for violin and bass (Berlin, Th.), and 1 solo for violin (Mendel).

FRANZ LAMOTTE (LAMOTTA), b. Vienna (or in the Netherlands?), ca. 1751; d. Vienna, 1781 (in the *Magazin*, 1780 (494), he is, however, mentioned as already dead). He was called the young Englishman, as an English merchant had bought him from his mother, and as he showed early talent had him trained as a violinist that he might accompany him as such on his journeys. On Dec. 31, 1766, he made his début in Vienna, where he had recently arrived ("Wiener Diarium"). Mozart praises his brilliant (perfect) staccato. In 1767 Gerber

Austria

(Lex. i) heard him at Hiller's in Leipzig. In 1769 he appeared in Paris, where he defeated Giornovichi (*see* below); during 1776 he was in London (Pohl, ii, 370). He was member of the Court chapel, Vienna, from 1772 to 1780 (Hanslick, 107; Köchel, i, No. 1218; Gerber and Fétis have anecdotes of doubtful authenticity and are otherwise inaccurate). Composed: Concertos, sonatas (3 in a collected volume by Welcker), and solo sonate p. le v. av. acc. de B. oe 5 (Paris, Leduc) (on the title page he styles himself 1st violinist of the Emperor); 6 airs mis en variations pour violon et basse (Paris, Leduc).

Fétis relates that by dissipation and bad friends he contracted heavy debts in London, for which he was imprisoned for several years until the prison was stormed by the Gordon rioters and he, with many other prisoners, was released and fled to Holland. That he died there is evidently an error by Fétis. He is perhaps better informed when he says that he had a remarkable technique of the left hand and the most brilliant staccato that had ever been heard till then.

He is mentioned in 1768 in connexion with Campagnoli. Wasielewski suggests that he might possibly be identical with Franz Lamotte, whom the Austrian Emperor had ordered to travel in order to perfect himself and who was in 1767 in Leipzig and Prague, and in 1769 in Paris. He belonged to the virtuoso school, and Reichard in his account of Karl Benda ("Briefe eines aufmerksamen Reisenden," vol. i, pp. 162, etc.) speaks about Lamotte's brilliant staccato in single and double notes.

Wasielewski says: At the age of 12 he played a concerto of his own composition before the Austrian Emperor, who at his expense ordered him to travel for further studies. Afterwards he was for a time a member of the Imperial Chapel in Vienna. In Paris he met Giornovichi, who, hoping to drive him from public favour, challenged him to a public contest. Lamotte offered to play at first sight any of Giornovichi's concertos if he would play a solo the former would place before him. Giornovichi accepted but was ingloriously defeated. Lamotte gave another proof of his good musicianship at Prague when the secretary of Prince von Fürstenberg tried to lay a trap by placing before him a difficult concerto in F sharp major, but Lamotte tuned his violin during the tutti, unnoticed by the others, a semitone higher and played the concerto, to the astonishment of everybody, with the greatest ease.

PAUL WRANITZKY (really WRANICZKY), b. Neureisch, Moravia, Dec. 30, 1756; d. Vienna, Sept. 28, 1808. He received his first education, both scientific and musical, at a neighbouring monastery; afterwards at Iglau and Olmütz. He then devoted himself chiefly to the study of the violin. In 1776 he entered the Imperial Seminary for Theology, where he was already able to function as conductor; he also studied composition under Jos. Kraus; for some years was violinist in the chapel of Count Johann Esterhazy von Galantha (O. E. Deutsch) and from 1785 to his death he was concert-meister of the Court opera, Vienna. He was a prolific composer in every branch of his art, and his compositions, consisting of operas, symphonies, music to dramas, concertos for cello, and for flute, quintets, quartets and trios for strings, also pianoforte trios, etc., were very popular in his time, but lacking in inspiration and originality; apparently he wrote neither concertos nor sonatas or pieces for violin.

ANTON WRANITZKY (really WRANICZKY), b. Neureisch, Moravia, 1761; d. Vienna, 1819. Studied the violin from early childhood. After absolving the Premonstratensian school at Neureisch, he studied philosophy and law at Brünn, then he went to live with his elder brother Paul at Vienna, who was his teacher of the violin, while he studied counterpoint under Albrechtsberger and received advice in composition from Haydn and Mozart. He became a popular and highly successful teacher for the violin and leader of Prince Lobkowitz's orchestra. He was also esteemed as a composer. For the violin he wrote a concerto, op. 11; sonatas with bass, op. 6; duos, op. 20, a number of variations and a tutor; also string quintets, numerous quartets, some masses, pianoforte pieces and songs.

He wrote a little tutor of some 18 pages in which he recommends pupils "to practise the 'Violin examples by Fux' (Jos. Fux). From time to time also other 'Galanterie Beispiele' (florid or drawing-room pieces) may be used to preserve the pupil's taste for these. As the legato kind (?cantabile) is the most excellent, pupils should be kept chiefly to this.

Austria

Therein the immortal Corelli and Tartini will meanwhile render them the most essential service."

T. WODICZKA. An 18th-century violinist and concertmeister in Vienna. He published under the name of Lustig a short tutor for the violin, translated from the German into French and Dutch (Amsterdam, Olofsen, 1757). Violin solos (?) by Wodiczka were pub. by Preston, London.

KAROLINE BAYER, b. Vienna, 1758; d. there in 1803. The daughter of a trumpeter at the Austrian Court. She commenced touring in 1775, and gained fame as violin virtuoso from 1780 to 1800 at all the various German Courts. Contemporary reports also praise her compositions, but they do not appear to have survived. (Gerber, i, 2.)

The story that Frederick the Great admired her playing so much that he accompanied her on his flute, has been shown by Pougin to be a fallacy, as Frederick was at that time no longer able to play, having lost his teeth.

MATTHIAS (MATTHEUS?) ALTMUETTER (ALTMITTER), b. Bollendorf, Austria, Feb. 11, 1760; d. Vienna, Sept. 16, 1821. He was the son of a peasant who showed musical talent, and therefore was sent to the Convict (Piarist Grammar School) in Vienna, where choir-boys learn singing and the playing of the organ or string instruments. Later on he became a violinist in Schikaneder's orchestra and then at the Kärnthnertor theatre. In 1807 he became a Royal and Imperial chamber musician, which position he retained, achieving the reputation of a good and modest artist.

MICHAEL KERZEL (KERZELLI), b. Vienna, ca. 1760. Violin virtuoso and composer. He lived in Moscow from 1786 and composed Russian operas which were performed there, also string quartets and trios, duets and solos for violin, etc

ADALBERT FAUNER, ca. 1760, Vienna (Breitkopf Cat., 1761). 6 trios for 2 violins and bass (2 in Munich library).

AUGUST (ALBERT?) FERDINAND TIETZ (TITZ), b. Lower Austria, ca. 1762, educated in a monastery, went to Vienna where he was engaged in an orchestra (Court chapel, Wki.). He afterwards settled at St. Petersburg, according to Gerber, from 1789 till after 1802, when Spohr heard him there and said that he played passages with the old-fashioned springing bow (Autobiography i, 45). About 1799 he was at Dresden, Leipzig, Berlin, Prague, giving concerts until 1810, from when he disappears from the *Allgemeine Leipziger Zeitung*. Several unsubstantiated statements in Fétis and Wasielewski say that he was in the Dresden and Vienna Court chapel (*see* Hanslick and Köchel).

He composed sonatas for violin and bass (Leipzig, Breitk. and Haertel); sonata for pianoforte and violin obligato (Gotha and St. Petersburg, 1797); 1 violin concerto and violin duets remained in MS. as well as 4 string quintets; 6 string quintets (Vienna, 1789); 3 do., op. 9 (Bonn, Simrock); Rondeau brilliant for string quartet (Ib.); 2 sonatas for violin and bass (MSS. Musikfreunde, Vienna).

FRANZ ALEXANDER PÖSSINGER, b. ca. 1767; d. Vienna, Aug. 19, 1827. Violinist in the Court chapel, Vienna, from Mar. 26, 1798, to the time of his death (Köchel). The *Leipzig Zeitung* has notices of numerous compositions of his. Still in existence are duets for 2 violins; violin and viola; trios for 2 violins and viola; violin, viola and violoncello; violin, flute and bass; and various other combinations; 18 quartets; 3 allemandes for string quartet; 1 quintet for flute, violin, 2 violas and bass; variations for flute and bass and a vocal quartet (Eitner).

JOHANN IGNAZ WILLMANN, b. Vienna (?), 17. .; d. there, 1821. In 1765 concertmeister at Montjoie, Eifel. During 1767–74, violinist in the Bonn Court chapel, and 1777 in Vienna, where, in 1787, he was Musical director to Count Joh. Palffy.

FRANZ SCHLEGER. Violinist in the Court chapel, Vienna. Composed 6 violin trios, op. 1 (2 violins and bass?), pub. Paris (1770), which he visited in that year.

PANCRAZ HUBER. Violinist at the theatre "on the Wien" in 1772, and Court ballet master. Composed 6 duos for violin and viola, op. 1, pub. in Paris; 4 quartets for flute, violin, viola and bass, pub. at Lyons; also symphonies, trios for violin, etc., pub. in Germany. Burney, who heard several of his compositions, speaks well of them.

THADDEUS HUBER (HUEBER). From 1789 to the time of his death on Feb. 25, 1798, violinist in the Court chapel, Vienna.

ANTON WRANITZKY   KARL DITTERS VON DITTERSDORF

These portraits are reproduced by kindness of Prof. O. E. Deutsch.

IGNAZ SCHUPPANZIGH   FRANZ KROMMER

FRANZ BENDA

JOHANN PETER SALOMON

Austria

He composed divertimenti for 2 violins and bass, MS., also a symphony and several sets of string quartets, mostly in MS. (some in Musikfreunde library and some in the Royal library, Berlin). He wrote in the style of Haydn (Mendel).

KARL HUBER is mentioned by Hanslick ("Geschichte des Konzertwesens," etc.) as a good violist of the late 18th century, living in Vienna.

A. WAGENHOFER. About 1772, 1st violin at the German theatre (Deutsches Theater), Vienna (Gerber, i). Composed sonata for violin and bass (Musikfr.).

IGNAZ SCHUPPANZIGH, b. Vienna, 1776; d. there, Mar. 2, 1830; son of a professor at the "Realschule." He first studied music as an amateur and was an excellent viola player. About 1792 (Wki., 1796) he exchanged that for the violin and chose music as a profession. Before he was 21 he proved himself an able conductor, although Hanslick says that he was neither a great virtuoso, nor a good conductor. He was, however, an excellent chamber-music player, and Beethoven fully appreciated his ability as a leader of his quartets, though he often twitted him about his Falstaffian figure. From 1795 to 1813 he conducted the Augarten concerts, which through his skill as conductor became very popular and successful. Afterwards he left Vienna for a time. He became the leader of Count Rasoumowsky's quartet in 1808 and chose Weiss as viola and Linke as violoncello. Schuppanzigh was the first to give public quartet performances. The first of his quartet academies were given in the winter 1804–5, with his pupil Mayseder as 2nd violin, Schreiber, chamber musician of Prince Lobkowitz, viola, and Anton Krafft, violoncello. (G. Kinsky, "Beethoven und das Sch. Quartett," *Rhein. Musik. and Theater Zeitung*, xxi, 235 f.) From 1827 to 1830 he was violinist in the Imperial Chapel. He was also an ardent admirer of Schubert, several of whose chamber works were first performed by his quartet (Hanslick, 71; Thayer, iii, 48; Köchel, i; *Leipzig Zeitung*, xviii, 423; xxxii, 618; Newman Flower, "Schubert"). Of his compositions only a solo pour le violon con acc. de *Quatuor*, Vienna, Diabelli & Co. (Musikfr.), survives.

The quartet was dissolved when Schuppanzigh entered the service of Count, afterwards Prince, Rasoumowsky, and reconstituted with himself as leader; Sina, 2nd violin; Weiss, viola; and Krafft, alternating with Linke, violoncello; it became generally known as the Rasoumowsky quartet which, under Beethoven's own guidance, produced his quartets at the Palace of Prince Lichnowsky.

In 1816 Prince Rasoumowsky gave up his house-quartet and the artists toured as the Rasoumowsky quartet with great success in Germany, Poland and Russia. On their return to Vienna in 1824, they resumed their quartet soirées, and Schuppanzigh was appointed as member of the Imperial Chapel. In 1828 he became conductor at the Imperial Opera, but died two years later from an apoplectic stroke. Criticism of his playing in Wasielewski. The most eminent of his pupils were Mayseder and Joseph Strauss.

FRANZ CLEMENT, b. Vienna, Nov. 17, 1780; d. there, Nov. 3, 1842. His father, a servant and musician of Count von Harsch, gave him music lessons from his fourth year, continued by Kurzweil, the concertmeister of Prince Grassalkowitsch, when he was in his seventh year. In a short time he was able to appear at the Hofburg theatre with such success that his father decided to take him on tour in Germany, Holland and England. At his concerts in London, 1791-2, Haydn and Salomon conducted the orchestra. The *Allgemeine Musik Zeitung* (vol. vii, pp. 242 and 500) contains enthusiastic notices about his playing of a concerto by Rode, etc., extolling his extraordinary technique, elegance of style and purity of intonation, which place him in the rank of the most perfect violinists, adding, however, that he had not the power of tone nor the deep emotional power of the Viotti school. The writer of those articles seems to have overlooked the fact that he was barely eleven years old. On June 2, 1790, he played at a concert under the patronage of the Prince of Wales, a concerto together with Bridgetower, who was about the same age, after which both became pupils of Giornovichi during their sojourn in London. On his return to Vienna, Clement became solo violinist at the Court theatre, and on account of his facility in score reading and accompanying on the pianoforte, he also became the assistant of the capellmeister, Süssmayer. In 1802 he became conductor at the newly built theatre on the Wien, but in 1811 he went with a Polish nobleman on a tour to Russia. On arrival at Riga he was arrested as a spy, and brought to St. Petersburg and, although innocent, deported to Austrian territory. Deprived of all means, he gave concerts in several Bohemian and Hungarian towns, thus working his way back to Vienna, where he found that his place had been filled again and he was obliged to accept a position as violinist in the orchestra of the neighbouring Baden. In 1813 he went as concertmeister to the national theatre at Prague, where C. M. von Weber had just become the conductor. In 1817 he went on tour again in Germany until he was recalled to the theatre on the Wien as conductor in 1818. He remained there till 1821, when he went on tour with Madame Catalini, managing and conducting her concerts. In 1829 he went on tour once more, after which he lived in Vienna, where he died in very reduced circumstances in consequence of mismanagement and irregular habits. Clement was a virtuoso as well as a musician of a very high order, but unfortunately he stooped frequently to low tricks of virtuosity to curry favour with the public, for which he was censured in the *Wiener Musik-Zeitung* of 1820 (p. 206). That he was capable of higher things is amply testified by the high esteem in which he was held by Beethoven, who wrote for him the "Kreutzer Sonata" as well as the violin concerto, the MS. of which, in the Imperial library, Vienna, bears his autograph inscription: "Concerto per Clemenzo pour Clement, primo violino e Direttore al Teatro à Vienne, dal L. v. Bthvn. 1806," and Clement had the privilege to introduce that immortal work to the public at a concert on Dec. 23, 1806. It appears evident that Beethoven had Clement's style and technique in mind when he wrote the rich and difficult figuration with the frequent use of high positions for the solo part. There are several accounts of Clement's extraordinary memory. In Dec., 1805, he was present at the Palace of Prince Lichnowsky, when his friends persuaded Beethoven, after stormy discussions, to contract the three acts of his "Fidelio" (then called "Leonore") into 2 acts. Roeckel, the tenor, who afterwards sang Florestan, left an account of the incident, in which he says: "Princess Lichnowsky played at the pianoforte the opera from the score, and Clement, who was sitting in a corner of the room, accompanied on his violin the whole opera from memory, playing all the solo passages of the various instruments (Thayer, Beethoven, ii, 295). A still more astounding feat, related by Spohr, was that after repeated hearing of Haydn's "Creation" he made, with the help of the textbook, a complete pianoforte score thereof which he showed to "Papa Haydn," who at first was confounded, fearing that his score had been stolen or secretly copied. He found the piano score so correct that he allowed Clement to revise it from the score and then adopted it for publication. Clement composed church, operatic and chamber music, also violin music which is of no particular value.

SANCZEK. Mentioned as violinist living at Brünn ca. 1780, in Gyrowetz autobiog., p. 8.

JOSEPH VON BLUMENTHAL, b. Brussels, Nov. 1, 1782; d. Vienna, May 9, 1850. The son of an Austrian chamber musician at Brussels who was pensioned after the Belgian revolution and went to Prague, where Joseph received a thorough musical education, especially when Abbé Volger took him under his particular care, and eventually in 1803 obtained for him a place as violinist at the theatre on the Wien. Joseph then settled at Vienna, where eventually he became choirmaster at the Piarist church, which post he held to the time of his death. He was an excellent violinist and a fertile composer in all branches of music. For the violin he wrote 40 numbers of duets and trios; duets, and a tutor which enjoyed great popularity. His brother LEOPOLD became chamber virtuoso in the private band of a Hungarian magnate, and another, CASIMIR, became director of music at Zürich, and died at Lausanne in 1849.

IGNAZ SCHWEIGL. In 1783 a violinist in Vienna, where he pub. his tutor: "Verbesserte Grundlehre der Violine zur Erleichterung der Lehrer" . . . 2 parts (Fétis: 1785) in 1786; a second ed. of "Verbesserte Grundlehre," also pub. by himself, appeared, first part in 1794, second part 1795; it was printed at Prague (Widmann). According to Gerber this tutor does not exceed the standard of Leop. Mozart's tutor, except for some instructions about harmonics.

STEPHEN FRANZ, b. Vienna, 1785; d. there after 1850. His father taught him the elements of music, singing and violin-playing before he was five years old. Endowed with a fine voice, he became, at the age of 9, a choir boy at the Piarists in the Josephstadt, where he studied also the humanities. His violin studies were also continued, and Dominik Ruprecht, who taught him pianoforte-playing, obtained for him lessons in theory and composition from Albrechtsberger, while Haydn, a friend of his father, gave him frequent and willing advice in the latter art. His father, fearing he might not be able to afford the expense of his higher musical education, apprenticed him to a merchant. In his leisure hours he took part in quartet practices at a rich nobleman's house, who offered him a permanent engagement as music teacher of his children, and first violinist in his quartet. There he remained from 1803 to 1806, when he went in a similar capacity to Pressburg, but early in 1807 he went as director of a private orchestra to a landowner in the county of Stuhlweissenburg. This position left him ample leisure for the study of the violin and for composition. He remained there for six years, played with great success in various Hungarian towns, and married in 1810. At the end of the six years he became 1st violinist at the theatre "An der Wien," Vienna. Count Kuefstein, and Salieri, who heard him about that time, became his patrons, and recommended him to the Emperor, who in 1816 appointed him as violinist in the Court chapel at the moment that he was offered, but refused, an important position in Russia. Until 1818 he was frequently heard as soloist in concerts playing mostly his latest compositions. In 1818 he retired from the opera and in 1820 he also gave up concert playing to devote himself more to teaching. In 1824 he accepted, however, the secretaryship of the Musicians' Pension Fund "Haydn," for which he had done already a great deal. This procured him the patronage of Count Moritz von Dietrichstein, the President of that society, on whose recommendation he was in 1828 appointed as orchestral director (conductor) of the music at the Burgtheater, which position he occupied until 1850. For that theatre he composed 15 overtures, ca. 90 entr'acts, etc. He composed also symphonies, a mass, and many chamber-music works of all kinds. Of his violin compositions only some "Airs variés" were pub.

JOSEPH KRAUS. Violinist in the Esterhazy chapel, under Haydn. A fertile composer, and from 1785 Court capellmeister in Vienna. He became the teacher of Paul Wranitzky.

JOHANN FUX. In 1788 violinist in the chapel of Prince Esterhazy, under Haydn.

HEINRICH EPPINGER. A pupil of Zissler, under whom he became not only an excellent violinist but also a distinguished quartet player, appearing publicly in Vienna as violinist in 1789. He was an amateur belonging to a Jewish family and possessed a moderate private income which enabled him to devote himself entirely to music. He was on friendly terms with Beethoven and was a regular guest in the houses of nobility which Beethoven also visited, and where Eppinger took part in the private concerts (Thayer, ii, 48). In 1802 he had a trio published and in 1808 an operatic scene. Other (MS.?) compositions of his for violin and for voice are in the libraries of the Friends of Music in Vienna and the Milan Conservatoire. He was one of the elect to compose the aria "In questa tomba" (see Mollo).

LEOPOLD HIRSCH. Until 1790 he served in Esterhazy chapel, under Haydn. The chapel was dissolved in the latter year. He composed 6 duos for 2 violins, op. 3, besides quartets, variations, etc., for flute, violin and violoncello, which were all pub. in Vienna. Fétis mentions 15 opus numbers and a cassation. After the dissolution of the Esterhazy chapel, he settled in Vienna, where he lived still in 1811 and was violinist at the Court opera.

Hirsch is considered to have played in the quartets of the aristocracy and was esteemed by Beethoven.

JOSEPH TIEMER. Composed sonate per il violino e basso Stb.—concerto for violin with string quartet in Stb. (Musikfr., Vienna). He lived during the 18th century, but no date is ascertainable.

TÜRKE. During the late 18th century he was a pupil of Wranitzky in Vienna (Wki.).

JOHANN TOST (II), b. Hungarian-Hradisch, Moravia, in the latter half of the 18th century; d. 1829, in Vienna. He was a rich cloth merchant in Vienna, an excellent violinist and conductor who exercised a great influence upon musical life in Vienna and was actively interested in the foundation of the Society of the Friends of Music. Spohr engaged to let him have all his compositions for a term of three years, for a high honorarium. In 1813 he had serious losses in business which led to his imprisonment in 1827 in which he died two years later (Pohl, iv, 229 ff.).

CHAPTER 19

Belgium

HENRI JACQUES DE CROES, son of Henri, sen., capellmeister in Brussels Court chapel. Baptized, Antwerp, Sept. 19, 1705 (Gregoire); d. Brussels, August 16, 1786. He held an appointment as 1st violinist and deputy capellmeister at church of St. Jacques (James), Antwerp, leaving there on Sept. 4, 1729, probably to take over the post as capellmeister in the Turn and Taxis Court chapel at Ratisbon, which post he left in 1745 (Mettenleiter, i, 272). On July 23, 1749, he became temporary director at the Brussels Court chapel, being definitely appointed to that post on Aug. 13, 1755. He was a prolific composer of masses, symphonies, sonatas, etc. Eitner only succeeded in tracing a few works, including 6 sonatas en Trio (Paris, Leclerq). He does not give the instruments. (A copy is in the Hofburg, Vienna.)

PAUL BAUWENS (*see* GRÉGOIRE). A violinist in the Court chapel at Brussels, 1729 till after 1742—he is missing in the lists from 1745. Another Bauwens was 2nd violinist in the chapel ca. 1746.

HERMANN FRANÇOIS DE LANGE, b. Liège ca. 1717; d. there. Studied composition and chiefly violin at Naples and was eventually appointed to the modest position of 1st violinist at St. Paul's, Liège, which he retained to the end of his life. He composed instrumental music, an opera, and church music.

GUILLAUME GOMMAIRE KENNIS, b. Lierre, Feb. 9, 1719; d. Louvain, May 10, 1789. He was at first choirboy at the church of Lierre, where he played also the violin in the church orchestra. On Mar. 2, 1742, he was appointed capellmeister there, although he was not a priest. He left there Nov. 28, 1749, and in 1750 became capellmeister at St. Peter's, Louvain, which post he held to the time of his death. As a violinist he possessed a remarkable technique of the left hand and his playing so pleased the Empress Maria Theresa that she presented him with a violin by Jac. Stainer, who at that time was placed above Amati and even Stradivari. Burney (1, 62) praises his compositions for the violin, which consist in sonatas for 1 and for 2 violins, duets for 2 violins ("creditable works of medium difficulty," E. v. d. Str., in Cobbett's Ency.), and for violin and violoncello, trio sonatas for 2 violins and violoncello. He also wrote 6 sinfonie a quattro, op. 3. Mich. Corrette included one of his violin pieces in his "L'Art du Violon."

FRANÇOIS CUPIS DE CAMARGO, b. Brussels, Mar. 10, 1719; d. ca. 1764 at Paris (Gregoir). A pupil of his father and brother of the famous dancer Camargo, in 1738 he made his début in Paris with great success. In 1741 he was appointed violinist at the Paris opera. On his printed works he calls himself Cupis. He wrote several books of sonatas for violin and bass; part of op. 1 has been republished in Eitner, ii. Daquin characterizes the playing of Franc. Cupis thus: "Connoisseurs whom one cannot accuse of partiality have assured me that he combines the feeling and tenderness of Leclair with the astonishing fire of Guignon." (Also Caffieux, "Histoire de la Musique.") His two sons, called CUPIS, L'AÎNÉ, and JEAN BAPTISTE CUPIS, LE CADET, were both violoncellists. (*See* E. v. d. Str., "The Violoncello.") CHARLES DE CUPIS was a member of the orchestra of the Paris opera in 1746. Campardon, who mentions the fact, does not state his instrument, which however was probably the violin.

PIERRE VAN MALDERE, b. Brussels, May 13, 1724; d. there, Nov. 3, 1768. He entered the Brussels Court chapel under Croes as choirboy, studied the violin and received a place as 2nd violin in the chapel. On Aug. 13, 1755, he became 1st violin and in Sept., 1758, he received from the Governor of the Netherlands the title of "Valet de chambre du Prince Charles de Lorraine," and surrendered his place in the chapel to his brother. In 1761 he went with the Prince to Paris, where several of his works were pub. and where his opera "La Bagarre" was performed at the Comedie Italienne on Feb. 18, 1762, but failed. In the same year he returned to Brussels. Dittersdorf mentions him as a violin virtuoso in his auto-

Belgium

biography. Gregoir in the *Artiste* gives a newspaper criticism of 1761. He composed a number of sonatas for 1 and 2 violins and bass, numerous symphonies, overtures, string quartets and an opera in the style of Stamitz. His symphonies and chamber-music works have artistic merit and belong to the best of their time.

FRANÇOIS JOSEPH GOSSEC, b. Jan. 17, 1733, at Vergnies (Belgium); d. Feb. 16, 1829, at Passy, Paris. As choirboy at Antwerp cathedral he received instruction in violin playing and studied composition by himself. In 1757 he became leader of the orchestra of General La Popeliniere, later on, at Ramearis' recommendation, of that of Prince Conti. Afterwards he devoted himself chiefly to composing and conducting, instituting the École Royale du Chant, of which he became the director, and which was enlarged into the Conservatoire de la Musique in 1795, where he functioned as one of the inspectors. He retired in 1815 and went to Passy. He wrote for the violin a set of 3 duos, op. 4 MS. (Darmst.), and trios a 2 violins et bass, op. 1 and op. 9. Gossec was also the founder of the concerts des amateurs and the first composer of symphonies in France, a form previously unknown in that country (*see also* Fétis.)

JEAN BAPTISTE HOOF, b. Lierre, 1735; d. Antwerp, Feb. 4, 1813. From 1754 violinist at the Opera and the cathedral at Antwerp. He composed duets and quartets pub. at Paris and at Brussels (Gregoir, "Artistes and Panth.," vi, 48).

JEAN BAPTISTE VAN MALDERE, also called l'aîné, elder brother of Pierre. In the time of Capellmeister Croes he was 2nd violin in the Brussels Court chapel, where he succeeded his brother in 1785 as 1st violin. Croes describes him as a good musician.

JEAN JADIN. An 18th-century violinist and pianist, who was for some years a member of the chapel of the Archduke, Governor of the Netherlands at Brussels. Afterwards he went to Versailles and was appointed as musician in the Royal chapel. He died as such at the outbreak of the Revolution. He composed trios for 2 violins and bass, quartets and symphonies, pub. at Brussels. His sons, Louis Emmanuel and Hyacinth, born at Versailles respectively in 1768 and 1769, were both distinguished pianists and composers.

The History of the Violin

EUGÈNE CHARLES JEAN GODECHARLE, b. Brussels, Jan. 15, 1742; d. there, ca. 1814; son of Jacques Antoine Godecharle, master of the music at St. Nicolas, and member of the Court chapel (in list of 1749). He was a choirboy in the Royal chapel, Brussels, then completed his studies in Paris, and thereafter appointed violinist in the Royal chapel, Brussels, Mar. 8, 1773, with a salary of 140 florins. After Croes' death in 1786, he became capellmeister at the church of St. Géry, and in 1788 1st violinist in the Royal chapel (Str., v, 171).

Fétis enumerates symphonies and sonatas, op. 1–8, by him. Eitner only knows sinfonie a 8, Paris (Paris Nat.) without christian name, hence doubtful if by him. Several members of this family were members of the Royal chapel and opera and in churches during the 18th century.

JEAN FRANÇOIS REDIN, b. Antwerp, baptized in the cathedral Nov. 5, 1748, as third son of Joseph Redin, citizen, and Frau Jeanne Françoise Hansewyck; d. there, Feb. 24, 1802. He became 1st violinist at the cathedral. His op. 4 was pub. in London, but there is no proof to show that he was ever there himself. Fétis, Straeten and Gregoir enumerate instrumental works of his which Eitner has failed to trace. Composed 2 books of 6 violin duets each, op. 1 and 2; 6 symphonies; 6 string quartets. Fétis states he was afterwards in the service of the Archduke Charles of Lorraine, Governor of the Netherlands, and died at Brussels, 1789 (?), but Mendel says d. Antwerp, Feb. 24, 1802.

GUILLAUME ALBERT TENIERS, b. Louvain, ca. 1748; d. Amsterdam, Feb. 12, 1820. At first he was violinist in a theatrical company, but in 1790 he became 1st violin at the theatre La Monnaie, Brussels, afterwards 1st violin at Théâtre Français, Amsterdam (Gregoir Galerie). Composed concertos and variations for violin (Böhme, Hamburg), sonatas for viola; 1780 "Maître des Symphonies" at the Hague Opera (Gregoir, "Panth.," iii, 80; viii, 154); 3 sonates p. alto avec acc. d'alto a Mr. C. F. H. Duguenoy, Maître de Mus. du Spectacle Français a Hambourg, op. VI; according to this he appears also to have been at Hamburg.

FÉMY, PÈRE, b. ca. 1750. Singer at Ghent cathedral and 1792 violinist at the Ghent theatre.

Belgium

FÉMY, CADET. In 1789 a violinist at Brussels theatre, and 1791 contra-bass player at theatre Feydeau, Paris.

FÉMY, FRANÇOIS, b. Oct. 4, 1790, at Ghent, where his father was a musician. In July, 1803, he became a pupil of Kreutzer at the Paris Conservatoire, where he gained the first prize for violin in 1807. He was for some years at the theatre des Variétés, then toured in France and Germany, and in 1827 he was engaged at the theatre at Frankfort a/Main, and in 1828 he had an opera and a symphony performed there. In 1834 he settled in Holland, where he was highly esteemed as a violinist. The time of his death is unknown. He composed 3 concertos and many duets for violin, also quartets and symphonies. (Wki.)

FÉMY, ADÈLE, born towards the end of the 18th century; daughter of Fémy, Père or Cadet, from whom she received her musical education. She excelled equally as violinist and singer, and having toured with marked success in her double capacity in Belgium and England she went to America, where she was known in 1847, and probably died there.

DIEUDONNÉ PASCAL PIELTAIN, b. Liège, Mar. 4, 1754; d. there, Dec. 10, 1833. One of the best pupils of Giornovichi. He was appointed at the Concert Spirituel, where he played a concerto of his own composition in 1779 (notice from contemporary paper in Gregoir, "Panth.," iii, 72). In 1782 he appeared in London, where he was appointed as 1st violinist at the Abingdon concerts (Pohl, ii, 370; Gregoir, "Galerie"). In 1793 he went to St. Petersburg, then to Warsaw, Berlin, Hamburg, etc., returning to Liège in 1800. He lived the rest of his life in easy circumstances from the fruits of his tours and as a beloved and honoured citizen. He composed 13 concertos, 6 sonatas, 12 duets for 2 violins, 12 airs variés, and 12 quartets.

JOSEPH GEHOT, b. ca. 1756 (Wki.). Belgian by birth; travelled in France, Germany, England, 1781 (Pohl, ii, 370), 1784 (Wki.?) in London. Composed 6 violin duets, op. 3; trios for 2 violins and violoncello; 6 trios for violin, viola and violoncello, op. 2; 6 duets for violin and violoncello, op. 9; string quartets, military music, "a treatise on the theory and practice of music," published mostly in London, some in Berlin (see Fétis, Gehot); wrote a tutor: "The Art of Bowing the Violin," "A Complete Instructor for every Instrument" (London, 1790), and also a theoretical treatise (London, 1784).

WILHELM VAN MALDERE. A 2nd violinist in the Court chapel at Brussels, from 1755, and from 1763 1st violinist. From 1783 his salary was 900 florins. He was also violinist at several churches in Brussels.

DE LA NEUVILLE, ca. 1766 (according to Gregoir, 1767); 1st violinist at Brussels opera (Delhasse's "Annuaire dram.").

VAN DER OUTEN, AÎNÉ. In 1767 1st violinist at Brussels opera (*see* Gregoir, "Panth.," vi, 131).

LAMBERTI, L'AÎNÉ. In 1767, 1st violinist and conductor at the Brussels opera (Gregoir, "Panth.," vi, 131); Straeten, iii, 48, says that he was in 1767 1st violinist and conductor at the theatre at Ghent.

PIÊRRE JEAN DE VOLDER, b. Antwerp, July 27, 1767; d. Brussels, June 24, 1841. A pupil of Redin. His first appointment was as violinist at the church of St. Jacques in 1783, then he became violinist at the theatre, and finally leader of the concert orchestra. In 1794, however, he devoted himself to organ building, for which he became famous. He started at Ghent, but in 1831 transferred his business to Brussels. He composed 3 violin concertos and 9 string quartets.

JEAN PIERRE GUILLAUME, b. 1771 at Liège; d. Feb. 9, 1846. An excellent violinist who educated three sons, ALEXANDRE, LAMBERT, and LOUIS, who were all distinguished musicians (Gregoir, "Panth.," iii, 129 and 45).

JOSSE BAUWENS, b. Bruges, 1771; d. there, Sept. 1856. A 1st violinist and town musician, afterwards capellmeister at Notre Dame there. Composed masses, motets and instrumental compositions. (*See* Gregoir.)

MALHERBE, L'AÎNÉ, b. Liège, lived ca. 1772 at the Hague (Burney, iii, 247). In 1780 he was 1st violinist and conductor there. (Gregoir, Pantheon, iii, 60.)

MALHERBE, CADET, is mentioned as second 1st violin about that time in the same orchestra.

CORNEILLE VAN DER PLANCKEN, b. Brussels, Oct. 25 (22, 23 ?), 1772; d. there, Feb. 9, 1849. There are contradictory notes

Belgium

by Gheeland (Louis Schoonen), biogr. (Gregoir, "Panth.," vi, 149, and vol. iii, 103), and Fétis; see also Wasielewski, Pougin, etc. According to Wasielewski he was a pupil of Godecharles, became 1st violinist at the Brussels theatre in 1797 and also a member of the Royal chapel. He was highly esteemed both as conductor and teacher and counted among his pupils Meerts, Robberechts, and Snel.

CHARLES ORTS, b. 1775 at Brussels; d. there, 1845; settled at Ghent as teacher of music and wrote operas and church music (Pougin and Fétis).

NICOLAS JOSEPH DELHAISE, b. Huy, near Liège, Nov. 25, 1776; d. there, 1835; violinist and composer. (*See also* Gregoir.) He was originally a stonecuttter whose love for music determined him to abandon that trade for the study of the violin. At first he had to earn his living by playing at dances; by dint of perseverance he became a talented player and fashionable teacher for Huy and the surrounding country. He composed some elementary and progressive duets and easy studies for the violin, also contredances for clarinet and violin.

JOSEPH TERBY, b. Louvain, Dec. 25, 1780; d. there, Feb. 23, 1860. A violin pupil of Pauwels at Brussels; in 1808 he founded a school for violin at Louvain to which he afterwards added a school for singing. In 1833 he became capellmeister at the church of St. Peter, and in 1842 founded the Lyric Choral Union. He left an important collection of instruments and of music, including instrumental music from the middle of the 16th century, in chronological order. His sons JOS. and FRANÇOIS TERBY were also good violinists.

JEAN HERMAN COPPENEUR, b. Liège, ca. 1780; d. Chaudfontaine, May 21, 1850. He studied law and went to Paris, where he practised as barrister (avocat), cultivating the violin as an amateur. Ca. 1806–10 he studied under Gretry, exchanged his profession for that of a musician, and became 1st violinist at the opera, retiring eventually to Chaudfontaine. Gregoir mentions some of his compositions as being in the possession of a relative of his wife.

JEAN HENRI SIMON, b. Antwerp, Apr., 1783; d. there, 1861. A pupil of Lahoussaye, Rode (for violin), Gossec, Lesueur, and Catel (for composition) in Paris; acquired a high reputation both as soloist and as teacher, counting among his pupils Meerts, Janssens and Vieuxtemps. Composed 7 concertos and a number of other pieces, etc., for violin, also several masses, oratorios, motets, etc.

ADOLPHE CLAES, b. Hasselt, Belgium, 1784; d. there, Sept. 19, 1857. An excellent amateur violinist who acquired great merit in promoting the musical life of his native town.

NICOLAS LAMBERT WÉRY, b. Huy, near Liège, May 9, 1789; d. Bande, Luxemburg, Oct. 6, 1867. His first teacher on the violin was Delhaise of Huy. At the age of 16 he became the pupil of Gaillard, a good violinist at Liège. Compelled by conscription, he had to serve in a regiment stationed at Metz, but at the end of one year he was allowed to find a substitute and to return home. There he studied for two months and then resolved to settle at Metz, where he had been well received. He started on the journey, giving concerts at every town on the way, but when he reached Sedan he received such favourable offers that he decided to remain there. For a number of years he went annually for some time to Paris to study under Baillot. In 1822 he settled in Paris and was for some time conductor of the Vauxhall amateur concerts, but in 1823 he gained, in a competition, the place of solo violinist to the King of the Netherlands and in 1830 was also appointed as professor for the violin at the newly founded Brussels Conservatoire, occupying that position until he was pensioned in 1860. He was an excellent teacher, Singelée, Collyns, and Dubois counting among his pupils. He composed several concertos, variations and other solo pieces, and several works of studies which were used at the conservatoires of Brussels and Paris.

JOSEPH FRANÇOIS SNEL, b. Brussels, July 30, 1793; d. Koekelberg, near Brussels, Mar. 10, 1861. His first master for the violin was C. van. der Plancken; later on he became a pupil of Baillot at the Paris Conservatoire from 1811–13, studying harmony under Catel and Dourlew. Returned to Brussels, he became 1st violin at the theatre, afterwards succeeding Gensse as 1st solo violin, which position he held for ten years. During that time he became the teacher of M. Haumann and Jos. Artot, who were destined to play prominent parts in the history of the violin in Belgium. After the revolution of 1830 Snel was appointed as conductor of the theatre, a place which

Belgium

he twice occupied and twice resigned. In 1828 he became director of the Military bandmaster school; in 1829 Inspector-General of army music schools; 1831 conductor of the society of the Grand Harmonie (military band), and 1837 capellmeister of the civic guard. In 1835 he had also been appointed capellmeister at the church of SS. Michael and Gudule. Most of his numerous compositions are for the church, the theatre, and military band, apart from a violin concerto for his pupil J. Artot, and 2 duos for piano and violin (Paris). His latter years were troubled by family and financial misfortunes. He was solo violinist to King William I of the Netherlands and afterwards master of the private music. In Brussels he founded, ca. 1814, a school of music where the Meloplast system was introduced, and another school on the system of Wilhelm, which had about 400 pupils.

JEAN ANDRIES, b. Ghent, Apr. 25, 1798; d. there, Jan. 21, 1874. 1835 Professor of violin and chamber music of the Ghent Conservatoire; succeeded Mengal as principal in 1851 and honorary director from 1856; also solo violinist at the theatre until 1855. He wrote some music-historical works.

HENRI SNOEK, ca. 1783, 2nd violin in Royal chapel, Brussels, with a salary of 250 florins (Straeten, v, 172).

GOESSENS. In 1790, 1st violin in the Court chapel, Brussels (Gregoir, "Panth.," vi, 154).

GENSSE, ca. 1813, 1st violin at Brussels theatre (Grégoire, "Documts. relatifs," 11136).

CHAPTER 20

Bohemia: to 1750

THE Bohemian Czechs are a naturally very musical people, whose cultivation of the violin was already advanced in the 17th century, and it was jocularly said of them, that whenever a boy was born, they placed a few months after a violin on one side of its cradle and a piece of money on the other side. If it took hold of the violin first he became a fiddler, if he took the money first . . . we better leave it at that. They were mostly roaming fiddlers who played their national melodies with a temperament and perfection which never failed to excite their audiences. In the monasteries the violin, as well as other instruments, were used for more serious music, and many excellent artists owed their early training to the monks, as for instance Franz Benda. With W. Pixis the violin school of the Prague Conservatoire begins to occupy an important part in the history of violin-playing. It gave to the world a considerable number of eminent virtuosi who exercised a great influence in the development of their art.

GEORG IGNAZ KELLER, b. Chlumetz, Bohemia, ca. 1699; d. Vienna, May 27, 1771, aged 72. He was first chamber valet of Count Kinsky, meanwhile studying the violin. He was appointed violinist at St. Stefan's Cathedral in 1730 and later also in the Court chapel (Pohl, iii, 47; Köchel, i).

JOH. IGN. ANGERMAYR, b. ca. 1700, Bilin, Bohemia. Was one of the violins at the performance of Fux's opera, "Constanza e Fortezza," at the Coronation of Charles VI at Prague in 1723, and was considered one of the best violinists in the Imperial Chapel, where he served until 1727. He was probably a brother of the famous painter, Joh. Albert of Bilin. Several violin concertos of his remained in MS.

Bohemia: to 1750

JOHANN CHRYSOSTEMUS NERUDA, b. Rossicz, Bohemia, Dec. 1, 1705; d. Monastery of Strahov, Dec. 2, 1763. A distinguished violinist, and brother of JOH. BAPTIST NERUDA (q.v.). After some years of successful activity as violinist at Prague he became a monk in the Premonstratension Monastery of Strahov.

FRANZ BENDA, b. Alt-Benatek, Bohemia, Nov. 25, 1709; d. Potsdam, Mar. 7, 1786: his autobiography is in Ledebur. Son of Hans Georg Benda, a linen weaver, and a good amateur musician, he received singing lessons at the age of seven from the Cantor Alexius and became a choirboy at Neubenátek. Two years later, on account of his beautiful soprano voice, he was chosen for the choir of St. Nicholas, Prague. There he was offered an engagement in the Dresden Court chapel, and as the authorities at Prague would not release him, he left there clandestinely and received his appointment at Dresden, where he devoted himself also to the study of various instruments, and Hiller tells us that he practised diligently the violin concertos by Vivaldi and also played the viola at the music practices of the boys of the chapel. After eighteen months his roving propensity took hold of him, and he asked to go to Prague. Having become very useful, he was refused permission, but followed his former tactics and decamped, hiding in a barge going up the Elbe. He, however, did not get farther than Pirna, when he was recaptured and ignominiously brought back to Dresden. Soon, however, his voice began to break and he was allowed to depart. In 1723 he was contralto singer at a Jesuit seminary and at the same time made his first attempts at composition. As he had to earn his own living, he next joined a gipsy band in which there was a clever blind Jewish violinist, Doeb, who played the national dances with extraordinary feeling and temperament and a great amount of technique. Benda took him for his model and by zealous study advanced his technique very considerably. As he took a higher flight he went to Prague, where he had the good fortune to find a patron in Count von Kleinau and commenced to study under the violinist Koniczek. The Count, who intended to take him permanently into his service, wished him first to study for some time in Vienna and sent him there in the suite of Count Ostein, who happened to be on a visit at Prague. In Vienna he made the acquaintance of the famous violoncellist Francischello (at the house of Count Uhlenfeld), from whose advice he benefited considerably, as he did also by hearing many great artists. For two years he studied with great zeal but without any particular master. During that time he had made friends with the musicians Czarth, Höckh (excellent violinists) and Weidner, and they resolved to tour together in Poland, where the Starost Suchaczewski (Mendel: Szaniawski) at Warsaw engaged all four, Benda becoming his capellmeister. The duties were exacting, Benda having sometimes to play 18 concertos in one afternoon, but for want of anything better he remained for three and a half years, after which he was engaged for the chapel of the Elector of Saxony, the famous August the Strong, at Warsaw. When the latter died in 1732 (Wki.: 1733) he lost that position, and went to Dresden, where he made the acquaintance of Quantz, who engaged him for the chapel of the Crown Prince of Prussia at Ruppin (Rheinsberg?), where he renewed his study of the violin under J. G. Graun and composition under Quantz. In this manner the influence of the school of Tartini was transmitted through Graun to Benda, and from him to his pupils. On the accession of the Crown Prince in 1740 as Frederic II, Benda became a member of the Royal chapel and after the death of Graun in 1771 he succeeded the latter as concertmeister. His contemporaries agree, in their appreciation of his playing, that although he possessed a perfect technique of both the left hand and the bow, his strength lay in the expressive playing of an Adagio. Schubart quotes Lolli, who heard him in Berlin, when his hands had already become stiffened by gout, as having said: "O, if I could only play an adagio like that! but I have to be too much of a harlequin, to please my contemporaries." J. A. Hiller speaks of him in a similar manner, and says also: "His tone was one of the most beautiful, fullest, purest, and most pleasing," and Burney, who heard him in 1772, when he had suffered from intermittent attacks of gout for about five years, says: "His style is so truly cantabile, that scarce a passage can be found in his compositions, which it is not in the power of the human voice to sing; and he is so very affecting a player, so truly pathetic in an *Adagio*, that several able professors have assured me he has frequently drawn tears from them in performing one" ("The Present

Bohemia: to 1750

State of Music in Germany, etc.," vol. ii, p. 128); and on p. 140 he adds: "His style is not that of Tartini, Somis, Veracini, nor that of the head of any one school or musical sect, of which I have the least knowledge: it is *his own*, and formed from that model which should be ever studied by all instrumental performers, *good singing*."

He was a most lovable character, devoted to his family, for whom, especially his parents, he cared in every possible way; even the blind Jew Loeb he remembered still gratefully in his age.

Burney's remark that he belonged to no school but founded one himself must not be taken literally, as he had no doubt learned much from Francischello, Graun and Pisendel whose friendship he gained at Dresden. The cantabile style of good singers served him as a model in the playing of slow movements, especially as he himself received his first musical training in that art, and at Ruppin, at the Crown Prince's Court had often to sing some arias; moreover, he trained two of his four daughters to become excellent singers. Although he mastered the technique of the violin to its fullest extent, he never employed it for the mere exhibition of virtuosity. Arpeggios he employed in the most varied form, also in his compositions, and this makes some of them still useful as studies for the bow, to which they give a great amount of freedom, lightness and elegance. He had a style which was perpetuated in varying degrees by his pupils. His works, the total number of which Gerber estimates at a hundred, consist of violin concertos, trios, sonatas, solos, caprices, variations, studies, etc., as well as concerti grossi, and odes mostly in MS. A sonata in A major has been re-edited by A. Moffat in his "Meisterschule" (Berlin, Simrock), 1 Symphony, and 1 "Violin solo im Birnstiel" (MS. Karlsruhe). In Dresden Mus. MSS., 4 concerti a violin concerto with string quartet, some with addition of 2 horns; 20 soli a violino e. B., score; 4 sinfonie, strings and woodwind.

KONIZEK. Was living at Prague ca., 1724. The first important violin teacher of Franz Benda.

JOHANN BAPTIST NERUDA (also Joh. Georg, and Joh. Bapt. Georg), b. Rossicz, Bohemia, ca. 1707; d. Dresden, 1780. Violinist and violoncellist. After being attached to the principal churches at Prague, he became violinist in the Dresden Court chapel in 1750 and was pensioned in 1772. His sons LUDWIG and ANTON FRIEDRICH were also members of that chapel, Ludwig becoming an Electoral chamber musician in 1764 at a salary of 120 thaler per annum. Joh. Baptist, an ancestor of Wilma and Franz Neruda, composed 4 violin concertos, 6 violin solos, 24 trios for 2 violins and bass, a sonata for viole d'amour, violin or flute with B.c. (MS. Berlin libr.), and 18 symphonies. Only 6 trios for 2 violins and bass were pub. (Leipzig, Breitkopf, 1764).

GEORG CZARTH (ZARTH), b. Hochten, near Deutschbrod, Bohemia, 1708; d. Mannheim, ca. 1780 (in Forckel's *Almanach* he is mentioned as violinist in that chapel in 1782). He studied at Prague, the violin under Jos. Timmer and Ant. Rosetti, and the flute under Biarelli. He next entered the service of Count von Pachta in Vienna, which he found so oppressive that with Franz Benda, Höckh and Weidner he went to Warsaw, where they were all engaged by the Starost (Count) Suchaczewski until 1833, when Czarth became a chamber musician in the Polish Royal chapel. In 1734 he entered, on Benda's recommendation, the chapel of the Prussian Crown Prince at Rheinsberg and on the accession of the latter in 1740, as Frederic II, he became a member of the Royal chapel, Berlin. In 1758 he went to Mannheim, where he entered the Court chapel as 1st violinist, appearing in the lists from 1758 to 1778 as Georg Zardt, at 800 florins per annum. He composed numerous symphonies, quartets, and solos for the violin and the flute, on which he was an excellent executant. On his pub. 6 solos for violin and his 6 solos for flute, he spells his name Zarth. One piece of his is contained in M. Corrette's "L'Art du Violon."

HERMANN ANTON GELINEK (called CERVETTI), b. Horzeniowecz, Bohemia, Aug. 8, 1709; d. Milan, Dec. 5, 1779, on a concert tour. In Italy he called himself Cervetti. Studied philosophy and law and entered the order of the Premonstratenses at Seelau, Nov. 1, 1728, and after that studied law in Vienna. He excelled as violinist and composer and became organist at his monastery of Seelau. He left the monastery secretly and appeared as Cervetti in public as violin virtuoso and composer, and toured in Italy several times. None of his

Bohemia: to 1750

compositions has been found so far. In 1760 he went to France and played before the King, who presented him with a golden snuffbox set with brilliants. Thence he went to Naples, where he remained for several years under the name of Cervetti. The Superiors of his Order discovered his whereabouts and compelled him to return to Bohemia. He obtained permission to go for some time to Prague and stay with the Grand Prior of the Order of Malta. The latter recalled him to his duty to return to his monastery, but his love for music caused him to escape once more, though no longer young. He went again to Italy, and some time later capellmeister Pichl found him there lying expiring on his couch, his violin in one hand, the bow in the other, and he announced his death to his brother canons at Seelau. Some of his concertos and sonatas were pub. in Germany. His organ pieces and church music remained in MS.

THADDEUS ANTON STAMITZ, b. Deutschbrod, Bohemia, 17..; d. there, 1750; brother of JOHANN W. A. STAMITZ; was likewise a noted violinist in his younger years and as such was for some time concertmeister at the Mannheim Court, but afterwards he became a canon at the monastery of Altbunzlau and died as a dean in his native town.

ANDREAS KOHLERT, b. Graslitz, Bohemia, 1710; d. Prague, 1788; was in his latter life principal violinist at the Dom and St. Nicolaus churches, Prague.

ANTON GIRANEK, b. in Bohemia, ca. 1712; d. Jan. 16, 1761, at Dresden. He lived first at Prague, then at Warsaw, where he was 1st violin in the Royal chapel and is said to have been finally violinist and capellmeister in the Dresden Court chapel, but is not mentioned by Fürstenau. The once famous singer and dancer, Madame Francisca Koch, was his daughter (Dlabacz). Eitner mentions concertos and symphonies by him, mostly in MS. (Pougin: 24 violin concertos and other instrumental works.)

FRANK (FRANZ?) GIRANEK. Lived in the 18th century. Is known by 2 sonatas for 2 violins and bass, the latter incomplete (MS., B.B.).

FRANZ FOYTA, b. Bohemia, ca. 1712; d. 1776 in his 64th year. He was related to the schoolrector Erasmus Foyta. A good violinist, for many years director of music at the Prague theatre and 1st violinist in the "Kreuzherrenkirche." Wrote sacred music, symphonies, and chamber music which has disappeared; some may still be in Prague church libraries (Dlabacz).

PAUL KÖCHER, b. Taus (Domažlic), Bohemia, 1719; d. Kukus, Bohemia, Feb. 21, 1783. He entered the order of the Brothers of Mercy, Prague, in 1737 (Fétis: 1736), where he took the vows in 1738. An excellent violinist and violoncellist. Occupied high positions in various Austrian monasteries. He composed numerous concertos for violin, violoncello, and also several for viol d'amour (Dlabacz), which he played with great virtuosity.

IGNAZ FRIEDRICH VON FRIEDENBERG, b. Prague, 1719; d. there, Jan. 7, 1788. A Benedictine monk, violinist and violoncellist, who composed concertos, etc., for violoncello (Geeber, i). He was a friend of Stamitz, who taught him violin playing. His virtuosity was acknowledged in flattering terms by Frederic the Great. Under his Italianized name, PACEMONTI, he composed numerous concertos and partitas, which appear to have been lost. In his latter years he devoted himself to the teaching of violin-playing and singing.

HAVECK. A family of musicians (of Bohemian origin?).

FRANZ XAVER SIMON HAVECK went from Munich to Bonn in 1725 and was appointed in the Electoral chapel as violoncellist or violinist; re-appointed Nov. 4, 1735; d. 1756. ERNST HAVECK, his son, was appointed in the Electoral chapel (Thayer, i, 23, 26, 30), Mar. 27, 1756, as violoncellist; afterwards viola player at 150 florins per annum, when he sat beside Beethoven (Thayer, i, 30, 32, 150). JOHANN PHILIPP HAVECK, d. ca. 1769, was appointed June 22, 1729, as 2nd violin in the Electoral chapel (Thayer, i, 25, 48).

JACOB HUTTARI, b. Schüttenhofen, Bohemia, 17..; d. Podiebrod, 1787. He is described by Dlabacz as a violinist of uncommon ability as well as a composer, who stood high in the estimation of his contemporaries. He lived for some time at Boemisch Brod, whence he removed to Podiebrod. He left in MS. a large number of concertos, sonatas and solos for violin.

Bohemia: to 1750

JOS KAFFKA (or Engelmann), b. Bohemia, 1720 (Mendel: 1730); d. Ratisbon, 1796. Entered the chapel of Prince Thurn and Taxis at Ratisbon in 1743, remaining till he retired, 1790. Fétis describes him as a violinist of very remarkable talent. He left some solos of his composition in MS.

FRANZ FISMAN, b. Altzedlitz, Bohemia, 1722; d. Vienna, July 15, 1774. Violinist and composer. Monk of the order of the Brothers of Mercy, entering the order in 1742 of which he afterwards became Prior in Vienna and where his compositions are said to be preserved in the reconvalescent house (Rekonvaleszenten Haus). More particulars are given in Dlabacz. Fétis says he studied at the monastery of the Brothers of Mercy at Prague and joined the order in 1742. The Superior (abbot) having recognized his talent for music, placed him under Capellmeister Seuche and Tuma. Afterwards he went to Vienna, where he played with great success before the Emperor and made many friends among eminent musicians, thus improving his knowledge and technique. He became director of music before being made Prior of the monastery at Vienna, and eventually was sent as Provincial of the general assembly of his order at Rome, where he studied the Italian style of music and where his playing was greatly admired by the Pope, the Grand Duke of Tuscany, and at Naples by the King. At Rome he formed a valuable collection of ancient church music which he took with him to Vienna, where, on his return, he became a close friend of Joseph and Michael Haydn and remained so to the time of his death. A great many of his compositions are preserved in the monastery at Vienna.

DISMAS HATTASCH, b. Hohenmaut, Bohemia, ca. 1725; d. Gotha, Oct. 13, 1777. From 1751 he was violinist in the Court chapel at Gotha, and married the sister of Franz Benda, a singer, who was engaged at that Court. 2 solos in sonata form, 3 movements for violin and B.c. in MS. by him are in the Schwerin library, and Joh. Michel Schmidt's collection contains some songs. In 1780 he wrote some numbers (? Eitner) and also composed 2 grand symphonies.

FRANZ KREIBICH, b. Zwickau, near Kamnitz, Bohemia, June 2, 1728; d. Vienna, Dec. 3, 1797. After studying the violin at Dresden, he was appointed in 1770 by the Emperor, as his private musician (Privatmusicierer), and in 1772 as chamber musician in the Court chapel at a salary of 400 florins, which position he retained till he died. The Emperor called him a clown and "Gänseschnabel" (goose-beak) in speaking about him to Dittersdorf, but could not do without him. Both Kreibich and Dittersdorf intrigued against Haydn and Mozart to prevent being replaced by them (*see* Reichard, Autobiog.). Gerber (ii) gives a critique of his playing: "The Musikfreunde" has a Sonata per violino e basso in M.S. by him. Fétis says: "He was renowned for his preludes (improvisations?) on the violin and retained his youthful fire in the execution of the works of the great masters even in his age." He left a considerable fortune, as well as a collection of valuable violins, of which latter, unfortunately, we possess no particulars.

FRANZ XAVER POKORNY, b. Bohemia, 1729; d. Ratisbon, 1794. He was a pupil of Riepel at Ratisbon; violin at the Court of Oettingen, afterwards 2nd violin at that of Thurn and Taxis (Bibliog. in Mellenleiter, i, 276). His brother, JOSEPH POKORNY, was pianist at the latter Court.

GOTTHARD POKORNY, b. Bömischbrod, Nov. 16, 1733; d. Brünn, Aug. 4, 1802. A violinist who became capellmeister at St. Peter's, Brünn, ca. 1760. His daughter was praised by Mozart as a singer. He wrote a large quantity of church music of a lighter nature, which once was very popular.

JOHANN BAPTIST POKORNY was for some time violinist at the Court of Bamberg when, on Mar. 16, 1796, he was made Court musician at 200 florins per annum and 2 florins 24 kronen weekly for board. He was a pupil of Fracassini. On Jan. 30, 1800, he became vice-director of music, and Nov. 23, 1802, Court director of music, at a salary of 399 florins 24 kreutzer and 8 simra of corn. After the disbanding of the chapel he conducted, from 1820, the musical society, married Eva Maria Berthold and died as pensioned director of music at Munich at the beginning of the forties. In Darmstadt is the MS. of a cembalo concerto, with orchestra, by him.

F. S. KUNTE, b. Bohemia. From 1750 to 1770 he was in the service of Count Bugnois at Prague, and afterwards a teacher, being an excellent violinist. His violin concertos were highly esteemed in Bohemia, but remained in MS.

Bohemia: to 1750

FRANZ STROBACH, b. Zwittau, Bohemia, Dec. 2, 1731. In 1764 he was 1st violin at the Prague opera (Dittersdorf, Autobiog., 134); capellmeister of Prince Lobkowitz's chapel at Prague (B.B. MS. 6141) in 1786, and director of Bondini's theatre company, Prague, in 1786 (Reichard, 1786, p. 165). From 1796 to 1810 he was choirmaster at Loretari Church (Gerber and *Leipzig Zeitung*, 12,806). Composed 12 songs with pianoforte, pub. Prague, 1792.

KLOEKEL. A Bohemian violinist of note during 1753-88. He is mentioned by Pougin without further particulars.

VINCENZ JAVŮREK, b. Ledecz, Dec. 7, 1730; studied philosophy and entered the Dominican Order in 1754. He excelled as violinist and conductor of church music in his order. After the dissolution of the monasteries, he retired to St. Plegidius at Prague, where he died in the last years of the 18th century (Dlabacz).

JOSEPH JAVŮREK, younger brother of Vincenz Javůrek, b. Ledecz, near Kuttenberg, Bohemia; d. Prague, May, 1805. An excellent violinist, engaged at several churches as well as at the opera, and was director of music at the Holy Virgin's church at St. Joseph. Dlabacz knew a number of his compositions for violin and some are in the possession of Mr. Gotthard Hlawa at Prague.

JOSEPH STROBACH, b. Zwittau, lordship of Birkstein, Bohemia, Dec. 2, 1731; d. Prague (?), Sept. 10, 1794. Being destined for the Church, he studied at Liegnitz and the universities of Breslau and Prague. His passionate love for music, however, decided him to devote himself entirely to the violin and the study of music in general. After being attached as violinist for thirteen years to the regular canons of the Cross (Chanoines réguliers de la croix, Kreuzbrüderschaft?), he occupied successfully the post of director of music at the churches of St. Paul, St. Gall, St. Wenceslaus and St. Nicolas, and at the same time he conducted with a marked ability the orchestra at the theatre. He composed violin concertos, sonatas and caprices, which remained in MS. He was an intimate friend of Mozart.

FRANZ JOSEPH ANDERLE, b. Podiebrod, Bohemia, July 7, 1733; d. in Hungary, Feb. 12, 1765. He was the son of a well-to-do brewer, and showed an early love and talent for the violin which found no encouragement from his father, who induced him to join his business, which he did. He married and had a numerous family, but his love for the violin increasingly took possession of him. He avoided the company of other people, practising whole nights through, and finally in 1762 he stole secretly away from home and wandered to Poland, where he created quite a sensation by his naturalistic, rhapsodic playing. From Poland he went by stages to Hungary, where he became a favourite of the big landowners, but soon he became demented, smashed his violin and shortly after took his own life in a fit of raving madness.

WERNER HYMBER, b. Jochnitz, Bohemia, 1734. In 1755 he entered the order of the Brothers of Charity in the monastery of Kukusen. Sent by his order to their monastery at Vienna, he studied the violin under Hoffmann, Fismann and Hunggi, and composition under Seuche. He was made director of music of his monastery and sent as Prior to the monastery of Prosnicz in Moravia. In 1796 he was director of music at Kukusen. He composed concertos, symphonies, masses and other church music. He was also a good pianist and mandola player, besides playing several other instruments.

SIMON JOSEPH TRUSKA, b. Raudnitz, Bohemia, Apr. 5, 1734; d. Strahov, Jan. 14, 1809. He followed first his father's craft of a cabinet-maker in which he worked at Prague till 1757, when the siege of the town by the Prussian army caused him to flee to Vienna. Returning in the latter part of the year, he entered the monastery of Strahov on Dec. 8, 1758, as a lay brother, becoming a monk on Jan. 1, 1761. Henceforward he devoted himself entirely to music, which he had cultivated from early boyhood. He became an excellent violinist, viol da gambist and violoncellist, and a fertile composer of chamber music as well as dances which were very popular at the balls of Prague in 1774-6. He became also an organ builder, pianoforte, violin, and viol maker, whose instruments were sought after abroad, as well as in his own country. He composed sonatas for viol da gamba, violin, viola, and violoncello, string trios, quartets, and quintets which were greatly esteemed in Bohemia. He died in his monastery at the age of 75.

Bohemia: to 1750

LENARD DONT. Famed as a violin virtuoso; lived about the middle of the 18th century as a Cistercian monk at Ossegg in Bohemia.

JOSEPH MISLIWECZEK ("Mysliweczek" on French publications), called IL BOEMO or VENATORINI, b. in a village near Prague, Mar. 9, 1737; d. Rome, Feb. 4, 1781. Studied philosophy at Prague but devoted himself to music after his father's death and became violinist at a church at Prague. He studied counterpoint under Habermann, and organ under Seegert, devoting himself afterwards to opera composition. In 1777 he was in Vienna, where Mozart visited him. For the violin he composed 6 divertimenti with orchestra (MS. Musikfreunde); 6 orchestra trios for 2 violins and violoncello (London, Welcker); 6 trios, 2 violins and violoncello, op. 1, 6 trios, 2 violins and bass, op. 4, both pub. in Paris. (*See* Eitner.)

ANTON KOLBE, b. Seestaedtel, near Brüx, Bohemia, 1740; d. Prague, Aug. 30, 1804. A distinguished violinist who lived at Prague, where he was engaged from 1775 at the opera and at the churches of St. Aegidius and St. Jacob. His style in solos and concertos was full of grandeur and was greatly admired. The latter years he passed in a state bordering on misery and ill-health partly with the Minorite friars, partly in the hospital of St. Jacob. He was a pious and benevolent man who would willingly give lessons without charge to pupils who could not afford to pay, although he was poor himself. He composed concertos, solos, serenades, etc., which remained in MS.; mostly in the hands of his pupils; Konzertmeister Klockel, who belonged to their number, was in possession of several of his compositions. (*See* Fétis.)

CHYTRY, b. Holobaus, Bohemia, ca. 1740. He studied first at Prague, then became a law student at Vienna, where he had the good fortune to play the violin before the Emperor Joseph II, who was so charmed with his performance that he gave him an appointment in the Imperial chancellery. In 1798 he held a Government appointment at Prague. Kucharz considers him one of the best Bohemian violinists. (Dlabacz, col. 281.)

ANTON KAMMELL (KAMEL), b. Hanna, Bohemia, ca. 1740; d. before 1788. Count Waldstein, Lord of Hanna, sent him to Italy to study the violin under Tartini. After his return he went to Prague and thence to London, where he is mentioned as violinist and viola player in 1769 and 1774 (Pohl, ii, 370). Dlabacz related that he married a rich lady and became Royal chamber musician. In 1788 he is spoken of as deceased. He wrote concertos, sonatas and duets with and without bass for violin, divertimentos for violin and tenor or 2 violins, etc., and a large amount of chamber music as well as symphonies, overtures, etc. (*See also* Gerber. *See* list in Eitner, also Riemann.) His compositions, which are very melodious, enjoyed a great popularity. He was particularly praised for his expressive playing of the Adagio.

KARANK. A Bohemian violinist of note, ca. 1760, mentioned by Pougin without further particulars.

WENCESLAUS PICHL, b. Bechin, Bohemia, Sept. 25, 1741; d. Vienna, Jan. 23, 1805. He commenced his musical studies at the age of 7 under John Pokorny, rector of the local school (*see* Fétis). In 1753, as choirboy at the Jesuit seminary at Brzeznicz, he attended also the Latin school; he next went to Prague, where he studied philosophy, theology and law at the University and became a violinist at the St. Wenceslaus seminary. In 1760 he became a pupil of Dittersdorf and in 1762 1st violin (Chorgeiger) at the Thein church, studying at the same time musical theory under Segert. On Dittersdorf's recommendation (*see* Autobiog.) he became vice-director at the Episcopal chapel at Grosswardein, wrote poetry and several Latin operettas for Dittersdorf. He refused an offer to go to St. Petersburg in 1769 and entered the service of Count Louis von Hartig at Prague. Two years later he became 1st violinist at the National theatre, Vienna, and in 1775 he went by the invitation of the Empress Maria Theresa to Milan, as musical director at the Court of the Archduke Ferdinand; during his twenty-one years there he visited all the chief towns in Italy, forming friendships with the principal artists of that time. When the French entered Lombardy in 1796 he had to flee precipitately, leaving behind all his belongings, including his compositions, library and a history of Bohemian musicians, the fruit of long research, which the French stole and he never saw again. In 1800 he calls himself capellmeister to his Imperial Highness Archduke Ferdinand in Vienna. In 1802 he visited Prague with his daughter, an excellent singer. (*See* his biography in Dlabacz, who knew him; also Wki., etc.) He was a prolific composer for his instrument as well as in all branches of music. A full list is in Dlabacz, still traceable; works in Eitner; Gerber says he died while playing at Prince Lobkowitz', on Jan. 23, 1805.

WENZEL PRAUPNER, b. Leitmeritz, Bohemia, Aug. 18, 1744; d. at Prague, Apr. 2, 1807. Studied theology as well as music, to which eventually he devoted himself entirely. At the seminary of St. Wenceslaus, Prague, he was an excellent violinist, organist and composer, who played violin concertos in church at the age of 14 and who filled various appointments at Prague, where he was highly esteemed. He became conductor at the private theatre of Count Rink, finally becoming capellmeister at the Kreuzherren Parish church at St. Franz, and in 1794 choirmaster at the metropolitan (Haupt) church on the Thein. After the death of Strobach he succeeded the latter as musical director at the Prague opera. The death of his wife affected him so deeply that it led to his death not long after. He composed violin concertos, symphonies, operas, masses and other church music including organ pieces, which all remained in MS.

FRANZ ANTON ERNST, b. Georgenthal, Bohemia, Dec. 3, 1745; d. Gotha, Jan. 13, 1805. He received his first lessons on the violin from his grandfather, after whose death he continued his musical as well as general education at Kreibitz and finally under the town organist at Warndorf. On a visit to the monastery of Neuzell, he was engaged there as choirboy, but after six months he went to the Jesuits at Sagan where he made four years' preparatory studies for the University, after which he went to Prague to study law, and then became Syndic in his native town. Soon, however, Count Salm, who admired his violin playing, engaged him as his private secretary. In that position he heard Lolli and became his pupil. Encouraged by the latter he went on tour as a violin virtuoso. At Strassburg he met Franz Stade (Stad), who exercised a considerable influence in developing that expressiveness which was so admirable in Ernst's playing. In 1773 he returned to Prague, and 1778 he became Ducal concertmeister at Gotha. Of his numerous compositions for the violin, only a few, including his masterpiece, a Concerto in E flat major, have been published. According to Fétis he proposed in 1798 to publish a treatise on the violin, in 2 parts, the first part dealing with the construction of the instrument, the second with the art of playing, but apparently his plan did not materialize. He occupied himself in his latter years chiefly with violin-making, and he also contributed some important articles on that subject to the *Leipziger Allgem. Mus. Zeitung*.

JAN STEFANI, b. Prague, 1746; d. Warsaw (Powonski), Feb. 24, 1829. He was at first capellmeister to Count Kinsky, then violinist in the Vienna Court orchestra, and from 1771, 1st violinist in the chapel of Stanislaus August Poniatowski at Warsaw, where he became afterwards capellmeister at the opera and at the cathedral. He composed operas and instrumental music, but apparently nothing for the violin.

JOHANN JOSEPH GEORG GAYER, b. Engelhaus, Bohemia, Apr. 17, 1748; d. Homburg, 1811. Studied the violin as a boy, also singing and pianoforte, and in neighbouring towns the horn and trumpet, as well as thorough-bass. He soon became organist at Engelhaus, but after two years he went to Prague to study the violin under Pichl, and composition under Loos. Afterwards he toured in Germany and stayed for several months in Darmstadt, where he benefited by his friendly intercourse with Concertmeister Enderle. There he received, in 1774, the appointment as concertmeister at the Court of Homburg, where he remained until his death. He composed 40 violin concertos, numerous concertos for wind instruments, 30 symphonies, an oratorio, masses, motets, 4 pianoforte sonatas, solos for various instruments, etc.

FRANZ BAUER, b. Gitschin, Bohemia, ca. 1748. He had studied theology and become a subdeacon, when partly his love for the violin—in the playing of which Mozart, who heard him at Prague, had encouraged him—and partly to enable him to marry, he decided to exchange his profession for that of a musician. With his wife, who played the psalterion (a kind of dulcimer), he went first to Russia where they gained not only materially but also in repute; then they continued their tour through Germany to France, Italy, Spain and Portugal, meeting everywhere with the greatest success. Bauer is said to have distinguished himself also as composer, but nothing is known of his compositions, which were never published. After amassing considerable wealth they returned to their native country in 1794, and from 1798 ceased to appear in public.

JOSEPH OBERMAYER, b. Nezabudicz, Bohemia, a domain (lordship-Herrschaft) of Prince Fürstenberg, 1749. He was a pupil of Kammel; afterwards, Count Vincent Waldstein sent him to Italy, where he became a pupil of Tartini. On his return to Bohemia he resumed his functions as valet to Count Waldstein and was seldom heard in public. In Prague he appeared with great success in 1801, and on July 4, 1803, his playing was greeted with applause at a musical festival at the church of Strahov monastery. He was still living in 1816, but from that time no particulars are available. He composed several concertos, which remained in MS.

CHAPTER 21

Bohemia: to 1800

JOSEPH FOYTA, b. Prague, ca. 1750. Son of an organist at Prague and probably a relative of Franz Foyta (q.v., 1712). For a considerable time he was violinist at the theatre orchestra and the "Kreuzherren" church, then accepted an engagement at St. Petersburg but returned to Prague in 1791 as teacher at the Thein principal school (Hauptschule). He wrote symphonies and church music, which remained in MS.

JOHANN PRAUPNER (the brother of Wenzel), b. Leitmeritz, Bohemia, June 24, 1750; d. after 1807. He studied Humaniora, went to the University at Prague, where he devoted himself to the violin, then entered the theatre orchestra and became choirmaster at the Kreuzherren church at St. Francis (St. Franz) (Dlabacz).

WENZEL KRUMPHOLTZ, b. in Bohemia (?), ca. 1750; d. Vienna, May 2, 1817 (Thayer, "Chron. Cat.," says May 3). A pupil of Haydn at Esterhaz and Eisenstadt, he played 1st violin in the orchestra there and after the dissolution of the chapel went into that of Prince Kinsky. In 1796 he was appointed to the Vienna Court Opera, though Köchel does not mention him. He was a close friend of Beethoven and one who was thoroughly convinced of Beethoven's greatness. Beethoven venerated him as his best friend and composed "The Song of the Monks" in his memory (Thayer, ii, 48; Pohl, iv, 102). Krumpholtz wrote 2 violin pieces, "Abendunterhaltung" (Evening Entertainment) for solo violin and "Eine Viertelstunde für eine Violine" (A Quarter of an Hour for a Violin), and a song of his is in Musikfreunde. His brother was a famous harpist.

JOSEPH KACZKOWSKI, b. Tabor, Bohemia, in the second half of the 18th century. Fétis states that he toured (probably as

Bohemia: to 1800

violin virtuoso) in Germany. He wrote a number of compositions, concerts, duets, solos, etc., for violin (a list is in Eitner).

BATKA. A numerous family of 18th-century Bohemian musicians. The father, LORENZ, was capellmeister at several churches at Prague. Of his five (?) sons, who were all excellent musicians, MARTIN (d. Prague, 1779) succeeded his father in his church appointments, being a virtuoso on the violin, and left in MS. some violin concertos and studies. MICHAEL BATKA, b. Sept. 29, 1755, was living in Prague in 1800, and was also an excellent violinist; no compositions of his are known. His son, JOHANN BATKA, was a distinguished pianist and a successful composer who lived at Budapest early in the 19th century.

JOHANN THEODOR BRODECZKY, b. Bohemia, 17... Violinist and harpsichord player who toured in Germany and the Netherlands, ca. 1770, and settled at Brussels as musician to the Archduchess of Austria, governor of the Netherlands. He composed some studies for the violin, pianoforte trios, quartets for harpsichord and strings, 6 symphonies and violoncello pieces, which, apart from the trios and quartets, remained in MS.; some pianoforte sonatas were pub. (Brussels, 1782).

MARTIN SCHLESINGER, b. Wildenschwert, Bohemia, 1751; d. Vienna, Aug. 12, 1818. Lived first at Königgrätz; in 1771 he was violinist in the chapel at Pressburg; in 1788 solo violin and director of the concerts of the Cardinal-Archbishop there. Afterwards he went to Vienna and entered the service of Count Erdödy as chamber virtuoso, ca. 1808 (Becker, iii; Pohl, iv, 53; Thayer, iii, 47; Fétis). Composed violin pieces published at Leipzig and Vienna; theme and variations with orchestra (Leipzig, Fleischer); Rondo hongrois for violin and pianoforte (Vienna, Mechetti, etc.); left also concertos in MS.

MANSWET STRZOSKY, b. Geyersberg, Bohemia, Dec. 11, 1753; d. Prague, May 8, 1807. He studied as choirboy at the Servites of Krulich, and afterwards at Prague, violin, pianoforte and composition. In 1799 he was violinist at the famous monastery church of Strahov; afterwards at Prague cathedral, and at the opera of that town. He composed quintets, quartets, and trios for strings, and 5 salutaris in 1800, for Strahov church, which all remained in MS.

STEPHAN KLACKEL (also called PATAN), b. Beraun, Bohemia, ca. 1753; d. Kositz, Bohemia, Mar. 19, 1788. First a choirboy at St. Egidius and pupil at the Latin school at Prague. Afterwards he studied the violin for two years under his brother at Böhmisch-Krummau and finally he studied physics for one year at Linz. After that he was appointed violinist at the Imperial theatre in Vienna, and then became capellmeister to Count Auersperg. The Emperor Joseph II gave him the means to study the violin in Paris for six months, at the end of which he toured as virtuoso in Germany and then resumed his position with Count Auersperg. Finally he became a member of the chapel of Count Thun in Bohemia, where he died prematurely of a fever. During the latter part of his life he composed diligently for the violin, but it is not known what became of his MSS.

ANTON JANITSCH (JANITZSCH), b. Bohemia, 1753; d. Burg-Steinfurt, Westphalia, Mar. 12, 1812. A pupil of Pugnani; concertmeister in the chapel of the Elector of Treves at Koblenz with a salary of 2,000 florins per annum, 1774–9. He was violinist at the Court of Count Oettingen at Wallerstein during 1782–5, after which he was expelled on account of his debts. He then went on tour and was, from ca. 1790 to ca. 1794, conductor in Grossman's theatre orchestra at Hanover. He visited Salzburg, where Leopold Mozart heard him (Jahn, Mozart, ii, 77). On Sept. 22, 1776, he gave a concert at Frankfort a/M. (Israel, 59). In 1794 he intended to visit England but broke the journey to spend the summer at the Court of Burg-Steinfurt. Meanwhile the war broke out and the unsettled conditions all over Europe caused him to remain in the service of the Count to the end of his days. Schubart praises his technique as well as his thoughtful rendering and adds that he was equally strong as soloist and as accompanist. Of his much-admired compositions none were published. Schilling gives a full biography of his life.

PETER FUCHS (FUX), b. Jan. 22, 1753, in Bohemia (?); d. Vienna, July 15, 1831. Studied at Prague, where he had already become prominent to some extent in 1768. Dittersdorf engaged him for the Episcopal chapel at Pressburg (Dittersdorf, Autobiog., p. 134), went thence to Esterhaz (1781/2) and from Mar. 1, 1782, to the time of his death, was a member of the Vienna Court chapel (Pohl, iv, 18). Köchel (i) gives, in one instance erroneously, the time of his death as Jan. 1. Composed violin sonatas with bass, some with violoncello and variations "a 3 soggietti" for 2 violins.

MATHIAS SOGKA, b. in Bohemia, 1755; distinguished violinist and organist. In 1788 he was in the service of Count Millesimo at Willinov, Moravia. He left in MS., concertos and sonatas for violin, apart from chamber music, symphonies and masses, which are highly praised.

FRANZ GÖTZ, b. Straschitz, Bohemia, ca. 1755. Received his first musical and general education as choirboy of the Jesuits of the Holy Mountain near Pribram, and afterwards at the seminary of St. Wenzeslaus. After taking his degree of B.A. and studying ecclesiastical history at Prague University he intended to join the Order of St. Benedict but changed his mind and accepted the offer of the place of 1st violin at the theatre at Brünn. After several years he left that position and went to Silesia, where he was successively conductor of the orchestra at several Abbey churches. During a sojourn at Breslau he made the acquaintance of Dittersdorf, who procured him the position of leader-conductor of the chapel of Johannisberg. When the chapel was dissolved he returned to Breslau, where he played at the coronation of King Frederic William II. Soon after that he was recalled to Brünn by Baron Kaschnitz, and entrusted with the direction of the theatre orchestra. In 1787 he became capellmeister of the Archbishop of Olmütz and was still there in 1799. During that period he wrote most of his compositions: symphonies, concertos, sonatas, trios and duos for violin, all of which remained in MS. Some of his symphonies were performed at the coronation of Joseph II in 1791 and of Franz I in 1792. (*See* Fétis, Mendel, Dlabacz.)

JOSEPH SCHUBERT, b. Warnsdorf, Bohemia, 1757; d. Dresden, July 28, 1833. He received his first music lessons from his father, a cantor and schoolmaster. Afterwards he went to Prague for his literary education, where he studied counterpoint under Abbé Fischer, and became a distinguished violinist. In 1778 he continued his violin studies under Kohn in Berlin. In 1779 he became a violinist at the Court of Schwedt, and in 1788 was appointed as viola player in the

Court chapel at Dresden. Mendel and Reissmann give a list of his numerous compositions, including 15 concertos, sonatas, and duets for violin, apart from other instrumental works, and several operas. A great number remained in MS.

JAKOB SCHELLER, b. Schettal, near Rackonitz, Bohemia, May 16, 1759; d. at a village in Friesland in 1803. He was a typical Bohemian vagrant musician, who started out as a small boy with a troupe of strolling players, when some Jesuits of the college at Prague recognized his talent and took him in charge to give him a general education. His love for an itinerant life, however, gained the upper hand, and soon he ran away to join a kind of gipsy band in Vienna, where he also heard good players who aroused his ambition, and these he strove to imitate. Thence he went to Munich, where he studied for some time under Cröner, then to Mannheim where, for two years, he was a member of the Court orchestra and received lessons in composition from Abbé Vogler. The desire to perfect himself in his art caused him to tour in Switzerland and Italy and to go on to Paris, where he became acquainted with Viotti and St. George and remained for three years studying hard to acquire the style of Viotti. After that he became concertmeister in the chapel of the Duke of Württemberg at Mömpelgard, where he remained till 1792 but lost that position through the French occupation. From that time he led a vagrant life, which brought about his moral and physical downfall. Gerber heard him in 1794, when he was already on his downward course. Rochlitz, in his "Freunde der Tonkunst" (vol. ii, p. 223), gives a graphic account of a visit which he received from him in 1802, when he had descended still lower. Both speak of his marvellous technique, his perfect purity of intonation, his brilliant staccato, as well as runs in octaves and thirds, and Rochlitz praises his soulful rendering of a simple folksong, upon which he improvised in the most musicianly manner. Both writers also tell us that he descended to all the tricks of charlatanism that would have delighted the audience of a low-class music hall, in the way of programme music and various imitations. Rochlitz records that while he looked shabby and showed the unmistakable traces of debauchery, his demeanour was dignified, not without self-conscious pride, adding that his motto was, even then, as it had been before, "One God—One Scheller," which he often repeated, as well as "Crying and laughing," as applied to his own playing.

FRANZ CHRISTOPH NEUBAUER (NEUBAUR), b. Horzin, Bohemia, ca. 1760; d. Bückeburg, Oct. 11, 1795. Studied music and science under the rector of a local school and showed remarkable talent. Later, he went to Prague for some time, then to Vienna as violin virtuoso. There he made the acquaintance of Haydn, Mozart, and Wranitzky, from which he derived great advantage, and also wrote an opera for Schikaneder. Afterwards he toured as violin virtuoso in the Rhineland and led a vagrant, adventurous life, now and again remaining for a time at some German Court or other. In 1789 he became capellmeister at the Court of Weilburg. When the chapel was dissolved on the invasion of the French, Neubauer fled to Minden, where he remained until the Prince of Lippe called him back to Bückeburg as composer to the Court by the side of Chr. Fr. Bach, who was somewhat jealous of Neubauer's new harmonic and orchestral effects, which were more advanced than his own, though sometimes marred by carelessness. He was full of talent and might have achieved more but for his instability and want of concentration. On the death of Bach he became first capellmeister, and married a young lady of good family, but died not long after from the effects of his irregular life. He composed: 8 sonatas for violin and viola; 3 sonatas do. do., op. 13; duets for 2 violins, violin and viola, violin and violoncello, and two violoncellos; symphonies, quartets, church music, operas, songs, etc.

ANTON WOLLANECK, b. Prague, Nov. 1, 1761; d. there 1849. A good violinist and organist. For several years he was conductor of the German and Bohemian theatres at Prague, then, in 1797 and 1798, in the same capacity at Leipzig. After that he was for eleven years organist at the Collegiate church of the Wischehrad, Prague; then violinist at the parish church of St. Adalbert, and from 1812 choirmaster of the church of St. Peter, for which he wrote some church music. He also composed violin sonatas, symphonies and dances for pianoforte, all pub. in 1807-9.

JOHANN WESSELY, b. Frauenberg, Bohemia, June 27, 1762; d. Ballenstedt, 1814. Studied the violin under his uncle, a Benedictine monk at Prague. He became an excellent violinist and composer in the style of Pleyel. In 1797 he was appointed to the theatre of Altona, and afterwards as 1st violinist at the theatre at Cassel. In 1800 he became concertmeister at the Court of Ballenstedt. He wrote a considerable number of trios and quartets for various instruments, also two operas and other vocal music, but nothing of importance for the violin.

FRANZ PECHATSCHEK, b. Wildenschwert, Bohemia, 1763; d. Vienna, 1821 (Wki.) (Mason Clarke: Sept. 26, 1816). He was a pupil of Lambert and Dittersdorf. In 1783 he went to Vienna, where he became one of the most popular violinists and favourite waltz composer. In 1790 he became conductor of the Kärntnertor theatre, for which he wrote 2 grand and 10 comic operas and 30 ballets of which "Das Waldweibchen" (The Little Woman of the Forest) obtained great popularity. He also composed 12 symphonies, masses and other church music, but it was chiefly his dances that endeared him to the Viennese of his time.

ADALBERT GYROWETZ, b. Budweis, Bohemia, Feb. 19, 1763; d. Vienna, Mar. 19, 1850. He showed very early talent for music, received the first music lessons from his father, choirmaster at the Cathedral, and began to compose as a pupil at the Piarist College, where he excelled also in all other studies. He entered Prague University for the study of law, but poverty and ill-health compelled him to abandon this after two years, and devote himself entirely to music. Count Fünfkirchen engaged him as his secretary and took him to Brünn to study the violin under Sanczek. Mozart introduced him as a composer to the Vienna public, who received his first symphonies enthusiastically. After that he studied counterpoint for two years under Sala at Naples. Through Count Batthyani's recommendation he became violinist in Prince Ruspoli's chapel, travelled, ca. 1787, with him over the greater part of Italy and earned laurels everywhere as a virtuoso. The Academy of Bologna made him an honorary member, and in Rome he made the acquaintance of Goethe, who soon after left for Naples. Gyrowetz went to Paris, where he found a publisher in Imbault. At the outbreak of the Revolution he went to London, where he was honoured and patronized by the Prince of Wales; but after a sojourn of three years, illness,

Bohemia: to 1800

caused by the English climate, compelled him to return to the Continent. After many tours he became, in 1804, capellmeister at the Imperial Court theatre in Vienna. When the management changed in 1827 he was pensioned and lived for the rest of his life in Vienna. He was one of the most fertile composers in all branches of music. A list of his works is given by Fétis, Mendel, etc. He had a facile talent for pleasing melody and excellent form, but lacked originality.

LORENZ SEICHE (SEICHERT), d. Prague, June 28, 1765. Started in 1712 as choirboy at St. Niklas, Prague, became violinist, and gave and appeared in concerts as soloist; had numerous pupils and composed many concertos for the violin (none enumerated in Eitner—*see* Dlabacz).

JAKOB JOHANN RYBA, b. Przesstiez, Bohemia, Oct. 26, 1765; d. Roczmittal, 1815. He received his first musical tuition from his father, an organist, from the age of 4. When 8 years old he was able to play faultlessly, concertos and sonatas by Wagenseil; he became equally efficient as violinist, cellist, harpsichord player, organist and composer. In 1780 the liberality of a relative enabled him to pursue his studies at the seminary of St. Wenceslaus at Prague. In 1788 he was appointed rector of the Gymnasium (college) at Roczmittal. He was a prolific composer with a strongly marked nationality, but only some German and Bohemian songs of his were published, the rest remained in MS.; these comprised 38 concertos, 87 sonatas, 130 sets of variations, 56 duets, etc., for various instruments, a large number of chamber-music works, orchestral and church compositions, also operas and melodramas.

ANDREAS BERNER, b. Bohemia, ca. 1766; d. Bonn, Aug. 5, 1791 (same as André Berner—Mendel, 564). An excellent violinist and good composer for his instrument (according to Neefe and Gerber). He was violinist in the Electoral chapel at Bonn. A symphony of his is said to have been pub. by Westphal, Hamburg, 1774. (*See* Eitner.)

JOHANN JANITZEK (JANICZEK?), b. Koschentin, Upper Silesia, 1768; d. Breslau, Apr. 8, 1806. Was chief huntsman of Count von Sobek, who gave him the opportunity to study music. In 1794 he was violinist and conductor at Wäser's theatre, Breslau, and conducted the "Richtersche Concert." Produced afterwards, in conjunction with Schnabel, big oratorio performances as leader of the orchestra. He died of a nervous fever.

MAXIMILIAN MAX, b. Winterberg, Bohemia, Dec. 27, 1769. Received his first musical and general education as choirboy of Passau cathedral; afterwards he studied theology at Prague and in 1792 he entered the Premonstratension order at Tepel. After the suppression of the monastery he went to Neumark and afterwards to Czihana. He is described as one of the best Bohemian violinists, who was also an excellent pianist and viol d'amour player. He composed trios for 2 violins and violoncello (Prague). (Fétis; Dlabacz).

JOHANN EYMANN. A violinist of great ability, ca. 1769, at Prague theatre (Dlabacz).

FRANZ HESSMANN. A native of Bohemia, who was a noted violin virtuoso at Prague, ca. 1770 (Gerber, ii; Dlabacz), where he was at that time considered the greatest violinist of Bohemia.

THOMAS MÜLLER, b. Strakonitz, Bohemia, ca. 1774. He was at first violinist at the "Theater Marinelli," Vienna, and afterwards went as capellmeister to Switzerland, where he died, 18... Dlabacz and Fétis enumerate 8 instrumental works by him as sonatas, duos, quartets, etc.

FRANZ MRAW (MRAF), b. in Bohemia. Earlier than 1784 he was in the chapel of the Count Kolowrat at Prague; from 1784 to 1786 in the chapel of Prince Esterhazy; then went, 1786, into Prince Batthyani's service at Pressburg, and died 1792 in the service of Prince Grassalkovicz in Hungary. (Pohl, iv, 18; Dlabacz.)

DOBWERIZIL, b. in Bohemia. During the last quarter of the 18th century he was 1st violinist at the German opera in Vienna. In 1783 he received the title of an Imperial chamber virtuoso (Gerber, i) on account of his remarkable technique.

ZYKA. An 18th-century Bohemian family of musicians of which at least six were members of the Berlin Court chapel. The following are mentioned there as violinists: ANTON, ca. 1786; FRANZ; JOSEF. The last-named was already violinist in the Royal chapel in 1783. In 1797 he composed operettas, also a stabat mater which he dedicated to the Tsar of Russia, who presented him with a valuable diamond ring. Two other members were violoncellists, of whom the elder JOSEPH B. ZYKA acquired fame as a virtuoso and composer; another, FERDINAND ZYKA, was a viola player.

FRANZ HOSSA. A Bohemian violin and viola (Mendel) virtuoso, ca. 1790 at Erlangen, who appeared at the Gewandhaus concerts at Leipzig, 1791–4 (Dörffel, ii, 25), went thence to Vienna (Gerber, ii).

ANDREAS PERNER, b. Prague, came from Frankfort a/M. to Bonn, where he was engaged as violinist at the National theatre and died there, still young, on Aug. 6, 1791. He was an instrumental composer, but no works are mentioned in Eitner (Thayer; Beethoven; Reichardt, 1791, mentions him as violinist in 1789).

WENZEL BRAUTNER. An excellent violinist and conductor at Prague, 1796; ca. 1800 choirmaster at the Thein- and Kreuzherrn churches there; composed masses, motets, etc., which were widely popular in his time. He also enjoyed a wide reputation as singing-master, though somewhat eccentric. He brought together a fine collection of stringed instruments.

CARL WLICECK, b. Prague, 1794. 1st violinist at the National theatre, Prague, and teacher of the violin. Wrote a violin tutor in the Ceskian language (Prague, 1833) which appeared also in a German ed.

FRANZ GLÄSER, b. Obergeorgenthal, Bohemia, Apr. 19, 1798; d. Copenhagen, Aug. 29, 1869 (Riemann: 1861). A pupil of Pixis at the Prague Conservatoire; an excellent violinist who devoted himself, from 1817, entirely to conducting, and the composition of operas and numerous other works for the theatre.

KARÁZEK. Lived during the second half of the 18th century. A Bohemian violin virtuoso who composed symphonies, concertos, etc., which were pub. (Dlabacz). Fétis says: He made himself known by his concertos for bassoon and violoncello and symphonies, which remained in MS.

WENZEL KRAL. About 1800 he was a violinist in the theatre orchestra at Prague. The *Leipziger Zeitung*, 2505, praises him as possessing a good technique and good taste and style. A "graduale" of his in MS. is in Kloster Neuburg.

VINCENZ HODSPOTZKY. A violinist of the 18th and 19th centuries. Began as choirboy at Salzburg cathedral, together with his brother GEORGE HODSPOTZKY, who became afterwards Court and chamber musician at Munich. Vincenz distinguished himself as violin virtuoso and died 1832 (Peregrinus, 121).

PICKEL (PICKL). A Bohemian, who was a pupil of Ferd. David, and concertmeister in St. Petersburg (Wki., 461).

CHAPTER 22

France: to 1725

THE self-sufficient despotism of the Twenty-four Violins of the King on one side, and that of the Confrérie de Saint-Julien" (Musicians' Guild) on the other, had a paralysing influence on the progress of Music in France, which by nature was not musical in the higher sense, as we know from the utterings of J. J. Rousseau; Vidal (les instrument à archet) says when singers, coming from a practice or performance of their choral union, want to sing something by their own initiative, they invariably sing out of tune; the opinion of the Mozarts, father and son, was no better, and Gluck is reported to have said that if he should receive 20 lires for an opera, he ought to be paid 20,000 lires for training the singers and players to perform it. This explains the vigorous and vicious persecution by the above-named corporations of any musician who by his or her superior talents might prove a danger by exposing their ignorance and incapacity.

Some members of the Confrérie went so far as to prosecute the Canon, who was also organist of a Cathedral, for giving organ lessons to some of his choir boys, without being a member of the guild, and a priest who was choirmaster at his church was told that he must only call himself dancing-master, to force him to join the Confrérie. Have we not a parallel to this even to-day! Several Acts of Parliament appeared to curtail and even revoke their privileges, but they continued their nefarious proceedings, whereof some of their foremost musicians became the victims, until the musicians of the whole country rose up against them, petitioned the King, and obtained a decree for the abolition and suppression of their lieutenants-general in the provinces and all their traffic in privileges, but it was not until 1776 that, after the abolition of the rois des violons, the Confrérie de Saint-Julien was finally dissolved.

These circumstances make it easily comprehensible why the art of violin playing remained at a low standard during the greater part of the 18th century in spite of the appearance of such excellent artists as Anet, Sénallié, Francœur, L'Abbé fils, the great J. M. Leclair and others who, however, had all to suffer from the intrigues of their above-mentioned countrymen, who even murdered Leclair, the greatest of their number.

It was not until the arrival of Gluck in Paris, in 1773, that a distinct change in the musical conditions of the city set in. With untiring zeal Gluck worked at the improvement of orchestral playing and succeeded within a comparatively short time to raise the standard of the opera orchestra appreciably. This roused the spirit of emulation, and led to the improvement of all other Paris orchestras. The most epoch-making event in the French history of violin playing was the arrival of Viotti in Paris in 1782. He transplanted the school of Corelli, Vivaldi, and Tartini to the latter city and became the Father of Modern Violin playing, transmitting the teaching of the classical masters of Italy to the whole of Europe through his direct pupils, as well as those who had taken him as their model, by a close study of his style from personal observation, like Kreutzer and Baillot, and by the study of his compositions, especially his concertos, several of which have retained their artistic as well as their violinistic value to the present time. Viotti is also credited, by his advice, with a share in the final perfecting of the shape of the bow which was achieved by François Tourte (1747–1835), who brought the bow to its highest perfection by the perfect proportions of the thickness and camber of the stick and the elegant shape of the head. He is also credited with the addition to the nut of the slide and the ferrule, but, as Hy. Saint-George ("The Bow," etc., p. 37) pointed out, these were also used by John Dodd (1752–1839), the famous English bow-maker, who was born only five years later than Tourte, and probably never saw a specimen of the latter's workmanship.

JEAN FRANÇOIS DANDRIEU, b. Paris, ca. 1684; d. there Jan. 16, 1740. The famous clavecin composer and organist at the Royal chapel wrote: Trios for 2 violins, dessus de violon, and bass, op. 1, Paris, 1705 (Paris, Nat.); Livre de 6 sonates a violin, seul, op. 2, Paris, 1710, Foucault; 6 sonatas (copy in Brit. Mus.); other ed. Amsterdam, Roger. Also a suite de pièces for violins [?*sic.*] called "Les caractères de la guerre" (Fétis), Paris, Boivin, 1729.

BAPT. ANET, pupil of Corelli from 1696 to 1700, when he returned to Paris where he was hailed as the greatest French violinist; this, under the circumstances, did not mean much. Louis XIV, who was biased by his Twenty-four Violins, did not receive him favourably, and in 1738 we find him at the Court of the Polish Ex-King Stanislaus Lesczinski. He died at Lunéville, 1755 (Jacquot, "La mus. en Lorraine"). He wrote 3 books of violin sonatas which were published. He was generally known as "Baptiste" (*see* under "Batiste" at Warsaw Court—Eitner). Daquin says that when Anet played to Corelli some of that great master's compositions, he was so touched by his playing that he embraced him and presented him with his bow. (Pougin relates several anecdotes to prove Anet's importance.)

JEAN MARIE LECLAIR, L'AÎNÉ, b. Lyons, May 10, 1697; assassinated in Paris, Oct. 22, 1764; son of a lacemaker who also played in the Lyons orchestra. The Marquise de Mésangère charged herself with his upbringing. He first played the violin at dances and even was engaged as a dancer himself at the Rouen theatre. Afterwards, ca. 1722, he became first dancer and balletmeister at Turin, where he attracted the attention of Somis, who took him as a pupil. In 1723 he was in Paris. In 1728 he made his first very successful appearance at the Concert Spirituel and by 1729 he was violinist at the opera with a salary of 450 francs, raised to 500 francs in 1735. In 1731 he became chamber musician in the King's chapel. On the second book of his sonatas he calls himself "Ordinaire de la musique de la chambre du Roy." At that time he lived in the rue St. Benoist du coté de l'Abeis, Faubourg Saint-Germain. Through a quarrel with Guignon, leader of the 2nd violins, he resigned from the opera in 1735 and lived by teaching and by his compositions, which his wife engraved on copper and also published partly after his death. On a journey to Holland he made the acquaintance of Locatelli, who exercised a distinct influence over his style of composition. About his compositions *see* elsewhere (also M.f.M., xx, 164, 169). Works in Eitner.

The History of the Violin

At the age of nineteen Leclair married a young girl at Lyons who died after only a few years of married life, and in 1730 he married Louise Roussel, aged 30, the clever engraver who engraved his second book of sonatas and all later, including his posthumous, works. After the death of his first wife until that time he had lived with his wealthy patron Bonnier, to whom he dedicated his first book of sonatas. Between his sojourn in, and his first journey to, Turin in 1722 he appears to have stayed some time in Paris, there meeting Bonnier and his son, and also studied composition under André Cheron, afterwards inspector of music and conductor at the opera. Laborde states that the basses of his first sonatas were the work of Cheron, to whom he inscribed his concertos, op. VII; in the dedication he says: "If they contain any beauties, they are due to the excellent lessons I have received from you." On his first journey to Holland he met and benefited by the advice of Locatelli; when is not known; but his second visit was in 1740. He was assassinated near his house by the unknown hand, through jealousy of the musicians.

LOUIS TRAVENOL, b. Paris, ca. 1698; d. there, ca. 1783. Violinist at the Grand Opera from 1739 to 1759, when he was pensioned. He was noted for his pamphlets attacking Voltaire, who caused both him and his aged father to be imprisoned. They were however released after five days and awarded substantial damages against their accuser. He defended French music against the criticism of Rousseau in two pamphlets (1754). He appears also to have quarrelled with his colleagues at the opera. He wrote "Premier livre de sonates pour violon seul avec la basse, par Travenol le fils, Paris," 1739; also "Histoire du Théâtre de l'Opéra" (1753), together with Durey de Nounville. An undeveloped 11-bar movement in Cartier's collection is insufficient to form an opinion of his work.

LE COCQ. All violinists at the Court chapel, Brussels: JACQUES LE COCQ, ca. 1660 and still in 1673. GUILLAUME LE COCQ, ca. 1673. FRANÇOIS LE COCQ, before 1729 (composer of guitar pieces). JEAN LE COCQ, ca. 1729, taille or viol (E. v. d. Str., v, 153). NICOLAS LE COCQ, ca. 1742 till after 1745 double bass (E. v. d. Str., v, 181).

France: to 1725

FRANÇOIS REBEL (REBEL FILS), b. Paris, June 19, 1701; d. there Nov. 7, 1775. Dates vary, apparently, with Grove. Pupil of his father; became violinist at the opera, 1714, with a salary of 600 livres and from 1735 with an additional gratuity of 500 francs. During the festivities at the coronation of Charles VI at Prague he became a close friend of Francœur, together with whom he composed operas; they also shared the same appointments, first as inspectors of the Royal Academy of Music (opera) and, 1751 to 1767, as directors. In 1760 his salary was 3,000 francs; then superintendent of Royal Music; by 1772 he was general administrator of the opera; retired Apr. 1, 1775 (Pougin; Gregoir, "Panth.," v, 109). For a poem on his opera "Ismene" in 1760, Louis XV made him a knight of the Order of St. Michael. L. de La Laurencie (Grove): during 1733-44 Rebel and Francœur were joint leaders at the opera, and in 1753 managers, but they soon retired on account of petty vexations. In 1757 they obtained the *privilège* of the opera, which they held until 1767 and considerably raised its standard. Fr. Rebel composed some cantatas, a Te Deum and De Profundis, but all that survived of his music is a dance tune from his opera "Pyrame et Thisbé," written as a "pas seul" for the famous dancer Camargo, which became known as "La Camargo."

ANTOINE REMI LECLAIR (called LE CADET), b. Lyons, Sept. 23, 1703; d. there Nov. 30, 1777; a brother of Jean Marie Leclair. He composed: 1er livre de sonates a violin seul et B.c. (Paris). Fétis thinks that these 12 sonatas were pub. ca. 1760. Maupetit's Minuets contain one number by him. Pougin states that he composed 2 books of sonatas. He was first violinist in the concert orchestra and at the opera at Lyons until he died.

DUPLESSIS, L'AÎNÉ. From 1704 to 1748 a violinist in the Paris Opera. Composed 2 books of Sonatas for the violin (Chansons in Ballard's Airs of 1702 and 1710).

DUPLESSIS, LE JEUNE, a brother of above, and violinist in the Paris Opera, with a salary of 450 livres. He was director of "Magasin de l'Opéra" music school in 1748, from which he retired in Dec., 1749. Composed "Les fêtes nouvelles," in 3 acts, performed at the opera on July 22, 1734.

The History of the Violin

GABRIEL GUILLEMAIN, b. Paris, Nov. 15, 1705; committed suicide on the journey from Paris to Versailles, Oct. 1, 1770. The name of his master is not known, but it is believed that he owed most of his art to natural ability, and the study of Corelli's works. Pougin says that some think that he went to Italy in early youth and studied under Somis, and that on his return he was for some years a member of the Dijon Concert orchestra. In 1738 he became a chamber musician in the Royal chapel, Paris. He was also a member of Mme Pompadour's private orchestra, but, being of a modest disposition, he never used his high patronage to further his own interests. He had a brilliant technique, especially of the left hand, and appeared with great success at the Court concerts both as soloist and in duets together with Guignon; but an invincible timidity born of a lack of self-confidence, prevented him from ever appearing at the Concert Spirituel, where he was known only by his compositions. Guillemain delighted in overloading his compositions with difficulties of every description, but as, unlike those of Le Claire, they lacked the stamp of genius, and were conceived merely for the display of virtuosity, they failed to interest the few who could master their technical difficulties. Pougin says that in a fit of frenzy while walking from Paris to Versailles he stabbed himself 14 times with a knife as he was approaching Chaville. He had composed by then 14 works of sonatas and trios. His divertissement "La Cabale" was successfully performed in 1749. After that he wrote three more works, the last, op. 17, appearing in 1759. Riemann, who gives a list, says that his sonatas, op. 13, are among the earliest ensemble works in which the harpsichord and the violin are treated as *concerted* instruments (i.e. as of equal importance).

FAVRE. A violinist in the Paris opera orchestra, ca. 1705, which he left in 1730 when he retired to Lyons, where he died in 1747. Fétis enumerates Sonatas, pub. Boivin, before 1729, and Menuets for 2 violins and bass of his composition. The Paris National Library has Sonates pour violon, 2^d livre (1731).

LOUIS QUENTIN, L'AÎNÉ and LE JEUNE. Fétis mentions only one, LOUIS—violinist at the Paris Grand Opera 1706–49, when he retired on a pension. He is said to have brought out 4 books of violin sonatas and 3 books of trios for 2 violins and bass. Eitner only knows "Sonates pour Violin," 1ʳ livre, Paris, 1730, Boivin; Paris Nat. in catalogue as "l'aîné." The same library has by Q. le jeune "Sonates pour Violon," 1, 2, 3 livres, Paris, No. 1, dated 1724, Boivin, folio. The Paris Conservatoire has also "Sonates de Violin," but in catalogue without further distinction.

CHARLES LA FERTÉ. One of the Twenty-four Violins of the King (Louis XIV). Wrote: "Premier livre de sonates pour le violon et la basse," Paris, Camus Sellier, 1707. Fétis says that he lived at Bordeaux in 1743, when he wrote a book of sonatas for violin solo, pub. in Paris. It appears doubtful whether this refers to a second book or whether it is based on an error on the part of Fétis in mistaking the date of the pub. of the first book.

DE VAL. A violinist who taught Birckenstock in Paris ca. 1708/9 (Wasielewski, p. 237). According to Pougin the same as: FRANÇOIS DUVAL, d. Paris, Jan., 1723 (*see* Besson, p. 246). Violinist of the chapel of Louis XIV and XV from 1704 to the time of his death. He was the first French musician who wrote violin sonatas in the Italian style. Of such sonatas he wrote 7 books, all pub. in Paris. He was greatly esteemed by the Dukes of Orleans and de Noailles, on whose recommendation he played also before the King, who accepted the dedication of his 3rd and 5th books of sonatas; books 1 and 2 were dedicated respectively to his Ducal patrons; the 2nd book consisted of trio sonatas for 2 violins and bass, the 1st contained "sonatas and other pieces" for violin solo and bass. Book 6 is entitled "Amusements pour la chambre" and book 7 "Les idées musiciennes"; both consist of solo sonatas with bass. He called himself "Symphoniste ordinaire" of the chamber and chapel of the King and violinist attached to the private music of the Duke of Orleans. Pougin says that apparently he was the first French violinist who used double stopping, and that he deserves a high place among French violinists.

PIERRE LECLAIR, b. Lyons, Nov. 19, 1709. Brother of Jean Marie (*see* p. 237). Pierre wrote a book of 6 duos for 2 violins, op. 1, published by Lemeru, Paris, 1764; the year in which Jean Marie Leclair died. As his brother Antoine, he was a violinist in the concert and theatre orchestra at Lyons.

JEAN BENOIT LECLAIR, b. Lyons, Sept. 25, 1714, another brother of Jean Marie, is probably identical with the J. B. Leclair who in 1749 was director of the theatre at Liège and afterwards of that at Brussels, where on Apr. 2, 1749, he had a grand ballet of his composition performed. In 1750 he was director of the theatre at Gand in company with a man named Langlois.

JOSEPH EXAUDET (EXAUDÉ), b. Rouen, ca. 1710 (Pougin: 1700); d. Paris, 1763. 1st violin at the concert (Academy) at Rouen; thence he went to Paris, where he became one of the Twenty-four Violins of the King and a member of the Opera Orchestra in 1749, which position he held to the end. He was also violinist in the orchestra of the Concert Spirituel. He is best known by his famous Minuet. He wrote 6 trios pour 2 violins et bass oe. 2 (Paris); sonates a violin seul avec bass oe. 3 in MS. The Wagner library has: 6 sonates pour violin et bass, Dedie a Mr. Chartraire de Bourbonne.

JEAN JOSEPH CASSANEA DE MONDONVILLE, b. Narbonne, Dec. 24, 1711; d. Belleville, near Paris, Oct. 8, 1772; he came of a good but impoverished family. After his marriage he added his wife's name "de Mondonville" to his own family name of Cassanea. He began in early youth to study the violin, becoming an eminent executant. From Paris, where he was in 1733, and published 6 violin sonatas with bass, he went to Lille, where he was for some time conductor of the public concerts. In 1734 he made his successful début at the Concert Spirituel in Paris, returning to Lille until 1737, when he settled permanently in Paris, where henceforth he was often heard either alone or in duets with Guignon at the Concert Spirituel, where both were great favourites of the public. Possessing a genius for intrigue, he succeeded by his elegant manner and suppleness to win the good graces of Mme de Pompadour, and with this powerful support he began to compose motets and even oratorios which were performed at the Concert Spirituel from 1738 to 1770 and met with such success that in 1755 he succeeded Royer as director of that institution, and occupied the post until 1762, showing great ability both as conductor and administrator. Royer,

France: to 1725

up to the time of his death, had paid him 1,200 livres per annum for all his latest compositions with the reservation that they were to be performed only at the Concert Spirituel. He became a Royal chamber musician in 1739, and in 1744 he succeeded Gervais as intendant of the Royal chapel at Versailles. He also composed a number of operas, some of which had at least a passing success and contained some graceful music. In connexion with his activity in that direction, Weckerlin tells an amusing anecdote in his "Dernier Musiciana," which shows the facility with which he composed. A friend who had supplied him with the book for an opera, called to see how it was getting on. Mondonville, who had not written a note of it yet, told him: "It is quite finished"—Splendid! Let me hear some of it.—(Search for the score in various drawers without result.)—Never mind! Give me the book. I shall remember. He sits down to the harpsichord and improvises the first act recitatives and all. The friend goes away delighted and tells all Paris about the new masterpiece. He had evidently a strong sense of humour, which is shown also by his setting in cantata form, pub. in 1760, of the "Privilege du Roy" which had to be printed with every musical publication of the time. It is written for voices, strings, oboes, and horns. Mondonville was credited by his compatriots with the invention of the harmonics, although they were known before his time, but he appears to be the first to use them in a systematic manner. This he did in "Lessons Harmoniques. Sonates a violon seul avec la basse continue" ... op. 4. In a preface he explains how they are to be produced and adds a diagram showing their position on the strings of the violin. The fifth of these sonates has been re-pub. in Alard's "Maîtres Classiques, No. 43" (Schott). He also wrote 6 sonatas for harpischord and violin, op. 3, which were also pub., for violin and flute, etc., by Walsh. The Air from the fifth sonata appeared in the *Mercure de France* of Jan., 1761, as a song with the words, "Tendre Amour," etc. The first sonata was played by members of the Dolmetsch family at the Haslemere Festival of ancient chamber music, 1929, and proved so delightful that part of it had to be repeated. Another book of violin pieces is entitled "Pièces de clavecin avec voix ou violon," op. 5, dedicated to the Bishop of Rennes; it consists of settings of

Latin texts from the psalms in eight separate numbers and contains instructions for the manner in which they should be studied: he adds a note to the effect that "Persons who play the harpsichord but have no voice, can have that part played by the violin. In default of both voice and violin, the accompaniment may be played as a piece by itself." Mondonville had an eye to business. (For a detailed description of his sonatas *see* E. v. d. Str., "Eighteenth-Century Violin Sonatas," *The Strad*, May and June, 1921.)

A son of Mondonville, b. Paris, ca. 1740 (Fétis ca. 1748), d. there 1808, was also a violinist whom Gerber knew as such in Germany in 1767. In that year 6 violin sonatas by this Mondonville were pub. in Paris. He became afterwards an oboe player.

JEAN MONDONVILLE, called Le Jeune or Le Cadet; b. Narbonne, Apr. 15, 1716; is mentioned in Grove's Dictionary as a younger brother of Jean Joseph, who was an "Ordinaire de la Musique du Roi." He composed a collection of sonatas in 1767 and is lost sight of after 1769. There appears to be some confusion with the son of Jean Joseph.

ANTOINE, DAUVERGNE (D'AUVERGNE), b. Clermond-Ferrand, Oct. 4, 1713; d. Lyons, Feb. 12, 1797; son and pupil of the 1st violin in the "Concert" of Clermont. He went to Paris in 1739 for further study, and appeared in 1740 at the Concert Spirituel with such success that in 1741 he was appointed to the Royal chapel, and 1742 to the Grand Opera. From 1751 to 1755 he was conductor at the opera and afterwards director, a post which he held with some interruptions till 1790. In 1752 he wrote a ballet "Amours de Tempé" and in 1753 an opéra comique "Les Trompeurs." In 1755 he bought the position of composer for the Royal chapel and the reversion of the place of master of the Royal chamber music, which compelled him to resign his post at the opera. In 1762 he succeeded Mondonville as director of the Concert Spirituel. 1769 to 1776 he was superintendent, and 1780–2 director of the Royal Private Musick again. These positions he exchanged several times until the outbreak of the Revolution, May 9, 1790, when he fled to Lyons, remaining there till his death. He composed for the violin: "Sonates de violon oe. 2," Paris, 1739; 12 sonates a violon et basse (MS., Dresden

France: to 1725

Museum). Pougin says that he pub. a collection of 92 violin Sonatas, and another of trios for 2 violins and bass: 6 of his sonatas have been re-pub. in Alard's "Maîtres Classiques," one by Eitner (ii), and an allegro composed in 1739 appears in Cartier's collection.

JOSEPH MARCHAND, d. ca. 1737, at Paris. He was a violinist in the Court chapel at Paris from 1717, in which his father Jean was lutenist and violinist (dessus), ca. 1691, and his uncle Jean Noel a violinist, ca. 1686. He composed "Pièces et Sonates pour le Violon," dedicated to the King (Paris, 1707) (Paris, Nat. Library). Fétis mentions also "12 sonates pour flute trav. ou hautboy ou violin avec B.c.," Paris, 1709, 4° with a 2nd ed. in 1732, which Eitner failed to trace. He also composed a pastoral and other plays for Court festivities. Pougin enumerates the following members of the same family, all members of the Twenty-four Violins of the King, viz. PIERRE MARCHAND, appointed Oct. 31, 1695, as successor to his son Joseph II, appointed Jan. 12, 1695; JOSEPH MARCHAND, III, appointed Aug. 20, 1706; CHARLES PHILIPPE MARCHAND, apparently son of Joseph II, appointed Mar. 1, 1731, in succession of the latter.

PIERRE DUPONT. A music and dancing master who wrote in 1718 a little tutor, "Principes de violon par demandes et par reponses, par lequel toutes personnes pourront apprendre d'eux-mêmes a jouer dudit instrument." Although a poor work, written in bad French, it is historically interesting as it gives advice for shifting into the second and third positions, thus proving that their use was generally known at that time. Apart from the very elementary tutor by Monteclair, the above appears to have been the only one in more or less general use, for even as late as 1740 Boivin brought out a new edition, and it was not before 1760 that L'Abbé's "Principes du Violon" appeared: this was the first serious book of its kind in France.

GERVAIS, ca. 1719. Violinist and conductor of the chapel of the Duke of Orleans and also violinist at the Paris Opera. His sister, a principal dancer there, married his colleague, Perignon, 1st violinist at the opera.

LOUIS AUBERT, b. Paris, May 15, 1720; eldest son of Jacques Aubert, was in 1798 in retirement on a pension of 1,000 francs from the opera. He joined the opera in 1731, aged 11, and a few years later he appeared at the Concert Spirituel. In 1755 he became leader of the 1st violins at the opera and therewith deputy of Chéron "for beating time." This post he retained till his retirement in 1771. His pub. compositions for violin comprise 6 books of solos, 6 books of duets, 2 concertos and several other works, including dance tunes for the opera. (Fétis.)

EMIL ROBERT BRIJON, b. Lyons, ca. 1720. He became a professor of music in that city, and wrote "Réflexions sur la musique et sur la vraie manière de l'exécuter sur le violon," Paris, 1763, 4°; also another theoretical work.

ANDRÉ NOEL PAGIN, b. Paris, 1721. A pupil of Tartini. He appeared in 1750 at the Concert Spirituel, Paris, in compositions by his master only, which the Paris musicians resented so much that they deprecated and boycotted him. Tartini thought so much of Pagin that he dedicated a book of sonatas to him. He retired from public life, received an annuity of 6,000 francs from his patron the Duke of Clermont, and henceforth only played in private circles, devoting his life to his art. Burney heard him in 1770 and praises him. Compositions: "6 sonatas for violin and bass, op. 1," Paris, Boivin, 1748; a sonata in Elis. Hare's "six sonatas;" adagio in Cartier, and sonata 5 in Alard, Maîtres Classiques, No. 47.

LEONARD ITIER. A lutenist and violinist under Louis XIV, ca. 1721–80. (La Borde, 143; Pougin, with documents.)

CHARLES ANTOINE BRANCHE, b. Vernon-sur-Seine, 1722. Was violinist at the Comédie Française, Paris, for thirty years. He composed 6 sonatas for violin solo, book 1; pub. Paris, 1748. Farrenc notes compositions: 12 sonates œuv. 1, fol.

GABRIEL BESSON. He succeeded F. du Val on Jan. 26, 1723, as one of the famous Twenty-four Violins of the King of France, and composed two books of sonatas for violin, pub. Paris, ca. 1720 (12 sonatas, for violin solo, 1er livre, Paris: Fétis).

CLAUDE JACQUES MARSELLE. Is mentioned in 1723 as chamber musician for the violin in the Munich Court chapel.

M. DENIS. At the beginning of the 18th century, master of the music at the cathedrals of Tourney and of St. Omer.

France: to 1725

Afterwards he was engaged in many French and Belgian towns as a musician. Composed 2 books of violin sonatas with bass, the first appearing in 1723. (Pougin.)

JEAN LAMOLINARY (LAMONINARY), b. Valenciennes beginning of 18th century. 1st violin at concert there: composed 3 books of trios for 2 violins and bass oe. 1, 2, 3 (Paris, 1749), and string quartets, op. 4 (Paris, Nat.).

ANDRÉ JACQUES MARC. Was a violinist in the Royal chapel in Paris about the beginning of the 18th century. He composed "Livre 1er de pièces de dessus et pardessus de viole" (Paris, 1724). The Christian names are given according to Fétis, who dates the work 1739. He calls himself "Violon du concert de Reims" on 6 sonates a violon seul avec une basse chiffrée, Paris et Reims, chez l'auteur (from copy once in the possession of Liepmanssohn).

DR. PEER. A Frenchman who studied the violin in Paris at the expense of the Landgrave of Cassel, at the beginning of the 18th century, and was appointed to his Court chapel at a high salary. He was also an architect and captain of engineers. (Eitner.)

BÉNARD. An early 18th-century French violinist who composed a book of violin solos, pub., according to Walther, in 1729.

MECHEL. Wrote 7 books of sonatas for violin (Gerber, ii), pub. Paris (?), early 18th century. Probably misprint for Michel (q.v.).

CHAPTER 23

France: to 1750

JOSEPH TOUCHEMOULIN (TOUCHMOLIN, DOUSMOLIN), b. Chalons, ca. 1727; d. Ratisbon, Oct. 25, 1801. He entered the chapel of the Elector of Cologne, at Cologne and Bonn, where his salary as chamber musician amounted (Mar. 11, 1753) to 1,000 florins. The Elector enabled him to visit Italy, where he perfected himself under Tartini and in 1761 he became capellmeister at Bonn. Under the Elector Max Friedrich his salary was reduced to 400 florins. He resigned, and received a post at the Court of Thurn and Taxis at Ratisbon. In 1754 he played at the Concert Spirituel in Paris (Thayer, i, 28, 32). He composed some sonatas for violin and bass (4 in MS., Bruss. Cons.), also symphonies and pianoforte (harpsichord) concertos, and a mass. Mendel says he left in MS. many masses and other church music, operas, symphonies and concertos.

Schubart says about him: "His taste (style) is quite French, soft and sweet; although he plays the violin with power, yet in a manner which cannot please everybody."

His son LUDWIG was already playing concertos on the violin at the age of 12. According to Gerber he became deaf in later age.

JOSEPH BARNABÉ DE SAINT SÉVIN, called L'ABBÉ LE FILS (from his clerical garb as church musician), b. Agen, June 11, 1727; d. at his house near Charenton (according to Fétis in 1787). Son of Philippe Pierre de Saint-Sevin, at that time musician at the church. He came to Paris on Nov. 11, 1731; became violinist at the Comédie Française in 1739, studied under Leclair, appointed to the orchestra of the Grand Opera, May 1, 1742. At the age of only 14 he played, together with P. Gaviniés, a sonata for 2 violins by Leclair at the

Concert Spirituel. He retired in 1762 to Charenton without a pension, as the government considered him too young, although entitled to it by the twenty years of service. He wrote 8 books of violin sonatas with bass and several sets of airs for 1 and 2 violins (the latter also for pardessus or 1 flute or oboe with 1 violin), and a tutor "Principes du Violon" (Paris, 1772). From 1741 to 1755 he gave regular and well-patronized subscription concerts, which increased not only his reputation as an artist, but brought him also a considerable fortune, enabling him to buy a country seat near Charenton, where he lived in retirement from 1776, highly esteemed both as man and as artist.

His "Principes du Violon" is the first French tutor for the violin of any real value; although the text is rather poor. The book was intended to serve also as a tutor for the treble viol (pardessus de viole); *see* E. v. d. Str., "The Romance of the Fiddle."

PIERRE GAVINIÉS, b. Bordeau, May 11, 1728; d. Paris, Sept. 9, 1800. He was the son of a violin maker. It is not known from whom he received his first instruction in violin playing, nor did he continue his studies under any one particular master, but he gathered knowledge and experience by keen observation of the great virtuosos who appeared in Paris. Pougin suggests that when in 1741 at the Concert Spirituel, at the age of 13, he played with sensational success a sonata for 2 violins by Leclair with l'Abbé, aged 14, that great master's pupil, Leclair would naturally have supervised their rehearsals and given technical advice also to Gaviniés; also that he may have continued to do so without the former becoming a regular pupil, and that with his great musical intelligence, Gaviniés absorbed a great deal of Leclair's art of playing, and it may be said that he was the real successor of that great master in the evolution of the French school of violin playing by the use of his method and his compositions.

He was of a very impressionable character, and became involved in a love affair with a married lady, which was discovered. To escape the vengeance of the husband he fled from Paris, but was captured and suffered a year's imprisonment. During this time he composed a piece which as the "Romance de Gaviniés" became very popular, and never failed to touch the hearts of his listeners when he played it with improvised variations. In 1762 he became leader at the Concert Spirituel, but resigned that post in 1764; however, in 1773 he became director of that institute together with Leduc aîné and Gossec. He had frequently played as a soloist at these concerts as well as together with his pupils and became a great favourite of the public, which greeted his directorship as the beginning of a new era. Leduc died in 1777 and both Gossec and Gaviniés withdrew from the directorate. When the Conservatoire was founded in 1794 Gaviniés was appointed professor for the violin, a post which he occupied to the time of his death. He possessed a technique which showed a great advance on that of his predecessors and his "vingt quatre matinées" are still among the most difficult studies for advanced students. Viotti called him the French Tartini, but if he surpassed the latter in technique, he possessed neither his soul nor his genius. He was, however, a most successful teacher, and among his foremost pupils may be mentioned: Lemière l'aîné, Paisible, Leduc l'aîné, Imbault, Baudron, Verdiguier, Robineau, Capron, Guénée and Dufresne. Of his compositions, only the matinées are still of practical value; the others are: 6 violin concertos; 6 solo sonatas with bass, op. 1; 6 do. do., op. 3; and 3 posthumous solo sonatas, of which one is entitled "Le tombeau de Gaviniés."

JEAN JOSEPH RODOLPHE (RUDOLPH) (Dlabacz, Schilling, Sittard). He gives his Christian names on the title of his opera "L'Aveugle de Palmyre." B. Strassburg, Oct. 14, 1730; d. Paris, Aug. 18, 1812. (Eitner, Fétis; Jahn, ii, 276; Schubart, p. 154; Pohl, ii, 373; Pougin.) From the age of 7 he studied the horn and the violin. He had already distinguished himself as an excellent horn player when at the age of 16 he went to Paris to perfect himself on the violin under Leclair. Afterwards he was engaged as 1st violin at Bordeaux, then at Montpellier and other towns in the provinces in the middle of France. Ca. 1754 he entered the Court orchestra at Parma, where Traëtta became his master of composition and also wrote a horn obbligato for him on an air for Signora Petraglia. In 1760 he went to Stuttgart, where he finished his theoretical studies under Jomelli and wrote the music for some ballets. In 1763 he returned to Paris, where he appears to have devoted himself chiefly to the horn, and in 1784 became professor of musical theory at the Conservatoire, lost his position in 1789, but was appointed in 1799 as singing-master and was pensioned in 1802. During several years he was violinist at the Théâtre Français. His compositions consist of 3 books of duets and studies for violin, operas, concertos and 2 theoretical works, both adversely criticized by Fétis, though one, the "Elements of Music," was widely used at one time.

ANTON RODOLPHE (RUDOLPH), b. Vienne (?), ca. 1770. Much of his biography requires investigating. He was a son of the preceding Jean Jos. Rodolphe. (*See* Eitner, "Q.L.")

PIERRE VACHON, b. Arles, 1731; d. Berlin, 1802. A pupil of Chabran (Chas.) at Paris for violin and composition. In 1758 he played his own compositions at the Concert Spirituel with success. He became 1st violin to Prince Conti in 1761, wrote numerous instrumental works and began to write for the opera. In 1772 he visited London (Pohl, ii, 370). He was at the Court of Mayence (Cramer, ii, 218) in 1772 and by 1786 was concertmeister at Berlin, next to Benda. He was pensioned in 1798 (Fétis, Ledebur). Compositions: Solo sonatas with bass, op. 1 and op. 3; concerto for violin and violoncello ('cello part by J. P. Duport); 1 duet for violin and violoncello in G; trios, 2 violins and bass; quartets, symphonies, 1 overture, very feeble operas and songs. Laborde ("Essai sur la Musique," vol. iii, p. 488) says that his talent as a violinist showed itself particularly in the playing of violin trios and quartets. Fétis in the list of Vachon's works mentions: 3 violin concertos, op. 1 (Paris, Venier); 2 do., op. 4 (Paris, Chevardière); 6 violin sonatas with bass, op. 3 (Paris, Venier); 6 do. (London, 1770); 6 trios, 2 violins and bass, op. 2 (Paris, Venier). In the Brit. Mus.: 6 easy duettos for 2 violins, op. 5 (1775); 6 sonatas, op. 1 (1760?); 6 trios, 2 violins and thorough-bass, op. IV (1775?); 6 divertimentos for 2 violins and thorough-bass by Pugnani, Vachon, etc. (1780) (*see* "Eighteenth-Century Sonatas," *The Strad*, July, 1923).

JEAN CLAUDE TRIAL, b. Avignon, Dec. 13, 1732; d. Paris, June 23, 1771. Was a choirboy at Avignon cathedral, afterwards violinist in concert orchestra there. He perfected himself under Garnier at Montpellier, went to Paris and entered the chapel of Prince Conti, where he became director of music, and at the Prince's recommendation he became director of music at the Opera. He died in his 39th year. He collaborated with Berton in 2 operas and composed another for the Comédie Française, also a Pastorale Heroique, performed five days before his death, and ariettas, etc. Fétis says: "The desire to know Rameau brought him to Paris, where he became 1st violin at the Opéra-Comique, for which he composed some successful overtures. At the same time he was engaged as 2nd violin in Prince Conti's chapel, of which he soon became the conductor. The Prince's protection procured for him the place of musical director at the opera conjointly with Berton. His compositions consist chiefly in cantatas for Prince Conti's chapel, overtures and operas."

JULIEN AIMABLE MATHIEU (MATHIEU FILS, also called LEPIDOR), b. Versailles, Jan. 31, 1734. Son of Michel Mathieu, whom he followed as 1st violinist in the Royal chapel in 1761; master in the Royal chapel in the place of Abbé Blanchard in 1770. Castil-Blaze mentions him as still in that position in 1791. He composed 2 sets of sonatas for violin and bass, op. 1, 4; 6 duos faciles for 2 violins; 6 trios for 2 violins and bass, op. 2; also a Domine salvum. Several violin concertos, symphonies, a mass and 45 motets remained in MS.

PIERRE LAHOUSSAYE, b. Paris, Apr. 12, 1735; d. there at the end of 1818. As a small boy he began to play the violin without a teacher, but from the age of 8 he became a pupil of Piffet called "Grand nez," a violinist at the Grand Opera, and before he had reached the age of 10 he made his début at the Concert Spirituel. Some time after, at the house of Count Senneterre, he attended a music meeting where many of the great violinists then in Paris each played a sonata. Noticing the enthusiasm of the youth, Ferrari handed him his violin and after preluding in a brilliant manner he played several parts of a sonata by Tartini which he had just heard for the first time. This so impressed Pagin, who was present, that he took him as a pupil and afterwards recommended him to Count Clermont, who engaged him as violinist for his concerts. His great ambition was to hear Tartini, and this was realized when the Prince of Monaco engaged him in 1757 and took him to Padua, where he met Tartini, who was so pleased with his playing that he accepted him as a pupil. He was soon

France: to 1750

recalled by the Prince, but when he arrived at Parma, the Infante Don Philip gave him an advantageous post at his Court, where Traëtta became his master in composition and made him write, for exercises, ballet music for his operas. Although he received many tokens of kindness and appreciation from Don Philip, he longed to see Tartini again, whom he called the master of masters. He therefore returned once more to Padua, where he received lessons from Tartini until 1769. Then he became a conductor in various Italian towns and gained a great reputation in that capacity. In 1772 he went with Guglielmi to London as conductor of the Italian opera. He returned to Paris in 1775, became conductor of the Concert Spirituel in 1779 and of the Comédie Italienne in 1781. In 1790 he shared that position at the theatre de Monsieur, afterwards theatre Feydeau, with Puppo. When that theatre was united with the theatre Favard after (?) 1800, he lost that post without receiving a pension. The same misfortune befell him on the reconstruction of the Conservatoire, where he had been a professor of the violin from its inception. This told upon him to such an extent that he gave way to habits of intemperance and fell upon evil days, so that he had to accept a place as 2nd violin at the Opera, but general weakness and deafness led to his dismissal in 1813. Fétis speaks of him as a handsome, venerable old man with flowing locks of white hair. Of his playing he speaks in most eulogistic terms and says that he heard him play Tartini's "Devil's Trill Sonata," when he was already advanced in years, in a manner that was as astonishing as it was pleasing. He combined perfect command of the bow with breadth of style, power of tone and a great technique of the left hand. He composed a set of violin sonatas with bass, pub. Paris (ca. 1765?), and 7 church concertos for violin, 7 more books of sonatas and 3 books of duets, which remained in MS. A translation of Tartini's "Trattato delle Appoggiature" by Lahoussay as "Traité des agréments," etc., was pub. by Pietro Denis, Paris, 1782.

CLAUDE JEAN FRANÇOIS DESPRÉAUX, b. Paris, ca. 1735; d. as a victim of the Revolution. Son of an oboist, he entered the orchestra of the Grand Opera in 1759 as violinist, became leader of the 1st violins in 1771 and retired in 1782. During the Revolution he was member of the tribunal and committed suicide on Thermidore 9. Fétis mentions sonatas of his for violin and pianoforte (harpsichord?). His two brothers were also distinguished musicians and teachers at the Conservatoire.

E. MANGEAN (MANGEANT), d. Paris, 1756. He was violinist in the orchestra of the Concert Spirituel in 1750, where he also appeared occasionally as soloist, playing the concertos by Guillemain. Composed "Ier et IIe suites en Trio" ... (Paris, ca. 1735); sonates (6) a violin seul e bass, op. 4 (Paris, 1744), and 2 books of duets for 2 violins.

CHARLES XAVIER VAN GRONENRADE (called DEBLOIS), b. Luneville, Sept. 7, 1737; pupil of Giardini and of Gaviniés. About the time of the French Revolution and for twenty-eight years he was one of the 1st violins at the Comédie Italienne, Paris, where he often took the place of conductor, and where, in 1784, an operetta by him was performed, which is adversely criticized. He does not appear to have composed anything for the violin unless it be a sonata mentioned by Fétis without saying for what instrument it is. As well as the little comic opera, he wrote 4 symphonies, etc.

JEAN BAPTISTE DAVAUX, b. Côte Saint-André (Isère), 1737 (Fétis says: in the Dauphiné, ca. 1740); d. Paris, Feb. 22, 1822; one of fourteen children who received nevertheless a good education, especially in music. At the age of 23 he went to Paris as violinist and composer; he devoted himself chiefly to composition. He wrote a considerable amount of violin music including concertos, duets, trios, etc., of which a list is given by Fétis. His chamber music was greatly esteemed, and a quartet consisting of Giornovichi, Guerin, Guenin and Duport used to meet once a week at his rooms to perform his works, needless to say with great efficiency. When Viotti came to Paris, Davaux was overshadowed by that master. Davaux gave probably the first impetus to the invention of the metronome by an article in the *Journal Encyclop.* of June, 1784. An opera of his was performed at the Comédie Italienne in 1785.

JACQUES HEUZÉ, b. Paris, ca. 1738; d. there between 1790 and 1800; studied violin at Paris, went to St. Petersburg, ca. 1760. In 1764 he went to Frankfort for the coronation of the Emperor, and was engaged as 2nd concertmeister in the Court

France: to 1750

chapel at Cassel, where he became 1st concertmeister in 1769. On account of some lapse he was dismissed in 1776, but reinstated soon afterwards. His salary was 1,000 thaler. After the dissolution of the chapel in 1786 he returned to Paris. His wife, *née* Scali, was an excellent singer (Gerber, i, from verbal communication).

LOUIS ANDRÉ HARANC, b. Paris, June 12, 1738; d. there, ca. 1805. Studied 1758–61 in Italy. It is said that at the early age of 6 years he could play the most difficult sonatas by Tartini in a technically and musically perfect manner. In 1770 he became 1st violinist at the Royal Court chapel, Paris. He was teacher of the Dauphin, father of Louis XVI, who chose him as his teacher of the violin in 1763 and took lessons from him, and in 1775 he became director of the Queen's Musick. The revolution of 1789 ruined his prospects and deprived him of his fortune which depended upon the Court, and he was obliged to accept the position as 1st violin at the theatre Montpensier in 1790. He composed 6 sonatas for violin and B.c. (Paris, Boyer), and 6 duos faciles for 2 violins (Ib.). He travelled in Italy 1758–61. On his return he was appointed to the Royal chapel.

PETIT, a pupil of Tartini who appeared at the Concert Spirituel, Paris, in 1738 (*see* Wki., p. 151).

PETIT, for thirty years violinist at the Opéra-Comique, Paris. Composed 3 sets of violin duets (Paris, Nadermann). 2 books of 6 duets each, op. 1 and 2, are in the Paris National Library. One of his sons, CHARLES, was a good horn player; another, CAMILLE, was a pianist and teacher of some note.

DE TREMAIS. According to H. Blanchard (*Gazette Musicale*, Aug. 11, 1839) a pupil of Tartini; lived in Paris; composed sonatas for violin solo, etc., with B.c. (Paris, 1736); sonatas for 2 violins, and a violin concerto. An adagio from his ninth sonata is in Cartier's "L'Art du Violon." (*See* E. v. d. Str., "Eighteenth-Century Violin Sonatas," *The Strad*, Dec., 1920.)

JEAN BAPTISTE DUPONT, appeared 1739 as violin virtuoso at the Concert Spirituel and was one of the best violinists in the orchestra of Paris from 1750 to 1773, when he was pensioned. He was a pupil of Le Clair and orchestrated the slow movement of one of the latter's sonatas, generally known as Le Tombeau, which was performed on the first anniversary of the death of Le Clair at the church of Les Feuillants (monks of St. Bernard) in 1765. He composed 2 violin concertos on operatic airs (Gerber), and wrote also 2 books, "Principes de Musique" and "Principes de Violon."

ADRIEN GARNIER, b. Lyon, ca. 1740; d. Paris, Nov., 1787. Went to Paris 1775, and from 1777 in the Paris Opera orchestra. Composed 6 solos pour le violin, op. 1, pub. Lyon, 1770.

LOUIS GRANIER, b. Toulouse, ca. 1740; d. there, ca. 1800. Became director of music at Bordeaux, then 1st violin to Prince Charles of Lorraine. In 1766 he was capellmeister at the Brussels Opera (Gregoir, "Panth.," iii, 101; vi, 131) where he produced his "Athalie" by Racine; went thence to Paris as 2nd violinist at the Opera (Gregoir, 1767; Fétis, 1766) and retired to Toulouse in 1787. He composed the opera "Tancrede," divertissements, ballets, etc., according to Mendel, also sonatas and other pieces for violin. Fétis says he entered the orchestra of the Paris Grand Opera in 1766 as 2nd violin, which place he held for twenty years, etc. Mendel says: "His ballets, divertissements, and especially his operas 'Bellerophon' and 'Theonis,' composed together with Bertou, were so successful that he was one of the heroes of the day, and became inspector of the Grand Opera in 1780. He was a very successful teacher of the violin, one of his foremost pupils being Jean Claude Trial."

FRANÇOIS HIPPOLYTE BARTHÉLEMON, b. Bordeaux, July 27, 1741 (Fétis, 1731); d. London, July 20, 1808. He went to Paris when quite young and became an officer, but turned chiefly to music and wrote a little opera, "Le Fleuve Scamandre," for the Théâtre Italienne. The Earl of Kelly, who was interested in his musical achievements, induced him to go to London in 1766 (1765?), where his opera "Pelopidas" was produced with so much success that Garrick paid him a visit to ask him if he could set English words to music. When Barthélemon answered in the affirmative, Garrick wrote down the words of a song to be introduced in the play of "The Country Girl," which he handed to Barthélemon with the words: "There, sir, is my song." To which Barthélemon replied, "And there, sir, is my music to it," handing him the MS. Garrick was so delighted that he invited him to dinner, together with Dr. Johnson. The song proved a great success, and Garrick promised him to make his fortune. As a beginning he employed him to write the music to a farce, "A Peep behind the Curtain," which was so successful that it brought Garrick a net gain of several thousand pounds. The latter rewarded Barthélemon with the munificent sum of 40 guineas instead of the 50 which he had promised him. His excuse was that the "dancing cows" cost him so much that he really could not afford to pay more. Barthelemon was the greatest interpreter of Corelli in his time, which at his death elicited from Salomon the words: "We have lost our Corelli! There is nobody left now to play those sublime solos."

Fétis records: "In 1774 his opera, 'The Maid of Oaks,' was performed at Drury Lane, but the treatment of theatre managers so disgusted him that in 1777 he went on tour as violinist in Germany and Italy, where he met with great success. The Queen of Naples was so delighted that she entrusted him with a letter to her sister, Marie Antoinette, which he handed to her in person at Versailles. He remained but a short time in France, and having received the offer of an advantageous engagement as conductor at the Rotunda in Dublin, went there with his wife, an excellent singer whom he had married in Italy in 1784. Clarke mentions him as still in Dublin in 1794. Soon after, he went to London again." Haydn esteemed him greatly for his *cantabile* style. He died as conductor of the Vauxhall orchestra (Eitner queries this as Dublin).

ANTOINE LAURENT BAUDRON, b. Amiens, May 16, 1743; d. Paris, 1834. A pupil of Gaviniés, he entered the orchestra of the Théâtre Français in 1763, and became conductor there in 1766. He composed for the theatre, including music to J. J. Rousseau's "Pygmalion" and to Beaumarchais' "Figaro," which awakened the interest of Mozart on his visit to Paris. He retired in 1822, receiving in consideration of his long service a pension to the amount of his full salary. None of his works were pub.

MLLE MARCHAND, b. Caen, 1743 (?). She appeared at the age of 12 as a violinist prodigy, with enormous success, at the Concert Spirituel, Paris (Pougin).

MARIE-ALEXANDRE GUÉNIN, b. Maubeuge (Nord), Feb. 20, 1744; d. Paris, 1819; violinist and composer. From 1760 he was a pupil of Capron and Gossec in Paris, and appeared as composer and violinist at the Concert Spirituel in 1773 and 1777 (Mendel, 1765?). He conducted the concerts of Prince Condé; in 1778 was admitted to the Royal chapel and in 1780 became solo violin at the Opera. Fétis says he was 1st solo violin in the Chapel Royal, but had to cede that position to Kreutzer in 1800, remaining however in the orchestra from which he retired in 1810, but not among 1st violins, and entered as 2nd violinist the chapel of Charles VI (IV?) of Spain, but returned to Paris in 1814, where he died in straitened circumstances. He composed trios for 2 violins and bass, op. 1, 3, 13, 15 (Paris); sonata in D for harpsichord and violin (Mannheim MS.); 6 sonates pur le violon avec un 2 violon ad lib. ouvrage methodique Oe. 9 and 10 (Mayence, Schott fils); 10 symphonies and 6 string quartets; 1 sonata for violin and clavier (clavecin?) in "Marzius," 1783; 3 sonatas for clavecin and violin, op. 5 (1781). His symphonies had at one time a high reputation in France, where they were even held to be equal to those of Haydn, although their only merit is good musicianly workmanship.

GUILLAUME (called JULIEN) NAVOIGILLE (L'AÎNÉ), b. Givet, ca. 1745; d. Paris, Nov., 1811. Came to Paris when very young and lived for a time with a Venetian noble who adopted him at Menimontant; after his benefactor's death he founded a school for violin playing in Paris. In 1789, through Monsigny, he became leader of the second violins at the theatre de Monsieur, later on at the theatre de la Cité, and had then still several changes (*see* Fétis, who considers him the composer of the "Marseillaise"). Composed 6 duets a 2 violons, op. 2; 6 sonatas violin solo and bass op. IV; recueil de trois airs var. e 3 caprices a violon seul, op. 7; also 2 operas and a pantomime. In 1806 he and his brother were engaged by Plantade for the Court chapel of the King of Holland. At the temporary amalgamation of Holland and France he returned to Paris. Fétis says: "In 1794 he resigned from the theatre

France: to 1750

de Monsieur and became conductor at the Pantomime Nationale, afterwards the theatre de la Cité. The bankruptcy of that theatre in 1798 left him without position and in straitened circumstances." Wasielewski records that his most remarkable pupil was A. J. Boucher.

PAISIBLE, b. Paris, ca. 1745; d. St. Petersburg, 1783. A pupil of Gaviniés; he entered the orchestra of the Concert Spirituel and the service of the Duchess of Bourbon Conti, whence he took leave and went on tour in France, Germany and the Netherlands. The biography in Cramer, i, 1390, mentions 2 concerts of his at Königsberg. Thence he went in 1778 to St. Petersburg, where Lolli's presence outshone him. He had hoped to play before the Empress Catherine, but this was prevented by Lolli's intrigues. He produced a number of oratorios there for the first time. Neither did he meet with success at Moscow, and getting more and more into debt, he shot himself. The biography in Cramer copied by Gerber, i, appeared in 1783. Composed 2 concertos, op. 1 (Paris, Boivin), also 6 quartets (London), and 6 quartets, op. 3 (*see* Eitner).

LE CHEVALIER DE SAINT-GEORGES, b. Guadeloupe, Dec. 25, 1745; d. Paris, June 12, 1799. He was the son of M. de Boulogne, a high government official, and a negress, and was educated in France from childhood. He had a splendid physique, and was a master in fencing, dancing and every kind of sport. He studied the violin under Leclair and soon became one of the best players in France, shining particularly in the brilliant execution of his master's concertos. After joining the musqueteers, he became a squire to Mme de Montessou, who was secretly married to the Duke of Orleans; then he was made captain of the guards of the Duke of Chartres, whose friend and confidant he became. With Gossec, his master in composition, he founded the Concert des Amateurs in which he was a director and leader of the violins. His ambition urged him to compose operas, of which one at least was not unsuccessful. At the beginning of the Revolution he engaged in political intrigues in the interest of the Royalists and distinguished himself by his bravery as colonel of a cavalry regiment, but was arrested as a suspect, and only the reaction of July 27, 1794, saved him from the scaffold. He was set at

The History of the Violin

liberty, but deprived of all his means; he died in poverty at the age of 54. His sonatas for violin and bass, op. 1, trio sonatas for 2 violins and bass, 5 concertos and 6 concertante symphonies for 2 violins and orchestra are not without merit. One sonata has been republished in Alard's "Maîtres Classiques" (*see also* E. v. d. Str., "Eighteenth-Century Violin Sonatas," *The Strad*). Cramer, i, 344, says: he was a composer, ca. 1780, whose works were played a great deal.

LOUIS FRANCŒUR (called L'HONNÊTE HOMME), d. Paris, Sept. 17, 1745. He was a Royal chamber musician and violinist at the Paris Opera.

FRANÇOIS FRANCŒUR (LE CADET), b. Paris, Sept. 28, 1698, d. there, Aug. 6, 1787; younger brother of Louis F. He was sent (probably at the King's expense) for further study to Germany, with a prolonged sojourn at Prague and Vienna, where J. J. Fux was then at the height of his fame. On his return he was appointed violinist at the Opera where he became the close friend of Rebel. He purchased a place in the Twenty-four Violins of the King, became a chamber musician and in 1733, together with Rebel, inspector and, in 1751, director of the Opera; then, in 1760, superintendent of the Royal Music, retiring in 1778. He died after several operations for stone. His wife was a daughter of Adrienne Lecouvreur, who brought him a dowry of 60,000 livres; their son was the famous mathematician Francœur who died in 1849. Francœur composed 10 operas and 2 books of violin sonatas. On the title page of the first book (pub. 1715) he calls himself Francœur le Fils. He used the left thumb for stopping the lower notes in some chords.

LOUIS JOSEPH FRANCŒUR, LE FILS; b. Paris, Oct. 8, 1738, d. there, March 10, 1804; son of Louis, who was his first master, and then he became the pupil of his uncle François, who had adopted him and in 1746 procured his appointment as a student violinist in the Royal Chamber Music. In 1752 he became violinist at the Opera; in 1754 he was promised a place as lutenist, but that was suppressed; 1764 saw him second—1767, first, director, and 1779, conductor at the opera. In 1776 he became director and superintendent of the Royal Chamber Music, and in 1792 he took over the management of the Opera, but, through constant intrigues, was superseded in 1800. He wrote theoretical works and composed for the theatre but apparently nothing for the violin.

FELIX JEAN PROT, b. Senlis, ca. 1747; d. Paris, beginning of 1823. A violin pupil of Desmarais and of composition under Gianotti. In 1775 he played the viola in the Comédie Française, from where he retired in 1822. Composed numerous duets for 2 violins, operettas, symphonies, etc., also symphonie concertante for 2 violas (Paris, Lachevardière); 6 duos for do. (Paris, Leduc).

ROUSSEAU, b. Versailles, 1748; d. Paris (or Versailles?), 1821; elder brother of Frederic Rousseau, the violoncellist. He entered the orchestra of the Opera, Paris, in 1776, and remained there as violinist until 1812. He composed 2 books of popular airs (airs connus) for 2 violins and bass, and 2 books of violin duets, op. 3 and 5, all pub. in Paris.

SIMON LE DUC L'AÎNÉ, b. Paris, ca. 1748; d. there, ca. 1777 (Fétis, 1787). A pupil of Gaviniés. In the latter years of his life he was director of the Concert Spirituel, together with Gaviniés and Gossec, where he also appeared as soloist in 1763. He composed 3 concertos, 6 sonatas, op. 1, with accompaniment of a viola, a bass or harpsichord (Paris, ca. 1770); second book of sonatas for violin, op. 4 (Paris, author); one posthumous violin sonata (1781?); 6 duos for 2 violins, several symphonies and 5 divertimento a 4, MS.

HENRI GUÉRILLOT, b. Bordeaux, ca. 1749; d. Paris, ca. 1805. Henri showed talent for the violin from early youth. From 1776, he was 1st violin at the Grand Theatre, Lyons; went to Paris in 1778; appeared 1785 at the Concert Spirituel, playing a concerto of his own. From 1784 to the time of his death he belonged to the orchestra of the Opera as one of the 1st violins, and was teacher at the Conservatoire from its foundation, but lost that position on the reconstruction in 1802, since when he became a bitter antagonist of the Conservatoire. He wrote duos for violin; his first concerto for the violin was pub. Lyons, 1782.

ETIENNE BERNARD JOSEPH BARRIÈRE (Pougin says the correct name is Barrier, but gives no Christian names), b. Valenciennes, Oct. 1749. Went to Paris at the age of 6 and became a pupil of Pagin, pupil of Tartini, studying composition under Philidor. After making his debut at the Concert Spirituel he was appointed as one of the solo violins of this and the "Concert des Amateurs." In 1801 he played a symphonie concertante with Lafont at the "Salle Olympique." He composed several books of concertos, duos, trios, quartets and symphonies, pub. in Paris (Fétis).

HUBERT JULIEN NAVOIGILLE (LE CADET), b. Givet, 1749; the more talented of the two brothers. He made his debut at the Concert Spirituel, ca. 1775, with great success and shone as virtuoso at the amateur concert at the Hôtel Soubise and afterwards at the Salle Olympique. In 1789 he lived in Paris as private teacher, but in 1806 he and his brother were engaged by Plantade for the Court chapel of the King of Holland, and on its dissolution returned to Paris, where he seems to have disappeared from musical life. Fétis said that although he was the better virtuoso, he had not his brother's talent as conductor. He composed 6 string quartets, op. 1, and a symphony concertante for 2 violins and orchestra, both Paris, La Chevardière. Mendel says that after 1775 he was 2nd violinist in theatre orchestras. His daughter was a well-known harpist in Paris.

LOUIS JOSEPH FRANCHE. In 1749 1st violin at the Comédie Française, composed a book of sonatas for violin solo, pub. Paris, no date (Mendel: 1749).

ETIENNE PIFFET (nicknamed "LE GRAND NEZ"), ca. 1750. He was violinist at the Grand Opera, Paris, and appeared as soloist at the Concert Spirituel, Apr. 23, 1753, and on later occasions. In 1762 he appeared as soloist in London (Pohl, ii, 370). According to Fétis he composed sonatas for 2 violins and bass and cantatas for 1 voice and B.c.

PIFFET (LE CADET), ordinaire de la chambre du Roy; composed (according to a catalogue by Liepmanssohn) 6 sonatas a violon seul et basse and sonates en duo pour le violon, qui peuvent se jouer sur la Muzette et Vielle; both works dedicated to Mr. de Roisy.

MADAME HABAULT. French violinist who made her debut at the Concert Spirituel, Paris, in 1750. Daquin, in the Siècle de Louis XV, speaks of her style and technique in most eulogistic terms. She was a sister of the equally famous Mlle Levy, and, like the latter, she excelled on the pardessus de viole (treble viol) as well as on the violin.

MARC. An 18th-century French violinist, ca. 1750 in the concert orchestra at Rheims; pub. a book of 6 violin sonatas with B.c. about that time.

L. LASSERNE. Mentioned by Pougin as a French violinist who composed a book of violin sonatas, pub. ca. 1750 (no other particulars).

CLAUDE JACQUES, of Marseille, 1750. Violinist in the Court chapel at Munich with a salary of 350 florins per annum.

THÉODORE SCHMIDT, b. Paris, first half of the 18th century; d. after 1783. He was born in Paris of German parents and became 1st violin at the theatre de Beaujolais. His first works were published in 1765 and in 1783 his name appears for the last time in almanacs, according to Fétis, so that he probably died soon after. He composed 6 duets, op. 2, for violin and violoncello; 18 trios for 2 violins and bass in 3 books; 6 symphonies, which were all pub. by Bailleux, Paris, between the above-mentioned dates. (Eitner: 6 duets, etc., op. 2; 6 sonatas à 3, op. 3; 6 symphonies à 8, op. 1.)

CHARTRAIN, b. Liège, 17..; d. Paris, 1793. Became violinist at the Opera, Paris, in 1772; played several concertos of his own composition at the Concert Spirituel. His style was distinguished by boldness and firmness of tone. He composed 3 violin concertos, op. 2, 3, and 7 (Paris Sieber); 6 duos for violin and viola, op. 9; string quartets, symphonies, and 2 operas.

CHAMPION. An 18th-century French violinist at the Paris Opera, well known in social circles, gave private concerts on every Saturday during the winter at his house, rue des Vieux-Augustins. The above information is given by Pougin without dates or source.

CHAPTER 24

France: to 1775

MICHEL WOLDEMAR, b. Orleans, Sept. 17, 1750; d. Clermont Ferrand, Jan., 1816. His real name was Michel, that of a well-to-do merchant's family; but at the request of his godfather, Marshal de Loewendahl, he took the name of Woldemar. He received a good general education and cultivated music in particular from early youth, Lolli, whom he resembled in eccentricity and vanity, becoming his master for the violin. Adverse fortune compelled him to seek the means for his existence in the exercise of his art and he joined a travelling company of comedians as their bandmaster. Afterwards he settled at Clermont-Ferrand, where he remained until his death. He constructed a violin with an additional string tuned to c, thus combining the compass of the viola with that of the violin. This instrument he called violon alto. He also composed a concerto for it, which he used to play. Urhan revived the instrument in later times. He composed 3 violin concertos; 4 sonatas fantomagiques, entitled "L'Ombre de Lolli, l'Ombre de Mestrino, do de Pugnani and de Tartini"; numerous solos, duets, etc., which are of no value. He also announced, according to Gerber, his invention of a "Correspondence lyrique" as a universal musical language, which consisted in an attempt to convey to his audience by means of violin pieces: (1) The Monologue of Beverlei the Gambler, from Saurin's tragedy; (2) Monologue of Medea after the murder of her children; (3) Part of a sermon of the ex-Jesuit Bauregard, and similar subjects. He also wrote tutors for the violin, the viola, and the clarinet, a book of instruction to compose all kinds of music without knowledge, and a system of musical stenography, none of which are worth considering. 6 caprices, violin elementaire, L'Ombre de Lolli, etc. see above. Sonate Pantomagique; they are of no particular value.

France: to 1775

LEBLANC, b. Paris (?), ca. 1750; d. there 18... A French violinist of great talent and promise; at first leader-conductor at the theatre Comique et Lyrique; in 1791 at the theatre des Jeunes Artistes, and soon after, as composer, at the theatre d'Emulation, where he remained until 1801. From that time onward he followed a downward path, occupying positions as 2nd violinist at second- and third-rate theatres; finally he earned a precarious living by copying music. His earlier very successful compositions showed great talent and augured well for his future, but having to write for inferior theatres and indifferent orchestras he became more and more lax. He wrote operas, ballets, pantomimes, etc. Cartier pub. in his collective work a violin sonata "La Chasse" in four movements, which is not without merit.

PAPAVOINE, ca. 1750, violinist at Rouen; Mendel says: "In 1760 he was concertmeister at Marseilles, then joined the orchestra of the Comédie Italienne, Paris, in the same year as leader of the 2nd violins. In 1762 he became 1st violinist and director at the Ambigu-Comique; in 1780 he went to the Hague as 1st violinist and Maître des pantomimes et répétiteur" (Gregoir, "Panth.," iii, 60). Fétis states that in 1789 he went to Marseilles as musical director of the theatre and died there in 1793. Composed violin sonatas with B.c., op. 5 and 6 (1769); duos à la grecque, op. 7 (1764); an opera, pantomimes, 6 quartets. In the Paris Nat. there are some symphonies, op. 1.

THEODOR JEAN TARADE, b. near Château Thierry, 1751–76. A pupil of Leclair. Violinist at the Grand Opera, Paris; as pensionnaire he received a salary of 400 livres (compardon). In 1755 he played at the Concert Spirituel. The Ges. d. Musifr. have 6 sonate per il violin e bass, op. 1, in score signed with Taradi (uncertain whether the same). Liepmann had once a "Traité de Violon," by T. Tarado (Paris, Gerard) (ca. 1760). He composed several operas. He was still living in 1788. His opera "La Réconciliation Villageoise" was successfully given at the Comédie Italienne, July 15, 1765; he was called at the end of the performance, but when he appeared with his score under his arm the audience began to laugh and he retired discomforted.

LEMIÈRE, L'AÎNÉ. Entered the orchestra of the Paris Opera

in 1751 as violinist; retired Apr., 1771, and died in that year. He was a pupil of Gaviniés and the teacher of Berthaume, and composed, according to Fétis, 2 books of sonatas and 1 book of duets for violin.

ISIDORE BERTHAUME, b. Paris, 1752; d. St. Petersburg, Mar. 20, 1802. Pupil of Lemière and, according to Pougin, of Gaviniés. He made his debut at the Concert Spirituel in 1761; became 1st violin at the Opera in 1774, and was principal violin at the Concert Spirituel 1783–8, being at the same time violinist at the Opéra-Comique and the Concert d'Émulation. On the outbreak of the Revolution (1791) he went to Germany, where he was concertmeister at the Court of Oldenburg at Eutin from 1793–1801. In 1802 he went to St. Petersburg via Copenhagen and Stockholm, as 1st violin in the Imperial Private Chapel, but died a few weeks after his appointment. He had evolved his technique from the study of the Italian masters. It was well developed in every detail and his intonation faultless, but his style was more elegant than broad or powerful. He composed sonatas in the style of Lolli, op. 1; 6 solos, op. 2; 6 duos with little airs, op. 3; sonatas for violin, op. 4; concerto for violin, op. 5; symphony concertante for 2 violins, op. 6; sonatas for pianoforte with accompaniment of violin, op. 7; 6 little sonatas for pianoforte, op. 8. He was a successful teacher; his best pupil was Grasset, who became professor at the Paris Conservatoire.

PIERRE LE DUC (L. LE JEUNE), b. Paris, ca. 1755; d. in Holland, Oct., 1816. He appeared at the Concert Spirituel as violinist, but afterwards, ca. 1775, he acquired the music publishing business of La Chevardière in the rue Traversière de Saint-Honoré (still in existence as Alphonse Leduc). He was a brother and pupil of the violinist SIMON LE DUC (q.v.).

J. AVOLIO (F. D'AVOGLIO?), b. Paris, mid. 18th century (*see* Eitner). Composer of violin sonatas and duets, pub. in Paris, 1770. Gerber: "F. d'Avoglio" played at Concert Spirituel in 1755, and pub. 6 works for violin (quartets, duets and solos) between 1780 and 1784 in Paris.

ANTOINE LACROIX, b. Remberville, near Nancy, ca. 1756; d. Lübeck, towards the end of 1812. A pupil of Ant. Lorenziti at Nancy, went to Paris in 1780, where he appeared

France: to 1775

as virtuoso, but, driven out by the Revolution, he went to Germany and Denmark. In 1794 he was at Bremen and on Jan. 22, 1796, he was appointed town musician at Lübeck where, in conjunction with Königslöw, he played at the subscription concerts. In 1803 he started a music-seller's business in that town. He composed sonatas, a considerable number of duets and variations for violin, also some string quartets. (*See* Wki., Gerber, ii, under Croix.)

ANDRÉ-JOSEPH FAUVEL, L'AÎNÉ, b. Bordeaux, 1756. Teacher of Rode (ca. 1763–9). He went to Paris in 1787, where he was a member of the Opera orchestra from 1794 to 1814. (Fétis says as viola player.) His wife, *née* Frey, was a pianist and composer. 3 quatuors, op. 1 (Paris, 1798), and 3ième livre de duos pour 2 violons, op. 7, are in the Paris National Library. Fétis mentions also 12 studies, followed by 6 studies as duets, op. 3 (Paris, 1801); 6 very easy elementary trios for 2 violins and bass, op. 4 (Ib., 1802); also a symphony for 8 instruments.

PIERRE DAVID AUGUSTIN CHAPELLE, b. Rouen, 1756; d. Paris, 1821. Went to Paris in his early youth, and played two violin concertos of his own composition at the Concert Spirituel. He devoted himself afterwards chiefly to the composition of operas, of which 10, mostly in one act, were produced between 1772 and 1794. He was for twenty years violinist at the Comédie Italienne and afterwards at the Vaudeville. For the violin he wrote 6 concertos (pub. in Paris); 6 books of duets for 2 violins; rondo for violin solo; sonatas, op. 14; and some airs with variations.

L'ABBÉ ANTOINE SIBIRE, b. Paris, 1757; d. there after 1826. Amateur violinist. He wrote "La Chélomanie, ou le parfait luthier" (Paris, 1806), based upon communications by Lupot (*see* Fétis).

C. LINTANT, b. Grenoble, 1758; d. there, Mar. 17, 1830. After receiving his elementary music lessons at Grenoble he went to Paris at a very early age and became a violin pupil of Berthaume. When his brother-in-law, Sageret, took over the management of the theatre Feydeau, he engaged Lintant as 1st violin under the conductorship of Lahoussaye and Blasius; when Sageret failed he lost his position but continued to live in Paris, depending chiefly on guitar lessons, on which instrument he had acquired great mastery. From ca. 1810 he became a lessee and manager of various theatres, the last being 1810 at Grenoble, where he died. He composed 3 duos for 2 violins, op. 7, and 3 "grandes sonates" for guitar and violin; 2 sets of string quartets, op. 1 and op. 4; songs, etc.

JACQUES FRANÇOIS D'AUTRIVE, b. St. Quentin Aisne, 1758; d. Mons, Belgium, Dec., 1824. He was one of the best pupils of Jarnovich (Giornovichi) and combined great expression with purity of intonation. At the age of 35 he became deaf and this prevented the realization of the hopes which his earlier career had awakened. He composed several violin concertos, duos, one of which is dedicated to Kreutzer; several of his compositions for violin remained in MS. Fétis praises his melodious vein.

THÉODORE LEFÈVRE, b. Paris, ca. 1759; d. after 1820. Son of a ballet master at the Comédie Italienne, Paris, and brother of Mme Dugazon. He became violinist at the Comédie Italienne, and in 1794 at the theatre in the rue Feydeau. In 1801 he became conductor at the Opéra-Comique, and retired in 1820. Composed operas and symphonies.

CARDON, b. Paris, 175.; third brother of Louis Cardon, harp player. Is mentioned by Fétis as a "distinguished violinist" without further particulars. A LOUIS CARDON composed several sets of sonatas for harp and violin, pub. Paris, ca. 1780 (see "Eighteenth-Century Sonatas"). Perhaps same as above.

CHARLES LOUIS MAUCOURT, b. Paris, ca. 1760; pensioned in 1813. Violin pupil of his father, and of Harenc; appeared as soloist at the Concert Spirituel in 1778; went on tour, was for some time at Mannheim, then at Brunswick, where he was appointed concertmeister in the Ducal chapel from 1784. Afterwards he was in the chapel of King Jerome of Westphalia; 1813 saw the end of Jerome's kingdom and in the same year a malady of his right arm compelled him to abandon his career and retire into privacy. His father was a harpsichord teacher in Paris, who wrote some pieces for harpsichord and violin pub. in 1758.

CHARLES LOCHON, b. Lyons, ca. 1760. A pupil of Berthaume; entered the orchestra of the Grand Opera, Paris, in 1787, and was pensioned Apr., 1817. He was also a member of the Concert Spirituel. He composed 6 duos for 2 violins, op. 1 (Lyons, 1780).

MAHONI LE BRETON. Ca. 1760 violinist at the Théâtre Italienne, Paris. Composed trios and duets for violin and flute (Fétis). Gerber, i, states that he wrote in 1787 the operetta, "Les Promesses de Mariage."

ANTOINE BAILLEUX. A music-teacher and seller of the mid 18th century. Composed numerous symphonies, a violin tutor (Paris, 1779; 2nd ed., 1798), a singing tutor (1760), and "Solfeges pour apprendre facilement la musique vocale et instrumentale."

CHARLES DUBREUIL (DUPREIL). From 1762 violinist at the Court chapel, Munich, with, from 1770, a salary of 500 florins; later, 575 florins. On May 14, 1796, his death is reported to the Elector.

CAPRON. One of the best pupils of Gaviniés, of whom neither the Christian name nor the dates and places of birth and death are known. Bricaire in his "Lettres sur l'état present de nos spectacles, etc.," pub. in 1765, classes him with Gaviniés as one of the best violinists of the century. In 1762 he was leader of the 2nd violins at the Concert Spirituel, when Gaviniés was leader of the firsts. In 1767 he succeeded to the latter position and played there as soloist in 1768 (Fétis) (Brenet says 1767). He composed 6 sonatas for violin, op. 1, pub. 1769, and 6 string quartets, op. 2, pub. 1770. M. A. Guénin was one of his pupils. He married secretly the niece of Piron, who, after having become blind, pretended to know nothing about it, but sometimes Capron said, "When I am dead I shall have a good laugh, my good Nanette has the parcel." When eventually his will was opened it began, "I leave to Nanette, wife of Capron, musician, etc." (Fétis).

JEAN BAPTISTE BONNET, b. Montauban, Apr. 23, 1763. Pupil of Giornovichi and Mestrino. Had he gone to Paris he might have ranked among the virtuosos of his instrument, but having become successively 1st violinist at Brest and Nantes, he could not persuade himself to leave the circle of his friends. Ca. 1802 he retired to Montauban as organist of the cathedral. He composed for the violin concertos, duets, trios for 2 violins and bass, also symphonies and chamber music. Fétis gives a list of his pub. and unpub. compositions, which enjoyed a fair amount of popularity.

VISCOUNT EDOUARD JOSEPH BERNARDY DE VALERNE, b. Bonnicu, near Apt, Oct. 15, 1763. He was a violinist who had 28 opus numbers of his works pub., including symphonies, overtures, trios, duos. He also wrote an opera.

DUPRÉ, d. Paris, 1784. Was violinist at the Paris Opera until 1754, when he was pensioned; he composed 2 sets of 6 pianoforte trios each (Paris, 1763).

GILBERT. A Frenchman who, in 1763–8, was 1st violinist at the Court chapel at Cassel, whence he went to Metz as director of music. Apell says he wrote good (brav gesetzte) symphonies. Castil-Blaze mentions, according to Pougin, a P. Gilbert who became one of the Twenty-four Violins at the French Court in 1723.

ALDAY, L'AÎNÉ, b. 1763 in Paris, made a successful debut at the Concert Spirituel in 1787. About this time he wrote a symphony concertante in C for 2 violins and viola (Paris, Sieber), and this was followed by another for 2 violins, which he played with his brother at the Concert Spirituel (Amsterdam, Hummel). Ca. 1795 he settled as music publisher and seller at Lyons where, apart from a set of string quartets and airs with variations, he pub. a "Méthode de Violon" containing among other things 16 trios for 3 violins, 6 progressive duos, and exercises for learning to modulate.

ALDAY, LE JEUNE, b. Paris, 1764, said to have received lessons from Viotti. He was far more talented than his elder brother and appeared on several occasions at the Concert Spirituel from 1783 till 1791, when he went to London, where Lavenu published his trios for 2 violins and bass. In 1806 he settled as director of music in Edinburgh. The date of his death is unknown. He left a number of concertos, trios, quartets, duets, variations, etc., which are entirely obsolete. Mendel-Reissmann says, however: His violin concerto in D minor (pub. Paris, 1780), was a favourite of all virtuosos and advanced violinists of that time and is distinguished by fine artistic traits.

PERRONARD, b. ca. 1764, appeared at the age of 15 or 16 as solo violinist at the Concert Spirituel, Paris, in 1779, and

France: to 1775

met, according to the contempory critics, with great success (Gregoir, "Panth.," iii, 70).

JEAN BAPTISTE BÉDARD, b. Rennes, Brittany, ca. 1765; d. Paris, ca. 1815. At first music teacher and 1st violin and director of music at the theatre of that town; violin virtuoso; settled 1796 in Paris. Composed duos for 2 violins, op. 2, 3, 4, 28, 53, 58; suites of duos for violin (double stops); Méthode de violon courte et intelligible (Paris, Le Duc, 1800); Airs variés and potpourris for violin; also 2 symphonies and various other instrumental works. He was also a virtuoso on the harp.

JOHN JOUSSE, b. ca. 1765 (Fétis 1760), probably at Orleans; d. London, Jan., 1837; French refugee in the time of the Revolution, settled in London 1789 as teacher of, and writer on, music. Wrote "The Theory and Practice of the Violin" (London, R. Birchall, 1811). It was pub. at £1 1s.—a higher price than ever before charged for a tutor. The book contains some interesting points, *see* description in "The Romance of the Fiddle," E. v. d. Str. He also wrote various other tutors.

JEAN BAPTISTE CARTIER, b. Avignon, May 28, 1765; d. Paris, 1841. Son of a dancing-master. He received his first musical training from the Abbé Walraef, canon of St. Peter's. In 1783 he went to Paris and became a pupil of Viotti. Not long after this he became, at Viotti's recommendation, accompanist on the violin to Queen Marie Antoinette, and retained that position until the outbreak of the Revolution. In 1791 he became deputy leader at the Opera, where he often played solos, and was pensioned after thirty years' service. Paisiello engaged Cartier for the chapel of Napoleon in 1804. At the Restoration he became a member of the Royal chapel, to which he belonged until its dissolution through the July revolution in 1830. Cartier was an excellent teacher; he composed a number of airs with variations, a "Sonata in the style of Lolli" (not a desirable model!), op. 7 (Paris, 1797); 6 caprices on études for violin (1800); 6 duos melodiques for 2 violins, op. 2 (1801); 3 grands duos dialogués et concertants for 2 violins; a fourth book of duos, op. 14 (1801); also violin concertos, symphonies and operas which remained in MS. Of more lasting value than his own compositions is the comprehensive collection of early violin sonatas by which he made his countrymen for the first time acquainted with the works of the great Italian masters, which up to that time were only partly known to them. The work contains, moreover, records of pieces of which hardly any other record now exists. The first ed. appeared under the title: "L'Art du violon, ou collection choisie dans les sonates des trois école italienne, française, et allemande, etc." (Paris, Décembre, 1798, fol.). The second ed. is entitled: "L'Art du violon ou division des écoles servant de complément à la méthode de violon du conservatoire," Paris, 1801. Although he was never on the staff of the Conservatoire he has done a great deal for the advancement of violin playing in France, and especially for the raising of its artistic standard. According to Pougin he was also occupied with a history of the violin for which he had collected a great amount of material, and written out the greater part, but unfortunately the MS. was lost after his death; an extract or chapter from it, entitled "Dissertation sur le violon," was pub. in the "Revue Musicale," vol. iii, p. 103.

BORNET, L'AÎNÉ. A violinist at the Opera, Paris, 1768–90; wrote a "Méthode nouvelle de violon et de musique," etc. ("Tutor for the Violin and Musical Theory, in which the necessary gradations have been observed to teach both arts together, followed by new airs from operas"). He also pub. a *Journal de Violon* which appeared from 1784 to 1788. In 1765 he wrote a ballet for the "Comédie Italienne." His brother, known as Bornet le jeune, was violinist at the Théâtre de la Pantomime Nationale in 1797 and afterwards at the Opéra Buffa, where he was still in 1807.

NICOLAS JACOB, French violinist and music theorist; d. Paris, 1772. Pupil of Gaviniés; entered the orchestra of the Grand Opera in 1765. Some motets of his were performed at the Concert Spirituel. He wrote "Méthode de Musique sur un nouveau plan par Mr. Jacob" (Paris, 1769). Fétis says it was not by him but by Nicolas J. of the Académie Royal de Musique. As that *is* the Grand Opera it confirms the above and shows, moreover, that his Christian name was Nicolas.

ÉTIENNE SCIO, b. Bordeaux, ca. 1766; d. Paris, Feb. 21, 1796. Violinist and composer, first engaged at the theatre at Toulouse; then 1st violin at the Marseille theatre, where he

FRANCOIS FRANCOEUR

JEAN JOSEPH CASSANEA DE MONDONVILLE

PIERRE RODE

RODOLPHE KREUTZER

JEAN MARIE LECLAIR

LEOPOLD MOZART
From his Violin Tutor.

composed several ballets and divertissements. Married the famous singer Créci, became conductor at the theatre Molière, Paris, in 1791, for which he wrote several operas. 1792 he went to the theatre Feydeau. Fétis enumerates his operas, which Eitner was unable to trace.

RODOLPHE KREUTZER, b. Versailles, Nov. 16, 1766; d. Geneva, Jan. 6, 1831. He was a pupil first of his father, member of the Royal chapel, then of Stamitz. At 13 he played at the Concert Spirituel a concerto of his own composition. He succeeded his father in the Royal chapel in 1782, when both his parents died. He was then considered the equal of the greatest virtuosos and began to compose operas performed, first at Versailles before the Court, and later on at the Théâtre Italienne, where he became 1st violin in 1790. On his opera "Paul et Virginie," in 1791, he calls himself "Musicien en ordinaire de la musique des Italiens." In 1796 he went on a concert tour through Italy and other countries after having been appointed by the Republic at the newly founded Conservatoire. By 1798 he was in Vienna (Thayer, ii, 21), and in 1801 he became solo violin at the Grand Opera, 1816 second, and 1817 first, capellmeister there. From Napoleon he received the title of chamber virtuoso, which was confirmed by Louis XVIII. In 1810 he broke his arm and had to give up playing (*Leipzig Zeitung*, 12, 968). He retired in 1826. In 1827 he offered his last opera to the directorate of the opera, who rejected it. This rebuff told on his already enfeebled health. He sought recovery in Switzerland, but death overtook him at Geneva. With Cherubini, Mehul, Kreutzer, Isouard and Boildieu he established a publishing business at Paris. For his numerous compositions *see* Eitner (Fétis Wki., Pougin). His studies have remained standard works to this day.

DU BOIS, appeared as violin virtuoso in London in 1770. A J. P. J. du Bois was collaborator of Vignole in "Le lire maçonne" in 1766 (Eitner).

HENRY-MONTAN BERTON, b. Paris, Sept. 17, 1767; d. there, Apr. 22, 1844. Son of Pierre Montan Berton, director of the Opera and the Royal chapel. He commenced his musical career as violinist in the orchestra of the Opera at the age of 15 as supernumerary, but afterwards as a regular member. After having studied musical theory under Sacchini he became opera composer, professor of harmony at the Conservatoire and director of music at the Italian Opera. Composed oratorios, operas, etc.

LOUIS DE VALMALÈTE, b. Rieux, ca. 1768. Studied elements of music under Foncés, afterwards violin under Turlet of Toulouse. In 1787 he went to Paris, where he studied for two more years under Puppo, Gervais, and Gaviniés, and composition under Liron. He set to music the 2 St. Cecilia odes by Dryden and Pope, and wrote words and music of 3 romances (pub. Paris), one of which, "Amans plaignez ma destinée," became very popular (Mason Clarke).

JEAN JACQUES GRASSET, b. Paris, ca. 1769; d. there, Aug. 25, 1839. Violinist and conductor at Théâtre Italienne from 1801 to 1829. Particulars in Fétis, who mentions 3 concertos, 5 books of duets, op. 9, and sonatas, op. 3, by him. Eitner knows only concertos, op. 1, 2 and 4. He was a pupil of Berthaume, but at the outbreak of the Revolution forced to enter the army and serve throughout the German and Italian campaigns. During the latter he studied the Italian music. Back in Paris, he competed for the professorship of the Conservatoire which had become vacant through the death of Gaviniés in 1800. Fétis, who heard him for the first time on that occasion, says that his superiority over his competitors, Guénin, Gervais, Guérillot, etc., was evident from the outset, to the audience as well as to the judges, and he was chosen accordingly. He also became violinist at the Grand Opera and conducted in 1802 the concerts in the rue Cléry. He succeeded Bruni as musical director of the Italian Opera and held that position until 1829, when he retired. He had a brilliant technique and his tone was pure and sweet but of little volume. He composed for the violin 3 concertos, a sonata with pianoforte, op. 3, many duets and airs-variés for 1 and 2 violins.

LOUIS LUC LOISEAU DE PERSUIS, b. Metz, July 4, 1769; d. Paris, Dec. 20, 1819. He had just finished his studies and become an excellent violinist when he fell in love with an actress of the Metz theatre whom he followed to the South of France and lived for some time at Avignon as teacher of the violin. In 1787 he went to Paris, where his oratorio, "The Passage

France: to 1775

through the Red Sea," was performed at the Concert Spirituel. In 1790 he became 1st violinist at the theatre Montansier, and 1793 he left it for a similar position at the Opera, but this was but of short duration on account of his differences with Rey, the conductor. In 1804 he was, however, recalled to that institute as chorus master, and his ability being noticed he was elected to the committee of administration and the selection of new works. In 1810 he succeeded Rey as conductor and 1814 as inspector-general of music at the Opera. Persuis was of a haughty and quarrelsome nature which led to constant dissensions with Choron who was the director of the Opera. These came to a head when the latter tried to prevent the revival of an opera by Persuis which in 1812 had proved more or less a failure. Persuis through his friends agitated at the Court, Choron was dismissed, and he succeeded him on Apr. 1, 1817, as first director of the Opera, which flourished under his management; but this came to a comparatively early end by his death from a chest complaint at the age of 50.

Besides the above activities, he was from 1794 professor at the Conservatoire, but lost that position on the reduction of the staff in 1802. In that year however he became maître de musique (assistant conductor) in Napoleon's private orchestra, in 1814 deputy capellmeister under Lesnuer, and in 1816 he succeeded the latter as superintendent of the King's Music. His compositions consist chiefly of 20 operas and ballets. On Dec. 5, 1819, Louis XVIII decorated him with the Order of St. Michael and settled upon him a pension, half of which to revert to his wife.

JOSEPH GRAVRAND, L'AÎNÉ, b. Caen, Apr. 2, 1770; d. there, ca. 1847. Studied violin under Queru, a pupil of Capron, afterwards finished his studies under Baillot at Paris. He became violinist at theatre Caen, and conducted the amateur concerts there. Composed 3 duos concertans pour 2 violins (Berlin J. J. Hummel); 3 duos concertans, do., op. 7 (Leipzig and Berlin, Bureau). Fétis: Duets op. 1, 2, 3, 4, 5, 7, 8, which he says were justly celebrated, and a trio for violin, viola, and violoncello, op. 6.

AUGUSTE GIRAULT, b. ca. 1770 at Paris; d. there, ca. 1806. First violin at theatre Montpensier. Composed duos for 2 violins (Paris, Pleyel) (Gerber, Fétis).

AUGUSTE GLACHANT. From 1770 to 1778 violinist at the Paris Opera, and in 1791 1st violin at the theatre Louvois; composed chamber music and pub. a collection of airs (Pougin).

GLACHANT, son of above, also violinist. Became conductor at the little theatre "Délassement comique," Paris, for which he wrote several operettas (Pougin).

ANDRÉ REMI MICHAUD. From ca. 1770 to the time of his death in 1788 violinist at the Grand Opera, Paris. Composed 6 duos each for 2 violins, op. 1 and 2; 4 recueils d'airs pour violin (Paris, Bailleux), etc.

MICHAUD, LE JEUNE. 1st violin of the "Concert de Besançon", wrote 3rd collection of variations for violin (pub. Paris, 1782).

J. B. MICHAUD. Composed 6 sonàtes à violin seul avec la basse, op. 1 (Paris, chez l'auteur).

L'ABBÉ ALEXANDRE ROBINEAU. An 18th-century amateur violinist. He was one of the best pupils of Gaviniés. He composed a concerto for violin and orchestra and 6 solos (pub. Paris, 1770). After the revolution of 1789 he emigrated and died in Germany. Eitner traced only "Sonates à violon seul et basse" (Paris). One sonata in A flat major appears as No. 44 in Alard's "Maîtres Classiques."

PIERRE MARIE FRANÇOIS DE SALES BAILLOT, b. Passy, near Paris; Oct. 1, 1771; d. Paris, Sept. 15, 1842. Son of a barrister. He began to play the violin as a little boy, without a master. When he showed distinct talent, Polidori of Florence, a mediocre violinist but good teacher, took charge of his studies, and when his father settled in Paris, in 1880, he became a pupil of Sainte-Marie. In Paris he had the opportunity of hearing Viotti, whom he henceforth took for his model. In 1883 the father was sent as Procurator General to Bastia, Corsica, and Pierre was thrown upon his own resources. A few months later his father died and the Intendant de Bouchepron sent him with his own children to Rome, where for 13 months he studied under Pollani, a pupil of Nardini, and played with marked success in public. He then followed his guardian to Corsica, Bayonne, Pau, and Auch, where they lived alternately. During that time he acted as private secretary to de Bouchepron, while part of the period was devoted to his general education. In 1791 he went to Paris, where, on the recommendation of Viotti, he was appointed a 1st violinist at the theatre Feydeau. A few months later he was offered, and accepted, a post in the Ministry of Finance, which he occupied for several years, without neglecting the study of the violin. He even appeared from time to time in public with great success. After having, compulsorily, served in the army for 20 months, he returned to Paris in 1795, and becoming acquainted with the works of Corelli, Tartini, Geminiani, Locatelli, Bach, and Handel, he decided to devote himself entirely to music, and was appointed teacher of the violin at the newly founded Conservatoire, where he also studied harmony under Catel, and composition under Reicha and Cherubini. In 1802 he entered the private band of Napoleon, and 1805-8 he toured in Russia with the 'cellist Lamarre, both of whom earned fame and money. In 1812 he toured in the South of France, and in 1814 he instituted quartet-soirées, which did a great deal to popularize chamber music in Paris, and proved him a great master in that art, in which for a long time he found but little public support. In 1815 he toured Belgium and Holland, but he did not visit Germany, it is said, to avoid a comparison with Spohr. In 1816 he toured in England, and on Feb. 26 he played at a concert of the Philharmonic Society of which he afterwards became a member. During 1821-31 he was leader at the Grand Opera, Paris, and from 1825 he belonged to the French Royal chapel in the same capacity. In 1833 he made his final tour in Northern Italy and Switzerland; from that time till his death he lived as the revered head of the French school of violinists in Paris.

Baillot was the last representative of the classical French school of violin playing and formed the link between that and the modern school. He was an enthusiastic champion of Mendelssohn's chamber-music works, and Mendelssohn, in his letters, praises Baillot's interpretation of his quartets and his octet. Ferd. Hiller also refers to him in his writings in a laudatory manner. Spohr, in his autobiography, says that Baillot's technique was almost as perfect as that of Lafont, without being restricted to the narrow limits of mere virtuosity. He praises his bowing as nimble and dexterous, and rich in colouring, but adds that it was not as free as

Lafont's, and his tone consequently not as beautiful, that moreover the change from up- to down-bow and vice versa was a little too noticeable. His compositions he describes as very correct and pure in style and not devoid of a certain amount of originality, but somewhat artificial, not without mannerism, and old-fashioned, and that therefore they leave one cold. Baillot's most important activity was that of a teacher, and in that he ranked with the greatest of his time. When the Paris Conservatoire had started on its career Baillot was asked by the directorate to fix the principles of violin playing and embody them in an instruction book. He called in the assistance of Rode and Kreutzer and the work appeared as "Méthode de Violon par Messrs. Baillot, Rode et Kreutzer, rédigée (edited) par Baillot" in a French as well as in a German ed. They embodied in their work what they considered best in the tutors by Geminiani, Corrette, Leop. Mozart, Dupont, and L'Abbé le fils. It appeared in several eds. between 1771 and 1842, and was repub. in the Universal Edition in Vienna in recent years. Baillot was not satisfied with the results, and in 1834 he produced his "L'Art du violon, nouvelle Méthode," after some 8 or 10 more or less important newer instruction books had made their appearance. At the beginning of this larger work he says that when 30 years before he and his colleagues were asked to write a method for the use at the Conservatoire, they had no information about the most useful manner to study the instrument, and their instruction had not risen beyond some wavering conceptions and incomplete traditions. "We had", he says, "to battle for years with error before we could approach the so-called secrets of the art, and the older works belonged to an epoch, too far removed to offer the flexibility of the means, which modern compositions demand more and more."

The result, however, although a great advance over the older works, remained still a long way behind the systematic, gradual progression, required for a really useful instructive work. He includes many things which do not belong to the domain of a tutor, while really essential matters are dealt with quite inadequately. The same fault in a greater or lesser degree is observable in all instruction books until we come to the works by Joachim-Moser, and Wilhelmj-Brown, at the end of the 19th and beginning of the 20th century. Baillot

France: to 1775

collaborated also with Baudiot and Levasseur in a violoncello tutor for the Conservatoire.

His published compositions are: 9 violin concertos with orchestra; 1 sonata for violin and pianoforte; 6 duos for 2 violins; 15 trios for 2 violins and bass; symphonie concertante for 2 violins with orchestra; 30 airs-variés; 12 études, 24 preludes, a number of solo pieces for violin, and 3 string quartets. In a literary capacity he became favourably known as the author of a "Notice sur Gretry" (1814) and a "Notice sur Viotti" (1825). Baillot's claim to remembrance lies not in his compositions, which, apart from his studies, are entirely obsolete, but in the part he played in improving the musical conditions of his country, and as the teacher of many eminent violinists, foremost among whom were: Habeneck, Dancla, Mazas, Guérin, Wéry and others.

JEAN BAPTISTE DESPRÉZ, b. Versailles, 1771. Pupil of Richer. Composed 6 duos dialogués for 2 violins, op. 1 (Paris, 1798). In 1799 he was conductor of the revived concert at Versailles, and was also a writer on music.

LOUIS JULIEN CASTELS DE LABARRE, b. Paris, Mar. 24, 1771. He came of a noble family of Picardy, received in his youth some lessons from Viotti. In 1790 he went to Naples, where he studied composition under Sala at the Conservatoire della Pieta and returned to France in 1793 to continue his theoretical studies under Mehul. After playing for two years as 1st violin at the theatre de Molière he entered the orchestra of the Grand Opera in 1799. A few years later he left that position for an appointment in the family of the Emperor Napoleon. He composed 3 sets of duets for 2 violins, caprices and airs with variations for violin, an opera, songs, etc., pub. in and after 1800.

PIERRE JEAN VACHER (also called LEVACHER), b. Paris, Aug. 2, 1772; d. there, ca. 1819. A pupil of André Monin and Viotti, he left Paris at the outbreak of the Revolution and entered the orchestra of Bordeaux, returning in 1794 to Paris, where, as 1st violinist at the Vaudeville theatre, he became known by his little airs and romances which were sung there and became popular. Later he became 1st violinist at the theatre Feydeau, and finally at the Grand Opera. Fétis gives 5 instrumental works, known are "Premier Livre de Trios pour 2 Violins et Bass," op. 3 (Paris, Nadermann), and songs.

IMBAULT. The dates and places of birth and death are unknown; he probably died in Paris where he had since ca. 1780 a flourishing music publishing business of French compositions of which, according to Mendel (Reissmann "Mus. Convers. Lexikon," v, p. 380), the catalogue of 1792 had grown to 12 large folio pages. He was a pupil of Gaviniés and in 1773–7 a 1st violinist at the Concert Spirituel in Paris. In 1780 he appeared successfully as soloist at Geneva. There he met Viotti who, in company with his master Pugnani, had arrived on his first concert tour, and a lasting friendship was established between the two virtuosos, who, when they met again in Paris, played together Viotti's concertante symphonies for 2 violins at the French Court. In 1786 Imbault was leader of the 2nd violins at the Concert d'Emulation, and in 1787 he was still heard as soloist in Paris. He was a member of the "Société Académique des Enfants d'Apollon."

CHARLES ERNEST, BARON VON BAGGE. An amateur violinist, who lived in Paris ca. 1783; d. there, 1791. He was a liberal patron of musicians, for whose talent he had the greatest admiration and discernment; but although himself but an indifferent player, with faulty intonation, he believed himself a great master and invited well-known violinists to become his pupils; when they objected, he offered to pay them for doing so, which some accepted, driven thereto by poverty. This gave him the nickname of "Francallen (francallen = free property allodium) du violon." The Emperor Joseph II once said to him: "Baron, I never heard anybody play the violin like you." He had also a mania for composition and had a symphony, 6 string quartets, op. 1, etc., pub. (the latter in 1773), also a violin concerto (Paris, 1782) which Kreutzer, then still very young, played with great success in public. Hoffmann has made Bagge the subject of one of his tales, where one finds the cachet of his original talent (Fétis). It is said that he was poisoned by his mistress.

J. J. DREUILH, b. Bordeaux, ca. 1773; d. Niort, Nov. or Dec., 1858. Eitner says "violinist and composer" without mentioning a single instance of his violinistic activity; he says:

"Pougin devotes a longer biography to him," but Pougin does not mention him in "Le Violon."

DENIS LOTTIN, b. Orléans, Nov. 19, 1773; d. there, 1828 (Fétis, 1826). Pupil of Fridzeri, who recognized his talent and in 1786 took him as one of his pupils to Rennes, where he remained for three years, after which he returned to Orléans and continued his studies. In 1805 he became 1st violinist at the Orléans theatre and conductor of the amateur concerts. He composed violin concertos, sonatas, duets, symphonies and "Principes élémentaires de musique et de violon" (Paris, Leduc).

PIERRE RODE, b. Bordeaux, Feb. 16, 1774; d. at the Château de Bourbon, Nov. 25, 1830 (Mendel, Nov. 13). His first teacher was Fauvel, aîné, ca. 1782 to 1788. In the latter year he played in a concert of Punto in Paris, who introduced him to Viotti, and only appeared again in public in 1790; became leader of 2nd violin at theatre Feydeau and also played concertos by Viotti in public (*see* various biographies, including F. M. F. Moser, Berlin, 1831, if accessible).

Fétis gives fuller details: In 1787 he was introduced to Viotti, who took the greatest interest in him and bestowed the greatest care on the development of his talent. He brought him out at the theatre de Monsieur in 1790 when he played Viotti's concerto during the entr'acte of an Italian opera. In the same year he joined the orchestra of the theatre Feydeau as leader of the 2nd violins. There he played at the concerts given during Holy Week 4 concertos by Viotti. The 18th, by the beauty of the composition as well as the brilliant rendering thereof by Rode, obtained a triumphal success for both composer and executant, and by special request on the part of the public it had to be repeated at three subsequent successive concerts. But soon after, in 1794, he left for a concert tour to Hamburg in company of the famous singer Garat, thence he went to Berlin, where he played before Frederic William II. He returned to Hamburg to embark for Bordeaux, but a gale drove the ship to the English coast and being so near his revered master he decided to revisit him in London, where he also gave a concert for the benefit of widows and orphans, which found but meagre support on account of his French nationality. Disappointed, he returned to Hamburg and thence gradually returned to France, giving many successful concerts in Holland and the Netherlands on the way. About the time of his arrival in Paris the Conservatoire was founded by decree of the Government, and Rode was appointed as professor for the violin. After playing with renewed success at the theatre Feydeau concerts he went to Spain, where he became very friendly with Boccherini, who orchestrated several of his, Rode's, concertos for him. After his return to Paris in 1800, Napoleon appointed him as 1st solo violin of his private music. Rode had now arrived at the zenith of his fame and soon he received a most tempting offer from the Russian Court. In 1803 he accepted and went with his friend Boieldieu to St. Petersburg, where the Tsar Alexander made him his 1st violin, at a salary of 5,000 silver roubles and the sole obligation to play at the Court and the Imperial theatre. On the journey he met Spohr at Brunswick, who was so impressed with his playing that he tried to make Rode's style his own. He remained for five years, during which time he met with ever-increasing success and popularity; but the constant excitement of the life at Court placed a great strain on his nervous system, and this had a derogatory effect on his technique, which even his friends could not help noticing at his concert at the Odéon after his return to Paris in 1808. He did not meet with the enthusiasm that greeted him in former years. The recent appearance of Lafont may have contributed to this. Rode felt hurt and withdrew from the public platform, devoting himself to the playing of chamber music in the circle of his friends, and Fétis describes the playing of his own string quartets by himself with Baillot and Lamare (he does not name the viola player) as truly exquisite. Meanwhile his inactivity was pressing upon him and in 1811 he went on tour once more, this time in Bavaria, Switzerland, Hungary, Styria and Bohemia. Spohr, who heard him again at Vienna in 1813, felt disappointed and found him now mannered and wanting in technique and style (see Spohr (ii. 197) also Wki., p. 380); Beethoven also heard him when he played his Sonata in G major, op. 96, with the Archduke Rudolph in a soirée at Prince Lobkowitz', and was dissatisfied.

In 1814 he settled in Berlin and married. Later on he returned to Paris, where in 1828 he was tempted once more to appear in public but with disastrous results, which so unnerved him that his health began to decline. He retired to his Château Bourbon, near Damazon, where he died from the effects of an apoplectic stroke. His wandering life prevented him from the complete training of any particular pupil, but several benefited from his teaching for a longer or shorter period: among these were Jos. Böhm (Vienna) and Ed. Rietz (Berlin). About his compositions, *see* Wasielewski, Moser, etc. His compositions stand on a higher level than those of most of his contemporaries. The concertos testify to nobility of thought, although they show no true inspiration. The concerto No. 7 in A is still occasionally heard, as well as his famous variations. His 24 caprices, however, are standard works and indispensable for all students of the violin.

L. LOULIÉ (LOULLIER), b. Paris, ca. 1775; d. after 1832. A pupil of Gaviniés; became violinist at the Opéra-Comique in 1801 and retired 1832. It is said that he died soon after (Fétis). Pougin says that there were two of this name, that the elder was 2nd violinist at the Comédie Italienne from 1766 to 1786; was probably the father of the above, and the composer of duets and sonatas for violin as well as of sonatas for viola with bass (2 books of 3 each).

LOUIS DE BAILLOU. A French violinist and composer of the second half of the 18th century; d. Milan, 1809. A pupil of Capron, he became leader and conductor at La Scala, Milan, for which he wrote, between 1777 and 1809, operas and ballets. Fétis mentions 20 operas. Milan Conservatoire has by him, in MSS., 4 symphonies, 1 overture; Passo a due and Allemanda, for orchestra and a violin duet in G.

LAGARDE. A mid-18th century French violinist and opera composer, who was chamber musician in the Royal chapel. Under Louis XVI he rose to the position of superintendent of the music of the Count of Artois and music master of the Royal children, which position he held still in 1788. His best known opera was "Eglé"; he also wrote violin solos and chamber music.

MICH. AUG. D'AMBREVILLE. An 18th-century violin concerto with string quartet by him, is in the library of the Musikfreunde, Vienna.

FR. XAVER RAMBACH, of Dunkerque, second half of 18th century. Composed: sei sonate a violino solo e B., gravés par Mme Leclair, op. 11a (Paris, Leclerc).

XAVER MAX RAMBACH, late 18th century. Wrote 6 duets for 2 violins, op. 6 London (Brit. Mus.).

CHAPTER 25

France: to 1800

MLLE DESCHAMPS. A pupil of Capron. From 1775 to 1790 or after she performed at the Concert Spirituel concertos by Capron, Giornovichi, and, it is said, even by J. S. Bach, and is praised in eulogistic terms by all who heard her. *Le Mercure* of Jan., 1785, speaking of her in terms of highest praise, compares her to Maddalena Sirmen; apparently recently married, she was then Madame Gautherot, and in 1790 she counted still among the most eminent violinists (Pougin).

FERDINAND ROUSSEL. In 1799 a violinist at the theatre Lyrique, Paris. Wrote "Guide musical, ou théorie pratique abrégée de la musique vocale et instrumentale" (Paris, 1775).

CHARLES FREDERIC KREUBÉ, b. Luneville, Nov. 5, 1777; d. at his country house near St. Denis in the spring of 1846. Studied the violin at Luneville and became musical director at the Metz theatre. In 1800 he went to study under Rod. Kreutzer at Paris; joined the orchestra of the Opéra-Comique in 1801, where he became 2nd conductor (leader) in 1805 and 1st conductor (chef d'orchestre) from 1816 to Nov., 1828, when he retired with a pension to his country house near St. Denis. From 1814 to 1830 he was also in the Royal chapel. Fétis gives a list of his numerous compositions, including 16 operas for the Opéra-Comique.

ÉLOY DEVICQ, b. Douai, ca. 1778; d. Abbéville, 18..; of an old and distinguished Flemish family, who, driven out by the Revolution of 1792 with the loss of their fortune, found asylum at Hamburg, where Éloy, who had studied the violin from childhood, became their support by giving lessons and playing at the theatre. After some time he went to Russia and lived for several years at St. Petersburg and Moscow. During that time he benefited by his friendly relations with Rode, Baillot, and the famous violoncellist Lamare. In 1809 he returned to France and married at Abbéville, where he settled down, cultivating the violin henceforth only as an amateur. All who heard him play admired his grand classical style and his profound musical feeling. To his enthusiasm for his art Abbéville owes its Conservatoire, which has produced many excellent pupils. He composed Russian airs with variations for violin, with violin, viola, and violoncello, or pianoforte (Paris, Pacini).

ALEXANDRE JEAN BOUCHER, b. Paris, Apr. 11, 1778; d. there, Dec. 29, 1861. He showed very early signs of musical talent, so that the elder Navoigille, in an entirely disinterested manner, took him as a pupil for the violin with such brilliant success that at the age of 6 he played at the French Court, and in his eighth year at a Concert Spirituel. The poverty of his parents compelled him to play for dances and in low-class theatres. For some time he was servant to the violinist and harp player Vicomte de Marie; then he appeared on the stage of the theatre de la Cité, as fiddler in a popular farce, where he was rapturously applauded for his grotesque buffoonery, which unfortunately helped to develop the latent eccentricity of his character. Later on he joined the revolutionary army and distinguished himself by bravery, but this did not help him to find a remunerative employment in his native country. In 1796 he went to Madrid, where his playing was greatly admired, and there he gave most successful quartet soirées with Boccherini. These attracted the attention of the king, who appointed him violinist in the Royal chapel. In 1805 he returned to Paris; when asked if he still indulged in his eccentricities in playing, he replied that he was not only the Alexander but also the Socrates of the violin. Henceforth he was generally nicknamed Socrates. Yet the next time he played a concerto by Rode he added so many runs, tricks and flourishes that it became disfigured beyond recognition. About that time he married the talented harpist Céleste Gallyot, with whom he toured all over Europe until she died in Feb., 1841. He visited Germany repeatedly and his meetings with Goethe and with Beethoven are recorded in the "Goethe Jahrbuch," vol. xii. He had a striking resemblance to Napoleon, which he exploited by imitating the latter, not only in dress but also in his manner of walking, speaking, etc. In Lille he announced his last concert in the following terms: "An unfortunate resemblance compels me to expatriate myself; I shall therefore before leaving my beautiful native country, give a farewell concert," etc. In St. Petersburg he was dressed up at the command of the Czar Alexander in a military uniform and succeeded in deceiving the Dowager Empress until he began to play. Innumerable anecdotes were published about him which would fill a book, and which, needless to say, did not always correspond to fact. This all tends to prove that there is no doubt about his charlatanry, but all the most reliable critics of his time agree that his technique was perfect in every detail, that there were no difficulties which he did not master with ease, and that only Paganini surpassed him in that respect. At times he would, moreover, play an Adagio in the most soulful manner and a Rondo with the most ravishing delicacy in a manner worthy of the greatest artist. In 1844 he visited Germany for the last time and played at Frankfort a/Main. From that time he divided his residence between Paris and Orleans, near which town he had a house. In 1859 he concluded his musical career by a grand and solemn farewell concert in Paris.

JEAN VERDIGUIER, b. Paris, Apr. 11, 1778; d. after 1830. He was a pupil of Gaviniés at the Paris Conservatoire from the time of its foundation; received 1st prize, 1799; was appointed to the opera in 1804 and pensioned 1830. Composed 3 duos, op. 1; 3 sonatas with bass, op. 2, both pub. in Paris (Liepm.). There was also an ed. without op. as "Premier livre des sonates."

JEAN NICOLAS AUGUSTE KREUTZER, b. Versailles, Sept. 3, 1778; d. Paris, Aug. 31, 1832. Studied the violin first under his brother Rodolphe, then entered the Paris Conservatoire, where he gained the 1st and 2nd prize. In 1798 he was appointed to the orchestra of the Opéra-Comique and 1802 in that of the Grand Opera, from which he retired with a pension in 1823. In 1825 he succeeded his brother as professor of the 1st class at the Conservatoire. He composed concertos, duos, and sonatas. He was also in the Court chapels of Napoleon, Louis XVIII and Charles X till 1830. He was rather delicate, and died of pulmonary disease. Spohr says: "The younger Kreutzer let me hear a very brilliant and graceful trio by his brother. The manner in which he played it brought to mind his brother's style, and convinced me that it is the purest, most solid, of the Parisian violinists. The young Kreutzer lacks physical power, he is sickly and often not allowed to play for months together. His tone is consequently somewhat weak, but apart from that his playing is clean, fiery and full of expression."

FÉLICITÉ LEBRUN, b. 1779 (?). A pupil of Baillot, who gained the 2nd prize for violin playing at the first competition of the Paris Conservatoire in the hall of the Odéon, Oct. 25, 1797. The *Citoyenne Lebrun* was then 18 years old and two years later, on a similar occasion, she was awarded the 1st prize.

HONORÉ COMPAN. An 18th-century violinist and harpist in Paris; in 1798 he was still violinist at the theatre de la Pantomime Nationale. His compositions pub. between 1779 and 1783 are all for the harp. He also wrote a "Petite méthode de Musique" (Paris, Frère).

BONAVENTURE HENRY. Appeared as soloist at the Concert Spirituel, Paris, in 1780, in a concerto of his own composition, pub. 1781, which had little success, and became 1st violinist at the theatre Beaujolais, where he was still in 1791. He was also esteemed as a teacher. Fétis enumerates concertos, sonatas, and studies for the violin by him, also a "Méthode de Violon" (Paris, Imbault).

H. J. PERIGNON. From ca. 1780 1st violinist at the Grand Opera, Paris, and at the Concert Spirituel (Gerber, i). Gerber (ii) mentions him still in 1800. Pougin says he was at the opera 1775–1800. His portrait appeared in engraving. He married one of the principal dancers at the opera, the sister of his colleague the violinist Gervais.

JEAN FREDERIC LOISEL. Lived about 1780 in Paris as violinist and died young. According to Fétis he composed 3 violin concertos, op. 2 (Paris), and 6 quartets, op. 1 (Paris, Offenbach, André).

FONTESKI. An 18th-century violinist who introduced Haydn's symphonies in Paris ca. 1780 (Pohl, iv, 175).

J. PUJOLAS. A military music master in France, at the end of the 18th and the beginning of the 19th century; settled at

Orleans as violinist and teacher of music; d. there 1806. He composed violin concertos, trios, and duos (6 duos for 2 violins, advertised 1808).

FRANÇOIS ANTOINE HABENECK, b. Mezières, June 1, 1781 (others: Jan. 22 or 23); d. Paris, Feb. 8, 1849. Son of Adam Habeneck, a Mannheim musician and pupil of Stamitz and Fränzl, who enlisted in a French regiment, and was the first teacher of François and his younger brothers. In Brest, where the father's regiment was then stationed, he studied without assistance, and by 1798-9 he had composed violin concertos and three operas. At the age of 20 he became Baillot's pupil at the Paris Conservatoire, where in 1804 he gained the 1st violin prize and became assistant teacher (Repetitor). The Empress Josephine was so pleased with his performance at a concert that she granted him a pension of 1,200 francs. He supplemented his means by playing at the Opéra-Comique, but soon afterwards he joined the orchestra of the Grand Opera, where in 1818 he succeeded Kreutzer as solo violinist. He had already shown a remarkable talent for conducting at the school concerts of the Conservatoire until the latter was closed in 1815. From 1821 to 1824 he was conductor at the opera. A new concert society was formed at the Conservatoire in 1826 and Habeneck became its director. It was in connexion with these concerts that he acquired his greatest fame, for not only did he bring the orchestra to a high standard of perfection but he cultivated the music of the classical masters, and he was the first to acquaint Paris audiences with Beethoven's works, which they declared to be Barbarian; but Habeneck persisted in the face of all opposition, and eventually was crowned with victory. Afterwards he received the support of Cherubini, and in 1827 he was given a suitable room for his concerts, which became so popular that barely an eighth of those seeking admission could be accommodated, and they flourished under his direction for over twenty-two years. Schindler, Beethoven's friend, praises the perfection of the orchestra, its precision and delicacy. It was under his conductorship that Meyerbeer's "Robert," the "Huguenots," and Halévy's "La Juive" were produced in Paris as well as in the provinces. In 1830 he became 1st violinist in the Royal chapel, and in 1827 he succeeded Kreutzer as capellmeister of the Grand Opera (till 1846).

He was a man of rugged strength and firmness of character, yet much beloved by his friends and pupils, among whom were Alard, Cuvillon, Deldevez, Maurin, Léonard, Prume, Sainton, etc. He composed for violin: 2 concertos, duets, caprices, variations and solo pieces, also some numbers for an opera, which Bennincourt left unfinished; his compositions are of little value. His brothers both studied at the Paris Conservatoire.

JOSEPH HABENECK, b. Quimpercorentin, Apr. 1, 1785; d. (?). Became violinist at the Opéra-Comique, where he rose to the post of 2nd conductor in 1819.

CORENTIN HABENECK, b. Quimpercorentin, 1787. Joined the orchestra of the Grand Opera in 1814, was chamber musician in the Royal chapel until the July revolution, and succeeded Launer as 1st violinist at the "Academie Royale de Musique."

PIERROT BERTIN. Pensioner of the Imperial Academy of Music, Paris. Appeared with his 8-year-old son in a concerto for violin and viola at the Lycée des arts, Paris, on Brumaire 14 (Nov. 4), 1798, and on Jan. 15, 1806, he gave a similar concert at Brussels (Gregoir, "Panth.," vi, 179). Gerber (ii) mentions a Bertin who appeared in London as a pianist in 1793, and in 1796 Bertin is known as a composer in Paris, and 1799 as violinist at the Opera. In 1781 6 duos for 2 violins, op. 1, were pub. in Paris, and Gerber mentions op. 3, 5 and 6 for violin.

CHARLES PHILIPPE LAFONT, b. Paris, Dec. 1, 1781; d. between Bagnères de Bigorre and Tarbes, Aug. 14, 1839, through the overthrow of the mail coach in which he was travelling. He received his first lessons from his mother, a sister of Isidore Berthaume, and herself a violinist, and continued under his uncle, with whom he toured in Germany already in 1792, exciting admiration in public concerts at Hamburg and Lübeck by the purity of his intonation and his technique. Returned to Paris, he studied for two years under Kreutzer, while Navoigille and Berton instructed him in the art of composition. He studied singing by himself, his only guidance being to hear and watch Garat. About that time he sang at the concerts at the theatre Feydeau, French airs and romances with much expression which were greatly applauded. He then became a pupil of Rode, whose style he henceforth strove to emulate. In 1801 he started on a tour in Belgium, but it was through the concerts at the Paris Opera and the theatre Olympique in 1805 and 1806 that he laid the foundation of his world-wide reputation. Between 1806 and 1808 he made frequent and prolonged tours in the Netherlands, Germany, Northern Europe, Italy, and England. In 1808 he succeeded Rode as solo violin at the Court of the Tsar at St. Petersburg. He remained there for several years. In 1815 he was 1st violin in the chamber music of Louis XVIII and in 1816 (not 1812 as stated by many biographers) he went to Italy, where, according to his own account (*see* Stephen S. Stratton's "Paganini," p. 111), he gave, in conjunction with Paganini, a concert in March at La Scala Theatre, Milan, in which they played the concerted symphony in F major for 2 violins and orchestra by Kreutzer. Both have given a detailed account of the event. Lafont's is reproduced verbatim in Stratton's "Nicola Paganini," pp. 111, 112, and Paganini's in A. Niggli's "Nicolo Paganini," p. 298. Lafont says the concert was an amiable collaboration, objects to hear it spoken of as a contest, and says: "I was not beaten by Paganini nor was he by me," but he will not have him placed above the masters of the French school which he says is "the first in the world." Paganini, probably with the consciousness of his superiority, is more generous in saying, "Lafont possessed perhaps the advantage of greater beauty of tone, but the applause of the masses proved to me that I had not succumbed in the contest." Each of the two artists played several solos apart from taking part in the duet. It is interesting to note here what Spohr says with regard to Lafont: "In his playing he combines beauty of tone with the greatest purity of intonation, power and grace, and he would be an absolutely perfect violinist if he possessed also a deeper feeling and had not accustomed himself to the curious habit of the French school to accentuate always the last note of a phrase. Feeling, however, without which one can neither play well nor invent a good Adagio, seems to be lacking in him, as in almost all Frenchmen, for although he knows how to embellish (furnish) a slow movement with many elegant and pretty ornaments, he remains and leaves one rather cold with it. The Adagio seems here to be looked upon as the most unimportant movement of the concerto, which is retained only because it divides the two quick movements well from one another and heightens their effect. It is known that Lafont's virtuosity is always restricted to a few pieces at a time and that he practises for years the same concerto before he plays it in public. Since I have heard what perfection of execution he attains thereby, I will not blame him for the exertion of all his powers to the one end; but I feel incapable of imitating him and cannot understand how one can practise the same piece for 4 to 6 hours, still less how it is possible, by proceeding in such a mechanical way, not to become dead to all true art."

Some time after his appointment as 1st violinist of the King's chamber music he became also accompanist to the Duchess of Berry, and played frequently at public concerts, always meeting with an enthusiastic reception. In 1831 he went on tour in Germany with the pianist Henry Herz; two years later he visited Holland, and in 1838 he went on tour in France and met with the accident mentioned on p. 290. He composed 7 concertos, a large number of fantasias and airs with variations, as well as a number of duos for violin and pianoforte in collaboration with Herz, Kalkbrenner and other pianists; they are of a superficial, virtuoso nature. He also wrote 2 operas and ca. 200 romances. His most prominent pupils were F. Schubert, Ghys, and the sisters Milanollo.

CHARLES GUILLAUME ALEXANDRE. A celebrated French violinist of the second half of the 18th century who composed 6 violin concertos (Paris, 1782) and violin duets, which are of lasting value (not in Eitner). He also wrote operas and operettas which were very popular throughout France down to the time of the Revolution.

ANICOT. Wrote "Méthode de Violon" (Frère, Paris) between 1782 and 1792.

ANTOINE FRANÇOIS HEUDIER, b. Paris, 1782. Entered the Paris Conservatoire in 1792, where he joined the violin class of Gaviniés. He became conductor of the theatre at Versailles, and composed a violin concerto and a set of string quartets pub. at Paris, also some melodramas and ballets.

JACQUES FÉRÉOL MAZAS, b. Beziers, Sept. 23, 1782; d. 1849. A pupil of Baillot at the Paris Conservatoire from 1802 to 1805, when he gained the 1st prize. Soon afterwards he rose to prominence by his playing at the Odéon concerts several concertos by Viotti in a style which combined great breadth with elegance and gracefulness as well as sweetness and power of tone. At the Conservatoire concerts in 1808 he played a concerto in D specially written for him by Auber. After that he was engaged at the Opéra Italienne, but left that position in 1811 to tour in Spain, returning to Paris towards the end of 1813. In 1814 he toured in England, Holland, and Belgium, returning to Paris in 1815. In 1822 he visited Italy, then he toured in Germany, and thence went to Russia. This prolonged tour proved financially a failure, as we find him a few years later in Poland in a precarious position, to which his relations with an adventuress may have largely contributed, and in 1826 he was at Lemberg, ill and almost at the end of his resources. In the following year he revisited Germany and this time obtained brilliant success at Berlin and other large German towns. In 1829 he returned to Paris and played at the Conservatoire concerts, but even his best friends had to admit that as a soloist his powers had diminished and no longer possessed the charm of former years. In 1831 he accepted an engagement as 1st violinist at the theatre of the Palais Royal, which he left not long after for the post of professor and musical director at Orleans, and in 1837 he became director of the communal School of Music at Cambrai. He composed a concerto, fantasias, solos, quartets, trios, etc., which are all antiquated. His excellent tutors, one for the violin and one for the viola, his violin studies, and duets remained in use until quite recent times, and some are used still.

FRANÇOIS DUFRESNE, b. Paris, 1783 (Fétis: vers 1780) and still active in 1825. Son of a musician of the Comédie Française. As a pupil of Gaviniés he studied at the Conservatoire 1797–1800; was violinist at the Opéra-Comique till 1806, then concertmeister (Mendel: capellmeister) at the Nantes theatre, and from 1809 at several institutes in Paris. He composed violin concertos, duos, trios, and potpourris. (*See* Wki. who calls him Ferdinand, D., p. 370).

CHEVALIER J. J. O. DE MEUDE-MONPAS. An amateur violinist who was a black musketeer under Louis XVI. He devoted himself to music and composed 6 violin concertos with orchestra, which were pub. before 1783 (Fétis: 1786); he also wrote a "Dictionaire de Musique" which is absolutely worthless. According to Fétis he was a pupil of La Houssaye for violin and of Abbé Giroust for composition. He fled at the outbreak of the Revolution and afterwards was in Berlin, where he wrote and pub. some bad French poetry.

DUMAS. A violinist who appeared at the Concert Spirituel in 1784. (*See* Brenet.)

GEORGE EUGÈNE NEUKOME, b. Saint-Quentin, Mar. 14, 1784. Violinist and professor of Music at St. Quentin, where he received his first lessons in music and violin playing from Jumentier, the director of a singing school. Afterwards he was a pupil of Kreutzer in Paris and returned to St. Quentin as an esteemed violinist, teacher and composer. His first compositions appeared under the pseudonym of "Kuffner." He was still living ca. 1836. Composed under his own name some airs with variations and a rondo brilliant with orchestra, pub. in Paris, Richaut; also trios, quatuors, rondos, etc.

FELICIEN TIBURCE AUGUSTE DUPIÈRGE, b. Courbevoye, near Paris, Apr. 11, 1784. Studied the violin and composition under his father; violinist at the Opéra-Comique, Paris, until 1815, when he settled in Rome as teacher. He composed violin concertos, duo-sonatas, for violin and pianoforte, solos, violin duets, a tutor for the violin, etc. His compositions were held in high esteem by his countrymen.

PIERRE AUGUSTE LOUIS BLONDEAU, b. Paris, Aug. 15, 1784; d. there 1865. Studied the violin at the Conservatoire under Baillot, theory and composition under Gossec and Méhul. He distinguished himself chiefly as composer; duets, airs variés, romances, etc., for violin, concertos for various instruments, chamber music, an opera, cantatas, overtures, church music, etc. He wrote also several works on musical theory, and a history of modern music, Paris, 1827.

PIERRE CRÉMONT, b. Southern France, 1784; d. Tours, Mar. 12, 1848. In the year 1802 he entered the Paris Conservatoire, where he studied the violin and the clarinet until 1803. He then went on a tour which brought him to St. Petersburg, where he became conductor at the French theatre. He returned to France in 1817 and became 1st violinist at the Paris Opéra-Comique in 1821, and in 1824 conductor of the

France: to 1800

Odéon until he was appointed in that capacity at the Opéra-Comique in 1828, and in 1831 he accepted a similar position at the Grand Theatre, Lyons. He did not remain there long, but retired to Tours, where he led a quiet and solitary life until he died. He composed a violin concerto, violin duets, trios for 2 violins and viola, and fantasies for violin, also a clarinet concerto, pieces for military band, etc.

BÉCOURT, ca. 1785. A violinist at the theatre Beaujolais, Paris. Composed airs, and a contredanse, the "Carillon Nationale," which the Queen Marie Antoinette delighted to play on the harpsichord, and to which a street singer in 1789 wrote the words "Ah! ça ira," by which it became popular throughout France as the notorious Revolutionary song.

GEORG ANTON WALTER. Settled in Paris in ca. 1785 and became a pupil of Kreutzer; in 1792 he was appointed conductor at the opera at Rouen, where he was still in 1801. Fétis and Gerber ii mention a number of instrumental works by him which all appeared at the end of the 18th century. Fétis records: 3 trios for 2 violins and bass; violin duets, books I–VIII, and duets, op. 14; 6 sonatas for violin and bass, op. 24; also string quartets, op. 1, 2, 5 and 7, all pub. in Paris.

MARIE JOSEPH BOUVIER, b. Colorno, near Rome, (?); d. Paris, 1823. At the age of 7 he became a violin pupil of Antoine Richer of Versailles, one of the 1st violinists of the Duke of Parma. Bouvier entered the chapel of that Prince at the age of 12. Afterwards he studied under Pugnani, who recommended him to Viotti, who secured his debut at the Concert Spirituel in 1785. After several appearances at these concerts he became a member of the Comédie Italienne orchestra, which position he held till his death. He composed 6 sonatas for violin and some books of romances for voice. His daughter Jenny was a talented opera singer who died of consumption in 1801.

ANTOINE NICHOLAS MARIE FONTAINE, b. Paris, 1785. Received his first music and violin lessons from his father, a musician at the Opera. Afterwards he was successively the pupil of Lafont and Kreutzer. In 1806 he entered the Conservatoire, where he studied theory under Catel, Daussoigne, and Reicha; gained the 1st violin prize in 1809. (Wki. states that he also received instruction from Baillot.) At the end of his studies he began to tour in France, Belgium, and the German Rheinland, and continued his concert tours for ten years with but casual visits to Paris to publish some of his compositions. At the end of that time he became tired of this restless and trying existence and ca. 1825 he settled down in Paris and devoted himself to teaching. Charles X appointed him solo violinist in his Private Chamber Music, a place and title of which the Revolution of 1830 deprived him. His pub. compositions for violin consist in 3 concertos, airs variés, fantasias, duets, rondos, a serenade, etc., which in their time enjoyed a large measure of popularity.

DURIEN appeared at Concert Spirituel in Paris in 1785, also played at Concert des Amateurs, and had a music-shop. He wrote a tutor for the violin, pub. Paris, Durien (1796).

FRANÇOIS BONNAY. Eitner: In 1785 violinist at the Paris Grand Opera. Two little operas of his were performed at the "Theatre de Beaujolais," 1786. Only the overtures of these were pub. (Fétis).

DENIS PIRIOT. A French violinist of the 2nd half of the 18th century. He composed 5 symphonies, pub. by Imbault, Paris, 1786. Fétis says: Pierlot (. . .), a violinist attached to the Concert Spirituel in 1786, pub. through Imbault, Paris: 3 symphonies for 2 violins, viola and bass, 2 oboes, 2 horns, op. 1; 1st and 2nd concertante symphony for 2 violins and orchestra. Evidently the same.

ROSE. Violinist at the Comédie Française. Wrote a double concerto for 2 violins à 9, pub. Paris 1786 (Gerber, i).

ANGELO VARESE DETTO SANTANGOLINO. Ca. 1788, 1st violinist and conductor at the Opera Bouffe, Paris (Gerber, ii).

LANCEZ. Known by his portrait of 1788, on which he is described as: "Professor du violon," 1st violinist in the fourth row at the Grand Opera, Paris (Gerber, ii).

JEAN BAPTISTE LERICHE. Played, 1789, a concerto for violin and orchestra, of his own composition (Paris, Sieber), at the Concert Spirituel; composed also 24 petits duos for 2 violins, oe. 4 (Fétis).

PIERRE MARCON. In 1790 he was appointed as violinist in the Royal chapel in Paris, became a member of the theatre

France: to 1800

orchestra at Rouen ca. 1795 and one of the 1st violins at theatre Lyrique, Paris; in 1798 there as music teacher. Went to Nancy in 1800, where he established himself as teacher of music. In 1804 he went as teacher to Bourges and remained there to the time of his death, ca. 1820. He wrote a theoretical work, "Eléments théorétiques et pratiques," which appeared in 3 ed. between 1797 and 1804.

GABRIEL ANTOINE DELORTH (Fétis says "Henry") was violinist at the theatre Beaujolais, Paris, and wrote: "Moyen de rectifier la gamme de la musique et de faire chanter juste," pub. Paris, 1791.

JULIEN BAUX. Violin prodigy, appeared in London in 1794 (Pohl, ii, 370). In 1799 he appeared at Hamburg, where he played concertos by Viotti (Gerber, ii).

GUERIN (PUINÉ), b. Versailles (?), 17... Brother of the cellist E. Guerin, aîné. Entered the Paris Conservatoire in 1796, where he became an assistant teacher and afterwards professor of violin. In 1824 he became also 1st violin at the Opera. Brenet ("Les Concerts en France") mentions a Guerin who appeared as violin virtuoso at the Concert Spirituel in 1775, which evidently was of an earlier generation. There appears to be a good deal of confusion with regard to the Guerins which it would take more trouble to solve than their importance warrants.

LABADENS. A Frenchman who was violinist in the orchestra of the Grand Opera ca. 1797. He no longer appears in the lists from 1802. He wrote a "Nouvelle méthode pour le violon" (Paris, Nadermann, 1797).

TURLET, d. at the hospital of Toulouse, ca. 1799. Mentioned by Choron and Fayolle as a pupil of Tartini, who was called the "Tartini du midi"; he composed concertos, duets, and caprices for the violin.

DESNOSE. A violinist of the second half of the 18th century. Lived at Toulouse, and composed, according to Pougin: "Six quartuors dialogués d'un genre nouveau, pour 2 violins, A. et B. oe. 12."

HONORÉ COMER. Harp and violin teacher of the late 18th century (Eitner).

THÉODORE SEGURA, b. Lyons, 17... Violinist, guitarist and composer; settled in Paris ca. 1816, where a number of airs with variations for violin, with quartet and pianoforte accompaniment, were pub.

J. (GIOVANNI) FREY. Studied the violin at the Paris Conservatoire about the end of the 18th century. He started a music-publishing business at the beginning of the 19th century which, according to Fétis, he had still ca. 1830. In 1817 he became viola player at the Opera and also played that instrument in the Conservatoire concerts. He wrote and published a "Méthode élémentaire de violon," 4°, Paris. A MS. violin concerto with 2 violins and bass, in score, and a trio for 2 violins are in the Dresden Mus. library.

LADURNER (née MUSSIER DE GONDREVILLE—prof. name MLLE DE LA GONCHÈRE), d. Maison Royale de Saint-Denis, Oct. 25, 1823. An excellent violinist, pupil of Mestrino, who often played in concerts in Paris, wife of the composer Ladurner. After her marriage, which practically ended her brilliant public career as a soloist, she gave weekly private concerts at her house, where her remarkable talent delighted those amateurs who had the privilege of attending. By some unexplained peculiar circumstances she was, after the Restoration, appointed Directress of the Maison Royale of Saint-Denis.

MORITZ ALLEAUMES, b. latter part of the 18th century. An eminent violinist who was a Royal chamber musician at Munich. In 1835 he toured with marked success in Bavaria, Austria, and Württemberg. His talented son was murdered. No other particulars are available.

COUPRIN (COUPERIN ?). Dresden Mus., Autograph MS. Sonata a violon e bass score.

CHAPTER 26

Germany: to 1725

IN the course of the 17th century German violin playing had from the technical point risen to greater heights than that of any other country, but the German style was not capable of the development which the art of violin playing experienced at the hands of the Italians, especially those of Corelli. The German players were alive to the fact, but while they proved apt pupils, they assimilated all they learned in such a manner that it received the impress of their own mentality. Even the genius of Bach did not disdain to study the form of the Italian concerts, nor to benefit from the technical achievements of Walther and Biber, but he extended and raised them to far greater and mightier creations. His contemporaries, Pisendel and Telemann, followed more closely in the footsteps of their masters, especially those of Torelli. Pisendel amalgamated the style of Torelli with that of the French violinist Volumier, at Dresden, to a quite remarkable style of his own (*see* Schering, "Geschichte des Instrumental Konzerts," p. 119). His friend Franz Benda had a much greater influence upon the development of violin playing in Germany, as the founder of a school at Dresden and also of one in Berlin, while J. W. Stamitz founded, about 1745, the famous Mannheim School which, through his pupils, Carl Stamitz (his son), Fränzl, Cannabich, and Wm. Cramer, exercised its influence throughout Europe. Fränzl's pupil, F. W. Pixis, became the founder of the Prague school, and teacher of Mildner and Laub. J. T. Eck and his brother Franz, the teacher of Spohr, also proceeded from the Mannheim school, although the principal field of their activity was elsewhere.

The German art of violin playing was largely indebted to the Bohemians, the Bendas, Stamitz, Eck and others, who were either born in Bohemia, although coming to Germany in early life, or they were, like Eck, of Bohemian origin. The Bohemian musicians, on the other hand, were encouraged by the custom of the Austrian, and afterwards also by that of their own nobles, to maintain either a private orchestra, or at least a private quartet. Where the means were not sufficient to engage only professional players, servants or employees, showing any musical talent, received tuition at the expense of their master, and then had to join his orchestra. This created a friendly rivalry between the Courts of the nobles, and a demand for new compositions, specially written for one or the other, which gave employment to a considerable number of composers, many of whom were good violinists or well acquainted with the technique, like Dittersdorf, Gyrowetz, Krommer, Hoffmeister, the brothers Wranitzky, Wanhal, etc., and who contributed to the development of the art of violin playing. Important in this respect were also the sometimes prolonged visits to Vienna and Prague of many eminent Italian violinists.

One of the most important events in the 18th-century history of the violin was the appearance of Leopold Mozart's Tutor for the violin in 1756. Although Mozart was mistaken in believing that his was the first work of its kind, as he was evidently unacquainted with the tutors of Playford ("Skill of Music"), D. Merck, Geminiani, and Monteclair, his was far more thorough and systematic than any of the preceding ones. He carries on the traditions of Franz Benda and the Mannheim school and lays strong emphasis on the difference between good musicianship and mere virtuosoship. The violin he considers in the first instance as a *cantabile* instrument, and protests emphatically against the senseless abuse of embellishments in the Adagio, only too common during the later 18th and even the early 19th centuries. Based upon a close and conscientious study of the works of the older masters, especially those of Tartini, he developed a thoroughly sound system of violin playing, devoting a large part of his book to the art of bowing, illustrated by carefully chosen examples. His tutor, which appeared in at least five ed., in 1804 also simultaneously in Vienna and in Leipzig, remained for several generations the leading textbook for violin students, and the fact that it was translated into both the French and the Dutch languages shows how highly it was esteemed in foreign countries, as well as in its own.

JOHANN GEORG PISENDEL, b. Kadolzburg, Austria, Dec. 26, 1687; d. Dresden, Nov. 25, 1755. He showed musical talent in early youth and was taught singing by his father, a musician. The Margrave of Ansbach, who heard him in church in 1696, was so pleased with his voice that he took him as a choirboy into his chapel of which Torelli was then 1st violinist, and from him Pisendel learnt to play the violin, making such rapid progress that he soon became a member of the orchestra. In 1709 he went to the University of Leipzig as a law student, but his love for music supervened. In 1711 he played a concerto by his master Torelli at the Colegium Musicum, and J. Ad. Hiller tells with very amusing detail how he astonished his hearers to such an extent that they chose him as conductor of their orchestra and he received also the equivalent positions at the New Church and the Opera. He acquitted himself of all his duties with the greatest distinction and he was generally as much beloved for his upright and amiable personality as for his artistic excellence. About this time Volumier, then capellmeister at the Dresden Court, heard him play and engaged him for the Electoral Chapel, which he entered in 1712. In 1714 he and Volumier accompanied the Hereditary Prince to Paris, then to Berlin, and in 1716 to Italy, where he studied for some time, first under Vivaldi at Venice, then in 1717 under Montanari at Rome, afterwards visiting Naples and other Italian towns. In this manner he absorbed all he found best, both in the French and Italian style of playing, and transmitted it to his pupils, the most important of whom was Joh. Gottlieb Graun, by whom his achievements were handed down to the North German school of Berlin. In 1718 he visited Vienna on his return from Italy and was greatly admired as a virtuoso. He was not only in possession of a brilliant technique, but also a great artist in the rendering of the works he played, and particularly in the expression he gave to an Adagio. Quantz in his autobiography states that he learnt most in this respect from Pisendel. Türk also praises him in his "Klavierschule" (p. 113). After the death of Volumier in 1728, Pisendel took over his duties, at first temporarily, but on Oct. 1, 1731, he was definitely appointed as capellmeister to the Dresden Court. Both Gerber and Reichardt speak of the care he bestowed upon the training of his orchestra. Whenever Hasse had finished a new opera he used to consult Pisendel with regard to every detail required to ensure a perfect rendering, and as the orchestral parts left the copyist's hands they were given to Pisendel who would, with the minutest care, enter all marks of expression as well as for the bowing of the string instruments. In this manner he achieved an accuracy and perfection of ensemble which had hitherto been unknown at the Court. In 1734 he followed the Elector (as King of Poland) to Warsaw with some of the musicians of the Dresden chapel. Pisendel was the only notable virtuoso on Bach's viola pomposa (*see* E. v. d. Str., "Hist. of the Violoncello").

Many of his compositions are said to have perished in the bombardment of Dresden in the Seven Years War. There are, however, still in the Dresden Royal library, 8 violin concertos, 2 solos with bass, 3 concertos for 2 oboes with stringed instruments, 2 concerti grossi, 1 symphony, and cadenzas to violin concertos. One violin sonata edited by Studeny has been repub. by the Wunderhorn Verlag, and one concerto by A. Schering (D.d.T., vol. 29/30). A gigue in Telemann's "Musikmeister," p. 49.

JACOBUS NOZEMAN, b. Hamburg, Sept. 3 (Pougin, Aug. 30), 1693; d. Amsterdam (Idus), Oct. 10, 1745. Composed sonatas for violin and bass, 6 each, op. 1, 2, 5 (Amst., Le Cĕne). Mich. Corrette's "L'Art de Violon" contains 1 piece. He composed also pianoforte pieces. He was violinist at Hamburg till ca. 1724, and afterwards went to Amsterdam as organist of the Remonstrant church.

DANIEL GOTTLIEB TREU (called FEDELE), b. Stuttgart, 1695; d. Breslau, Aug. 7, 1749. From an assistant of his father, a printer, he received his first violin lessons as a child; at school he learned singing and pianoforte, and became a pupil of Kusser, who was his uncle. By that time he had composed instrumental music and operas, and ca. 1716 he produced a composition for the Duke's birthday and also played a violin solo at the Court, which so pleased the Duke that he gave him the means to study under Vivaldi and Bitti at Venice, where Treu had several operas produced, and was offered the post of capellmeister. In his autobiography in Mattheson's "Ehrenpforte" he relates the romantic adventures of his journey to Italy. He engaged at Venice a troupe of excellent Italian singers and musicians and with these he went to Breslau, where he became capellmeister in 1725. From 1727 he was in the same capacity in the service of several Silesian noblemen at Prague, and in 1740 of that of Count Schafgotsch at Hirschberg in Silesia. He devoted himself chiefly to the composition of operas and also wrote 2 Latin treatises on music.

IGNAZ STADLMANN. Köchel (ii, 230, 446, 448) calls him alternatively Stadelmair. B. ca. 1697. During 1734–41 he was Court scholar for violin in the Imperial Chapel. Köchel (i, No. 939 and 1081) mentions an Ign. Stadelmann who was violinist in the Court chapel from Jan. 1, 1736, to his death, aged 39, Feb. 24, 1753, with a salary of 400 florins; whether this is the same as above remains to be investigated; also whether he was related to Daniel Achatius Stadlmann (ca. 1680–1744), a good copyist of Stainer who made Haydn's baryton, and Joh. Joseph Stadlmann, also a copyist of Stainer of average merit, of the 18th century.

JOHANN PFEIFFER, b. Nürnberg, Jan. 1, 1697; d. Bayreuth, 1761. Studied at the University of Halle and Leipzig, and the violin under Fischer. His first appointment was with Count Reuss-Schleitz. Became violinist in 1720 and in 1726 was concertmeister in the Court chapel at Weimar. He accompanied the Duke in 1729–30 on journeys through Holland, the Netherlands, and France, and in 1734 was called to Bayreuth as capellmeister, remaining in that position till his death. Composed 7 violin concertos, overtures, partitas and a cantata.

GEORG GOTTFRIED WAGNER, b. Mühlberg, Saxony, Apr. 5, 1698; d. Plauen, Mar. 23, 1756. Son of a cantor who instructed him early in the playing of various instruments. He preferred the violin, which he played so well that on special occasions he was engaged at various German courts. From 1712 to 1719 he visited the school of St. Thomas at Leipzig, where he studied music under Kuhnau, and when the latter was succeeded by J. S. Bach, he remained three more years, in the Grandmaster's orchestra as leader. In 1726 he became, on Bach's recommendation, cantor at Plauen, Voigtland, where he remained to the end. His compositions, which were widely known and popular about the middle of the 18th century, but remained unpublished, comprised besides violin concertos and solos, trios, oratorios, numerous church compositions, overtures, etc.

JOHANN GEORG ORSCHLER, b. Breslau, 1698. He received his first music lessons from the organist Michel Kirsten; became a page of Count Zirotin, who sent him to Berlin to study the violin under Frey and Rosetti, and then to Fux, in Vienna, to study counterpoint. In 1730 he became capellmeister at the Court of Prince Lichtenstein at Olmütz, but afterwards returned to Vienna. In 1766 he was still active as violinist at the Court in Vienna. He composed 24 trios (for 2 violins and bass?) and 6 solos for violin, also church symphonies in 4 parts, but all remained in MS.

JOHANN GOTTLIEB GRAUN, b. Wahrenbrück, ca. 1698; d. Berlin, Oct. 27, 1771. He was educated at the Kreutzschule, Dresden, and studied the violin under Pisendel and Tartini. In 1726 he became director of the chapel at Merseburg (Friedemann Bach was his pupil), where he wrote his 6 violin and cembalo sonatas, thence he entered in 1727 the service of the Prince of Waldeck, whence he was called in 1732 to the chapel of the Prussian Crown Prince at Rheinsberg, and on the latter's accession in 1740 became concertmeister at Berlin with a salary of 800 thaler, afterwards 1,200 thaler (Schneider, iv, 169; Bitter's "Bach"; Ledebur; Burney, iii, 171 ff.; *see also* Wki., etc., etc.). He was a prolific composer; the MSS. of his works, including symphonies, overtures, concertos, trios, cantatas, church and secular vocal music, are in the Joachimsthal and the Royal libraries in Berlin. The Dresden Museum has the MSS. of 51 violin concertos with quartet; 18 solos with bass; 13 trios for 2 violins and bass; 11 do. with Christian name; symphonies, overtures, etc.

His brother was KARL HEINRICH GRAUN, the favourite capellmeister at the Court of Berlin, now best remembered by his cantata "The Death of Jesus."

EBERHARD REINWALD. Violinist and conductor of the concerts at Hamburg from 1700 to 1721. Mattheson (i, 132) says

Germany: to 1725

that he and Reinwald, "ein starker violinist," conducted the Sunday concerts in winter, 1700–1, given by Count von Eckgh to the crème of society (feinste Publikum), where they received ample payment and choice refreshments. Keiser was also there, but conducted himself more as cavalier than as musician.

ANTGARTEN. A numerous family of musicians, Kur-Köln, ca. 1700. ARNOLD ANTGARTEN was 1st violin in the Electoral Chapel at Bonn, and ordered to teach Musical Science to the boys of the chapel at 100 florins per annum. Appointed on Jan. 23, 1701, he held that position only till Sept., 1701 (Thayer, i, 12). Several other members of the family were in the Electoral Chapel during the first half of the 18th century, but no instruments are specified.

LUDWIG ALBERT FRIEDRICH BAPTISTE, b. Oettingen, Suabia, Aug. 8, 1700; d. Cassel, ca. 1770. At the age of 3 he went with his father to Darmstadt, where he remained till his 17th year. In 1718 he went to Paris, but the French music was not to his taste, and he set out for Italy, where he travelled about, afterwards visiting various other Continental countries, settling in 1723 as violinist and dancer in the Court chapel at Cassel. He composed 12 solos for violin; 6 solos for violoncello; 6 trios for oboes and bass; more than 36 solos and 12 concertos for viola da gamba; and 6 sonatas for flute travers, pub. at Augsburg. (Fétis, *see also* Eitner's list.)

JOHANN JOACHIM AGRELL, b. Löth, East-Gotland, Feb. 1, 1701; d. Nuremberg, Jan. 19, 1765. He was a violinist and Court musician between 1723 and 1746 at Cassel, where he also established a reputation as a harpsichord virtuoso. In 1746 he became capellmeister at Nuremberg. He composed concertos, sonatas, etc., mostly for the harpsichord, also symphonies.

KARL FRIEDRICH RIECK, d. 1704. Obercapellmeister of Friedrich I, virtuoso on the cembalo and violin (*see* Eitner).

KARL FRIEDRICH RIECK, violinist, 1710–12 (*see* Ledebur).

RIECK, b. Berlin, 1730. Entered Berlin chapel as violinist in 1755. During the Seven Years War he migrated to England, returned to Berlin as private musician, where he is mentioned in 1772. Composed symphonies and violin pieces. (Marpurs, i, 586, mentions him.)

RIECK, JUN., 2nd violin in Berlin Court chapel in 1712 (Schneider, 55).

FERDINAND SEIDEL, b. Falkenberg, Silesia, in 1705. A violin pupil of Rosetti in Vienna. Returning to Falkenberg, he and his brother Karl entered in 1732 the service of Count Zierotin, who charged himself with their education. Afterwards he went to Salzburg, where in 1757 he became Court composer to the Archbishop of Salzburg, and conducted the performances alternately with Eberlin, Cristelli, and Leopold Mozart (Walther; Gerber, i). He composed symphonies and violin concertos, which were said to have been very difficult. Only 12 menuets for violin were pub. (Leipzig, 1753).

JUSTUS BERNHARD WIEDEMANN. Was, on Jan. 16, 1705, appointed chamber musician and violinist in the Court chapel, Berlin. In 1712 he was 1st violin there, with a salary of 400 thaler (Schneider, 52). In 1713 the chapel was dismissed and he went to London as master of the King's band, where he preceded Stanley. Quantz met him in London in 1727 as a renowned flautist (?).

JACOB CRAMER, b. 1705 at Sachau (Fétis) in Silesia. The head of a long and numerous line of musicians, he became a member of the Mannheim Court chapel in the forties of the 18th century. *The Musical Almanach* of 1782 says: "He is one of the best soloists on the violin; his style and his compositions are very brilliant." Walter mentions him in the list of 1747–70. Mendel mentions him as flautist and says he died in 1770.

JOHANN NICHOLAS FISCHER, b. Behlen, Schwartzburg, 1707. A violinist of distinction, in the service of Duke Augustus William of Brunswick. He composed among other works, 6 violin concertos, solos for violin, and 6 symphonies for 2 violins, 2 flutes, viol and bass.

JOSEPH BLUME, b. Munich, 1708; d. Berlin, 1782. The son of a violinist in the Munich chapel, he was first appointed violinist in the same chapel, after that in the chapel of Prince Wielopolski, then that of Prince Lubomirski in Poland, and finally, ca. 1733, in the chapel of the Crown Prince of Prussia and after the latter's accession to the throne, in the Royal chapel in Berlin. His caprices for the violin enjoyed a wide reputation and were popular for a long time. In Marpurg, i, 546 (Exempl. BB.), is a marginal note: "lebt sehr kläglich" (lives in very poor circumstances).

JOSEPH IDELPHONSE MICHEL (MICHL), b. Neumarkt, Bavaria, 1708; d. Ratisbon, 1770. A violinist who studied composition under Wagenseil, became capellmeister of the Duke of Sulzbach and after the death of the latter in 1733 was called to the Court of Thurn and Taxis at Ratisbon. He is praised as an excellent violinist and composer who wrote for various Courts operas and oratorios but burnt all in a fit of melancholia except 6 violin concertos which remained in MS. in the Court library at Ratisbon. His younger brother FERDINAND MICHEL, b. Neumarkt, 1713, d. Munich, 1753, who was organist at the Jesuit church of St. Michel at Munich, but also a good violinist, wrote trios for 2 violins and basso continuo, under the title "XII symphoniæ tribus concertantibus instrumentis, scilicet violino 1 et 2 ac basso continuo, op. 1" (Augsburg, 1740).

FRIEDRICH VON ERLACH, b. Berlin, Aug. 2, 1708; d. there 1757 (according to Schilling, 1772). (Son of a captain of the Guards.) Blind virtuoso on the violin, harpsichord, flute à bec (recorder) and viol da gamba. He appeared frequently at the weekly concerts of the organist Sack, in Berlin (Ledebur), where he played the recorder, which he had improved and on which he was a virtuoso. He constructed also a recorder with two tubes tuned in thirds, see Walther's "Lexikon" (Fétis). In 1730 he lived at Eisenach, but returned afterwards to Berlin.

NAZARIO (Fétis writes NASSOVIUS) DEHEC, b. ca. 1710 in Germany. Appointed as 1st violin at S. Maria Maggiore at Bergamo. He composed Sei Sonate a Violino e Basso, op. 3 (Paris, Bayard), ca. 1760 (Cons., Paris). Fétis mentions 6 trios for the violin (2 violins and bass?), Nuremberg, 1760. Other compositions of his, which are known, remained in MS.

JOHANN SERTA. During 1710–29, violinist and teacher at the *Domstift*, Salzburg, afterwards concertmeister (Peregrinus, 93, 169), at the Episcopal Court.

MARTIN FRIEDRICH MARX (MARCKS). From 1711 violinist in Berlin Court chapel with a salary of 100 thaler, and from 1712 of 200 thaler.

SEBASTIAN BODINI (BODINUS: Eitner), b. Duchy of Altenburg, 17... Chamber musician in the Württemberg Court chapel before 1726 and ca. 1756, concertmeister of the Margrave of Baden-Durlach. Composed 6 works of 6 quartets and trios for various instruments, pub. at Augsburg, under the title of: "Musikalisches Divertissement," and 6 sonatas for violin and B.c. entitled "Acroama Musicum."

JOHANN GABRIEL SEYFFARTH, b. Reisdorf, Duchy of Weimar, ca. 1711; d. Berlin, Apr. 9, 1796. Pupil of Johann Gottfried Walther at Weimar. He went thence to Zerbst and studied the violin under Höckh and composition under Tasch; was appointed in the Chapel of Markgrave Heinrich in Berlin, and 1740 in the Royal Chapel and the Opera orchestra there, for which he had also to write the ballet music. He composed violin concertos, trios, symphonies, etc. (Gerber (i), Ledebur, Bitter (i, 26) calls him Seifarth and gives his salary as 300 thaler.) His ballet music in particular met with marked success.

JOSEPH SPIESS (SPIES). From ca. 1711 was 1st violinist in the Court chapel, Berlin, with a salary of 150 thaler, and from 1712 300 thaler (Schneider 55, H. 35). In 1718 he was premier chamber musician in the Court chapel of Cöthen under Bach (Spitta, ii, 985; Hosaens, 7).

JOHANN GRAAB. Known, 1712, as violinist and instrument-maker at the Electoral Court of Cologne; re-appointed July 12, 1725, by Clemens August, without salary! (Thayer, i, 23).

JEAN BAPTISTE VEZIN, b. Hanover, 1712, as ninth child of the Court musician Pierre Vezin. After the father's death he entered the Hanover chapel, and became concertmeister and director of it in 1765 with a salary of 355 thaler. As a young man he had visited Milan, Turin and London. Forkel (i, 134) mentions him in 1781. (Dr. Fischer, "Musik in Hanover," p. 33.) Whether he was a violinist is uncertain.

JOHANN GOTTLOB FREUDENBERG (FREYDENBERG), b. 1712 at Wachau (Dresden). Entered the Prussian Court chapel in 1743 with a salary of 200 thaler per annum. Reichard mentions him as still being a member of that chapel in 1777 (also Marpurg, i, 77, 548).

Germany: to 1725

BENDA. Apart from Franz (q.v.), its chief representative, there were seven members of the family as violinists at the Court in Berlin, while one occupied positions as violinist and conductor at Hamburg and Königsberg.

JOHANN WENZEL BENDA, b. Alt-Benatek, Apr. 16, 1713; d. Berlin, 1752. Was a violinist at the Court at Dresden in 1733, whence his brother Franz brought him to Rheinsberg in 1734 and gave him further tuition. In 1740 he became Royal chamber musician and violinist at the Opera. He composed 3 violin concertos which remained in MS.

GEORG BENDA, b. Jungbunzlau, 1721; d. Köstritz, Altenburg, Nov. 6, 1795. The third son of Hans Georg. When Franz, with the King's permission, reunited the whole of his family in Berlin in 1740, Georg became his pupil and progressed so rapidly that in 1742 he was appointed as 2nd violinist in the Royal chapel; meanwhile he studied the harpsichord, oboe and composition, and in 1748 he became capellmeister at the Court of Gotha. The Duke sent him to Italy for further studies in composition, and he became a composer of European fame.

JOSEPH BENDA, b. Alt-Benatek, Mar. 7, 1724; d. Berlin, Feb. 22, 1804. The youngest son of Hans Georg, and violin pupil of his brother Franz. In 1742 he became a Royal chamber musician; later on, deputy concertmeister, and on the death of Franz in 1786 he succeeded the latter as concertmeister. On the accession of Friedrich Wilhelm III, in 1797, he was given a pension of 800 thaler per annum.

FRIEDRICH WILHELM HEINRICH BENDA, b. Potsdam, July 15, 1745; d. there, June 19, 1814. Elder son and pupil of Franz; was a chamber musician in the Royal chapel from 1765 to 1810, when he was pensioned. He was also a good pianist and organist and studied composition under Kirnberger. He became favourably known as a composer of operas, 2 oratorios, cantatas, concertos for various instruments, trios, sonatas, etc.

ERNST FRIEDRICH JOHANN BENDA, b. Berlin, 1747; d. there Feb., 1785. The elder son of Joseph, studied violin and pianoforte, became a chamber musician in the Royal chapel in 1766. In conjunction with K. L. Bachmann he conducted from 1770 the very popular amateur concerts of which he was a co-founder. Of his compositions, only a minuet with variations (Leipzig, Breitkopf and Härtel) is known.

KARL FRANZ BENDA, b. Berlin, 1751; d. there Dec. 1, 1816. The younger son of Joseph, as his brother Ernst he became a Royal chamber musician. No other particulars are available.

KARL HERMANN HEINRICH BENDA, b. Potsdam, May 2, 1748; d. Berlin, Mar. 15, 1836. Younger son and pupil of Franz and most gifted of the younger members of that talented family. He approached nearest of all to his father in technique and tone, and in his incomparable rendering of the Adagio. Reichardt in his letters ("Briefe eines aufmerksamen Reisenden," vol. i, p. 162) gives a long detailed description of his style and technique, which contains, however, some fallacies in Reichardt's own ideas about violin technics. Karl became a member of the Royal chapel when he was barely 18 years old. Later on, he became assistant conductor of ballet rehearsals and in 1802 concertmeister. When the orchestras of the Opera and the National Theatre were merged into one, he obtained his pension. Karl was also greatly esteemed as a teacher of the pianoforte, King Friedrich Wilhelm III and K. F. Rungenhagen being among his pupils for that instrument. Among his compositions are a sonata for violin and bass, and 6 adagios for pianoforte, with observations on the rendering of the Adagio. These observations were published separately in the *Allgemeine Musik Zeitung*, Leipzig, 1810.

FRIEDRICH LUDWIG BENDA, b. Gotha, 1746; d. Königsberg, Mar. 27, 1793; (Baktie: Feb. 22, 1793; Riemann: Mar. 20, 1792). Eldest son and pupil of Georg; was conductor of Seyler's theatrical company in 1778, at the Hamburg theatre in 1782, when he married the then famous singer, Felicita Agnesia Reitz, with whom he gave concerts as a violin soloist at Berlin and Vienna. He then became chamber musician for the violin and court composer at the Court of Mecklenburg, but his unhappy married life, which led to a divorce from his wife, caused him to resign that position, and to accept an engagement as director of the concerts at Königsberg. He composed some violin concertos and several successful operas.

JUSTUS WERNER, b. Cassel. A pupil of Birckenstock, Veracini and Locatelli, who, at the age of 14, entered the service

Germany: to 1725

of a distinguished gentleman (Vornehmer Herr) at Amsterdam. In 1713 or 1714 he entered the Court chapel of Weissenfels, went to Gera and Bayreuth and was, during 1716–24 (Apell and Lynker say 1718–25), in the Court chapel at Cassel. After that he toured: visiting Berlin, Hamburg, Bremen and the Netherlandish provinces, returning in 1735 to Cassel, via Hanover. In 1736 he visited the middle-German towns of Eisenach, Gotha, Weimar, Rudolstadt, etc. (Gerber, i, from Walther's posthumous MS. notes.)

ECK. Court musician (violinist) in Weimar chapel 1714–16 (Spitta, i, 855). Unknown whether related to the Mannheim Ecks.

JOH. JOS. VILSMAYR. Is known by "Artificiosius concentus pro camera," distributus in 6 parts; "Seu Partias" a violon solo e B. belle imitante. Salisburgi, 1715 (Brit. Mus.). Gerber (ii) refers to VI Partie a violon solo e continuo, Augsburg, Lotter, 1730. The partitas prove their author, of whose personality no particulars have been discovered, to have been a late 17th- and early 18th-century violinist-composer who possessed considerable technical abilities as a player, and melodious invention as a composer. He makes extensive use of the scordatura (*see* E. v. d. Str., "Eighteenth-Century Violin Sonatas," *The Strad*, Feb. and Mar., 1918).

JOHANN WOLFGANG KLEINKNECHT, b. Ulm, Apr. 17, 1715; d. Ansbach, Feb. 20, 1786. Son and pupil of the concertmeister and second cathedral organist, Johann Kleinknecht. In his eighth year he was already playing as a violinist before the Duke of Württemberg, and toured in the surrounding country. In 1733 he became a chamber musician in the Stuttgart Court chapel and continued his study of the violin under capellmeister Brescianelli. After the death of the Duke he toured again and was for some time engaged as 1st violinist at Eisenach. In 1738 the Margravine of Bayreuth asked him to play at the birthday celebrations of the Margrave and they prevailed upon him to remain as concertmeister at their Court. There he met Franz Benda, whose style he adopted henceforth, and a lifelong friendship sprung up between them. After some time, however, Kleinknecht, conscience-stricken that he had left Eisenach clandestinely, returned thither and remained until he was recalled to Bayreuth, where he remained until the dissolution of the chapel in 1769, when he went, with other members thereof, to the Court of Ansbach and remained there to the end. He composed: 6 solos for violin (Paris, 1765) and Breitkopf, Leipzig, possessed, in 1773, the MSS. of 2 concertos and 8 trios for 2 violins and violoncello.

STEPHAN FREUDENBERG. Violist in Court chapel, Stuttgart, 1715, where, later, 1731, he received a salary of 550 florins per annum. (Sittard, ii, 92, 120.)

GEORG CHRISTOPH HEMPEL. b. Gotha, 1715 (Fétis and Mendel); d. Gotha, May 4, 1801. Violinist and chamber musician in the Court chapel at Gotha. Composed 2 concertos and 12 solos for violin, symphonies, etc., pub. from 1764 onward (Gerber, i, 2, and B. and H. MS. list of music). Fétis says his compositions remained in MS.

LEOP. AUG. ABEL, SEN., b. Köthen, 1717; d. Ludwigslust, Mecklenburg-Schwerin, Aug. 25, 1794. A brother of Karl Friedr. Abel and an excellent pupil of Franz Benda. He played first in Nicolini's orchestra at Brunswick, became concertmeister at the Court of Sondershausen in 1758; held the same position in the chapel of the Margrave of Schwedt from 1766, and in the Ducal chapel of Schwerin from 1769. He composed 6 concertos for violin (Hamburg, Böhme), symphonies (*see* Eitner) and easy studies.

AUG. ABEL, JUN., son of above (?), 2nd violin in Mecklenburg-Schwerin Court chapel, 1783.

BERNARD HUPFELD, b. Cassel, Feb. 28, 1717; d. Marburg, 1794. Agrell was his teacher for the violin from 1729 to 1732. In 1734 he went with the Count von Horn to Vienna, toured in Hungary and returned to Cassel, 1736. Count Wittgenstein appointed him as his capellmeister in 1737, and in 1740 he became bandmaster in a regiment of dragoons of Waldeck, in Austria, which was disbanded in 1749. Hupfeld then went to resume the study of the violin under Domenico Ferrari at Cremona and afterwards under Tranquillini at Verona, where he studied composition under a capellmeister named Barba. In 1751 he became capellmeister to Prince Waldeck at Arolsen, and in the following year concertmeister to Count Sayn Wittgenstein-Berlenburg, where he remained until that chapel was considerably reduced in 1775. Soon afterwards he was elected to a similar position at the University of Marburg, where he remained to the time of his death. He composed: Solos for violin, op. 1 (Amsterdam, Hummel); 6 trios for 2 violins and violoncello, op. 2 (Ib.), apart from a number of unpub. violin concertos, trios, quartets, concertos for various instruments, symphonies (some pub.), songs, etc.

JOHANN WENZEL ANTON STAMITZ, b. Deutschbrod, Bohemia, June 19, 1717; d. Mannheim, Mar. 27, 1757. A son of the rector of the local school, he showed very early talent for music, and studied the violin and composition under his father. About his further studies and early career we know nothing until 1742, when he went to Frankfort a/M. and appeared with great success as a violin virtuoso at the festivities connected with the coronation of the Emperor Charles VII. On June 29 he gave a concert there, when he played the violin, viola d'amore, violoncello and contraviolone. The Elector Franz Theodor who heard, and greatly admired him at Frankfort, appointed him concertmeister in his Court chapel and Director of the chamber music at Mannheim, where he remained from 1743 to the time of his death. He married in 1744, and on Sept. 8, 1754, he made his debut at the Concert Spirituel in Paris, when he played a violin concerto and a viola d'amore sonata, and conducted a symphony, with horns and oboes, all of his own composition, which made a great impression on the audience, with the result that his work exercised a great influence on the evolution of the symphony in France. It was however not only in France that this influence was felt, the "Mannheim symphony" of which Stamitz was the chief originator became the model, which was adopted by the classical masters of the second half of the 18th century, who evolved from it the modern symphony (see H. Riemann, "Denkmäler der Tonkunst" in Bayern, and Schering, "Zur Geschichte des Instrumentalkonzerts"). He also introduced the use of dynamic variations in the orchestra, which caused Mozart to be quite enthusiastic about his conductorship. His fame both as virtuoso and composer were such that Carl Stamitz, on the French publication of his works, found it of advantage to add to his name the words "fils du fameux Stamitz." Johann Stamitz composed 6 violin concertos,

3 sets of 6 sonatas each, and solos for violin, all pub. in Paris; 21 concertos and 9 solos remained in MS.; he also wrote 45 symphonies, 10 orchestral trios, etc., etc. (*see* Eitner).

SIMONETTI, ca. 1717, a concertmeister at Darmstadt (Marpurg, iii, 50). In the Dresden Museum there is a concerto a violino concertante con violin, viola a Bass in G minor; MS. Cx. 857, which Eitner thinks might be by the above.

JOHANN GRAF, b. Nuremberg, late 17th century; d. Rudolstadt, ca. 1745. In his early years he learned to play various instruments as well as to compose, and still in his youth became a violinist in the orchestra of the "Deutsche Haus," Nuremberg. Then he went as a bandmaster and music instructor of the Losselholz regiment to Hungary. Repeated sojourns in Vienna brought him into contact with many eminent musicians who were of great educational value to him. In 1718 he was appointed Court musician to the Elector of Mayence and Prince Bishop of Bamberg; after that he became concertmeister and finally capellmeister at the Court of Rudolstadt. Gerber mentions 12 violin sonatas and 6 partitas of his composition (pub. in Bamberg and Rudolstadt) as excellent works. His six sons all became good musicians, the youngest, FRIEDRICH HARTMANN (HERMANN) GRAF in particular was a composer of great merit, who in 1783–4 conducted concerts of his own compositions in London and received the degree of honorary Doctor of Music from the University of Oxford in 1789 under exceptional circumstances. His quartets and quintets were very popular.

JAKOB LUDEWIG EBEL, b. Küstrin, 1718. Pupil of Raab, ca. 1754, and violinist in chapel of Prince Charles of Prussia in Berlin (Marpurg, i, 159).

JOHANN GEORG LEOPOLD MOZART, b. Augsburg, Nov. 14, 1719; d. Salzburg, May 28, 1787. He was the son of a bookbinder, with the ambition to rise to a higher station in life, and consequently he studied at the University of Salzburg, from 1737 to 1739, with the intention of becoming a priest. Meanwhile he had also devoted much time to the study of the violin, which finally obtained the victory over theology, and in 1740 he was appointed violinist and valet (Grove says chamberlain) to Count Thurn and Taxis, a canon of Salzburg cathedral. In 1743 he became a chamber

Germany: to 1725

musician, in 1757 Court composer, and in 1763 capellmeister, to the Archbishop of Salzburg. He has a twofold claim to remembrance by posterity; firstly, that of being the father and teacher of one of the greatest composers of all times, secondly, as the author of the first important and systematic violin tutor, which passing through many editions, including such in French and Dutch, remained the standard method for over half a century.

He married Anna Maria Pertl, daughter of an official at St. Gilgen, in 1747. They were described as the handsomest couple in Salzburg. Only two of their seven children survived—Maria Anna and Wolfgang—whose musical talents soon absorbed almost his whole attention, and under his careful training they soon developed into prodigies without equal. He was a devoted father but a hard taskmaster, and the restless touring all over Europe to exhibit their marvellous gifts was undoubtedly a chief agent in undermining Wolfgang's constitution. Leopold was not only an excellent violinist but also a composer of no mean order, whose works would have attracted more attention if they had not been so completely overshadowed by those of his son. H. Mendel ("Musical Conversations," Lexikon, vii, 181) ranks his sonatas with the best of the pre-classical period. He composed also oratorios, symphonies, concertos, etc., etc., which remained in MS. Some of his sonatas, ed. by A. Seiffert, were pub. by Breitkopf and Härtel, Leipzig, 1908. His most important work is however his above-mentioned tutor: "Versuch einer gründlichen Violinschule," pub. by himself through J. Lotter, Augsburg, 1756 (attempt at a complete tutor for the violin, etc.). The introduction contains much valuable information about the stringed instruments of his time, many of which have since become obsolete. His instructions are clear, logical, arranged in systematic order, and illustrated by well-chosen examples. He shows himself in this work an artist of deep and earnest thought and high culture, and much of what he says holds good to-day. For a more detailed account *see* Wasielewski, "Die Violine," 1920, pp., 282, etc., and E. v. d. Str., "The Romance of the Fiddle," pp. 234–41.

LEOPOLD FRIEDRICH RAAB, b. Glogau, 1721. Became violinist in the chapel of Prince Ferdinand at Berlin; said to have distinguished himself also as composer (Marpurg, i, 156). From Fétis and Wasielewski is learned that he studied for some years at the Jesuit college at Breslau, where he was also a choirboy, afterwards receiving elementary violin lessons from Rau. He then went to Berlin and became a pupil of Franz Benda, whose style he assimilated to such an extent that it became difficult to distinguish the compositions of one from those of the other. He was engaged successively by the Margrave Charles, and afterwards in the chapel of Prince Ferdinand in Berlin, where he was still in 1784. His violin concertos remained in MS.

GEORG RITTER (father of the family), b. Bayreuth, Apr. 30, 1721. At first Court actor and musician of the Margrave Friedrich of Bayreuth. By 1756 he was violinist at Mannheim Court chapel, where he remained till he died. In 1776 and 1779 he gave concerts with his sons Heinrich and Peter, and a flautist at Frankfort a/M. (Israel, 59, 69).

HEINRICH RITTER, son of Georg, b. ca. 1768. Entered the Mannheim Court chapel in 1776 as "accessist" and was among the 1st violins in 1802 (W. Schulze, Peter Ritter).

PETER RITTER, b. July 2, 1763, at Mannheim; d. there Aug. 1, 1846. Studied the violin under his father, but soon devoted himself to the violoncello, acquiring fame as virtuoso and composer.

JACOB RITTER. Violinist in Mannheim Court chapel in 1759–63 (Fr. Walter, p. 225).

WILHELM GOTTFRIED ENDERLE (ENDERLEIN), b. May 21, 1722, at Bayreuth; d. Darmstadt, Feb. 18, 1790. Studied music at Nuremberg and the violin in particular in Berlin; entered the Episcopal Chapel at Würzburg in 1748. On May 16 and 23, 1749, he gave concerts at Frankfort a/Main. In 1753 he became concertmeister at Darmstadt. He is praised by Gerber (ii) as an eminent violinist as well as a good pianist (*Leipzig Zeitung*, 2d and 3d Jhg.; Forkel, i, 135; Thomas, iv, 77; Israel, 36, 42). He composed violin and pianoforte concertos, trio 2 violins and bass, many symphonies, overtures and vocal music, but nothing was published (list in Eitner).

FERDINAND FISCHER, b. Brunswick, 1723; d. there, ca. 1805. Distinguished violinist, chamber musician at the Court of

Germany: to 1725

Brunswick. He toured for some time in Germany and Holland, returning to Brunswick in 1761 and wrote for the Duke 6 trios for 2 violins and bass in 1763, and 6 symphonies in 9 parts in 1765. In 1800 he composed a birthday cantata for Paul I of Russia, who rewarded him with a personal letter of thanks and a richly ornamented golden snuff-box. At the age of 80 he conducted a grand vocal and instrumental concert. Of this Mendel says: On Aug. 17, 1803, he gave a grand concerto of his compositions at Brunswick on which he had worked for 26 years. It was for wind instruments, Janizari music, trumpets and kettledrums, and was based on a bizarre programme. It caused a great stir but was censured by seriously musical people. 6 string quartets of his remained in MS.

JACOB LE FEVRE, b. Prenzlau, in the Uckermark, ca. 1723; d. Berlin, 1777. A pupil of Graun and Ph. Em. Bach. He entered, in 1750, the chapel of the Margrave Henry of Prussia, but was dismissed a few years later; he was then a teacher of music and later on became director of the "Französische Theater," but died in the same year. He composed violin concertos, duos, trios, odes, psalms, and songs, partly published, partly in MS. (*see* Fétis).

JOHANN RIES (the elder), b. Benzheim, ca. 1723; d. Cologne o/Rhine, before or at the beginning of June, 1784. Was appointed Court trumpeter in the Electoral Chapel at Bonn, May 2, 1747, with a salary of 192 thaler. On Mar. 5, 1754, he became violinist there, and in 1784, after the Maximilian became Elector, a Court report says, "Johann Ries the elder is old and feeble-minded, he receives a 'Gnadengehalt' (pension) of 150 thaler; is married and has by order of His Grace the Elector been placed with the Alexian friars in Cologne." (Thayer, i, 28, 148; Forkel, i, 129.) He was the ancestor of a remarkable family.

KARL OFFHUIS. At first violinist, then concertmeister at the Court of Mannheim (according to Fr. Walter, p. 370, 1723–68, pensioned 1744). Eitner says "pensioned 1756" (Marpurg, ii, 570, calls him Ofthuis). Walther (216) says that he was allowed to retire with his pension to Brussels. He appears still in the pay lists in 1768.

JOHANN GOTTFRIED KORNAGEL. Ca. 1723–35 "Städtischer Kunstgeiger" (town Art-violinist) at Leipzig (Spitta, ii, 60).

CARL THEODOR, PRINCE PALATINE, b. 1724; d. 1799. Played the violin in his Court concerts under Kröner at Mannheim; he was also, according to Schubart, an excellent gambist.

JOHANN MARTIAL GREINER, b. Constance, Baden, Feb. 9, 1724; d. Kirchberg, 1792. Studied theology and violin; after three years he played a concerto in public so successfully that he was persuaded to devote himself entirely to music. To escape the objection of his parents, he fled to Innsbruck, where his art procured him a prolonged refuge, until a wealthy amateur took him to Padua and Venice, at which latter town his patron died. Soon afterwards he was at Munich, where he lived for three years in the house of Ferrandini, father of the Court capellmeister, and where, among many notable musicians, he met Angelo Colonna of Venice, under whom he studied composition for some time, and who procured him an appointment as 1st violinist in Padua under Tartini, whom he took for his model in playing. From there he went to Stuttgart, where for twenty-one years he was a member of the Court chapel under Jomelli. There he trained many excellent pupils. Apparently he remained at Stuttgart after the dissolution of the chapel in 1769, until he was called to Kirchberg as director of music at the Court of Prince Hohenlohe, where he remained to the end.

JOHANN MICHAEL GLASER, b. Erlangen, 1725. For some time violinist in the Court chapel at Anspach until 1774. In 1775 he became chamber and town musician at Erlangen, where he was still living in 1790. Composed 6 symphonies, op. 1, Amsterdam, 1748 (Gerber, i, 2).

JOHANN AUGUST (Mendel says FRANZ) BODINUS, b. Schwarzburg, ca. 1725; d. after 1792. A pupil of Franz Benda, and from 1750 the 1st violinist in the Schwarzburg-Rudolstadt Court chapel. In 1770 he became concertmeister and director of the Tafel (dinner) Musik, and in 1787 director of that chapel, which position he held to his death. About ten years before his death he lost his son, who, under his tuition, had already become a highly promising artist. This terrible blow preyed upon him and eventually affected his mind so that the last few years of his life he was incapable

Germany: to 1725

of following any artistic occupation, and was pensioned in 1792. A violin Sonata with B.c., concertos, concerti grossi, flute sonatas, etc., in MS. in Karlsruhe library, and a church composition in autograph in Berlin library.

JOHANN OTTO UHDE, b. Insterburg, East Prussia, May 12, 1725; d. suddenly, Berlin (?), Dec. 20, 1766. He was passionately fond of music from early childhood, but studied law as a profession and became a councillor of the Criminal Tribunal of the Court at Berlin. All his leisure he devoted to the study and practice of music. He studied the violin under Simonetti, harpsichord and composition under Schaffrath at Berlin, but the violin was his favourite instrument. He then studied law at the University of Frankfort on the Oder, from 1743 to 1746, continuing at the same time his musical studies. Returning to Berlin in 1746, he composed some violin concertos, symphonies, cantatas, and an opera, some of which were pub.

STOLZE. During the second half of the 18th century he was conductor of the academical concerts at Helmstädt. In earlier years, ca. 1725, he was violinist and bassoon player in the Court chapel at Brunswick, where he was a pupil for the violin of J. G. Graun, and for composition of K. H. Graun, the Court capellmeister. He had the peculiarity of using the bow with his left hand and, without altering the order of the strings, to hold the violin vertically against the right breast. This did not prevent him from becoming an excellent soloist as well as leader of the orchestra.

BIRCKENS. An early 18th-century violinist of whom nothing is known, except one piece in M. Corrette's: "L'Art de se perfectionner," etc. (Perhaps a corruption of Birkenstock.)

JOSEPH MECK. An early 18th-century violinist in the Electoral Chapel, Mayence, who composed several concertos for the violin with string quartet accompaniment, a piece in Corrette's "L'Art du Violon," XII concerti per il violino a 5 e 6 stromenti." (Amsterdam, Roger, ca. 1730). In Salzburg library is "Musica Partieen pro liutho, violino, Basso del Sigr. Meckh.," but it is doubtful whether by the above. He left many concertos and sonatas in MS.

JOHANN KARL KOLBE, b. Potsdam, early 18th century; d. Berlin, (?). A pupil of his father, a choirmaster and cantor at Potsdam and known as a good composer. Afterwards he studied the violin and pianoforte under Karl Haak, on whose recommendation he became a chamber musician in the chapel of the Crown Prince and continued so on the accession of the latter. Pianoforte variations and sonatas of his were published in 1793 and 1798. He was equally good as violinist and pianist.

LOBST. An 18th-century German violin virtuoso and pupil of Tartini. He was a chamber musician at the Court at Munich. In 1772, at an advanced age and after he had been pensioned for some time, he was still appearing in public with great success, and Burney heard him at Munich on his journey through Germany.

CHAPTER 27

Germany: to 1750

JOSEPH WODICZKA, b. ca. 1726; d. Munich, Apr. 26, 1794. Violinist in the Court chapel, Munich, from ca. 1753, at a salary of 195 florins; in 1778 he was 2nd violin, at 285 florins, and in 1765 Chamber virtuoso, "Joh. [*sic*], receiving 475 florins."

T. WODICZKA. Violinist in Munich chapel. Wrote "Instruction pour les commençants," etc., traduit de l'Allemand p. J. G. Lustig organist, Groningen. "Korte Instructie voor de Viool" (Dutch ed.), by Jac. Wm. [*sic!*] Lustig, Amsterdam, 1757.

WENZEL WODICZKA was concertmeister at Munich chapel from 1745. In 1750 he received a salary of 925 florins, continuing till his death in 1774. He composed 6 sonatas, op. 1, and 8 sonatas, op. 2 (Boivin), 1739; 2 sets of 6 solos, London (same?), all for violin and bass; 2 symphonies, and concerto a 5, flute and strings. Mendel states that he was for some time concertmeister in Vienna.

FERDINAND BLUEM was 2nd violin in Munich, 1726–78. In the latter year he became 1st violinist at a salary of 475 florins.

FRANZ BLUEM, a chamber musician in 1726, at 500 florins.

CLEMENS BLUEM, violinist, Munich, in 1788.

FRANZ XAVIER BLUEM, Munich; d. there 1743 as vice-capellmeister.

In 1780 (July 2) a Bluem is pensioned, but no Christian name is given.

GEORG SIMON LÖHLEIN, b. Neustadt a/d Heide, Coburg, 1727; d. Danzig, Dec. 17, 1781. Known mostly as a violin teacher. At the age of 16, on account of his tall stature, he was forcibly carried off to Potsdam while on a journey to Copenhagen and enrolled in a Prussian Garde-regiment. He went through several battles, was wounded at Kollin and left for dead on the battlefield. Austrian soldiers who found signs of life in him carried him to a hospital, where he was cured and returned to his parents, who still wore mourning for him. In 1760 he went to Jena, where he became director of music in 1761. After the peace of 1763 he went to Leipzig as teacher and there became violinist in the orchestra as well as harpsichord player at the Concert Society of the town. Soon after he instituted an amateur concert chiefly recruited from his pupils. He played all instruments and engraved his own compositions, which he had performed at these concerts. In 1779 he was called to Danzig as capellmeister, but the climate proved fatal to his delicate health. Among his numerous compositions are concertos for harpsichord and violin and a tutor for violin with 24 little duets for exercises, "Anweisung zum Violinspielen" . . . which appeared in three editions. (*See* E. v. d. Str., "The Romance of the Fiddle.")

JOHANN WILHELM HERTEL, b. Eisenach, Oct. 9, 1727; d. Schwerin (Mecklenburg), June 14, 1789. A son and pupil of Johann Christian, who studied the violin also under Benda. In 1757 he was concertmeister and Court composer to the Duke of Mecklenburg-Schwerin, resigned his post on account of failing eyesight in 1770 and devoted himself more to the harpsichord. In 1770 he became secretary to Princess Ulrike, and Court Councillor. He was a prolific composer and writer on musical subjects. For the violin he wrote concertos and sonatas with bass.

SCHWACHHOFEN (Mizler, vol. ii, part 4, p. 123, calls them SCHWAAHHOFER), four brothers who were in the Mayence Court chapel, ca. 1727:

IGNAZ SCHWACHHOFEN, concertmeister.
JOSEPH SCHWACHHOFEN, violoncellist (Mattheson, i, 115).
ANDREAS and ANTON SCHWACHHOFEN, violinists.

PANCRATIUS RÖBER. A violinist in the Court chapels of Mayence and Breslau; ca. 1727 he went to Prague (Gerber, i).

GEORG BERNHARD LEOPOLD ZELLER, b. Dessau, 1728; d. Strelitz, Mecklenburg, Apr. 18, 1803. Pupil of his father. He went to Berlin, where he received further instruction, was appointed violinist in the chapel of Prince Heinrich of Prussia at Rheins-

Germany: to 1750

berg, and became afterwards capellmeister at the Court of Strelitz-Mecklenburg (Marpurg, i, 86; Dulon mentions him 1783, and Reichard, 229, 1777). In Schwerin library is a sinfonia pastorale by Zeller without Christian name; composed violin and pianoforte pieces and 2 operas, performed at Strelitz.

FERDINAND J. SEBASTIAN SAMBER, son of Joh. Baptist Samber; valet and cathedral organist and teacher at Chapel Institute, Salzburg. Ferdinand was violinist and teacher of choirboys at the cathedral there, 1728–53, and teacher of the violin at the institute of the chapel of the Prince Bishop, 1729–43. (Peregrinus, 93, 169.)

ANTON BRAUN, b. Cassel, Feb. 6, 1726; d. there, ca. 1790. Violinist in the chapel of the Landgrave of Hesse-Cassel. His sons JOHANN (q.v.), JOHANN-FRIEDRICH, MORITZ and DANIEL were all distinguished musicians, as well as his wife and daughter, who were noted singers.

JOHANN BRAUN, b. Cassel, Aug. 28, 1753; d. Berlin, 1795 (Riemann). He had his first violin lessons from his father, Anton Braun (q.v.). Afterwards he went to Brunswick to study the violin under Posch, and composition under Schwanenberg (Eitner, Schwanenberger). On his return he entered the chapel of Hesse-Cassel, then the best in Germany. When this combination of famous artists was dissolved in 1786 (Mendel 1788) Braun went to Berlin as concertmeister to the Queen, and was still in that position in 1795. In conjunction with excellent artists he instituted concerts at the hotel "Stadt Paris" which became widely and favourably known. His pub. compositions consist of three sets of trios for 2 violins and bass and 2 violoncello concertos. In MS. he left 30 violin concertos and a large number of concertos for various other instruments, as well as a ballet; they were greatly esteemed in their time.

GEORG WILHELM GRUBER, b. Nuremberg, Sept. 22, 1729; d. there, Sept. 22, 1796. A pupil of the town musician Hemmerich for the violin, the organists Dretzel and Siebenkees for theory and composition, and from his seventh year he was also a choirboy. In his eighteenth year he toured successfully as a violin virtuoso in Germany, playing some of his own compositions, and remained for some time at Dresden to complete his studies in counterpoint under Umstadt, the capellmeister of Count Brühl. Returned to Nuremberg, in 1750, he was appointed violinist in the town orchestra. Ferrari's visit to that town, ca. 1750, had a great influence on Gruber's playing, so that about 1760 he was looked upon as the greatest violin virtuoso in Germany, and when the capellmeister Agrell died in 1765 he was chosen as his successor. To bind him still further to their town the Nuremberg Town Council bestowed upon him several honorary offices. He was a prolific composer, who wrote some concertos, etc., for the violin apart from chamber music of every kind and for various instruments, symphonies, oratorios, masses, and other sacred music, songs, etc. His son JOHANN SIEGMUND GRUBER was a lawyer and music historian who wrote several important works on that subject. (*See* Mendel, Reissmann.)

JOHANN GEORG HÄSER, b. Gersdorf n/Görlitz, Oct. 11, 1729; d. Leipzig, Mar. 15, 1809. Father of a numerous family of talented musicians, the most important of his sons being AUGUST FERDINAND HÄSER, composer, conductor, and writer on voice training. Johann studied law at Leipzig in 1752, but having to earn his living by giving lessons he soon turned to music, and in 1763 was appointed 1st violinist in the theatre orchestra and the "Grosse Konzert" by J. A. Hiller, later also in Gewandhaus concerts. During 1800–4 he was viola player there and from 1785 he was also director of music at University church and for a time also of the theatre orchestra. He founded the Orchestra pension fund and retired in 1806. (Dörffel, i, 6, 12; ii, 10, 236.) Compositions not known.

CHRISTIAN FRIEDRICH FRIESE. In 1729 violinist in the Court chapel of the King of Poland and Elector of Saxony.

JOHANN REICHARDT, b. Oppenheim a/Rh. in the early 18th century, went with Count Truchsess zu Waldberg to Prussia and became highly esteemed as a teacher. The violin and the lute were his principal instruments. His autobiography is in Schletterer's "Reichardt."

JOHANN FRIEDRICH REICHARDT, b. Königsberg, Nov. 25, 1752; d. Giebichenstein, June 17, 1814. Son of Johann (above); studied the violin under Veichtner, a pupil of Benda. At the age of 10 he was already able to play in the orchestra at a concert. During 1769–70 he studied at Königsberg University, where he attended the lectures of Kant, in 1771–2 he studied at Leipzig, and afterwards became capellmeister at the Court of Berlin as successor of Agricola. He was one of the first *Singspiel* composers and did a great deal for the development of the German Lied. He was also the first to find an adequate mode of musical expression for Goethe's lyrics. He wrote several books on music and of very interesting letters on the musical life and people in Paris, Berlin, Vienna, and of his travels. Autobiography in the *Berliner Musikalische Zeitung*, 1805, Nos. 55–89. A Schletterer's biography, vol. i, was pub. 1865.

KARL AUGUST PESCH, b. ca. 1730; d. Brunswick, Aug., 1793, where he lived as a teacher of music to the Hereditary Prince, as well as to the general public. The prince, according to Leop. Mozart, played so well that, as a professional, he could have made his fortune by it. In 1767 Pesch accompanied the prince to London, where 6 sonatas, each op. 1, op. 2 and op. 3, for 2 violins and bass, of his were pub. On his return he was made concertmeister and conductor. On Nov. 30, 1776, he gave a concert of his own compositions at Frankfort a/M. (Israel, 60). Burney (iii, 258) made his acquaintance as concertmeister at Brunswick. He composed, apart from the above, some sonatas and a solo, quartet and symphonies (*see* Eitner). Reichardt, in his notice of Franz Benda, places Pesch in a line with Dittersdorf and Fränzl, etc., for brilliance of technique, sweetness and purity of tone, and gracefulness of style.

VAUPEL, b. Dillenburg, ca. 1730. Was appointed violinist at the Court at the Hague ca. 1762 (Gregoir, "Panth.," iii, 107, Gerber, i).

ENGELMANN, b. Bohemia, ca. 1730; d. Ratisbon, 1796. According to Riemann this was the real name of Joseph Kaffka or Kawka (*see* p. 215).

JOHANN CHRISTOPH KAFFKA, the second son and violin pupil of Joseph Kaffka, was b. Ratisbon, 1759; d. Riga, Jan. 29, 1815. Studied composition under Riepel; became a violinist in the same chapel until 1778, when he made his debut on the stage in Berlin, afterwards appearing as an actor and singer at Breslau, where he occupied himself also with composition. In 1803 he settled at Riga as bookseller, and appeared occasionally again in public as violin virtuoso. He composed oratorios, operettas, symphonies, masses, etc., but apparently nothing for the violin. WILHELM, *see* p. 392.

HEINRICH CHRISTIAN ZEISING, b. Römhild (Sachsen Meiningen Hildburghhausen), violinist in the Court chapel, Durlach; from 1730 capellmeister at Hildburghausen Court chapel.

LORENZ SCHMITT, b. Obertheres, Würzburg, Apr. 27, 1731; d. Würzburg, June, 1796. Made his first literary and musical studies at the monastery of Theres. One of the foremost violinists of his time. At the age of 15 he entered the chapel of Prince Greiffenklau, who placed him under Enderle for further studies on the violin. In 1755 he entered the Würzburg Court chapel and in 1757 he began to tour through Germany to Italy and arrived at Padua, where he received lessons from Tartini. In 1774 he returned to Würzburg, where he received the title of concertmeister and became director of the Court chapel, a position which he held to the time of his death, leaving in MS. several concertos for the violin.

CHRISTIAN CANNABICH, b. Mannheim, Dec., 1731; d. Frankfort a/M. Feb. 22, 1798 (Riemann: Jan. 21). Son of a flautist in the Electoral Chapel. His first teacher was his father, who afterwards placed him under Johann Stamitz. On the completion of his studies under the latter master the Elector sent him to Naples, where he studied, 1783, under Jomelli (Riemann: 1758). In 1765 he was appointed as concertmeister, and 1775 (Riemann: 1774) as capellmeister at the Mannheim orchestra. In 1778 he followed the Court to Munich. Schubart, in his effusive, loquacious manner, gives a long and detailed account of Cannabich's style (quoted at length by Wasielewski) and technique, as well as of his compositions, which is sometimes contradictory. He credits him with an entirely new system of bowing, which probably refers to a few original features and mannerisms which are individual in every great artist. That he was such there is no doubt, neither that his technique of bowing was highly developed and combined power with lightness, grace and elegance. He did not, however, cultivate virtuosity so much as the art of leadership of the orchestra, in which from all accounts he achieved great perfection. His tone was apparently powerful yet flexible, and with his excellent musicianship and true artistic instinct he was the first to introduce dynamic shading in the Mannheim orchestra, with which he became acquainted through Jomelli, who, wrongly or rightly, has been credited by some writers with being the first to use them in any orchestra. Cannabich was an excellent teacher and his numerous compositions were greatly admired in his time. Mozart speaks admiringly of him in his letters. He died on a journey to Frankfort. For the violin he composed 3 concertos with string quartet; 6 trios for 2 violins and violoncello, op. 3; 4 books of airs from ballets for 2 violins and harpsichord (Mannheim, 1775); 6 duos for flute and violin, op. 4 (Mannheim, 1767); also string quartets for violin, flute, viola and bass (violoncello). His operas and symphonies, of which some were received with enthusiasm, are now quite forgotten. Although he did not carry the evolution of the symphonic form beyond the achievements of John Stamitz, he showed distinct progress in his orchestration, especially in the manner in which he lets all the instruments take part in the thematic development.

AUGUST KOHN, b. Königsberg, 1732; d. Berlin, after 1798. A pupil of his father and a violinist called Zachow, but was chiefly self-taught. He became a violinist in the chapel of the Margrave Charles in Berlin, ca. 1750, where he studied composition under Schaffrath. About 1760 he was appointed as violinist and chamber musician in the Prussian Royal chapel and was pensioned in 1798.

ZACHÄUS WM. ALBRECHT, b. 1732 in Berlin (see Eitner). About 1754, violinist to Prince Karl in Berlin (Marpurg, i, 159).

ANTON JOSEPH LIBER, b. Sulzbach, near Ratisbon, 1732; d. Ratisbon, 1809 (Mendel after 1807). A pupil of Riepel, concertmeister in the chapel of Prince Taxis. Composed many symphonies, masses, 6 sonates en trio for harpsichord, violin and bass (Mannheim, Götz) (Lipowski).

JOHANN CHRISTOPH SCHULTZE, b. 1733; d. Berlin, Aug. 22, 1813. From 1768 leader-conductor at the "Döbbelin'sche

Theater," and afterwards the National theatre, Berlin. Composed instrumental and vocal music but nothing for violin. On a 4-part chorus of which the music and words could be read forwards and backwards, Zelter had written: "This good soul was called Schultz. He taught me the violin for some time and was my friend to his death."

KARL GOTTLIEB GÖPFERT, b. Wesenstein, Saxony, 1733; d. Weimar, Oct. 3, 1798. Pupil and choirboy at the "Kreutzschule," Dresden, where he began to study the violin, and continued to do so with marked success while studying law at Leipzig University from 1753. In 1764 he met with Dittersdorf at the coronation at Frankfort a/M., who gave him much valuable advice which determined him to devote himself entirely to music. Returned to Leipzig, he became solo violinist at the great concert (Grosse Konzert) at the Three Swans (afterwards at the "Gewandhaus") in 1765, and afterwards leader and conductor at the "Richter" concerts until 1769, and it was said that he equalled or even surpassed in beauty of tone and facility of bowing the greatest virtuosi who came to Leipzig at that time. In 1769 he went to Berlin, where, at the end of a year, he was on the point of going to London, when the Dowager Duchess of Saxe-Weimar induced him to accept the post of a chamber musician in the Court chapel there. A few months later he became concertmeister and conductor and distinguished himself in both capacities, remaining in that position until 1798, when he had two attacks of apoplexy and died soon after. Gerber mentions 6 polonaises for violin of his, which at that time were considered almost unsurmountably difficult, but which he played with uncommon facility, fire and grace.

IGNAZ FRÄNZL, b. Mannheim, June 3, 1734; d. there, 1803. In 1847 accessist and from Nov. 28, 1750, member of the Court chapel. In 1774 he was concertmeister and afterwards director of music, in 1876 receiving a salary of 800 florins per annum. In 1700 he became director of music at the Mannheim theatre. Schubart says: "He is one of the loveliest (lieblichsten) violinists of our time and also his violin compositions are of value." Dittersdorf, in his "Autobiography," accounts him among the most excellent violinists of the time. In 1784 he went on tour with his son. He appeared in Vienna in 1786, when he did not disdain to amuse the public by imitating the sounds of animals, like Carlo Farina before and Paganini after him. Lipowski says he belonged to the first violinists of his time who knew the power of his bow, and the artistry of the passages in his violin concertos prove his knowledge of the fingerboard, above all, however, the training of his son Ferdinand. The Berlin *Musicalische Wochenblatt* of 1791, after praising him, describes his playing as "more of an orchestral than of a virtuoso character, and lacking sweet delicate singing quality by which the violin excels." He composed violin concertos, trios, quartets, etc., which were popular among the circles of his acquaintance but bore no comparison with the works of his son.

SCHARDT. In 1735 violinist of the Crown Prince of Prussia at Rheinsberg. By 1744 he is Royal chamber musician with a salary of 800 thaler (Bitter, i, 26). In the Royal House library, Berlin, under Schart: "Sonata per il violoncello solo e cembalo," MS.

GRUNER. In 1735 a violinist in the band of the Crown Prince at Rheinsberg; became on the accession of the latter, in 1740, Royal chamber musician in Berlin.

PRINCE ALEXANDER FERDINAND of THURN and TAXIS, b. Ratisbon, 1735. Austrian Postmaster-General at Venice; a pupil of Tartini; studied first with Riepel and was a good violinist as well as pianist. He also composed. It is said that Tartini bequeathed his compositions to him. He defended his master Tartini against Rousseau's attack in his "Dictionnaire" in the "Risposta di un anonimo al celebre Signor Rousseau" . . . Venice, 1769.

JOSEPH KARL RODEWALD, b. Seitsch. Gross Glogau, Mar. 11, 1735; d. Hanau, July 11, 1809. Pupil of Franz Benda for violin and Kirnberger for composition. He was one of the few German musicians retained by the Landgrave when he reconstructed his orchestra chiefly from French musicians. In 1762 he was 1st violin in Court orchestra at Cassel. He excelled also in composition; became music master of the Hereditary Prince, whom he accompanied to Marburg in 1789. In 1788 he received the title of concertmeister, and was later pensioned. (Gerber, i and ii; Apel, *Leipzig Zeitung*, 12, 63.) Of his compositions are known: 3 symphonies, an opera, Stabat Mater for 2 sopranos and orchestra (Schott, 1799), also a piece in collected vol. (Breitkopf, 9).

PATER (FATHER) ILDEPHONS HAAS, b. Offenburg, Apr. 23, 1735; d. in the monastery of Ettenheim Münster, Baden, May 30, 1791. Fétis: "In 1747 he commenced the study of the violin under Wolbrecht, a musician in the Court chapel of Baden. In 1751 he commenced his noviciate, and entered the order in 1752. A pupil of W. Stamitz, in his part of the country he was considered the best violinist and church composer. He wrote church music and arias, pub. by Lotter at Augsburg, but apparently nothing for the violin." He corresponded with most of the great men in art and science of his time and his noble and amiable character gained him many friends.

KARL GOTTLIEB BERGER, b. Olmarsdorf, near Pirna, 1736; d. Leipzig, Jan. 21, 1812. He lived as solo violinist at Leipzig, highly esteemed as artist and as man. For over thirty years he lived together in closest friendship with the cellist Johann Friedrich Berger (it is not known whether they were related). 6 caprices for violin by him were pub.

KARL MICHAEL RITTER (CHEVALIER) VON ESSER, b. Aix-la-Chapelle, ca. 1736 (Schubart, also Wasielewski says Zweibrücken). Toured from 1759 successfully over the greater part of Europe until 1763, when he became concertmeister at Cassel, but (according to Gerber) he left soon after and started again on a concert tour through Europe. In 1772 he was in Rome, where the Pope bestowed upon him the order of the Golden Spur. By 1774 he was in Paris, where he was preferred to all other violinists, and London proved for him a veritable goldmine as a reward for his playing in 1775–6. In 1777 he appeared at Berne and 1779 at Basle. He was also a famous virtuoso on the viol d'amour, and greatly esteemed as a composer. 6 duets for 2 violins, op. 2, were published in London in 1880 (1780?) A concerto for viol d'amour and a duet for the same and gamba in MS. are in the Brit. Mus. In 1786 he went on a tour to Spain, which proved a triumph. Schubart speaks of him in his usual terms of extravagant praise, and goes into ecstasies over the effect he obtains by striking the strings with a little stick. He probably means the col legno. Gerber says: "His extraordinary facility and elegance of style evoked the admiration of connoisseurs and the amazement of amateurs." In 1783 he composed, according to Reichard's "Calendar," a ballad opera, "Die drei Pächter," for Berlin. Two sets of 6 symphonies each were published in Amsterdam (see dates in Brit. Mus.) but of the second set only No. 3 is still in existence.

JOHANN WILHELM MANGOLD, b. Umstadt, 1736, d. Darmstadt, 1806. Son of Joh. Heinrich. From 1764 musician in Darmstadt Court chapel. Joh. Wm. went to Darmstadt, 1764; in 1781 was appointed violinist in the Court chapel. He left five sons, who all belonged to the same chapel.

GEORG MANGOLD, his eldest son, b. Darmstadt, Feb. 7, 1767; d. there, Feb. 18, 1835. A pupil of Schick, Mayence, held an appointment in 1780 as violinist in the Darmstadt Court chapel; 1801 director of instrumental music; received the title of concertmeister in 1804 with a salary of 830 florins (Thomas, pp. 22, 35, 37, 81) and became Court director of music in 1817. His son JOH. WILHELM, b. 1796, see later.

LUDWIG MANGOLD, also a son of Joh. Wm., b. Darmstadt ca. 1777; d. ca. 1829. Was likewise violinist in the above chapel.

Several other members of the family were distinguished musicians (E. v. d. Str., "Hist. of the Violoncello": A. D. Mangold).

RITSCHEL (RITSCHL) (Eitner: WENZESLAUS; Mendel: GEORG; Fétis: GEORGE), b. 1739; d. Munich, July 1, 1805. Entered the Court chapel, Mannheim, ca. 1776 as violinist with a salary of 400 florins; followed the Court to Munich in 1778 with a rise in salary from Jan. 12, 1787, and served in it to his death. Gerber (i), who calls him Georg, says he composed 6 quintets for flute, violin, viola, violoncello and bass (Paris, 1780, Mme Berault).

FRIEDRICH WILHELM RUST, b. Wörlitz, near Dessau, July 6, 1739; d. there, Feb. 28, 1796. His father was a high official at the Court of the Prince of Anhalt-Dessau, who died when Fr. Wilhelm, the youngest of four sons, was only 11 years old. He had already shown remarkable musical talents, and his eldest brother, Johann Ludwig Anton, who, while a student at Leipzig University, had played the violin in Bach's orchestra, now charged himself with his further musical education, and at the age of 13 he played the whole of the "Wohltemperierte Klavier" from memory. He received his general education, preparatory for the University, at the Lutheran Gymnasium at Köthen, while the Seven Years' War was raging all around, and left there in 1758, taking leave in an ode, depicting war as the greatest of temporal evils, which showed him possessed of poetical talent. At Halle, where he studied law for three years, he soon made the acquaintance of Friedemann Bach, who instructed him gratuitously in composition as well as organ- and clavier-playing, in return for secretarial work. When he returned to Dessau in 1762, the Prince, who had been his playmate in early boyhood, expressed the wish that he should develop the musical side of art at his Court, to which he willingly acceded. Eager to advance his own powers, he studied the harpsichord under G. Fr. Müller, from whom he inherited the technique of the Goldberg school, and in the same year he went to Zerbst to continue his study of the violin under Concertmeister Höckh. During 1763-4 he studied the violin under Franz Benda at Potsdam and clavier under C. Ph. Em. Bach, and when the Prince went to Italy in 1765, he took Rust with him, leaving him free, after arrival, to go wherever he liked to further his art in the land of music. He made the best use of his opportunities, met with all the eminent musicians of his time and heard the greatest singers. On Nov. 24 and 26 he was at Padua and visited Tartini, and although the latter was no longer able to play, Rust said afterwards that he had profited greatly from their intercourse. Next he started for Venice, where he visited the hospitals della Pieta and dei Mendicante, being greatly impressed by the angelic voices of the girls, and at the latter he also heard Maddalena Lombardini, then about 15, and a pupil there. At Venice he met Georg Benda, the brother of his master Franz Benda, and hoping to benefit by converse with that excellent master he travelled in his company via Ferrara to Bologna where they visited the famous Padre G. B. Martini and the singer Farinelli. On their journey from Florence to Rome they fell in with Laurence Sterne the author, and arrived at the Eternal City shortly before Christmas. The Prince arrived on Christmas eve and they spent the night in visiting various churches to hear the music,

Germany: to 1750

including Allegri's famous Miserere at the Sistine chapel. In Rome the Prince met J. J. Winkelmann, and Rust, who took an interest in all arts, was asked to take part in their meetings. On Feb. 21, 1766, the Prince, with all whom he had asked to accompany him, apparently also with Benda, went to Naples, where Rust made the acquaintance of Barbella, with whom he played together at the weekly concerts of the English Ambassador Lord Hamilton, whose then living first wife was an excellent harpsichord player. On March 11 all started on the return journey to Rome, but Rust and his friends did not follow the same route as the Prince; instead they went via Monte Cassino, where Rust delighted the monks by his exquisite organ-playing, which impressed them all the more as Rust tells us that he met few good Italian organists and still fewer good clavier players. Rust at that time had already become a virtuoso on every known musical instrument, including some Oriental ones. He was the last great lutenist and defeated all the best Italian lute players. In Apr., Rust went to Leghorn in order to visit Pietro Nardini, from whom he learned much about Tartini's style. He greatly admired Nardini's cantabile. During his sojourn there he appears to have cultivated to a large extent the viole d'amour, to which he was very partial, and in the possession of his descendants is the MS. of one sonata and two solos, the latter bearing the inscription "composta a Livorno," but from the form of the MS. they have been written at the same time, on his only visit to that town. This fact has been unknown so far. The writer was enabled to make a copy of the autograph of the sonatas, by the courtesy of Dr. Erich Prieger, Bonn, in whose care they were at the time. In Turin Rust met Pugnani, another pupil of Tartini, whose mastery over his instrument surpassed all his expectations. Their daily intercourse developed into real friendship and was fruitful of valuable results for Rust, who also had studied the art of singing during his sojourn in Italy. In July, 1766, he returned to Dessau via Venice, where he developed immediately an immense activity in all directions to improve the musical conditions at the Court and in the town. He instituted concerts, at first with very inadequate resources, which by his untiring zeal and energy soon increased. In his two pupils, Luise and Henriette

Niedhart, he trained two singers of outstanding talent, who became the greatest help in his vocal performances. In 1771 Basedow opened his Philantropin which the sons of noble and distinguished families from all parts of Germany visited for their higher education, the musical part being confided to Rust, and thence he derived in a short time additional players and singers for his performances. At his suggestion, a Society theatre was erected, and opened in 1774 and proved a great success with Luise Niedhart as prima donna. In 1775 he was formally appointed musical director to the Court and on May 10 he married his pupil Henrietta Niedhart, who bore him 3 sons and 3 daughters, all of whom were musically talented; the eldest son, however, was drowned in 1794 in the Saale, near Halle, where he was a student at the University. The shock contributed to shorten the life of his father. The eldest daughter, Henrietta, was a good pianiste, Carl Ludwig was a capable violinist, and Wilhelm Karl, whom Beethoven greatly esteemed and befriended, and whom he often asked to play him his father's compositions, an excellent organist, pianist and talented composer. Soon after his marriage Rust went to Potsdam with his wife and sister-in-law, where they performed before the assembled Court. Rust showed his great mastery on the violin and the viole d'amour, the Crown Prince accompanied the two sisters on the 'cello, and probably a trio for flute, violin and viole d'amour was performed before the King, which Rust had composed shortly before the journey. The singing of the two sisters stood the severe test of comparison with the great Mme Mara, who was also present on that occasion. The result was a very successful performance of Rust's "Inkle und Yariko" at the Berlin Opera house, which was repeated six times. Apart from some concerts in Saxon towns, and occasional visits to the Court of Ballenstädt, where they were received in a friendly, informal manner, Rust never left Dessau-Wörlitz, where his duties were very arduous and his salary so poor that he complained in a letter to a friend about his position, which he said was so deplorable that he had to waste precious time, which might be better employed, by giving lessons. His capacity for work must have been astounding, for in spite of all obstacles he wrote apart from cantatas with 6 and 8 part choruses and numerous other church compositions, operas, songs; 4 dozen pianoforte sonatas, with and without accompaniment; sonatas for pianoforte duet, some for 2 and one for 3 pianofortes; many sonatas for violin, viola, viole d'amour, 'cello, lute, and harp; concertos for violin, 'cello and other instruments; variations, fantasies, duets, trios, quartets, etc., for various instruments. His innate modesty and want of business instinct may be the reason that very few of his works were published in his lifetime, and a very large part of his MSS. were lost without hope of recovery.

An enumeration of Rust's works is given by his grandson, Dr. Wm. Rust, late Cantor of St. Thomas, Leipzig, in the biography of his grandfather in Mendel-Reissmann's "Musical Conversations Lexikon." We can deal here only with his violin compositions, none of which were published during his lifetime. Three Solo Sonatas, d min., B flat maj. and A maj., were published by Peters, Leipzig, 1853. Of these the one in d min. has been republished with a pianoforte accompaniment, and many arbitrary alterations, including a complete mutilation of the great fugue by F. David. In this disarrangement it became widely known as a favourite piece of Mme Norman-Neruda (Lady Hallé). (*See* E. v. d. Str., "Unpublished Violin Compositions," by F. W. Rust, *The Strad*.) The first two sonatas have been re-edited in their original form by Edm. Singer. The Sonata in A maj., with accompaniment of a second violin, bears on the title page the inscription: "Written during my last illness during the first weeks in February 1796"; on the 28th of that month the great master passed away. This sonata is a most remarkable work as it not only anticipates but even surpasses many technical features of Paganini's art, such as alternate pizzicato and bowed notes, and a whole variation in artificial harmonics in the highest positions. The sonata, in 3 movements, is written entirely for the E string, and in a note students are advised to practise it also on each of the three other strings! That leaves Paganini's Solo for the G string a long way behind. Another "Sonata a violino solo senza Basso," dated 1795, exists in photo-litho reproduction of the autograph, but this was unfortunately made only for private circulation. Dr. Erich Prieger in his pamphlet "Friedrich Wilhelm Rust, ein Vorgänger Beethoven's," points out that Rust is more closely related to Beethoven than any other master of that time. This is shown not only in several of his pianoforte works but also in his violin sonatas, especially in some parts of the unaccountably neglected "Sonata Seria," a noble work containing lofty ideas, especially in the third movement (Fantasia), worthy of the later master, pub. C. A. Klemm, Leipzig, 1889.

Four sonatas for violin and lute or pianoforte, written for the gondola parties on the lake at Wörlitz, ed. by Dr. Wm. Rust, were pub. by H. Pohle, Hamburg, 1892, the first three composed in 1791, No. 4 in 1795. To the latter is added Rust's song, "An die Laute" (to the lute) with lute or pianoforte, the swan song of the master and of the lute. The "Religioso e cantabile" of Sonata 1, in G maj., in its opening bears a striking likeness to the famous andante cantabile of Beethoven's trio in B flat, op. 97, and the second subject of the Coriolanus overture occurs note for note in an unpublished violin duet by Rust composed several decades earlier. In the pianoforte sonatas are several instances of similarity of thought and treatment.

EHMES. A violinist in the chapel of the Crown Prince Frederic of Prussia at Rheinsberg, who became chamber musician in 1740 and died about 1764 (Ledebur).

JOHANN RELZER. A Viennese who, ca. 1740, was chamber musician of the Bishop of Würzburg; said to have been an excellent violinist (Gerber, i).

JOHANN GOTTFRIED SCHWANENBERGER (SCHWANENBERG, SCHWANBERGER, SCHWANBERG), b. Wolfenbüttel (Fétis: Dec. 28, 1740); d. there, or in Brunswick, Apr. 5, 1804. He commenced his career as violinist in the Court chapel at Wolfenbüttel, with a salary of 200 thaler, went to Italy to perfect himself in opera composition and became Court capellmeister on his return; for further particulars *see* Eitner. For the violin he wrote only sonatas for 2 violins and violoncello (1767, Brunswick), but numerous operas, symphonies, etc. Schubart speaks slightingly of his music. Fétis mentions violin concertos, also violin trios, which he afterwards disavowed.

JACOB HERSCHEL, b. Hanover, ca. 1740; d. ca. 1792. A member of a family of excellent musicians, one of whom,

HEINRICH I. F. BIBER VON BIBERN
From a frontispiece of his Sonatas, by kindness of Prof. Dr. J. Wolf of the Berlin State Library.

CHRISTIAN CANNABICH

JOHANN WENZEL ANTON STAMITZ

FRIEDRICH WILHELM PIXIS
By kindness of Prof. O. E. Deutsch.

WILHELM CRAMER
By courtesy of Messrs. J. B. Cramer &

FRIEDRICH WILHELM RUST
From a contemporary engraving.

Germany: to 1750

Fr. Wm., became the famous astronomer, while a younger brother, Alexander, was a noted 'cellist. His biography appears to have become inextricably mixed up with those of his brothers. Certain it is that he ranked among the best violins of his time, that he was a member of the Court chapel at Hanover, went to Amsterdam 1771 (according to others 1775), where 6 pianoforte quartets were published, and ca. 1786 he was in London, where 2 symphonies and some string trios of his appeared in print. Some say that he died in London, ca. 1792, others that in that year he was found murdered at the Gate of Hanover.

JOHANN MICHAEL DEMMLER, b. Gross Altingen, ca. 1740; d. Augsburg, 1784. An organist of the cathedral. He was also an excellent violinist and pianist. Mozart, who made his acquaintance in 1777, held him in high esteem. Gerber, i, enumerates his compositions, an opera, symphonies, and piano pieces, of which apparently none were pub.

PETER ALBRECHT VON HAGEN, b. Hamburg. Gave a concert as violin virtuoso at Hamburg, May 12, 1740 (Sittard, i, 72, 166). In 1772 he was organist at Rotterdam, according to Burney, iii, 250.

NICOLAUS GÖTZE, of Rudolstadt, cembalist and violinist of the Prince of Waldeck. In 1740 he settled in Augsburg, where he brought out 6 sonate a clavicembalo obbligato con violino. Sonate 1 Augsburg, J. C. Haupt. Only one sonata in 4 movements in G major (Karlsruhe) is known to Eitner. The others never appeared. (*See* Fétis.)

FRANZ ADAM VEICHTNER, b. Regensburg, 1741; d. St. Petersburg, 1822. A violin pupil of Franz Benda at Potsdam, and, for composition, of Riepel. In 1763 or 1764 he was in the service of the Russian Count Kaiserling at Königsberg i. Pr., and composed violin concertos (Reichard, Autobiog.). During 1769–95 he was concertmeister at the Court of Courland (title to Russian symphonies, 1771); he obtained leave to go to Italy, where he shone in concerts, etc., but returned to Mitau until the chapel was dissolved. In 1798 he became chamber musician in St. Petersburg, where he remained till his death. He composed concertos (only Petersb.), 1 with orchestra (pub. Riga, 1775; in Eitner); sonatas (6 or more?) for violin and violoncello; solo in C for violin and bass (MS. Königsberg); symphonies, quartets, a mass, an oratorio, a Singspiel. Fétis enumerates the following compositions for violin: concerto for violin, string orchestra and B.c. (Leipzig, Hartknoch, 1771); 24 fantaisies for violin and bass, op. 7, lib. 1 and 2 (Leipzig, Breitkopf and Haertel); 24 sonatas for violin and bass, op. 8, lib. 1, 2, 3, 4 (Ib.); Air Russe varié, suivi d'un caprice, op. 9 (Ib.).

FERDINAND TREWER (TREVES, DREWERS), b. Bonn, 1741? Son of Theresa Trewer. Appointed in Court chapel, Bonn, Mar. 1, 1756 (*see* Thayer, i, 28, 44, 45, 85, 148). On Oct. 3, 1765, appointed a Court singer with a salary of $137\frac{1}{2}$ thaler. Cramer (i, 384) and Reichard (1791, 197) mention him as Bonn Court musician, and the latter mentions also Franz Trewer as accessist there.

HEINRICH AUGUST BREULL (BREUL), b. Lindenhardt, near Bayreuth, 1742 (Eitner: 1732); d. Erlangen, 1785. In 1765 he became violinist in the chapel of the Margrave of Anspach, but afterwards he became organist at Erlangen, where he remained to the end. He was also a good harpsichord player and left a number of instrumental compositions in MS.

FRANZ SIMON SCHUHBAUER. Was Abaco's successor as concertmeister at the Court of Munich from 1742 to 1743 (from Sandberger's "Einleitung zu Band I der Denkmäler der Tonkunst in Bayern").

GEORG ANTON KREUSSER, b. Heidingsfeld, Bavaria, 1743; d. early in the 19th century (*Leipzig Zeitung*, 13, 354, mentions him in 1811 as deceased). A pupil of his brother Adam at Amsterdam, he excelled in early youth as a violinist and played frequently in public concerts. He went to Italy to study composition; returned in 1775, became concertmeister. He toured in France and Holland, was for some years conductor and composer at Amsterdam in 1776 in the Court chapel of the Elector at Mayence and gave a concert of his own compositions at Frankfort on Nov. 12, 1779, which was followed in 1780 by a performance of his Oratorio of the Passion ("Der Tod Jesu?"). He became then capellmeister at the Frankfort theatre (*Leipzig Zeitung*, 13, 354). (*See also* Israel, 71; Cramer, i, 748 and i, 1350 about his

"Tod Jesu"). He composed two sets of "Sinfonie pour le clav. avec 1 violon," the first pub. by Hummel, Amsterdam. Also quartets, quintets, symphonies and "Der Tod Jesu," a cantata, words by Ramler (also used by Grann for his famous Passion music).

His brother, ADAM KREUSSER, b. Heiligenfeld, near Würzburg, June 22, 1727; d. Amsterdam, Apr. 19, 1791, played the French horn and the violin, and was concertmeister at Amsterdam.

JOHANN PETER SALOMON, b. Bonn, baptized Feb. 2, 1745; d. London, Nov. 28, 1815; buried in Westminster Abbey. Entered Bonn chapel 1758 at a salary of 125 florins; first payment, Aug. 30 (Thayer, i, 31); assigned already in 1765 (asked for a certificate, July 1, Ib., 44) and went on tour. In Berlin Prince Henry engaged him as concertmeister, but he left again in 1780 because he abhorred the Graun-Quantz-Kirnberger school and worshipped Haydn and Mozart. He had written several operettas, chiefly for Rheinsberg, where they were performed 1771–4 (Pohl), of which the autograph MSS. were sold at Puttick and Simpson's in 1863 (titles in Eitner). He went first to Paris, and soon after to London, where he made his debut as violin virtuoso Mar. 23, 1781, and after that took part as leader-conductor in many performances; in 1785 he conducted the Pantheon concerts, and in 1786 those at Hanover Square Rooms, where he introduced the symphonies of Haydn and Mozart which soon withdrew the public interest from the professional concerts. On Dec. 15, 1790, he started with Haydn from Vienna and arrived at Dover, Jan. 2, 1791. The history of their triumphs is known. He continued to play as virtuoso even in later years. Through a fall from a horse he broke his shoulder and died soon after. (Pohl, ii, 16, 18, 73, 89; Thayer also, iii, 363.) He composed a concerto for violin and orchestra (arranged with pianoforte by G. Masi), 6 sonatas for violin and bass (Paris, 1782), sonata for violin and bass and B.c. (MS., Brussels), 6 solos for violin and bass op. 1 (London), operas, 1 oratorio, glees, songs, etc.

CHRISTIAN FRIEDRICH DANNER, b. Mannheim, 1745; d. Karlsruhe, 1816. He received his first music lessons from his father and soon made such progress on the violin that he was accounted one of the best players of that instrument. In 1761 he was appointed as violinist in the Electoral Chapel and followed it on its removal to Munich in 1778. In 1783 he became concertmeister in the Court chapel at Zweibrücken, and from 1792 to the time of his death he was in the same capacity at the Court of Karlsruhe. A violinist Danner played at the Concert Spirituel, Paris, in 1783, but it is uncertain whether Christian is meant, as no first name is given. He was the teacher of Fr. Eck. Of his compositions one only knows of a concertino in F, with orchestra, pub. by Sieber in Paris. His father, GEORGE DANNER, formerly a violinist and chamber musician at Mannheim, died in his son's house at Karlsruhe in 1807.

WILHELM CRAMER, b. 1745 (Mendel: 1795) at Mannheim; d. London, Oct. 5, 1799. Son of Jacob, and pupil of Stamitz, Basconni and Cannabich. He appeared as a prodigy at the age of 7. Toured later (ca. 1761) through Holland and Germany and was then appointed to the Court chapel at Mannheim. In 1772, after the death of his father, he went to London, where he gave his first concert Feb. 20, 1773. His wife appeared later as singer and harp player and was counted among the best players of her time. Wilhelm soon came into prominence and conducted the Antient Concerts from 1780 to the time of his death. He was leader at the opera and at the Handel Festivals (Pohl, ii, 328; Israel, 47; Wki., i, 185) Schubart calls him a violinist full of genius, etc. (*see* Wki.). He composed concertos, sonatas, solos, trios for 2 violins and violoncello or bass, also a favourite concerto for the harpsichord. It is said that J. C. Bach gave the final polish to some of his compositions, which enjoyed great popularity in their time, but they are dated by it and now obsolete.

FERDINAND SEYDL. From Falkenberg, Silesia. During 1745-1774 violinist and concertmeister in the Court chapel at Salzburg (Peregrinus, 93). Marpurg (iii, 186) calls him Court composer.

KARL STAMITZ, b. Mannheim, May 7, 1746; d. Jena, 1801 (buried Nov. 11). Eldest son of Johann, who was his first master; afterwards he studied under Cannabich. In 1762 he became violinist in the Court chapel. In 1770 he went to Strassburg and afterwards to Paris, where he appeared as viola and viole d'amour virtuoso and was engaged 1775 by the Duc de Noailles for his Private Music. He left that post in 1785 and toured successfully in Germany and Austria. In 1787 he was for a short time concertmeister of Prince Hohenlohe-Schillingsfürst. From 1789 to 1790 he conducted the amateur concert at Cassel; thence he went to St. Petersburg, where he lived for several years. In 1800 he became conductor of the academic concerts of Jena and died there in 1801. Jean Paul has immortalized him in his "Hesperus." Composed 7 violin concertos (Paris, Bailleux); duets for 2 violins, violin and violoncello, violin and viola; 6 trios for 2 violins and bass, op. 1 (Offenbach, André); 4 concertante symphonies for 2 violins; 2 operas; 70 symphonies; 1 concerto for pianoforte and one do. for viola. Also 5 sets of string quartets (Riemann). Brenet mentions him among the soloists of the Concert Spirituel, 1773–7 (Wki., 267).

P. F. REMIGIUS FALB (BROTHER REMI). Early 18th-century Cistercian monk at Fürstenfeldbrück Kreis Iser. Composed: "Sutor non ultra crepidam, seu Symphoniæ 6, for 2 violins and bass," Augsburg, 1747, fol.

JOHANN GOTTLIEB FEIGE, b. 1748 at Zeitz; d. Breslau (?), ca. 1802. Actor and singer in Wässers company which played 1775 in Silesia and 1777 at Stettin and other towns. In 1779 he was member of the Court theatre at Strelitz, and afterwards stage manager (Reichard, 1780, 133, 245). He resigned that position and became violinist at the Breslau theatre in 1780. According to Reichardt ("Gotaischer Kalender," 1778, p. 224) he composed the operettas (Singspiele—ballad operas) "Die Kirmess" and "Der Frühling," words by Kellner, which became very popular.

PHILIPP DAVID STIERLIN (STIERLE, STIERLEIN), d. Stuttgart, Mar. 31, 1801, aged 90. Studied music from his youth, partly in Italy. Under Duke Karl Friedrich (Administrator of the Duchy, 1677–1733) he served as chamber musician. On Sept. 19, 1748, he became "Stift-Organist" (Sittard, iii, 30); he appears also as violinist. He composed an Arioso for 2 violins, cembalo and bass, signed P. D. Stierlein; MS. in Rostock.

BACHMANN, b. Berlin, 1749; d. there, Mar. 20, 1825. Second son of the Court musician and noted instrument maker Anton Bachmann. Entered the chapel of Prince Frederic William of Prussia as violinist in 1775, and on the accession to the throne of that prince in 1786, he became Royal chamber musician, and took over the direction of the amateur concerts founded by his brother Carl Ludwig Bachmann and E. F. Benda until their dissolution in 1797. He was pensioned in 1811 but continued to administer the orchestral widows' fund so admirably that he received a testimonial of public thanks.

HEINRICH CHRISTOPH KOCH, b. Rudolstadt, Oct. 10, 1749; d. Mar. 12, 1816. Received his first music lessons from his father, a member of the Prince's chapel; the Elector placed him under excellent masters for the violin and pianoforte, and under his capellmeister Scheinpflug, afterwards under Göpfert at Weimar, for further study of composition. At the age of 15 he was appointed by Prince Ludwig Günther to be 2nd violin in his chapel and he gave him a pension to continue his literary studies, which were of importance afterwards in his work in musical theory. In 1768 the Prince made him a 1st violinist and in 1777 a chamber musician. Engrossed in his studies, his life ran an uneventful course in the performance of his duties at the Court, until a stroke ended it and deprived art and his friends of a learned and amiable man. He is chiefly remembered by his musical dictionary ("Musikalisches Lexikon"), Frankfort a/M., 1802, an abbr. ed. of which appeared at Leipzig. His other works on musical theory are dealt with in Mendel Reissmann's "Musik.Lexikon." He composed cantatas and a drama, but nothing for violin.

ERNST HEINRICH OTTO RAAB, b. Berlin, ca. 1750. Son of Leopold Fr. Raab. Violinist in the chapel of Prince Ferdinand at Berlin. Toured and went to Russia in 1784 and became chamber musician at St. Petersburg (Gerber, i). Gerber describes him as a violinist of merit "because he knew how to combine Benda's style with the newer method in a sensible manner."

TADDÄUS HÖFFELMAYR, b. Rastadt, 1750. A 1st violin in the Court chapel of Mayence (Gerber, i; Cramer, i, 749). Prob-

Germany: to 1750

ably identical with that Höffelmayr who was chamber virtuoso in the Court chapel at Baden-Durlach, and gave concerts at Frankfort a/M. on Dec. 8, 1775, and in 1777, calling himself chamber virtuoso to the Elector of Mayence. His wife, a singer at the Court of Mayence, appeared as soloist on these occasions. He seems to have settled at Frankfort a/M. in 1776, where he produced important vocal works (Israel, 58-60). In 1783 he was director of a Bohemian company (orchestra ?) which played at Mayence, Frankfort and Cologne. He then styled himself court-musician (Reichardt, 1784, 229).

BERNHARD, FÖRSTER, b. ca. 1750; d. Breslau, Nov. 7, 1816. He was an admirer of Franz Benda, to whose school he adhered, though he was probably not a personal pupil. He had a great reputation as teacher and trained a considerable number of excellent violinists. No compositions of his are known.

WILHELM KASSKA, b. Ratisbon, 1750; d. there, ca. 1806. A pupil of Touchemoulin, who early became a member and afterwards concertmeister in the Court chapel of Thurn and Taxis. According to Fétis he composed some violin concertos which may still lie in one of the many libraries of Ratisbon.

CHRISTIAN (Eitner: CHRISTOPH) HERMANN JOSEPH BRANDT, b. Bonn, 1750, Weber's father-in-law. He became assistant violinist (accessist) in the Electoral Chapel at Bonn on Nov. 20, 1767. Afterwards he became violinist and tenor singer with a salary of 400 florins, and still appears in the lists in 1784.

J. J. KRIEGK, b. Bebra, near Merseburg, June 25, 1750; d. Meiningen, ca. 1813. He lost his father when quite young, whereupon his mother went to Meiningen. At the age of 12 he became a singer and violinist in the Court chapel. At the age of 19 he entered the chapel of the Landgrave of Hesse-Phillipthal, whom he twice accompanied to Holland, which pleased him so much that in 1773 he became a violinist at the Amsterdam opera. In 1774 he accompanied the Marquis de Taillefer to Paris, where he began to study the violoncello under Louis Duport and henceforth made this his principal instrument. After one year's study he was able to appear successfully in public as a solo 'cellist, and on Giornovichi's recommendation he was for four years in the service of the

The History of the Violin

Prince de Laval, Montmorency, as violoncellist, after which he returned to Meiningen, first as chamber musician, and from 1798 as concertmeister. He wrote some violoncello concertos and sonatas which were highly praised.

CRÖENER (CRÖNNER, KRÖNNER, KRÖNER, CRONER). (Particulars from "Kreis Archiv., München," taken by Eitner.) A numerous family of musicians, mostly violinists, all in the service of the Elector of Bavaria at Munich.

ANTON ALBRECHT VON CRÖNER (also ALBERT CROENER), b. Augsburg, ca. 1726; d. Traunstein, Upper Bavaria, 1769. According to Fétis (Lipowsky). Was a 1st violinist with a salary of 475 florins; 1750–65, 565 florins (gulden). Lipowsky, who gives the dates of his birth and death, calls him a violoncellist, appointed 1744 in the Bavarian Court chapel.

ANTON VON CROENER, d. before Apr., 1771. A chamber virtuoso, taking 600 florins, with a rise in 1768.

FRANZ KARL VON CROENER, d. June 10, 1780. He was for forty-three years in the Court chapel of the Elector of Bavaria, twenty-four years being as concertmeister. About 1770 his salary was 1,000 florins. In 1761 and in 1768 he gave concerts in Frankfort a/M. (Israel, 43, 49). Rudhart (130) says that he composed gamba pieces for the Elector at 10–12 florins per dozen.

FRANZ FERDINAND VON CROENER. The oldest of four sons of Thomas Croener—all of whom were raised to nobility in 1749; b. 1718, Augsburg; d. Munich, June 12, 1781. A 1st violin, at a salary of 745–835 florins, reduced in 1765 to 475 florins, in the Court chapel of the Elector of Bavaria from 1750–65. During the Austrian occupation of Bavaria he toured with his brothers in Holland, England, France, and other countries.

FRANZ CARL VON CROENER, b. Augsburg, 1722; d. Munich, Dec. 5, 1787. Brother of Franz Ferdinand. 1st violinist, received 475 florins in 1750 and 565 florins in 1778. Was a good violinist as well as flute and gamba player, likewise a good composer. In 1756 his oratorio "Joseph" was performed. He had to supply the Elector annually with 6 concertos for the gamba. Composed also, 6 trios for 2 violins and bass, said to have been pub. at Amsterdam, 1760.

Germany: to 1750

A number of symphonies, quartets and concertos remained in MSS.

JOHANN VON CROENER, d. before Aug. 19, 1785. Vice-concertmeister, pensioned in 1778.

JOHANN NEPOMUK VON CROENER, b. Munich, 1737; d. there, June 24, 1785 (Mendel, 1784). During 1750–5 he received 474 florins per annum as violinist. (*See* Wki., Gerber, Lipowsky.)

THOMAS VON CROENER. Violinist in Bavarian Court chapel from 1737. In 1750–5 he received a salary of 285 florins.

Six sonatas for 2 violins with thorough bass for harpischord or violoncello by Croner (London, Thompson & Son), are esteemed to be by one of the above.

LOUIS CELLA, b. at Bayreuth, ca. 1750; d. Vienna, 18... An eminent violinist and composer. He studied the law in his younger years, and was well versed in all arts and sciences. From 1775 he served in the Imperial army, but having in the latter year embraced the Roman Catholic faith, he had to leave the army as his family would no longer give him monetary support on account of his conversion. Thereupon he addressed himself to the Prince Bishop of Bamberg, who drew him to his Court and enabled him to continue his studies. There he wrote some books on legal subjects and acted as managing secretary to the eccentric Dom-capitulary Baron con Dahlberg. On Apr. 3, 1784, the Prince Bishop made him his chamber fourier (quartermaster). This position he relinquished to accept the position offered to him on Feb. 2, 1790 (by letter from Naples), by the Dowager Margravine of Erlangen, who offered to deposit in his name the sum of 8,000 florins Rhenish, and a salary of 800 florins Rhenish per annum with free housing and living, as her chamberlain at Erlangen. For the sake of a pretty actress he soon relinquished that position to found a theatre of his own at Bayreuth, which failed. From Oct. 8, to Dec., 1798, he was director of a travelling company at the Nuremberg opera house, and in the following year he went to Vienna, where he died in the early part of the 19th century, highly esteemed as a musician (Marschalk). He appears to have composed only pianoforte pieces.

AMBROSIUS TAUSCHMANN, d. Sept. 28, 1764. Chamber musician in Munich Court chapel, where he receives a rise on Oct. 12, 1750. On Oct. 16 he calls himself, on a petition, "concert-violinist to Count Koenigsfeld." During 1753 and 1755 his salary was 190 florins. At the time of his death he held the title of Electoral chamber virtuoso (registered as of Frauenkirche).

C. W. RAMNITZ. An 18th-century pupil of Franz Benda; violinist in the chapel of Prince William of Brunswick.

CHAPTER 28

Germany: to 1775

KARL HAAK, b. Potsdam, Feb. 18, 1751; d. there, Sept. 28, 1819. A pupil of Franz Benda, appointed violin in the chapel of the Prince of Prussia (afterwards Frederick William II), became concertmeister in 1782. On the accession of the Prince in 1786 he was appointed chamber musician, and in 1796 concertmeister in the Royal chapel. He was also an excellent pianist. In 1810 he gave his last concert in Berlin, and was pensioned in 1811. He was the chief representative of the school of Franz Benda, and Möser, Seidler, Maurer, etc., count among his pupils. His compositions stood in high repute; among these were 6 concertos for violin and orchestra, two sets of 3 sonatas each, op. 5 and 6, for pianoforte and flute or violin.

FRIEDRICH HAAK, his brother, b. Potsdam, ca. 1760, became also a remarkable violin virtuoso and as such was likewise a member of the Prince's chapel, but in 1779 he was appointed organist at Stargardt, Pomerania, and in 1793 director of music at Stettin.

JOSEPH SIMON HÄNTZ(E) (HEINZE, HINZE), b. Dresden, ca. 1751; d. Berlin, 1800. In 1793 leader (conductor) of the Berlin amateur concerts. Gerber, ii, heard him there and praises his playing. In the old Lexikon Gerber calls him Hinze, Heinze and Häntze, pupil of Neruda and Hundt, since 1779 concertmeister of the Margrave of Schwedt, went afterwards to Berlin. On Jan. 8, 1783, he gave a concert at Leipzig, where he is called Concertmeister Häntz on the programme. He played there several concertos and produced symphonies by Stamitz, Abel and Naumann (Dörffel, ii, 192). Reichard (1783, 290) calls him Heinze, concertmeister in Schwedt and (in 1786, 198) Henze Musikdirektor and Konzertmeister.

The History of the Violin

GOTTLIEB FEIGE, b. Zeitz, 1751; d. Breslau, May 24, 1822. Brother of Johann Gottlieb Feige. Studied the violin under his father and became an excellent virtuoso. In 1771 he joined a regiment and became in 1775 a non-commissioned officer, stationed at Danzig, where he became known as an excellent violinist. In 1786 he left the army, continued his study of the violin and toured with great success in Germany and Russia. In 1797 he was appointed as director of music at Riga, but accepted in 1800 an engagement as concert-meister to the Duke of Courland at Mitau, and finally he settled at Breslau. He was noted for his rendering of the concertos by Viotti and by Eck. When the war broke out in 1806 he rejoined the army as trumpeter in a Cuirassier regiment. At the Battle of Auerstädt he saved the life of Blücher, whose horse had been shot under him, by giving him his own. After the Peace of Tilsit he toured again as a violinist and his playing proved as full of life and brilliance as before. In 1810 he returned to Breslau as 1st violinist at the theatre. In 1813 Blücher, mindful of Feige's service to him, appointed him as his first staff trumpeter about his person, and in 1815 he was decorated for his bravery and his merit as an artist with the Russian Order of St. George. He returned to his former position at Breslau, where he remained to the end with the reputation of one of the foremost violinists in Prussia and Silesia.

CHRISTIAN FRIEDRICH MÜLLER, b. Rheinsberg, Dec. 29, 1752; d. Stockholm, 1809. A pupil of Salomon, he was for some time in the chapel of Prince Henry of Prussia. In 1778 he went on tour with the famous Mme Mara, then he married the singer Caroline Friderike Walther, whom he had induced to divorce her husband. They went to Stockholm, where they were engaged for a season. In 1782 they toured successfully in England, and in 1783 they returned to Stockholm, where they were engaged for a term of ten years. In 1782 they visited England and gave concerts with great success. After a few years his fickle wife left him and returned to Copenhagen while he remained at Stockholm. In 1801 he visited St. Petersburg, where he was greatly honoured and richly rewarded by the Tsar; after six months he returned to Stockholm for the remainder of his life. He was noted for his fine playing of the Bach sonatas. 6 violin solos by him were pub. in Paris and another 6 in Berlin, 1785.

FEDERIGO FIORILLO, b. Brunswick, 1753, as the third son and pupil of the Neapolitan mandolinist, lutenist and composer Ignazio Fiorillo. The time of his death is unknown, but in 1823 he lived still in Paris. He was at first a mandolinist, and exchanged that instrument for the violin and the viola, and excelled as virtuoso and composer. Apparently he had no other master than his father. In 1780 he toured in Poland and Russia and in 1782 was choirmaster at the Riga theatre until 1784 (Reichardt, 1783, 279). In 1786 he was in Paris, where he appeared as soloist at the Concert Spirituel. In 1788 he settled in London, where apparently he met with but moderate success as a violinist, and he appears as a viola player in Salomon's quartet and in the ancient concerts from 1791 (Wki., 1794; see Pohl, ii, 263, 371). After 1794 he left London and went to Amsterdam, but by 1823 he was again in Paris, where he underwent an operation, and after his recovery went to London again, where probably he died soon after. Of his numerous compositions for the violin, quartets, symphonies, etc., only his 36 études have survived, and they belong to the standard literature for the violin. Spohr added to them a second violin part, A. Tottenham a pianoforte accompaniment, and Ferd. David edited a more recent edition.

ADOLF FRIEDRICH WOLF (WOLFF). A violin pupil of Franz Benda and a high official in the war office in Berlin in 1753. He was an excellent violinist, composer, and conductor. During 1765–9 he was chamber director at Sondershausen and finally "Ober-Commissär" at Wolfenbüttel, where he died in 1788. Co-founder, secretary, and conductor of the "Musikübende Gesellschaft" (musical society), Berlin, about which he wrote a treatise pub. in vol. i, pp. 385–413, of Marpurg's Beiträge.

JOHANN ADAM FRIDL (FRIEDEL) is mentioned 1753 and 1755 as violinist in the Munich Court chapel at 950 florins per annum. He died Mar. 11, 1759.

GEORG and MICHAEL FRIEDL, his sons, were also violinists in the same chapel. Schubart (Wki., 316) speaks of the brothers Friedel as having great technique, beauty of style and being particularly strong in the playing of harmonics (it may be they are the above). Marpurg, ii, 568, mentions a JAKOB FRIEDEL as violinist at Mannheim, ca. 1756. Schubart says the brothers Friedel were unfortunately very dissipated, but their compositions were full of charm, and so many violinists learned from them that they almost founded a distinct school of their own.

JOHANN AUGUST ENGERT. About 1754 he was Royal chamber musician at the Court of Gotha (Marpurg, i, 270).

J. GOTTWALT. A German 18th-century violinist and instrumental composer who lived chiefly in Paris, where he pub. ca. 1754 sonatas, duets and trios. Some pianoforte sonatas of his were pub. by Breitkopf and Hartel in 1800.

JOHANN FRIEDRICH KIESEWETTER, b. Coburg; d. Anspach, 1780 (Fétis, Wki.). A pupil of Benda, who became a Court official (Kammerregistrator) at Anspach and from 1754 until his death 1st violinist in the Court chapel. He was held in high esteem as a violinist (Gerber, i), although amateur.

CHRISTOPH GOTTFRIED, KIESEWETTER, son of above, b. Anspach, Sept. 24, 1777; d. London, Sept. 28, 1827. Studied the violin and became chamber musician at the Court of Bernburg, but often changed his position and toured a great deal. (Fétis: studied under his father, whom he surpassed in technique.) Finally he went to London, where he does not appear to have met with much success, for he died there in poor circumstances. The Kiesewetter mentioned as engaged at the Court of Eutin (M.f.M., 28, 87) may be identical with Chr. Gottfried. Fétis says: He was of an unsociable disposition, which often created unpleasant situations which caused his frequent change of position, although touring successfully from early youth. He was greatly admired everywhere and was offered many good engagements. He first stayed for a time at Amsterdam, thence he went to Rastadt, where he met with brilliant success, but did not remain there long; from there he went for about eighteen months to Bentheim Steinfurt, then to Neundorf. At the end of 1801 he was engaged at Ballenstedt at a salary of 600 thaler per annum, but he left there in 1803 to become capellmeister at Oldenburg at a salary of 800 thaler, and proved himself not only a brilliant violinist but also an excellent conductor. In 1815 he went to Hamburg (Hanover? —see Wki., 260), remaining until he went to London in the winter of 1821, where he obtained a brilliant success, but met with the intrigues of mediocre musicians which were particularly strong in London. Although he continued to play at public concerts, and especially in oratorios, he found no permanent position and drifted into a state bordering on absolute misery. He left in MS. several concertos which he would never publish and they were dispersed after his death. (See Wki., 260, containing also Spohr's judgment of him, who praised his technique.)

JOHANN ANDREAS SCHICK, b. Goldbach, near Gotha. A violinist in the Court chapel, Gotha, ca. 1754 (Marpurg, i, 270), and in 1781 concertmeister in Coburg-Gotha Court chapel (Forkel, i, 140).

BALTASAR CHRISTIAN FRIEDRICH BERTRAM, b. Salzwedel, 17..; d. Berlin, 1787. A pupil of Joh. Gottlieb Graun and a member of the Royal chapel, Berlin, from 1754 until his death. His violin compositions remained unpub.

JOHANN FRIEDRICH KRANZ, b. Weimar, ca. 1754; d. Stuttgart, at the beginning of 1807. In 1778 he made his debut with a viola concerto, which pleased so much that it was immediately published and he was placed in the Ducal chapel. There he received violin lessons from concertmeister Göpfert until 1781, when the Duke sent him to Italy for further studies. In Italy he gained everywhere recognition as an artist and remained until 1787, when he went to Munich for one year, and returned to Weimar in 1789 as second concert- and capellmeister. Through his excellent work he attracted the notice and approval of Goethe, to whose "Gross Cophta" he wrote the music, and who mentions him in the "Annalen" of 1791. In 1803 he succeeded Zumsteeg as capellmeister at the Court of Stuttgart with a salary of 1,500 florins per annum. He composed a viola concerto and a great deal of music for plays, etc.

ANTON STAMITZ, b. Mannheim, Nov. (baptized Nov. 25), 1754; d. there ca. 1820. Son and pupil of Joh. W. A. Stamitz. He went to Paris in 1870 with his brother Carl, where, like the latter, he distinguished himself both as violinist and as composer, and became the teacher of Rodolphe Kreutzer. He composed one concerto each for violin and for violoncello; quartets, trios and duets for strings; 3 piano concertos; 13 symphonies, etc.

WILHELM KAFFKA, b. Ratisbon, ca. 1755. Elder son of Joseph Kaffka, whom he surpassed in virtuosity as a violinist and was considered one of the best soloists and orchestral players of his time. In 1788 he was already a violinist in the chapel of Prince Thurn and Taxis, as also was his father; Wilhelm became concertmeister in the chapel in 1806; he composed for his instrument as well as masses, which became very popular in Bavaria, but nothing was pub.

DR. FRANZ ANTON RIES (Father of Ferdinand), b. Bonn, Nov. 10, 1755; d. Bremen, Nov. 1, 1846. Became violinist, and chamber musician, in the Electoral Chapel. On Nov. 23, 1774, his salary was 25 thaler per quarter. On Apr. 15, 1779, he received leave for a journey to Vienna, returning before Mar., 1780. On Mar. 2, 1780, he petitions for a salary of 500 which, after repeated petitions, was fixed at 400 florins on May 2. A report to the newly appointed Elector Maximilian in 1784 says: "Fr. Ries is the best violinist for solo, of excellent conduct, still young, married, 27 (?) years old, with eighteen years' service, his salary is 400 florins." He succeeded Jos. Reicha as capellmeister in 1791. When the French invaded Bonn in 1794 the Elector fled, leaving the members of his chapel to their fate. Ries remained as private teacher, became town councillor in 1800. The University, on account of his many merits, bestowed upon him in 1845 the diploma of doctor honoris causa and the King decorated him with the Order of the Red Eagle of the 3rd class. When age compelled him to retire from his activities he went to Bremen, where he probably had a married daughter. There he celebrated his 90th birthday and died the following year. (Thayer, i, 53, 211; *Leipzig Zeitung*, 47, 880; Euterpe, vi, 31; Allgem. Deutsche Biog.)

WILHELM HEINRICH STÖWE. In 1755 violinist to Prince Heinrich in Berlin, and afterwards till ca. 1780 in the Court chapel of Schwedt, where he also played as concert virtuoso. In the Berlin-copy of Marpurg, i, 507, it says: "Jetzt ist er ein Herberger geworden." (Gerber, i.) (Now he lives in lodgings.)

KONRAD JACOBI, b. Mayence, 1756; d. Dessau, July 11, 1811. An excellent violinist who composed various pieces for that instrument. He succeeded Neefe, 1782, as choirmaster of Grossmann's theatrical company, was appointed successively at the National Theatre, Mayence, the Frankfort a/M. theatre, and finally became in 1802 director of the Court chapel at Dessau. (*Leipzig Zeitung*, 13, 579; Gerber, Hosæus). He composed concertos and solos for violin which he played in public with great success, but they were not pub. (Mendel). He died of apoplexy. The violinist of that name who appeared at Frankfort a/M. as virtuoso on the violin and on the Hand-Bassel in 1760-1 cannot be the same, the date being too early.

SAMUEL DIETRICH (Wki.; Theodor) GROSSE, b. Berlin, 1756; d. there, 1789. A pupil of Lolli who played with a fine tone and in the broad style of his master. Before 1779 he became a member of the chapel of the Prussian Crown Prince at Rheinsberg. In 1780 (according to Brenet, 1881) he went to Paris and played his first violin concerto, at the Concert Spirituel, with great success. He returned in 1782 and established his high reputation in Berlin. In 1783 his first concerto was published there and a French comic opera of his was performed. On the accession to the throne of Frederic William II in 1786 he became a member of the Royal chapel and in the same year a jubilee cantata of his for the French colony was performed at Potsdam. Three years later he was attacked by a fever which proved fatal. He composed 3 violin concertos, op. 1 (Berlin, Hummel); a symphony concertante for 2 violins, op. 2 (Ib.); 6 duos for violin and viola, op. 3 (Ib.); 3 trios for 2 violins and bass, op. 5 (Paris, Toubault).

JOHANN EICHHORN, b. ca. 1756 (Fétis, 1760). Violinist alternately at Berlin and at Bruchsal, Baden, he was in 1807 appointed to the Court chapel at Mannheim. Gerber (ii) mentions 3 quartets by him of the year 1794. Composed also 3 duos for 2 violins, op. 9, Carlsruhe, Schütt and Grande Quintetto for strings, op. 11 (Leipz., Kühnel, Musikfreunde). Fétis says, he was still at Mannheim in 1815. A concerto and some solos for violin were pub., Berlin, 1791; 3 duos for 2 violins (Leipz., Kühnel); 3 string quartets (Darmstadt, 1794) and a string quintet, op. 11 (Leipz., Kühnel).

NICOLAS HEROUX. During 1756–69 in Court chapel at Mannheim. He was an Alsatian. His son was probationer (accessist) for the violin in 1775–6.

FRANZ HEROUX. A good violinist and pianist (son of Nicolas?), was engaged in the orchestra in Frankfort a/M. in the early 19th century. He composed pianoforte pieces.

KARL AUGUST HEROUX, b. Frankfort a/M., 1786; d. there, Jan. 2, 1842. Son of Franz Heroux. He was an excellent musician and composer; for thirty-six years leader of the 2nd violins in the Frankfort orchestra.

JOHANN EISELT (JOHANN HEINRICH, in Gerber). In 1756 at the Court chapel, Dresden, where, according to Cramer (i, 1236), he was still in 1783 with a salary of 300 thaler per annum. Gerber (i) states that he was a pupil of Tartini and was known as a composer from 1766. Eitner mentions none of his compositions. Fétis says that he studied counterpoint under Tartini for three years, and made himself known in Germany by his compositions, which remained, however, in MS.

CHRISTIAN LUDWIG DIETER (DIETTER), b. Ludwigsburg, Württemberg, June 13, 1757; d. Stuttgart, 1822. Entered the famous Karlsschule in 1770, where he studied painting, and devoted his leisure hours to music, in which however he made such rapid progress that the Duke of Württemberg counselled him to devote himself entirely to it. He chose the violin as his principal instrument, which he studied at first under Seubert, receiving his higher training from Celestino. He learned also to play several wind instruments, especially the bassoon. Baroni gave him some lessons in composition, but it was chiefly from the study of the works of Jomelli and the great Italian masters that he acquired his knowledge in that art. He gained several medals for playing as well as for composition at the school, and he was still a pupil there when, in 1781, his first composition, a horn concerto, was pub. In the same year he became 1st violinist in the Ducal chapel, to which he belonged till 1817, when he retired on a pension. 3 concertos and 6 solos for the violin remained in MS. As a composer he was of more than average merit and his operas, symphonies, and concertos for wind instruments were held in high esteem.

Germany: to 1775

HEINRICH CHRISTOPH DEGEN, b. about the commencement of the 18th century near Glogau. Was in 1757 solo violinist and cembalist in the chapel of the Prince of Schwarzburg-Rudolstadt. His compositions, concertos, etc., for violin and harpsichord, as well as some cantatas, remained in MS.

FRIEDRICH WILHELM GRAFF (GRAF?) of Schwarzburg; violinist, oboist, and composer; probably a son of Johann Graff, and his successor ca. 1757 at the Court at Schwarzburg Rudolstadt (Marpurg, iii, 78).

PATER WOLFGANG, b. Donauwörth, Oct. 31, 1758; d. Ratisbon, July 23, 1840. Entered the monastery of Michelfeld in 1779 after he had appeared already in public as violinist from the age of 8. On the secularization of the monasteries he became organist at Ratisbon. He composed 5 violin concertos, masses and other church music which remained in MS.

BECK II, ca. 1758. According to Gerber (i), violinist at the church of the Fratres Misericordiæ at Prague, 1758. Due Divertimenti in "Hausbibl.," Berlin, author uncertain.

JOHANN EBERHARD BECK, b. Passau, where he was as concertmeister. Gerber (i) mentions him as violinist and composer.

WENZEL RUZICZKA, b. Jarmeritz, Moravia, Sept. 8, 1758; d. Vienna, June 21, 1825. Court organist, viola player at the Court theatre and violinist and music master at the "Convict" where, *inter alia*, the boys of the Imperial Chapel received their musical training and general education. At that school he was for some time the teacher of Schubert. He wrote Sonate pour piano et violon (Vienna, Mechetti).

JOHANN FRIEDRICH WEBERLING, b. Stuttgart, 1758; d. there, 1825. He entered the military school at the age of 12, but his love for music gained the upper hand and he devoted himself to the study of the violin, making such rapid progress that he became a 1st violin in the Ducal chapel, which post he retained until 1816, when he retired with a pension. He composed 3 violin concertos and violin solos, also 3 concertos for horn and duets, and variations for flute, all pub.

SAMUEL GOTTLOB AUBERLEN, b. Nov. 23, 1758, at Fellbach, near Stuttgart; d. after 1824. He commenced his long and adventurous career as violinist, studying under Enderle and Heinrich Ritter. After having toured in Switzerland, and a short engagement in the Stuttgart chapel, during which he studied composition under Poli, he filled several posts as director of music, and eventually he founded the great Suisse musical festivals and an important choral school. In 1817 he became organist and director of music of Ulm cathedral, where he was still in 1824. He composed songs, pianoforte pieces, etc., and wrote an interesting autobiography.

CHRISTIAN GOTTFRIED WEBER, b. Stuttgart, July 24, 1758. A violin pupil of Göz, became a member of the Court chapel in 1782. Composed Singspiele, cantatas, songs and compositions for harp, which he also played himself.

MATHIEU FRÉDÉRIC BLASIUS, b. Lauterburg, Alsace, Apr. 23, 1758; d. Versailles, 1829. He went to Paris in early youth. He commenced his career as military bandmaster and afterwards distinguished himself as conductor of the Opéra-Comique and professor at the Conservatoire. Apart from being an expert player on many wind instruments, he was an excellent violinist. Gerber mentions him as 1st violin and conductor at the Comédie Italienne, and in 1784 he appeared also at the Concert Spirituel (as violinist?). He wrote for violin: 3 concertos, 4 sonatas with bass, and 12 books of duets (Fétis says 10 books). One of the sonatas was repub. in Alard's "Maîtres Classiques." He also wrote a number of string quartets. A list of his numerous other works, including two operas, is given by Fétis. In 1816 he retired from the Conservatoire with a pension, and in Mar., 1818, from the Opéra-Comique after twenty-five years' service.

JOHANN WILHELM L'ÉVÊCQUE, b. Cologne, 1759; d. Hanover, 1816. He was the son of French parents, with whom he went to Paris. Although intended for the church, he studied assiduously the violin. Having become an excellent player, the love for music triumphed. Secretly he left his home, toured successfully in the French provinces and eventually he became concertmeister to the Prince of Oettingen-Wallerstein and a few years later to the Prince of Nassau Weilburg. When the wars of the French Revolution caused the dissolution of the chapel, he went to Switzerland for two years, toured a further period in Austria-Hungary and Bavaria, finally going to Passau as concertmeister of the chapel of the Prince-Bishop. Three years later, in 1801, he became musical

Germany: to 1775

director at the Court of Hanover until Hanover was merged into the Kingdom of Westphalia, after which he continued to reside at Hanover. His style was elegant and graceful, his phrasing delicate, intelligent and pleasing. According to Gerber (i), he composed concertos, solos, duos, trios and quartets, of which only the minor part was pub.

FRIEDRICH MAINZER, b. ca. 1760. A good violinist and composer. In 1785 violinist at the chapel of the Margrave of Brandenburg-Schwedt, which he left in 1795 for that of the Duke of Mecklenburg-Strelitz, and in 1807 he entered the Royal Court chapel at Munich. A rondo for violin with quartet accompaniment and a quartet for flute and strings are mentioned as of particular merit among his pub. compositions.

HEINRICH SIMROCK, b. Bonn, 1760. Brother of Nicolaus Simrock, the music publisher. Violinist in Bonn chapel; afterwards at theatre Montansier, Paris, where he kept a stock of his brother's publications, eventually returning to Bonn. Fétis knew him in Paris in 1807. He composed, among others, 3 duos pour violin and viola, op. 5 (Bonn, N. Simrock.)

Fétis says: "I believe he is the author of 2 books of duos for violin and viola, pub. in Paris."

JOHANN GEORG DISTLER, born in Vienna, ca. 1760. From 1780 as violinist, and from 1790 as concertmeister, in the Court chapel at Stuttgart. On account of a mental disorder he returned in 1796 to Vienna, where he is said to have died in 1798; but as he does not appear in the "protocol of the dead" of that town he probably died in the vicinity. He was a favourite pupil of Haydn and his compositions were very popular on account of their easy, pleasing and melodious style. He wrote, among others, 2 concertos for the violin, 18 string quartets, and 6 string quintets. The latter remained in MS.

FRANZ STADE. In Apr., 1760, he entered the Cassel Court chapel, left it in 1761, but returned in Sept., 1763, and became 2nd concertmeister with a salary of 666⅔ thaler. In 1764 he left again, but his dissolute habits brought him down, so that finally he played in beer houses (Apell). Fétis says that he was in Paris in 1765 where his 6 sonatas for violin and bass, op. 1, were pub. In 1773 he entered the theatre orchestra at Strassburg, and in 1782 he went to Vienna, where his 37 variations for violin and bass were pub. by Toricella (both in Brit. Mus.). Whistling's Handbuch also mentions Exercises (Paris, Sieber). The MSS. of 6 trios for pianoforte, violin and bass by him were in the possession of Breitkopf, Leipzig.

FRANZ KROMMER, b. Kamenitz, Moravia, May 17, 1760; d. Vienna, Jan. 8, 1831. A pupil of his uncle Anton Krommer, choirmaster at Turas. After studying violin and composition, he held various appointments as violinist or musical director in the houses of great noblemen, and finally in 1818 became Imperial Court capellmeister of the Court chapel, Vienna. His portrait is in Wiener Musikzt., ii (Köchel, i, biog. and appreciation). Prolific composer: violin concertos, violin duets (musically as violinistically valuable); trios for 2 violins and B.c.; quintets, quartets, string trios; symphonies, divertissements, concertos for various instruments, masses and other church music. He was a highly gifted musician but lacked the spark of genius. His duets are still used.

MAXIMILIAN HEISS (HESS, HEUS, HEUSS). From 1760 a violinist probationer (accessist) in Munich chapel, as he says in a petition to the Elector of 1780 that he had already served twenty years as violinist and concertmeister. In 1765 he was still probationer and was sent about this time to Italy to perfect himself. He received several increases in salary of 100 florins each. In 1778 a Heiss is mentioned as 2nd violin, at 250 florins, but this could hardly be the same. His father, PHILIPP HESS, was a violin player in the Munich chapel, mentioned as such in 1750, pensioned 1778 and died in 1791. A HEISS is mentioned as musician (?violinist) in Prince Lobkowitz' service at Prague in 1811; it is doubtful that he is Maximilian (Eitner).

FRITZ (really FRIDOLIN STEPH. JOH. MARIA ANDR.) WEBER, stepbrother of Carl Maria, b. Hildesheim, 1761, went thence to Cassel; d. Hamburg, 183?. In 1784 both he and Edmund became pupils of Haydn, and Fritz became a violinist in the chapel of Prince Esterhazy, but left again in Sept. of that year and studied under a music master at Ludwigslust. In 1791–2 he was conductor, viola player and bass singer in his father's operatic company. By 1809 he was conductor at the theatre at Freiburg i/B. and afterwards viola player at the Hamburg theatre, where he was still in 1832. Fritz Weber was the first teacher of Carl Maria, his step-brother, who in 1809 composed for him an "Andante e Rondo Ungarese per la Viola Alta" which appeared in 1813 as a composition for bassoon. An opera, "Der Freibrief," which appeared under his name was really compiled of music by Haydn, Mozart, Fritz and Carl Maria v. Weber. (See F. W. Jähn's article, *Allgem. Mus. Zeitung*, 1876, No. 48.)

JOHANN HEINRICH SCHRÖTER, b. Warschau, ca. 1762. Brother of Corona Schröter. Made his public debut at Leipzig with a violin concerto by Dittersdorf at the age of 7 (Gerber, ii, but not in Dörffel, ii). In 1782 he went on tour and is said also to have visited London, where 6 violin duets of his were pub. Very little is known about him. Six trios for violin, viola, violoncello, op. 3, of his were pub. by W. Forster, London (Brit. Mus.); Fétis gives a number of other works. He was also a virtuoso on the harmonica. His brother, JOH. SAM SCHRÖTER was a distinguished organist, clavecinist and composer, who lived in London from 1772 and died there 1788.

JOHANN MATTHÄUS KREUSER, b. Lengfurt, near Würzburg, Dec. 13, 1763. Brother of Ant. Kreuser and pupil of his father and Mart. Schmidt at Würzburg and afterwards of Schick at Mayence. He lived at Mayence until 1793, when he began touring as a soloist. On one of his tours he visited Berlin. From 1807 he lived in retirement at Mayence. His brother Anton surpassed him as virtuoso and especially as musician.

JOSEPH DEMAR, b. Gauaschach, near Würzburg (Bavaria), June 29, 1763; d. Orleans, 1832. A violin pupil of Lorenz Joseph Schmitt, concertmeister to the Duke of Württemberg at Würzburg. Demar was a virtuoso on the violin and viol d'amour and was a member of the Württemberg chapel in 1812. He composed many duets for 2 violins, and masses with full orchestra; he also wrote a violin tutor. Mendel says that he followed his brother Sebastian to France in 1804.

GEORG GLANZ. A violin virtuoso who gave a concert at Nuremberg in 1763, where he played several compositions of his own. The library of Schwerin has two symphonies by him in MS. At first, chamber musician at the Court of Württemberg, which he left to tour in Germany.

JOHANN KONRAD WILHELM PETISCUS, b. Berlin, ca. 1763. Preacher at the Reformed church, Leipzig; wrote on music and was a good amateur violinist. He wrote: "Abhandlung über die Violine" (Sept., 1808), ed. L. Mozart's violin school for Kühnel, Leipzig, and the "Méthode de violon du conservatoire de Paris" with German translation for Breitkopf and Härtel. He wrote "Ueber musikalische Lehrbücher," *Leipz. Mus. Zeitung*, vol. x. 161, 177, and other unsigned articles mentioned by Gerber (ii).

JOSEPH TIETZE. In Court chapel, Dresden, ca. 1764, with a salary of 120 thaler (Fürstenau, i, 156). Pupil of Weinlig (Viertelj., x, 366).

ANTON LEHNEISS, JUNIOR. Appointed violin in the Electoral Chapel at Dresden, 1764, with a salary of 120 thaler (Fürstenau, i, 156). Gerber (ii) mentions him as still there in 1782. One Anton Lehneiss is mentioned in a MS. in the B.B. "Libro del contrapunto del Tartini" as a pupil of Tartini who became concertmeister at the second Court at Dresden. This must be the above. In 1764 he became concertmeister with 1,000 thaler and retired Dec. 28, 1776, with a pension of 700 thaler (Fürstenau, i, 133, 155, 167). His father, KARL MATTHIAS LEHNEISS, was a violinist in the same chapel from 1729 with a salary of 200 thaler.

JOHANN GOLDBERG, b. Bonn, 1764. On Apr. 15, 1777, he was appointed as accessist (probationer) at 50 florins per annum in Bonn Court chapel. In 1782 he petitions for a rise. Reichard mentions him as still a member of the chapel in 1789. (Thayer, i, 54, 56; Reichardt, 1791, 197; Eitner.)

FRANZ JOSEPH OTTER, b. Nandlstadt, Bavaria, 1764. From May 21, 1809, to the time of his death, Sept. 1, 1836, at the age of 76 violinist in the Court chapel in Vienna (Köchel, i). Reichard in the Gothaer calendar (1798, 242) mentions him as concertmeister at the Court theatre and, in 1800 (p. 287), as Director of music in Vienna. During 1803–7 he was violinist at the cathedral, Salzburg (where he studied composition under Mich. Haydn), his salary being 200 florins; and his brother, LUDWIG, violinist, also held an appointment there, at a salary of 150 florins. Lipowski says Franz was born at Nandlstadt in Bavaria and sent to Florence for his musical education at the expense of the Bishop of Freising. He was a pupil of

Germany: to 1775

Nardini, composed concertos and sonatas, and pub. only a book of variations on "Ich bin liederlich."

BERNARDO LORENZITI, b. Kirchheim, Württemberg, ca. 1764. Brother and pupil of Antonio Lorenziti at Nancy. Went to Paris and became 2nd violinist at the Grand Opera in 1787. He wrote a large number of compositions for violin and for viola; concertos, sonatas, duets, etc., which are unfavourably criticized by Fétis, also "Principes ou nouvelle méthode de musique pour apprendre facilement a jouer du violon suivis de 12 duos progressifs" (Paris, frères Gaveaux).

JOHANN BLIESENER, b. in Prussia, ca. 1765; d. Berlin, Feb., 1842. Was a pupil of Giornivichi and became a member of the Dowager Queen of Prussia's private band in 1798 (Mendel) (Eitner: 1789), remaining until its dissolution after the battle of Jena in 1806. He was somewhat eccentric and announced in 1801 that he had invented a musical alphabet of 5 figures, which anybody could learn in half an hour and thereby would be able in 5 hours' time to play any instrument mechanically. He was a good soloist and composed a violin concerto, three books of 3 duets each, for 2 violins and one book of 3 duets for violin and viola, also a number of string quartets, including one in D major entitled "Friedensfeier," illustrating a celebration of peace.

PATER (PATNER), a family of Munich musicians: FERDINAND PATER, d. Apr. 23, 1793. 2nd violin at Munich Court chapel from ca. 1765 at a salary of 285–300 florins. FRANZ XAVER PATER. Violinist at the Court chapel, Munich, from ca. 1784; receives a rise of salary in 1790. JOS FERDINAND PATER. Viola player at Munich Court chapel from before 1751, at a salary of 190 florins. Another PATER played double bass there in 1789 and following years.

KARL VON HAMPELN, b. Mannheim, Jan. 30, 1765; d. Stuttgart, Mar. 23, 1834. Received his first musical education at Munich and became a prodigy as violinist and composer. From a very early age he was successively director of the Court chapels at Donaueschingen, Hechingen and, from Nov. 13, 1811, Stuttgart, where he was pensioned Dec. 31, 1825, on account of failing eyesight. He was highly esteemed as a violinist, especially in the playing of the quartets by Haydn and Mozart. He composed a symphony concertante for 4 solo violins with orchestra in E flat major (Offenbach, André); and a violin concerto with orch. (Augsburg, Gombart); also waltzes for orchestra and for pianoforte, and a mass with orchestra.

FATHER JOSEPH SCHMITT. Cistercian monk in the Abbey of Eberbach, Rheingau, from 1766, an excellent violinist; left the monastery 1780 and went to Amsterdam, where he married. Here he had numerous compositions published (Gerber, i and ii) in his own music printing and engraving works, some bearing dates 1780–5. Driven out by the Revolution, he re-appeared 1803 (Riemann: 1800) at Frankfort a/M., where he became musical director at the theatre and died ca. 1808. (List of compositions are in Eitner.)

KARL I. WENDLING. During 1766–78 a violinist and chamber musician first in the Mannheim, then in the Munich Court chapel. His wife, Auguste Elisabeth, was a singer in the Court opera, but should not be confounded with the more famous contemporary Dorothea Wendling.

JOHANN HEINRICH LÖWE, b. Berlin, 1766; d. Bromberg, after 1835. A pupil of K. Haack. He appeared in public as violin virtuoso in 1785, entered the service of the Margrave of Schwedt, later on went to Hamburg and, 1799, to Bremen as leader of the amateur concert. During the time of the French Terror he lost his position and retired to Bromberg, where he bought a brick-kiln, and was still living there in 1835. He composed several violin concertos, sonatas and duets, also trios, etc.

JOHANN FRIEDRICH MARPURG, b. Hamburg, 1766; d. Altona. He was the son of Friedr. Wilh. Marpurg, the famous theorist, etc. He appeared first in Hamburg as a violinist, Mar. 15, 1788 (Sittard, i, 169); then he became violinist at the German theatre, Berlin, and later on in the Court chapel in Schwedt, and in 1790 in that of Ludwigslust, where in 1791 he started a musical business. In 1802 he is said to have moved to Altona and to have died there. According to Ledebur he had to leave Ludwigslust on account of having been implicated in a conspiracy. He evidently had not inherited the learning and strict principles of his father.

CHRISTIAN LUDWIG KLEINKNECHT, b. Bayreuth, Aug. 12, 1766; d. Anspach, Mar. 11, 1794. He went with his father to

Germany: to 1775

Anspach, after the amalgamation of the two little states, and became a favourite of the Margrave Alexander, who sent him in 1784 to Leipzig to study law, and on his return in 1788 appointed him as violinist in his chapel. He was an excellent violinist and also good composer. A few of his compositions are known, including a birthday song for Frederick William II of Prussia.

JOHANN FRIEDRICH ECK, b. Mannheim, 1766; d. Bamberg, 1809 or 1810. Son of a Bohemian horn player in the Electoral chapel at Mannheim. He studied the violin from 1773 under Christian Danner, becoming eventually one of the most distinguished German violinists. He combined a remarkable left-hand technique with perfect intonation and beauty of tone. In 1778 he went with the chapel to Munich, where he received lessons in composition from the capellmeister Winter. In 1788 he became director of the Court concerts and conductor of the National Theatre. In 1801 he married for the second time a Countess of Taufkirchen, retired from the chapel, toured in France, visited Paris and settled at Nancy, retiring finally from the platform. Nothing is known of his life from that time except that he went eventually to Bamberg. He composed 6 violin concertos pub. at Offenbach and Paris, and a symphony concertante for 2 violins (Leipzig, Breitkopf). Reichardt, who bestows upon him words of highest praise, ends up by saying that no violinist gave him greater pleasure except Salomon, whom he heard in 1786 in London.

AEGIDIUS CHRISTOPH MÜLLER, b. Görsbach, near Nordhausen, Thuringia, July 2, 1766; d. Brunswick, Aug. 14, 1841. Violinist, Court musician at Brunswick. His four sons: KARL FRIEDRICH, FRANZ FERDINAND GEORG (both violin); THEODOR HEINRICH GUSTAV (viola), and AUGUST THEODOR (violoncello) founded the first Müller quartet. Fétis, who erroneously calls him Henri Frederic, mentions among a number of his compositions: Variations on a French air for violin, op. 6, and sonatas for pianoforte and violin, op. 11, both pub. Brunswick, Spehr.

KARL HUNT, b. Dresden, July 27, 1766. His father, Franz Hunt, a Court musician, began to teach him the violin when he was only 4 years old. In 1776 capellmeister Seydelmann became his master in composition and on Aug. 10, 1783, he was appointed as 1st violin in the Electoral Chapel; he still was there in 1810. He composed 10 violin concertos with orchestra; 2 concertante symphonies for 2 violins; 8 quartets, an opera, symphonies, church music, etc. (list in Fétis).

JACOB ANDREAS ROMBERG (see Eitner, *Niederrhein Zeitung*, 7, 357; Rochlitz, i, 70; Spazier's *Musik Zeitung*, Oct., 1793), b. Vechta, near Münster (Westphalia), Apr. 27, 1767; d. Gotha, Nov. 10, 1821. He belonged to a numerous family of eminent musicians; his father, Gerhard Heinrich Romberg, was capellmeister and clarinetist. At the age of 7 he already played the violin at a public concert in a duet with his cousin BERNHARD, the violoncellist, and they were with short intervals always playing and touring together until Andreas settled at Hamburg in 1801. At the age of 13 he toured with his father and Bernhard in Holland and France with unqualified success. In 1784 he visited Paris for the first time and played at the salon of Baron Bagge with such success that he was engaged for the Concert Spirituel for that season. In 1790 both he and his brother were engaged in the Electoral Chapel at Bonn, but left in 1793 on the approach of the French armies and went to Italy, where they gained the protection of Cardinal Rezzonico, who procured for them the favour of being the first musicians to give a concert at the Capitol on Feb. 17, 1796. They returned through the Tyrol, and Andreas went on to Vienna, where he met with a very friendly reception both as virtuoso and composer. Haydn, who attended the performance of his first string quartet, expressed himself pleased with the work. In 1897 he settled at Hamburg and in the following year he was for the first time separated from his cousin, who went alone on tour, but in 1800 the letter induced him to join him again in Paris. There he produced several of his larger works, but without any marked success, and when an opera, "Don Mendoce," which he had written in collaboration with Bernhard, met with no better fate when it was performed, he returned to Hamburg. There he became a friend of Klopstock, many of whose poems he set to music. He married about that time, remained at Hamburg and devoted much of his time to composition. In 1815 he succeeded Spohr as Court capellmeister at Gotha and composed and produced several of his more important works until several attacks of paralysis prevented him from further activity. He left his wife and six children unprovided for and several German towns honoured his memory by giving concerts for their support. The University of Kiel bestowed upon him the degree of honorary doctor (of Phil.?). His numerous compositions, extending over all branches of music, are full of merit, but as they opened up no new paths they shared the fate of the works of so many excellent composers. In their own time, however, they were very popular and much admired. The only work that survived until recent times is his pleasing setting of Schiller's "The Lay of the Bell." Spohr, who judges him very severely as a virtuoso, speaks with great admiration of his string quartets, but in both cases he exaggerated. Neefe spoke of him in 1793 as one of the most perfect violinists and other good judges placed him on a level with Benda, Fränzl, Pixis, Rode, etc. (*Allgem. Mus. Zeitung*, 1789, No. 8.)

HEINRICH ANTOINE (called CRUX), b. Mannheim, 1768; d. Munich, 1809. He went with his mother, Francisca, *née* Amberger, the famous actress, to Munich, where he became a pupil of the Court musician, P. Winter. Afterwards he studied for two years under Leopold Mozart at Salzburg. In 1786 he became chamber musician of the Elector of Trêves at Coblenz, then he toured in Holland and France, became solo violinist of Prince Bentheim-Steinfurt and married the singer Johanna Fontaine, with whom he went to Munich in 1791 and was appointed as chamber musician in the Electoral Chapel. He composed some solos for violin.

VALENTIN RÖSER. A mid-18th-century chamber musician to the Prince of Monaco. Riemann suggests that he may have been a personal pupil of J. Stamitz. Apparently he lived for some time in Paris and also in Vienna. He composed sonatas for pianoforte and violin obbligato, op. 10; 5 sonatas for 2 violins and B.c., 1768, imitations of Stamitz, op. 1; 6 sonatas for pianoforte and violin arranged from trio and symphony movements by Stamitz; a symphony (in Chevardière's "Sinfonie Périodique"), No. 34; a number of suites, marches, etc., for wind instruments; he also pub. a French version of Leopold Mozart's violin tutor (1770) and "Instructions for Composing for Wind Instruments."

The History of the Violin

KARL CANNABICH, b. Mannheim, Oct. 11, 1771 (according to Riemann); d. Munich, Mar. 1, 1806. At the age of 4 he received his first lessons from his father, Christian Cannabich. When he was 9 he became a violin pupil of Friedrich Eck, and Grätz and Peter Winter for composition. In early youth he toured with the oboe virtuoso, A. Lebrun, playing with great success in all the principal towns of Germany. On his return in 1784 he became a member of the Mannheim Court orchestra, but went to Italy in 1785 for further studies, and on his return he received still further lessons in composition from Winter. In 1796 he accepted, with the consent of the Elector, an engagement for four years as director of music at Frankfort a/M. without losing his position in the Electoral Chapel. At Frankfort he married, in 1798, the singer Josephine Woraleck. Two years later he was called to Munich to succeed his father as director of the Court concerts. There he had two of his operas performed with great success. In 1805 (?) he was sent to Paris to study the methods of teaching which obtained at the Conservatoire; on his return to Munich he was attacked by a nervous fever, from which he died. He composed for the violin: 6 trios for 2 violins concertante, op. 6; and concerto, op. 9; besides operas, a symphony, an overture, vocal music and pianoforte pieces.

PAUL ROTHFISCHER. Some of the particulars concerning this violinist are of a conflicting nature. Gerber gives his name as Rottfischer and Gerber (ii) calls him a Bohemian, while Lipowsky says that he was born at Altmannstein in Bavaria, which probably is correct, as he received his first schooling at the monastery of Westenburg and afterwards studied at the monastery of St. Emmeran, Ratisbon. He then devoted himself to the study of the violin, went on tour, and gave 2 concerts at Frankfort a/M. in 1770 (Israel, 51). In 1778 he was concertmeister to the Princess of Orange at Nassau-Weilburg, where he died, according to Gerbert, in 1785, after a sojourn in Vienna (Jähn, ii, 165). Gerber's statements are incorrect in many particulars. Schubart (p. 192) says that he was in Vienna as concertmeister-conductor at the Deutsche Theater in 1784, and he praises him as a skilful conductor and a thoughtful (einsichtigen) artist. He also confirms his position at the Court of Weilburg and praises his symphonies.

Germany: to 1775

KARL TRAUGOTT EISRICH (EISSRICH), b. Fonsbach, near Dresden, ca. 1770; d. St. Petersburg, 1833 (?) ("Guide Music", by Schott, 1881, No. 46). A violinist, pianist and composer. The only vocal compositions by him are mentioned by Eitner. Mendel and Fétis say: b. Bayreuth, ca. 1776, was equally talented as violinist and pianist, but he became best known in Germany by his numerous songs which are distinguished for the fine characterization of the words. About 1830 (?) he was director of music at Riga.

BRACKER, b. Berlin, ca. 1770; d. there, 1820. Violinist at the National Theatre; when this was reconstructed as the opera, he became a Royal chamber musician.

HEINRICH AUGUST FERDINAND HARTMANN, b. Hamburg, ca. 1770. Settled in Russia as violinist and was conductor (musical director) at the French theatre at St. Petersburg, ca. 1800. He composed solos for the violin (Mendel-Reissmann).

J. L. P. L. FREUBEL, b. Berlin, ca. 1770; d. Amsterdam (?). Settled at Amsterdam ca. 1802 as conductor. He was violinist, pianist and composer, and wrote for violin: "Symphonie concertante pour 2 violons principals, op. 3," Amsterdam, 1802.

JOHANN FRIEDRICH SCHUBERT, b. Rudolstadt, Dec. 17, 1770; d. Cologne, 1811. Studied successively under Hesse, town musician of Frankenhausen, Hausmann at Sondershausen and the violinist Hauk of Stettin. After a quarrel with Hausmann he left Sondershausen and took an engagement as violinist in Berlin. In 1798 he became violinist, conductor of and composer for the Döbblin theatrical company at Stettin. It was then that he received his finishing lessons from Hauk. In 1801 he was conductor at Glogau, and 1804 at Ballenstädt, whence he seems to have gone to Cologne. He pub. in the *Allgemeine Musikalische Zeitung*, Leipzig, 1804 (vol. v, p. 769), an article on the "Mechanical Construction of the Violin," besides other theoretical and didactical works. He composed 1 concerto and 2 books of 3 duets each, op. 1 and 2; an opera and other instrumental pieces.

PETER HÄNSEL, b. Leipa, Silesia, Nov. 29, 1770; d. Vienna, Sept. 18, 1831. A pupil of an uncle at Warsaw, and in 1787 violinist in the chapel of Prince Potemkin (under Sarti) in St. Petersburg. In 1791 concertmeister of Princess Lubomirski in Vienna. In 1792 he renewed his studies of composition under Haydn, and in 1795 his first compositions were published. He was a prolific writer of violin solos, 15 violin duets, 6 string trios; 55 string quartets, 3 do. for wind instruments, 4 quintets, pianoforte pieces, songs, etc. He had melodious invention and his music, which once was very popular, is not without merit, although it lacks depth of thought. During 1802–3 he lived in Paris; after that he returned to Vienna, where he succumbed to the cholera in one of those frequent epidemics which were a scourge of that town in the early 19th century. Seyfried describes him as "a modest artist and tasteful violinist who was highly respected."

JAKOB HELD, b. Landshut, Nov. 11, 1770, son of the Cantor Anton Held. Studied the violin with his father and progressed at the age of 7 so well that he could play a concerto by Stamitz in public. He finished his general education at the seminary, where at the same time he filled the post as organist. In 1782 (Mendel: 1788) he studied philosophy at Munich University, found a protector in Count Tauffkirchen, who enabled him to study violin under von Hampeln, and later under F. Eck, Danzi instructing him in the art of composition. He made successful tours as virtuoso and settled at Munich as a teacher of music. He then became a member of the Royal chapel at Munich, which post he still held in 1812. In 1811 he toured with his elder son (see Eitner's version), who was already distinguished as a violinist, though only 11 years old. They appeared with success on the Rhine, in France and Switzerland. He composed 3 violin concertos, 2 books of duets, 3 trios for 2 violins and violoncello; 5 airs with variations and overtures for orchestra.

HEINRICH ANTON HOFFMANN, b. Mayence, June 24, 1770; d. Frankfort a/M., Jan. 19, 1842. Studied law and philosophy as well as violin playing. When his father died at the outbreak of the French Revolution he was forced to turn his violinistic talent to account by becoming a chamber musician in the Mayence Court chapel. The siege of that city by the French drove him to Aschaffenburg, whence he went in 1796 to Frankfort a/M. as 1st violinist at the theatre, where in 1801 he became also choirmaster, then concertmeister, in 1817 deputy conductor, and in 1819 first conductor and joint managing director. When Guhr was appointed as capellmeister in 1821, Hoffmann remained 1st violinist and vice-director of music. In 1835 he retired with a pension and devoted the rest of his life to composition. Of his many compositions: Violin-concertos, duets, concertante for 2 violins, duets for violin and violoncello, string quartets, songs. Eitner mentions as still in existence: 6 duos for 2 violins (Paris, Nadermann), 3 duos, op. 5, and 3 duos, op. 6, for violin and violoncello (Offenbach, André), 3 quartets, op. 3 (Ib.), 2 symphonies and vocal compositions.

FERDINAND FRÄNZL, b. Schwetzingen, Palatinate, May 24, 1770; d. Mannheim, Nov. 19, 1833. A pupil of his father, Ignaz Fränzl, from the age of 5. At 7 he appeared successfully as soloist at the Court, and in 1782 he was already chamber musician in the Mannheim Court chapel. From 1784 he went with his father on prolonged concert tours. In 1785 he met with a very favourable reception at the Court of Munich and likewise in Vienna in 1786. Soon afterwards he made a prolonged sojourn at Strassburg for further studies under Pleyel and F. X. Richter, visited Switzerland, and then went to Paris, where he failed to make an impression in comparison with the great violinists of that city, headed by Viotti. In 1789 he became concertmeister in Mannheim with a salary of 1,000 florins per annum, and in 1790 went to Italy, where he studied counterpoint and composition for some time under Padre Mattei (not Martini as in Wasielewski) at Bologna, then visiting Rome, Naples and Palermo, meeting everywhere with great success. In 1792 he was musical director of the National Theatre at Frankfort a/M. (Reichard in "Gothaer Kalender," 1793, 142). In 1794 he became director of the private orchestra of a merchant, Bernard, at Offenbach. During a prolonged leave in 1799 he visited London and Hamburg, and afterwards he went repeatedly to Vienna and to Munich, where he was always greatly honoured and admired. During a prolonged sojourn at Strassburg he made further studies in composition under Pleyel and Richter. In 1802–3 he toured in Poland and Russia, and harvested in St. Petersburg and Moscow not only laurels but also considerable substantial reward. After his return he succeeded Karl Cannabich in 1806 as director of the Court chapel at Munich (on his op. 17 he calls himself "1st violin and director of the Royal music in Bavaria"). The *Leipzig Zeitung* of 1808, vol. ii, 157, calls him violinist and director of the Court chapel. From there he toured at various times to Frankfort, Offenbach and Mannheim, 1810 to Amsterdam and Paris, 1814 to Vienna, and 1816 to Leipzig. In 1823 he revisited Italy and was received with great honour, especially in Milan. In 1824 (Mendel: 1825) he resigned the conductorship of the Opera and was appointed as Bavarian Court capellmeister. In 1827 he was pensioned and went to Geneva, where he did a great deal for the advancement of music, and his departure was generally deplored when, in Apr., 1831, he retired to Mannheim for the remainder of his life. He composed for the violin: 9 concertos; 1 double concerto for 2 violins and orchestra; "Das Reich der Töne" (The Realm of Sound), concertino for violin, 5 solo voices, chorus and orchestra; solos, duets, and trios for 2 violins and bass, a symphony, overtures, several operas, and songs. His concertos in particular stood out from the majority of contemporary works both in form and invention, and would have taken a higher place, had they not been overshadowed by those of Viotti, whose influence they showed, and still more by the epoch-making works of Spohr. From all contemporary accounts we learn that his technique was neat and clean, that he played slow movements with great feeling, and in Nardini's manner with many runs and shakes, with great delicacy. His style was more intimate and graceful than broad and heroic. Spohr, who heard him in St. Petersburg in 1802, says: "The most distinguished violinist who was then at St. Petersburg was undoubtedly Fränzl. He holds the violin still in the old manner, on the right side of the tail piece, and therefore must bend his head in playing. In addition to this he holds his right arm very high and has the bad habit of raising his eyebrows in expressive passages. His playing is pure and clean. . . . As soon as he plays loud his tone becomes rough and disagreeable, because he bows too slowly and too close to the bridge and presses too much on the strings. The passages are distinct and pure but always in the middle of the bow, consequently without variety of forte and piano." In 1815

Germany: to 1775

Spohr heard him again and found both his composition and his style of playing antiquated; and of his former pre-eminence, his temperament only was left which, however, now sometimes caused want of clearness and impure intonation. From all this it is interesting to note the great change in the art of playing that took place at the end of the 18th century and that artists who in their youth stood out as shining lights were unable to cope with the higher demands made upon those of the younger generation.

LOUIS MASSONEAU, b. Cassel, ca. 1770, of French parents in the second half of the 18th century. Studied the violin under Heuzé and composition under Rodewald. He was also a viol d'amour player. In 1782 he was violinist in the Court chapel at Cassel. Thence he went to Göttingen as conductor of the academical concerts; in 1795 he was at Frankfort a/M. as 1st violin at the theatre; in 1797 at Altona in a similar capacity; and in 1802 he was director of music at Hamburg where Spohr made his acquaintance. The *Leipzig Zeitung*, 4, 765, merely calls him violinist at the Opera there, and says he was called as concertmeister to Schwerin in 1802. Kade in the Schwerin catalogue gives further particulars and states that he came there as concertmeister from Dessau, in 1803, and he appears in the "Diarium" of Ludwigslust until 1837. He was in great esteem there both as virtuoso and as composer. He composed violin concertos, duets for 2 violins, violin and viola, quartets, etc., symphonies, overtures, and a large number of greater and lesser vocal compositions. (Eitner; Gerber, ii; Fétis.)

PIERRE HENRI COURNON, b. Berlin, ca. 1770. A pupil of Braun, jun., and Heuzé; entered the Court chapel at Cassel in 1783. On the dissolution of the latter he went to Stockholm, whence he was called to Utrecht, where he received a salary of 800 florins for his services in the winter, while he went to Cassel during the summer. Apell and Gerber (ii) praise his mellow (sweet) tone, which was particularly suited to chamber music.

JOHANN KASPAR BÄUML, b. Eger, 17..; d. Bamberg, Feb. 17, 1796. Studied the violin under Lorenz Schmitt at Würzburg, a pupil of Tartini. He was appointed as violinist at the Court of Bamberg in 1771, and became 1st violin July 1, 1773.

On Apr. 2, 1779, he married the talented soprano Maria Barbara Bauerschmitt; both were highly esteemed as chamber musicians at the Court and elsewhere. On Nov. 16, 1782, he went to Frankfort to fulfil an engagement for 14 concerts during the winter season. In 1788 and 1789 Bäuml gave winter concerts at the "Black Eagle" at Bamberg. His wife, who survived him, became ailing in her later years, and this added to financial embarrassment, by which he had been beset during the whole of his life. Among his pupils were the Court musician, Braun, at Würzburg, and director of music, Uhlmann. (Marschalk.)

JOHANN CHRISTIAN(?) BOCK. War secretary of Hanover. Composed a solo for the violin, 1771 (Nuremberg).

PETER ANTON KREUSER, b. Lengfurt, near Würzburg, 1772 (Mendel: 1771). Violin virtuoso, who went to Paris, 1788, where he was appointed as violin in the Royal chapel; on the outbreak of the Revolution he went to London, where, in 1807, he was appointed to the Royal chapel. In Paris he wrote several operettas (Gerber, ii). In London also several little operas of his were performed. Apart from a considerable technique, he showed in his playing distinct individuality of style and expression.

AUGUST RIEMANN, b. Blankenhain, Thuringia, Aug. 12, 1772; d. Weimar, Aug., 1826. In 1790 was 1st violinist in the Weimar Court chapel; in 1806 conductor of rehearsals at the Opera there, and 1818 Court capellmeister. His violin compositions remained unpub.

MARIANNE CRUX, b. Mannheim (Mendel: Munich), 1772. Daughter of a Court ballet master, studied the violin under Fr. Eck, singing under Dorothea Wendling, and the pianoforte under Stritzl. She excelled in all three of these arts, and also had a perfect knowledge of English, Italian, and French, besides being very clever at drawing and needlework. In 1787 she played the violin and pianoforte and sang at Vienna before the Emperor Joseph II, who was greatly pleased with her performance. In 1790 she went with her father to Berlin, where she was received with great enthusiasm wherever she appeared. "Soon afterwards," says Mendel, "she married a so-called Holstein nobleman, and appeared at Mayence with great success as Mme Hollmann, thence she went to Frankfort

Germany: to 1775

a/M. and Mannheim, where her father obtained for her the offer of an engagement as singer at the Court of Munich, but she preferred to continue touring. She visited London and thence went to Stockholm, where, it is said, she was married to Gelbert, an officer of the engineers. In 1807 she was in Hamburg, but from that time nothing is known about her, and in 1811, according to Fétis, even her father did not know where she was.

FRANZ CRAMER, b. ca. 1772, at Mannheim; d. London, 1848. Second son of Wilhelm Cramer, of his first marriage. A pupil of his father, and during 1799–1814 director of the Ancient Concerts, London; Royal chamber musician; professor of the Academy of Music, and from 1834 Master of the King's band. He conducted many of the great Music Festivals (*Leipzig Zeitung*, 50, 560; Pohl, ii, 36). Fétis, who says that he was but a mediocre violinist, states that he was also conductor of the Philharmonic Society.

JOHANN MICHAEL MÜLLER, b. Schwetzingen, Aug. 8, 1772; d. Stuttgart, Dec. 13, 1835. Studied the violin at the Paris Conservatoire. In 1889 he went to Berne as leader of the concerts. After that he became director of music at Bayreuth and soon afterwards toured as virtuoso. In 1802 he became concert violinist at Frankfort a/M. and succeeded Cannabich when the latter retired as director of the Opera. In 1804 he became concertmeister at Weimar, and in 1806 he went on tour again and finally settled at Stuttgart as solo violinist and second capellmeister, except for three years when he was leader in the chapel of Prince Esterhazy in Vienna (A. d. Biog.; Eitner). He composed 2 quartets for harpsichord and strings (Musikfr.).

FRIEDRICH MÜLLER. Violinist (?), who lived ca. 1760 in Paris, where his "Sei sonate a violino solo col Basso" were pub. about that time (Eitner).

BENJAMIN FELIX FRIEDRICH KREIBE, b. Ballenstädt, ca. 1773. A pupil of Aghte and F. W. Rust, chamber musician, violinist in the Court chapel at Ballenstädt, and a fertile composer (Gerber, ii).

HEINRICH MARCHAND, b. Mannheim, 1774. A pupil of Leopold Mozart at Salzburg, and became one of the foremost

German violinists of his time. Brother of the famous singer Margarete Danzi. He was also a good pianist. His first engagement was in the chapel of Prince Thurn and Taxis at Ratisbon; afterwards he visited Paris. His pub. compositions are all for the pianoforte.

KARL MÖSER, b. Berlin, Jan. 24, 1774; d. there, Jan. 27, 1851. Son of an oboist in the Ziethen Hussars, who recognized the son's early signs of musical talent and fostered them; he became a pupil of Böttcher, made his debut as virtuoso Apr. 24, 1784. On the recommendation of Frederick William II he was engaged in the Court chapel of the Margrave of Schwedt; after the death of the latter he returned to Berlin and entered the preparatory class of the Royal chapel, making further studies under C. Haack. Jan. 1, 1792, he was appointed as Royal chamber musician. In 1796 he was exiled from Berlin on account of an amorous adventure with the Countess of Mark, natural daughter of the King, and went to Hamburg, where he met Rode and Viotti from whom he learned still more. Then he went on tour in Denmark and Norway and finally came to London, where Salomon engaged him but another love affair with an Italian singer at Copenhagen caused him to leave London, and after the death of the Prussian King in 1797 he returned to Berlin and was reinstated in his former position. During 1806-11 he lived at St. Petersburg, and after the War of Liberation on the re-organization of the Royal chapel he became concertmeister. In 1813 he instituted public Quartet performances, playing chiefly Haydn, Mozart, Beethoven, and in 1816 he added symphony and overture performances, and thus laid the foundation to the symphony concerts of the Royal chapel for the benefit of the orphan fund. In 1825 he became musical director, first concertmeister, and conducted the first performance of Beethoven's fourth symphony in Berlin, Nov. 27, 1826. In 1829 he celebrated his fifty years' jubilee, received the title of capellmeister, was pensioned but retained the instrumental class (Ledebur, *Rhein Zeitung*, i, 260). His compositions were unimportant. Returning to Berlin, he became the favourite of Prince Louis Ferdinand, who admitted him to his intimate circle of friends where he met Dussek, from whom he received much wholesome artistic impulse. In 1804 he went to Vienna, where he was praised by both Haydn and Beethoven for his playing of their quartets. The dissolution of the Royal chapel at the outbreak of the war in 1806 drove him from Berlin, and after touring in Poland he went to Russia. The celebrated violinist, C. Müller of Brunswick, was one of his pupils.

AUGUST MÖSER, b. Berlin, Dec. 25, 1825; d. on a tour in America, 1859; was his son and pupil. He composed some pianoforte pieces.

FRANZ ECK, b. Mannheim, 1774; d. Strassburg, 1804. Son of a horn-player, Georg Eck, in the Court chapel, Mannheim, Franz was an "accessist" violinist in Mannheim Court chapel in 1778, and went with the Court to Munich, where he was appointed violinist in the chapel on July 29, 1779. By 1789 he received a salary of 900 florins per annum, and a rise in 1790. Dismissed May 21, 1800, on account of a love affair with a noble lady, he travelled to Russia, lost his reason and was brought to Nancy by Johann Friedrich, who placed him in an asylum in Strassburg, where he died in 1804. Fétis says that Franz in 1801 went first to Riga, then to St. Petersburg, where he devoted himself to serious studies. The Tsar was so pleased with his playing that he nominated him director and solo violinist of the Court concerts; but soon after he was attacked by religious mania, which so affected his mind that the Tsar sent him back to his brother under escort. Franz was the teacher of Spohr.

LUDWIG TIETZ, b. Dresden, Apr. 26, 1774; d. there, Aug. 8, 1827. The son and pupil of a Dresden chamber musician, afterwards violin pupil of J. G. Scholtz. In 1790 he became a member of the Court chapel and undertook several tours as a violin virtuoso. In 1814 he became leader of the interludes at the theatre, and in 1818 was appointed Royal vice-concertmeister.

UDALRIC BALDENECKER. Violinist at the Court of Mayence, who wrote violin pieces; 6 trios for violin, violin and violoncello and church music, pub. Frankfort a/M., 1775–80; musical director of Marchand's theatre, Mayence. Composed 2 violin duets, op. 5, 6 trios for violin taille and violoncello.

JACOB KRESS, d. Darmstadt. In 1736 first concertmeister at the Court of Hesse-Darmstadt and composed 6 concertos for violin in 5 parts, op. 1 (pub. Nuremberg), sonate da camera a violino, oboe, basso o cembalo, op. 3 (Rostock), and minuets for violin and B.c., 6 sonate à 4, 2 violins, viola e bass, 11 sonate à 4 for violin, or flute trav. violin 11, viola and bass, Nos. 7–17; 2 of the violin concertos are for violin or flute trav.; many flute sonatas and solos; 1 trio for flute trav., viole d'amour and cembalo or 1 lute; trio for flute trav., 1 viola da gamba concerto with cembalo (MS.), all in Darmstadt; also a symphony and 1 overture (MS., Schwerin).

GEORG FRIEDRICH KRESS, b. Darmstadt; probably son of Jacob Kress; d. Göttingen, ca. 1775 (Fétis says 1783). His first appointment as violinist was in the Court chapel of Schwerin. In 1753 he became concertmeister at the Academy of Göttingen, where he remained till his death. Gerber, i, who gives some not very flattering accounts of his playing by contemporaries while it is praised by others, mentions some of his compositions.

EBERHARD FRIEDRICH SCHWARZ, b. Ansbach, 1775; d. Berlin, after 1835. Son of the bassoon player, Andr. Gottlob Schwarz. Studied the violin under Janitsch. He toured as violinist in 1795, played at Berlin before the King and became member of the Court chapel. He was also an excellent pianist. In 1835 he was pensioned, and died probably soon after. He did much to spread the knowledge of Mozart's and Beethoven's music (Ledebur).

JOHANN EISERT, b. Georgenthal, near Rumburg, Feb. 4, 1775. A violinist and chamber musician in the Dresden Court chapel. Though he does not rank among the great virtuosos he was a violinist of great merit. No compositions of his are known. His son, JOHANN EISERT, was a noted organ player and composer who settled in Vienna. (*See* Riemann, Grove, etc.)

CHRISTIAN SCHMIEDICHEN, b. 1775; d. Vienna, Apr. 24, 1812 (Becker, iii, 53). Evidently the same as H. C. Schmiedigen mentioned in the *Leipzig Zeitung*, vol. 9–15, as violinist from Oldenburg, who gave a concert at the Gewandhaus, Leipzig, on Oct. 20, 1807 (Dörffel, ii, 199, No. 163, under the same name). In the same year he appeared also at Dresden, and in 1812 in Vienna, where he died. *Leipzig Zeitung*, 1815, discusses variations by him.

Germany: to 1775

JOSEPH MORALT, b. Schwetzingen, near Mannheim, Aug. 5, 1775; d. Munich, Nov. 14, 1855. He was the eldest of five brothers, the others being JEAN BAPTIST, violin, JACOB, violin, PHILIP, violoncello, and GEORGE, viola. Joseph received his first music lessons from the town musician, Carl Geller, at Schwetzingen, and afterwards studied the violin under Lops, a chamber musician of Duke Clemens of Bavaria. After having played for some years as supernumerary in the Court chapel, he was appointed as full member in 1797 and became concertmeister in 1800. He toured as virtuoso in Switzerland, thence he went to France and England, meeting with great success at Lyons, Paris, London, and on his return journey in Frankfort a/M., where he gave several concerts, and in other German towns. After receiving his appointment as concertmeister on May 10, 1801, he started studying quartets by Haydn and Mozart with his brothers Jean Baptist, Jacob, and his twin brother Philip, and under his artistic leadership they attained to such perfection in their ensemble as had never been heard before. As Fétis tells us: "They appeared together in many German towns where they always met with enthusiastic receptions." Joseph retained his position in the Munich chapel to the time of his death. He became Royal director of music and conductor at the opera in 1827, and retired in 1836.

TRAUGOTT MAXIMILIAN EBERWEIN, b. Weimar, Oct. 27, 1775; d. Rudolstadt, Dec. 2, 1831. His first teacher was his father, a town musician, under whom the boy made such rapid progress that at the age of 7 he was already violinist in the Ducal chapel. According to the custom of the town musicians, he had to learn all the instruments then in use, and he also composed at that early age some dance and ballet tunes. In 1791 his father sent him to Frankfort a/M. to study musical theory under Kunze, and afterwards he perfected himself on the violin under Schick at Mayence. After a successful debut as violin virtuoso at Hamburg in 1796, he was appointed violinist in the Court Chapel of Schwartzburg Rudolstadt in 1797, as petty jealousies and intrigues among the musicians had driven him from Weimar. In 1803 he obtained leave from the Prince to go on tour, during which he visited France, Bavaria, the Tyrol and thence went to Italy. At Rome he wrote his first string quartets and then studied composition under Fenaroli at Naples. In 1804 he returned to Rudolstadt and was entrusted with the direction of the chapel in 1809, but only in the following year he received the official title of chamber musician, and in Sept., 1817, he became capellmeister to the Prince. Before that he had made some concert tours in Germany, especially to Berlin, where he gained the friendship of Himmel and Zelter. In 1817 he visited Vienna again, where he had previously made the acquaintance of Beethoven and Salieri; later he toured in Hungary and Bohemia, thence returned to Rudolstadt, where he remained for the rest of his life. He was a man of high ideals, who studied philosophy, sciences, art, medicine, and especially social politics. He was particularly active in the furtherance of musical art and conditions of musicians and mankind in general. With this object in view he instituted several musical festivals in various German towns and a Widows and Orphans Fund for the members of the Rudolstadt chapel. His compositions, amounting to some 100 works, include no violin concertos or solos although there are several for flute and clarinet. His best works are said to be the settings of some of Goethe's "Singspiele." Of his two sons, LUDWIG EBERWEIN, the younger, was a member of the Rudolstadt chapel.

SIMON (Gerber, i; Kade Cat., ii, 235, mixes him up with Johann Gottfried). Before Oct. 30, 1776, he was a violinist at the Court of Mecklenburg, but left there apparently before Sept. 20, 1785, as his wife Friderica, *née* Behrensen, of Schwerin, petitions the Duke on that date for subvention, as her husband, the Jew, had left her. Some sonate a clavicembalo et violino obbligato dedicated to Prince Francis (I) of Mecklenburg are in the Ducal library.

FRANZ FAUNER. An 18th-century composer. Musikfreunde have: Concerto for violin and quartet, divertimento for 2 violins and bass; duet for violin and bass; 3 sonatas for violin and bass. They call him von Fauner. Karlsruhe has: Concertino flute trav., violin, viola, bass, 4 movements. He is probably the same as Friedrich Fauner (Gerber, i), about 1780, in Paris, where he pub. 6 duets for 2 violins.

CHAPTER 29

Germany: to 1800

JOSEPH KÜFFNER, b. Würzburg, Mar. 31, 1776; d. there, Sept. 8, 1856. Studied law but turned to music. Appeared in public as violin virtuoso. In 1797 he was appointed provisionally in the chapel of the Prince-Bishop, only a few years later this was made definite with a salary of 125 florins. When Würzburg was joined to Bavaria in 1802 he became a military bandmaster, and wrote a great deal for brass band. His numerous compositions are of a superficial nature.

KARL LUGE, b. probably at Oppeln, where his brother Franz, an excellent musician, was b. 1776. Karl in 1805 was at Breslau as a violinist, and became choirmaster at the opera there in 1807 and afterwards its musical director. He wrote variations on a theme by Himmel for violin solo (Hoffmann) (Breslau, Foerster). According to Fétis, he belonged to the school of Rode, had an excellent tone and played with much expression. His best pupil was H. Panofka.

KARL HELLMUTH (HELMUTH), b. Wolfenbüttel. A violinist in the Court chapel of the Elector of Mayence, singer and actor in Seyler's theatrical company, part of which gave performances in Bonn 1777 to 1779. Hellmuth had meanwhile become co-director of the company together with Grossmann. He wrote a "prelude" (curtain-raiser), "The Look into the Future," with vocal music for the birthday celebrations of the Elector, performed at Bonn, May 13, 1779. From 1781 his name disappears from the members' lists of the company. (Reichardt, 1793, 253; Thayer, i, 67, 72; Gerber, ii; Gerber, i, is incorrect.)

FRANZ ZICH. Ca. 1777 a chamber musician, violinist, in the Dresden Court chapel. He was the teacher of Joh. A. Miksch (q.v.) (Mendel-Reissmann, "Music Lexikon.")

CHR. K. KARL KIESEWETTER, b. Augsburg, 1777; d. London, Sept. 27, 1827. At first the concertmeister (violin) at Oldenburg, after that, 1814–22, at Hanover, where he was supposed to be the first to give whole symphonies without breaking them up and dividing them between other numbers. Thence he went to London, where he appeared also as soloist at the Philharmonic concerts, but without much success, and he died there in reduced circumstances. (Riemann—appears to be identical with Christ. Gottfried, K., *see* p. 350.)

JOHANN BAPTIST MORALT, b. Mannheim, Jan. 10, 1777; d. Munich, Oct. 7, 1825. A pupil of Cannabich (*Leipzig Zeitung*, 28, 42, Obituary), violinist at Mannheim; in 1792 supernumerary in Munich chapel, and from 1798 till his death 1st violinist in the Court chapel at Munich. He and his brothers (*see* Grove) were excellent quartet players, Johann Baptist being the 2nd violin. Composed: "Leçons méthodiques pour le violon avec accompagnement d'un second violon" (Mayence, Schott); also violin solos, symphonies, a German mass, and other works for the church. The loss of a son in 1823 began to undermine his health (Fétis).

FERDINAND AUGUST (KARL) SEIDLER (Gerber, ii, calls him Ferdinand August), b. Berlin, Sept. 13, 1778; d. there, Feb. 27, 1840. A pupil of the violinist Bernard, who appeared as violinist-prodigy at the age of 6. Provided with letters of the Princess Friederika of Prussia he toured for some time, on his return resumed his studies under Haak, and was at the King's command made a member of the Royal chapel in 1798. When Möser left Berlin, he succeeded him in the court-quartet, and when the personnel of the chapel was reduced in 1806 he accompanied the art patron Count Yermolow to Russia. In 1812 he left there and went to Vienna, where he married the singer Caroline Wranitzki, and then returned to Berlin to become concertmeister in the Royal chapel in 1816. During the first performance of "The Brewer of Preston" on Apr. 28, 1839, he was attacked by a stroke of apoplexy which led to his death on Feb. 29 in the following year. He was generally admired for the beauty of his tone, purity of intonation and neatness of his technique, for which even so severe a judge as Spohr praised him. His beautiful violin (it does not say by whom), a present of King

Germany: to 1800

Friedrich Wilhelm II, became afterwards the property of L. Ganz. Of his compositions only a song to words by Schiller is known (B. Wagner).

KARL NEUNER, b. Auen, Munich, July 29, 1778; d. Munich, mid-July, 1830. Violinist in the Court chapel, Munich. Composed church music, ballets, etc., musical symphonies, overtures, but apparently nothing for the violin. He died from pulmonary disease, from which he had suffered for a number of years.

SCHINGE (SCHÖNGE). Violinist in Mannheim Court chapel with a salary of 130 florins and 125 extra. In 1778 he went with the chapel to Munich, received a rise of salary, July 29, 1779, and was still active there in 1799.

PETER BROCHARD, b. Munich, Aug. 4, 1779. The son of a ballet master and Evelina Brochard, an eminent opera singer. He received lessons on the pianoforte from 1787 and began to study the violin in 1792, first under the Court musician Held, then under Friedrich Eck. In 1797 he became supernumerary in the Electoral chapel, and in 1798 he was sent to Mannheim as violinist in the Court orchestra, but was recalled to Munich in the following year. In 1802 he accepted a two years' engagement in the Stuttgart chapel, at the end of which he returned again to Munich; where he was in 1811. According to Fétis, he was a talented composer who wrote sonatas, variations, ariettas, cantatas and five ballets for the Royal (from 1805) Theatre, Munich.

KONRAD LUDWIG DIETRICH ZINKEISEN, b. Hanover, June 3, 1779; d. Brunswick, Nov. 28, 1838. At first a pupil of his father, then of Rode at Wolfenbüttel. From 1801 to 1803 he was oboist in a military band at Lüneburg, and in 1803 became leader of the academical concerts at Göttingen, where he studied composition under Forkel. In 1819 he was appointed chamber musician in the Brunswick Court chapel. He composed 6 violin concertos, a concertante symphony for violin and viola; variations for violin and string trio; 2 duets for violin and viola; 3 string quartets; 4 overtures; a number of concertos, etc., for wind instruments and choral songs for mixed and for male voices. Many of his compositions remained in MS.

The History of the Violin

JOHANN GEORG HOLZBOGEN, b. Munich, in the first half of the 18th century; d. there in 1779, as pensioned chamber musician. He was already a member of the Munich Court chapel in 1753, when he was sent by the Duke Clemens of Bavaria to Padua to perfect himself on the violin and study composition under Tartini. After his return to Munich he was, in 1762, appointed Court-concertmeister. Burney, who heard him there, praises his brilliant technique, fiery temperament and beautiful tone. On June 19 and 22 he gave concerts at Frankfort a/M. with the hornplayer Leitgeb (Israel, "Chronicles of Frankfort Concerts," p. 51). Mendel ("Music Lexikon") mentions as known compositions by him: 6 symphonies, 6 string trios, and two for violin and wind instruments. Fétis states that he composed violin concertos, quartets, trios, and "Meditations for Holy Week" for the Jesuits at Munich. In the Munich library are 1 symphony, 1 trio, and 1 notturno for 2 violins and violoncello all in MS. None of his compositions were pub.

JOHANN BÖHM. Lived during the latter decades of the 18th century and beginning of the 19th. In 1779 director of a theatrical company, which bore his name. A highly esteemed violin virtuoso and conductor of various German theatrical companies, for whom he wrote operas suited to their limited powers and means, which proved very successful.

JAKOB MORALT, the twin brother of PHILIP MORALT (violoncellist), was born at Munich 1780, d. there in 1803. He studied the violin under Christoph Geitner, a member of the Electoral Chapel, in which he was already a violinist in 1797 but died at the age of 23.

GEORG MORALT, b. Munich, 1781; d. there in 1818. He also was a member of the Electoral Chapel and of the Moralt quartet as a viola player to the time of his death.

KUNISCH. Between 1780 and 1790 chamber musician in the Brunswick Court chapel and the first teacher of account of Spohr.

ERNST HESSE. In 1780 at the Court chapel at Darmstadt with a salary of 450 florins. In 1804 he became concertmeister with 830 florins. He died in 1821 (Thomas, 28, 37, 83). Not to be confounded with Ernst Christian Hesse.

Germany: to 1800

JOHANN LEONHARD HESSE, d. 1805, of Stargard, Pomerania. During 1780–5, violinist at the Court chapel, Berlin (Reichardt, 1786, 217). Marpurg mentions him as in 1754; Ledebur says 1754 to 1798, pensioned in latter year. Bitter (i, 26) says Hesse entered the chapel in 1740 as chamber musician; doubtful if the same.

FRANZ ANTON MORGENROTH, b. Namslau, Silesia, Feb. 8, 1780; d. Dresden, Aug. 14 (7?), 1847. Studied in Breslau. In 1798 at Warsaw in the war and domaine office; 1805, controller of the government pawn house. In 1806 he left on account of the war, went to Dresden and devoted himself to music. During 1810–11 he studied under Weinlig, entered the Royal chapel as violinist in 1810, and on Apr. 4, 1812, became chamber musician with a salary of 150 thalers, which was raised, 1817, to 300 thalers. His intercourse with Polledro and other artists benefited him so much that on Oct. 1, 1828, he became the vice-concertmeister, and after Rolla's death in 1838 concertmeister (Fürstenau, i, 177, 180; A. D. Biog.). Composed and pub. only songs. MS. in Dresden lib., also instrumental compositions and a theoretical work. Fétis adds: 2 concertos for violin and orchestra; Sicilienne with variations for do. do.; Thèmes variés for violin with quartet, op. 1 and 2; 2 symphonies and 2 overtures. With Lipinski and F. Schubert he was eager to advance the fame of the Dresden chapel and his excellent personal qualities gained him the love and respect of all who knew him.

JOHANN HEINRICH MÜLLER, b. Königsberg, Mar. 11, 1780 (Mendel: Mar. 19, 1781); d. St. Petersburg, Mar. 19, 1826. According to Mendel, after studying law, he went to Halle and studied composition under Türk. As he was obliged to choose something which would secure his livelihood, he took up the violin, and went to Paris, where he studied under R. Kreutzer and became an excellent player. As such, he was engaged in the Vienna Court chapel. In 1803 he became director of the German theatre at Pressburg. As this position was not congenial to him he resolved at the end of his contract to devote himself entirely to composition and teaching. For that purpose he withdrew from all contact with his friends and the outer world to study the pianoforte, and after one year he re-appeared as an excellent pianist. Among his pupils for composition were Field, Laput, Sussmann, Böhm, etc. He composed an oratorio, church music, string quartets and excellent studies.

GEORG KAUMEYER, b. Augsburg, Jan., 1780; d. Berlin, Dec. 1, 1858. Violinist and leader at the theatre on the Wien, Vienna. In 1825 he was appointed in the Royal chapel in Berlin, and pensioned in 1845 (Ledebur).

JOSEPH BAUMÜLLER, b. Mannheim, 1780. A talented violinist who through the influence of Franz Schemenauer became musician in the Munich Court chapel, and 1st violinist from 1800.

PAUL THIERIOT, b. Leipzig, Feb. 17, 1780; d. Wiesbaden, Jan. 20, 1831. A pupil of Baillot, Paris; toured a great deal as virtuoso, but his nervousness, artistic pride combined with his lack of social forms, and an idealistic outlook on life, embittered his existence and repressed his great talents, and, having a good general education, he had at times to resort to teaching languages. He had several fixed appointments as violinist, for instance, in the private orchestra of Mr. Peter Bernard at Offenbach, then as director of music at Neufchâtel, Switzerland, where he married, in 1812, Eva Hoffman, who was of a kindred nature. Finally he was teacher of music at the Boys' Institute of Delaspée at Wiesbaden (Schnyder von Wartensse, Lebensbeschreibungen, 1888, pp. 220 ff.). Thieriot was a friend of the great German author, Jean Paul (J. F. P. Richter).

FR. SCHWACHHOFER, b. Mayence, ca. 1780; d. Berlin, Mar. 3, 1846. Chamber musician in the Royal chapel, Berlin, 1804–45, then pensioned.

JOHANN GABRIEL REICHENBERG. At first concertmeister in the Brunswick Court chapel and from ca. 1780 in that of Berlin. Gerber, i, calls him "an agreeable and neat (angenehmen und netten) violinist."

KUBASCH. One of the best Silesian violinists of the middle of the 18th century, who died at Olmütz in poverty ca. 1780; he became known in wider circles as composer of two violin concertos. Apparently he never left his native country, the Upper-Lausitz.

Germany: to 1800

LUDWIG WOLF, d. Offenbach, 1817; ca. 1780 (Mendel: 1769). Violinist at the theatre, Frankfort on the Main. Composed violin solos; duets, op. 1 and op. 3; do. for violin and viola; trios for violin, viola and 1 violoncello, op. 2; pianoforte trio, op. 6 (particulars in Fétis); potpourri for two concertet violins, op. 5.

KARL BARON VON TAUBER VON TAUBERFURT. Imperial councillor, Graetz, d. there, Jan. 6, 1814. Wrote: "Ueber meine Violine" (about my violin), Vienna, Burtzboeck, 1780. Fétis describes it as "a Phantasy on various musical subjects, political, philosophical, æsthetical, etc. It contains 352 reflections of a capellmeister in a didactic style."

JOHANN WILHELM RUHE. In 1781 violinist at the "Grosse Concert," Leipzig. He played afterwards repeatedly as soloist at the Gewandhaus concerts until 1792 (Dörffel, ii, 22, 25, 37).

HEINRICH AUGUST MATTHÄI, b. Dresden, Oct. 30, 1781; d. Leipzig, Nov. 4, 1835. He learned to play several instruments from childhood, but the violin became his favourite. On a visit to Leipzig in 1803 he played at the weekly Gewandhaus concert with such success that he was engaged as solo violinist by the side of Campagnoli for these concerts as well as for the theatre. The interest which his talent and his person created decided some of his friends and patrons to supply him with the necessary funds to perfect himself under Rodolphe Kreutzer at Paris. And he returned in 1806 showing such results that they fully justified the aid his friends had given him. In the autumn of 1809 he formed a permanent quartet with Campagnoli, Voigt and Dotzauer for the production of the works of Haydn, Mozart and Beethoven. Their concerts were greatly admired at Leipzig. At a great musical festival in Thuringia on June 21, 1810, he played a concertante symphony with Spohr and proved himself a worthy partner of that great master, and he confirmed that opinion at a concert which he gave at Berlin on Dec. 16, 1811. After a very successful tour in Northern Germany he succeeded Campagnoli as concertmeister at Leipzig in 1817 and retained that post until he died. He composed a few solo pieces with orchestra; duets for 2 violins, op. 3 (Leipzig, Peters); 4 concertos (Ib.,

Peters and Hofmeister); string quartets and vocal quartets and songs. Fesca and Ulrich were the most prominent of his pupils.

FRIEDRICH CHRISTIAN HERMANN UBER, b. Breslau, Apr. 22, 1781; d. Dresden, Mar. 2, 1822. He was the son of the distinguished lawyer and amateur musician and composer, Christian Benj. Uber. He was destined for the law, but while studying at Halle University, Türk, with whom he studied composition, decided him to embrace music as his profession. Türk had handed over to him the conductorship of the winter concerts at Halle, where he produced in 1801 a violin concerto and a cantata of his own composition with great success. In 1803 he returned to Breslau, where he was to prepare for his career as an advocat, but the success of a second cantata, "The Triumph of Love," finally overcame his father's objections to the choice of his career. At the end of 1804 he accompanied Prince Radziwill to Berlin where, at Bernhard Romberg's recommendation, he became solo violinist in the chapel of Prince Louis Ferdinand; but the political events of 1806 deprived him of that position after he had given a concert at Berlin where he was greatly admired as a violinist. In 1807 he was engaged for the Court chapel at Brunswick, but in 1808 he left this to become 1st violinist and conductor of the German opera to the King of Westphalia at Cassel. There he produced several operas and cantatas of his composition, including several French opéras-comique. In 1814 that Kingdom was dissolved and in the same year he accepted the position of director of music at the theatre of Mayence. In 1816 he was musical director in the theatrical company of Seconda at Dresden, but he left this soon afterwards and resided for some time at Leipzig as a private teacher. In 1817, however, he was called to Dresden as cantor and musical director of the "Kreuzkirche"; there he produced operas, cantatas and an oratorio, "The Last Words of the Saviour," which was performed for the first time at the very hour of Uber's death. He had been ailing for some time. Of his many compositions only his violin concerto, op. 3, in E minor, 2 overtures and romances and songs to French words were published at Leipzig. His brother was the eminent violoncellist ALEXANDER UBER, who also died at the age of 41.

Germany: to 1800

ANTON BOHRER, b. Munich, 1783; d. Hanover, 1852. His father, an eminent double-bass player and trumpeter in the Electoral Chapel, gave him his first lessons on the violin and then placed him under Cannabich, in whose company he eventually went to Paris where he became a pupil of R. Kreutzer. On his return in 1799 he was appointed as violinist in the Electoral Chapel, and soon after he toured with his father, KASPER BOHRER, in Austria and Bohemia, and in the following year he and his brother, MAX BOHRER, the violoncellist, visited Switzerland, France and Germany, where they gave very successful concerts in all the principal towns. On their return, they started on a serious and severe study of ensemble playing, which was the cause of their subsequent phenomenal success. They started on their great tour in 1810 which took them all over Germany, Holland and back again to Poland, Bohemia, Hungary, and then to Russia, when Anton fell ill at Kieff, where they were consequently delayed for four months. From Kieff they went to Moscow, whence they fled at the approach of the French, but they were apprehended by a troop of Cossacks who brought them before General Seblowsky. The latter had orders to send all German prisoners to Siberia, especially subjects of the King of Bavaria, to whom the Tsar felt the strongest resentment. The General was, however, a great lover of music, and after he had heard the two young artists he was so pleased with their playing that he allowed them to proceed to St. Petersburg; to give them the necessary protection he sent them as government couriers. In St. Petersburg they met with so much success that they remained for a whole year, after which they toured through Finland to Sweden and Denmark, and from there they went to Hamburg, whence they embarked for London. Towards the end of 1814 they returned to Munich to rejoin their family. In the following year they visited France again and were received with enthusiasm—especially their unaccompanied fantasias for violin and violoncello were admired on account as well for the originality of their themes as for the brilliance and perfection of the ensemble. Fétis, who no doubt speaks from personal knowledge, attributes their success chiefly to Max Bohrer. Of Anton he says: "His tone is small, and his style, although elegant and graceful, lacks grandeur, but he seconds his brother well in their concerted pieces.

These are all composed by Anton." He also says about the latter: "His playing, although of pleasing finish, could not produce a vivid sensation in a town where one is accustomed to hear violinists of the most remarkable talent." There may perhaps have been just a little bias in favour of the great French violinists in his judgment, though on the whole it was undoubtedly true. After a second visit to England the brothers Bohrer returned to Paris, where they appeared at the Concerts Spirituels during Holy Week. In May of that year (1815?) they went to Berlin, where, in 1818, Anton received the title of concertmeister, and Max that of 1st chamber violoncellist. In 1820 they went on tour again, this time visiting the principal towns of Italy and returning to Berlin in 1824. Frictions arose between the two brothers and the quarrelsome, haughty Spontini, in consequence of which they left Berlin in 1826 and Anton persuaded his brother to accompany him via Hamburg to Munich. There they married two distinguished pianists, the sisters Dülken, daughters of the Court instrument-maker. Max married Louise, the elder, born 1805, and Anton the younger, born 1807. In 1827 they returned once more to Paris, with renewed success. After a few minor excursions they gave during the winter quartet and quintet concerts at the salons of Mr. Pape, with Tilmant as 2nd violin and the famous viola player Urhan. There they performed the latest compositions by Beethoven with remarkable perfection of ensemble and delicacy of phrasing. The Revolution of 1830 drove them away from Paris and for the first time they separated. After touring for some time, Anton became concertmeister at the Court of Hanover in 1835 till 1844, when he resigned, to tour with his daughter Sophie, a talented pianist. He was a prolific composer for his instrument as well as for chamber and orchestral music, of which Fétis gives a list, but his compositions are entirely antiquated.

GEORG GRIESBACH, b. Coppenbrügge, Hanover. Studied the violin under Wm. Cramer and was 1st violin in the Royal band in 1783 (Cramer, i, 1038). W. C. T. and H. Griesbach appear in the lists of violinists of the concerts of ancient music at the Hanover Square Rooms, London, in 1797; they belong possibly to the same family, of which several members resided in London in the 18th century.

Germany: to 1800

HEINRICH ALOYS PRAEGER, b. Amsterdam, Dec. 25, 1783; d. Magdeburg, Aug. 7, 1854. A violinist, guitarist, composer. He was for some time conductor of a travelling theatrical company; from 1827 to 1830 (Riemann: 1829–31) capellmeister at Hamburg; conductor at the Leipzig theatre and afterwards in the same position successively at the Magdeburg and Hanover theatres. His published compositions are violin duets and variations, 1 string quintet, 1 quintet for viola and wind instruments, 7 string quartets and 2 string trios, variations for various instruments; in MS., capriccios, and 3 books of violin studies.

KARL HERTEL, b. Berlin, Mar. 13, 1784; d. there, Nov. 16, 1868. He was a violinist in the Royal chapel, Berlin, ca. 1808, and about that time appeared also in public as a violin virtuoso with marked success. In 1811 he became a Royal chamber musician, was decorated with the Order of the Red Eagle in 1857, and pensioned in 1862. His son, PETER LUDWIG HERTEL, b. Berlin, Apr. 21, 1817, was a violin pupil of his father and Ed. Ritz, and studied the pianoforte under W. Greulich and composition under J. Schneider and B. Marx. He distinguished himself chiefly as composer, especially by his numerous ballets, mostly written to scenarios by P. Taglioni, many of which became very popular. In 1858 he became Royal Court composer and in 1860 director of the Royal Ballet music. He was pensioned in 1893.

KARL EBERWEIN, b. Weimar, Nov. 10, 1784; d. there, Mar. 2, 1868. The second brother of Traugott Maximilian Eberwein. He received his first music lessons from his father and afterwards from his brother, who also instructed him in the art of composition. He became chamber virtuoso and director of the Ducal chapel and conductor of Goethe's house orchestra. He was a man of a serious turn of mind and great musical talent, showing in his work a certain amount of originality, although his admiration for Mozart gained a strong influence over him which became noticeable in his compositions. He wrote for the violin a concerto with orchestra for amateurs, op. 15 (Leipzig, Hofmeister); 3 books of duets for 2 violins (Ib., Breitkopf, Hofmeister), string quartets, flute concerto, operas, cantatas, etc. His wife Emilie, *née* Hässler, was prima donna at the Weimar opera, and their son, MAXIMILIAN KARL EBERWEIN, was a pianist of European reputation.

GEORG MAURER. A violinist at the Court chapel, Berlin, from 1785; probably identical with the Maurer mentioned by Gerber, ii, and Ledebur as chamber musician in Berlin, 1788–92, who generally lived at Potsdam and composed sonatas for harpsichord and violin ad lib., op. 1 (3) and op. 2 (3), also some pianoforte pieces.

F. KLES, b. probably in Silesia, and lived at Breslau towards the end of the 18th century. Composed a concerto for violin with accompaniment (of orchestra?) and a concerto for viola with orchestra, both pub. in 1786 (Breslau?).

FRIEDRICH WILHELM PIXIS, b. Mannheim, 1786; d. Prague, Oct. 20, 1842. He commenced the study of the violin at the age of 5 under Georg Ritter, father of the eminent violoncellist and composer, Peter Ritter, and continued them under Luci or Luigi at Offenbach, and finally under Fränzl at Mannheim. In his ninth year he had already appeared in public, and soon after went on tour with his father and his brother Johann Peter, the eminent pianist. They appeared successfully in Karlsruhe, Stuttgart, Göttingen, Cassel, Brunswick, Zelle, Bremen and Hamburg. At the latter place they arrived in 1798, and young Pixis had a course of lessons from Viotti, who lived there at the time. In 1799 he toured again with his father and brother, visiting Hanover, Leipzig, Berlin, Dresden, and Warsaw, where great praise was bestowed upon the young artist. In 1802 he was at Königsberg, where Spohr heard him and, in an entry in his diary, condemned his playing in almost every particular, especially for holding his bow three inches away from the nut (a fairly general custom at that time). Spohr afterwards admits, however, that his judgment was influenced by that of his teacher Fr. Eck, who was very severe, and that when he heard him ten years later in Vienna he had developed into an excellent player and teacher. During 1804–6 he was a member of the Mannheim Court orchestra. After that he went again on tour, remained for some time at Vienna and thence went to Prague in 1810, where he became conductor at the theatre and afterwards professor of violin at the Conservatoire, proving himself an excellent teacher, as which even Spohr praised him.

Germany: to 1800

He remained in that position to the time of his death. His compositions, including variations on a popular air for violin and orchestra (Vienna, Leidesdorf), and a concertino for violin, are entirely antiquated.

LEHRITTER. In 1786 a violinist conductor, chamber musician to the Bishop of Würzburg. He was a stepbrother of the Abbé Sterkel, the well-known composer (Gerber, i).

ANTON BERNHARD (BERNARD). An excellent 18th-century violinist and viola player; chamber musician for violin in the chapel of the Crown Prince Friedrich Wilhelm of Prussia, on whose accession in 1786 he became a member of the Royal Opera orchestra in Berlin, where he was still in 1792.

AUGUST HEINRICH WENCK, b. Brüheim, Duchy of Gotha. A pupil of Hattasch at Gotha and of Georg Benda, with whom he went to Paris in 1786. He was also a virtuoso on the harmonica. Returning to Gotha, he occupied himself with pianoforte-making and in 1796 invented a chronometer of which he published a description in 1798. In 1806 he settled at Amsterdam. He composed a potpourri for violin and pianoforte, and some pianoforte sonatas, all pub. in Paris.

JOH. GOTTFRIED ERNST, and JOH. KARL EDUARD EICHHORN (brothers). They were the sons of Johann Paul Eichhorn, b. Feb. 22, 1787, at Neuses, near Coburg, an uneducated but naturally talented self-taught musician who was admitted as a musician in the Court chapel. He was married and his first son Ernst was born Apr. 30, 1822, but the wife died in child-birth. In order to have his son properly cared for he soon married again, and a second son, Joh. Karl Eduard, was born Oct. 17, 1823. From their tenderest age both boys, especially Ernst, showed a love for music. One day he was surprised to hear the two boys playing a soldier's march on two toy violins, perfectly correct and in tune. His astonishment was still greater when he found that both violins were tuned in perfect fifths, one however was at a higher pitch than the other, but by avoiding open strings and adjusting their fingering to the circumstances they played in perfect harmony. This caused him to give more time and attention to their musical education and when Ernst was barely 6 years old he played a concerto by Kreutzer at the Court in Mar., 1828, and Eduard, who had accompanied him, showed also quite exceptional talent. Two months later the boys were asked to give a concert before the Duke at the Palace, when their playing evoked the greatest interest and they were rewarded in a princely manner. The father now saw his way to improve his fortune. All other schooling, scientific, moral, or religious, was cut out and an intensive course of technical training began, ending in a tour through middle and southern Germany which met with immense success. This awakened the avarice of the uncultured father to its fullest extent and the boys were given no rest. The father ill-treated them in the most brutal manner when, from sheer exhaustion, their young hands refused to function. Other tours were undertaken, going always farther afield: Paris, London, Vienna were visited, and in 1835 they visited the Courts of Northern Europe. Ernst could now measure himself with the greatest players of the time, but only technically, for without any schooling of any kind except technical drill they had only become perfect machines. Ernst, the more talented and sensitive of the brothers, soon collapsed under the brutal treatment, and died at Coburg, June 16, 1844. Nor did Eduard fulfil the great expectations which he aroused, yet he became concertmeister at the Court of Coburg, where he died Aug. 4, 1896.

KARL WILHELM FERDINAND GUHR, b. Mielitsch, Prussia, Oct. 27, 1787; d. Frankfort a/M., July 22, 1848. His father, a cantor of Mielitsch, was his first teacher for the violin and pianoforte, then Capellmeister Faust became his violin teacher and afterwards Janitschek at Breslau, where Capellmeister Schnabel instructed him in composition, in which he received lessons also from Abt Vogler, while Berner and Wölfe were his pianoforte teachers. In his fourteenth year he was already a violinist at the church at Mielitsch, and a member of the chapel of Count Maltzahn at Breslau, for whom he wrote viola da gamba solos, concertos, sextets, quartets, etc. During 1804–7 he was at Mielitsch again. In 1810 he went to Würzburg as chamber musician, but when, soon after, Reuter became director of the theatre at Nuremberg, he engaged Guhr as conductor, who did much to raise the standard of music in that town and had some of his own operas performed, which were well received. After some years in that town, during which time he had married the singer Mlle Epp, he went as music director of the theatre to Wiesbaden, but the war of

1813 ruined that residence, and the Landgrave of Cassel appointed him director of his chapel and of the theatre, but he left that position in the following year for some unexplained reason. He remained without any fixed employment until Apr., 1821, when he accepted a twenty-two years' engagement as director of the theatre orchestra at Frankfort a/M., at a salary of 5,000 florins per annum, and from that time he remained there till he died. As a violinist he had at first followed the style of Rode, but after hearing Paganini he made a special study of the technical features of the latter's art and his observations in that respect are contained in his remarkable book, "Ueber Paganini's Kunst die Violine zu spielen" (about Paganini's art to play the violin) (Mayence, Schott, 1831). His pub. compositions for violin comprise 1 concerto "Souvenir de Paganini" in E, op. 15 and several solos. He composed a mass with orchestra, operas, symphonies, pianoforte sonatas and duets, etc. He is said to have been an excellent pianist. He also wrote down a number of Paganini's solos from hearing.

JOHANN ALBERT GROENEMANN (GRONEMAN), b. Cologne; d. The Hague, 1788; registered Feb. 15, 1732, at Leyden University. Settled at Leyden as violinist, where he was considered Locatelli's equal on the violin. During 1750–60 he was organist at The Hague, became melancholic and died soon after in an asylum. In 1756 he played at the Musical Society at Arnhem, as well as his brothers (?) Anton and Konrad, who are mentioned there also in 1758. Albert wrote 3 sonatas for violin and B.c. (MS., Brussels Cons.).

ANTOINE GROENEMANN. Wrote 6 sonatas a v. seul et B. oe. 2 gravé p. Mlle Vandôme, Paris, aux adr. ordin. fol. (Eitner).

FRIEDRICH ERNST FESCA, b. Madgeburg, Feb. 15, 1789; d. Karlsruhe, May 24, 1826, of consumption. His father was a good amateur violinist and violoncellist, and his mother, *née* Podleska, a pupil of J. A. Hiller, had been chamber singer to the Duchess of Courland. In his fourth year Friedrich Ernst could sing correctly any songs his mother taught him and learned to play them on the pianoforte. At the age of 9 he began to study the violin under Lohse, leader at the Magdeburg theatre. Very soon he despised all salon pieces and would only play compositions by Haydn and Mozart, and in his eleventh year he played repeatedly solos and concertos at

The History of the Violin

the subscription concerts of the Freemasons' Lodge. He also studied theory and composition. In June, 1805, he went to Leipzig, where he studied the violin under Mathäi, and composition under A. E. Müller. He showed particular interest for the study of ancient church music, and also composed several violin concertos which he played in public with conspicuous success. In the autumn of 1805 he became 1st violinist in the Leipzig orchestra, but in 1806 the Duke of Oldenburg engaged him for his chapel, and in the spring of 1808 he became solo violinist to King Jérome of Westphalia at Cassel, where he was in brilliant circumstances, but in 1810 attacks of illness began to show themselves, although he was still able to perform his duties, and to compose 7 string quartets and 2 symphonies. In 1813 Jérome's Kingdom came to an end and in Jan., 1814, Fesca went to Vienna, where a brother of his resided. By this time his health had become impaired so far that he had to renounce appearing in public as a soloist, and restricted his activities to leading performances of his quartets in private circles, where both his works and his playing were greatly admired. Soon afterwards he was called to Karlsruhe as leader of the Grand-Ducal chapel, in which he became concertmeister in 1815. About that time he turned his attention again more to the composition of church music. In 1821 attacks of hæmorrhage set in, which were still arrested but showed the signs of consumption and prevented him from accepting offers of more advantageous positions. Disillusionment and bitter experiences brought about a state of melancholy in which he became accessible only to intimate friends. At times he would brighten up, and in some of his latest works there are moments of joyousness and even of humour, more frequently than before. In 1825 he took a cure at Ems, from which he returned to Karlsruhe apparently greatly improved in health, and he wrote an overture for orchestra and a quartet with flute. In Jan., 1826, he had a serious relapse, from which he never recovered. He was a composer of distinct talent and some of his 20 quartets and 5 quintets for string and wind instruments will still prove attractive. Of his violin compositions only a few potpourris have been pub. He also wrote 3 symphonies, 4 overtures, 2 operas, a number of works for the church as well as songs for one and several voices. ALEXANDER ERNST FESCA, son of F. E.

Germany: to 1800

Fesca, 1820–45, was also a composer and violinist. He calls himself "Fesca, Conte di Lavagna" in a letter of 1871 respecting the sale of his surplus violins.

HEINRICH LUDWIG VETTER. An 18th-century regimental oboist, who became violin virtuoso and, ca. 1790, concertmeister of the Prince of Anhalt at Homburg. In 1800 he lived at Hanau without any fixed position. Composed 3 quintets (Speyer, Bossler), and symphonies (Offenbach, André) (Gerber, i).

WILHELM RUHE. Of Leipzig. From 1793 Musical Director of the Court theatre, Cassel; an excellent violinist and composer (Apell). Reichard ("Gothaer Kalender," 1798, p. 32) writes: 1797 musical director of Schauspieler Gesellschaft (theatrical company), Cassel.

HARTUNG. Was, ca. 1794, in the Court chapel at Brunswick. Started a music business but without publishing. He composed 2 books of violin duets pub. at Frankfort by Haneisen, and at Amsterdam by Schmitt in 1792.

KARL WILLMANN, d. Bonn, 1794. Was violinist in the Electoral chapel at Bonn.

MARCUS FRENO. During the latter half of the 18th century, a violin virtuoso, and member at the Court chapel of Munich in 1794. A pupil and colleague of Joh. Friedr. Eck, who was praised for his remarkable technique.

C. W. WESTERHOFF, d. Bückeburg, 1807; late 18th-century violinist. Concertmeister in the Court chapel of Bückeburg, also excellent viola player. He composed: Trios for 2 violins and bass, op. 1, book 1 and 2 (Amsterdam, Schmitt, 1795); duos for violin and viola, op. 8, book 1 and 2 (Leipzig, Joachim); 2 concertos for clarinet, 1 for flute, and a funeral music (MS.) for the Duke of Bückeburg (1799); also a "Music in honour of Vaccination by vaccine from Cows" (1801).

HÄMPELN. Intendant of the Court music of the Prince of Fürstenberg at Donaueschingen, and Polish Court councillor in 1795; distinguished himself as violinist and composer for the violin (Gerber, ii).

E. F. VILLARET. In 1795 concertmeister and soloist in the Leipzig Gewandhaus orchestra. He disappeared early in

1797 without even drawing the salary due to him in March of that year (Dörffel, i, 6, 2, 26).

THRANDORF. Ca. 1796, a concertmeister (violin) at the Ducal Court theatre, Brunswick (Reichard, "Gothaer Kal.," 1796).

STIEMER. An 18th-century violin virtuoso. He wrote a violin concerto, pub. by Hummel, Berlin, 1796. In 1807 he became organist at Danzig (Gerber, ii).

FRIEDRICH BUNTE. A late 18th-century German violinist known only by his variations on the air "Kind willst Du ruhig schlafen" (from Peter von Winter's highly successful opera "Das unterbrochene Opferfest," 1796) for solo violin with 2 violins and violoncello, op. 1 (Offenbach, André), and some books of violin duets; also (Eitner: Bunte F.) Sonate pour pianoforte avec acc. de V. oe 4 (Berlin and Amsterdam, J. Hummel).

HASSELBECK. Gerber, ii, believes that he was the much praised Court agent and violinist from "Siebenbürgen" (Transylvania), who in the "Great Academy" of von Kees in Vienna, was leader of the 2nd violins. He composed 12 "Deutsche" dances for clavier which were performed at the "Redoute" in Vienna in 1796.

ANTON DITTMAIER. At first known as an industrious arranger of concertos, he was appointed as violinist in the Court chapel of Bamberg, Oct. 10, 1798, with 150 florins per annum, and on Pokorny's accession to the post of musical director, Oct. 23, 1802, he became 1st violinist and concertmeister. He was a sound musician and a virtuoso with a great technique, but lacking in mental refinement and culture. On the abolition of the Principality he received a comfortable pension and in conjunction with other pensioned-off members of the Court chapel he formed the orchestra for the theatre newly called into life by Count Soden. This orchestra, augmented by town and military musicians, he conducted from 1802 to 1818. The story of the quarrel between Dittmaier and A. T. E. Hoffmann is very interesting, see in "Marschalk," p. 20.

JOSEPH BINDERNAGEL. A German late 18th-century musician (violinist) who lived as teacher in Paris, and composed ca. 1799–1800: Grande sonate for violin and harpsichord, op. 2

Germany: to 1800

(1799); 3 duos concertants for 2 violins, op. 4 (1800); 3 sonatas for violin and harpsichord, op. 5 (Fétis); 3 duos for 2 violins, op. 10 (Paris, Chapelle). In Vienna, Musikfreunde, 3 string quartets, op. 12, by Bindernagel (Paris, Decombe), apparently Joseph.

G. GURATZKY. In Dresden Museum a Concerto a violin conc. with string quartet (MS.). Sonata a violino e basso score.

ADAM FEICHTNER (VEICHTNER). In the late 18th century, a pupil of Franz Benda; concertmeister of the Duke of Courland (particulars in Reichardt's Autobiography, Berlin, *Mus. Zeitung*, 1805, p. 313, etc.).

LUDWIG PITSCHER. A pupil of Franz Benda and violinist in the chapel of Prince Heinrich of Prussia at Rheinsberg, 18th–19th century.

CHRISTIAN HEINRICH KÖRBITZ. From late 18th century to early 19th century, a violinist in the Bayreuth Court chapel. He was a pupil of Franz Benda.

JOHANN WILHELM MATHEES. A violinist in the chapel of Prince Heinrich of Prussia, 18th–19th century. Is mentioned by Wasielewski as a pupil of Franz Benda.

JOHANN ANTON HÄNSEL. Lived at the end of the 18th and the beginning of the 19th century. He was chamber musician to the younger Count von Schönberg at Rochsburg and wrote: "Untersuchungen über den Bau der Violine," 69 pp. (*Leipzig Zeitung*, 1811, p. 82).

PIGUOT, d. ca. 1827. Chamber musician at the Court theatre, Karlsruhe (Baden). His Stradivari violin is offered for sale for 35 Louis d'or in the *Leipzig Zeitung*, 29, Bl. 12.

KARL FEYER. Violinist-composer who lived in Berlin during the late 18th–early 19th century. He wrote: Concerto pour le violin, op. 1 (Paris, Imbault; Berlin, Hummel) and Concerto for do., op. 2 (Berlin, Hummel, and Offenbach, André, 1792) (Eitner).

JOSEPH MELCHIOR KIENINGER. In 18th-19th century, a 1st violinist of the Philharmonic Society of Steier. He was still living in 1836, when he wrote: "Theoretische und praktische Anleitung für angehende Violinspieler, nach den besten

Methoden eingerichtet"—"Theoretical and practical instruction for beginners on the violin, arranged from the best methods" [tutors] (Graetz, J. F. Kaiser, 1825, 40).

SANDMAIR. An 18th-century violinist who is mentioned by Schubart (p. 172) as solo violinist and ripieno player in the Court chapel of Baden-Durlach. When still a young man he went on tour with Abbé Vogler.

BERNHARD JOHANN, d. Frankfort a/M., 1849. Violinist and pianist at Frankfort a/M., wrote variations for violin, violin and pianoforte pieces. Also cembalo sonatas (?). He was violinist successively at the theatres of Karlsruhe, Amsterdam (opera) and Frankfort.

KARL JOSEPH BIRNBACH, b. Koepenick, near Neisse; d. Breslau, May 29, 1805. After leaving the village school he visited the college (gymnasium) at Neisse from the age of 10, where he made rapid progress and gave at that age lessons in music. By thrift and industry he amassed enough to rebuild at the age of 15 his parent's little house, which had been destroyed by fire. This act of filial piety touched the heart of Capellmeister Dittersdorf, who instructed him on the violin and in composition. After leaving college he entered the chapel of Count Hoym at Breslau, where he had occasion to pursue his studies. A few years later he was appointed for lifetime in the chapel of the Archbishop. About this time he married Caroline Wilhelmina Roehn, by whom he had fifteen children. When the Archbishop died his place was suppressed. A lawsuit against his successors went in his favour but was not made final, and he lost 5,500 thalers (£825) which were legally due to him. For some years he supported his family by music lessons in Berlin. His eminent talent as a violinist secured him a place in the Royal Chapel, but in 1803 he went with his son Henry to Warsaw, having obtained a pension of 300 thaler (£45). He was a prolific composer but few of his compositions were pub. His 10 concertos, and 15 solos for violin remained in MS. Mendel says he remained at Warsaw, where he died of an epidemic.

CHAPTER 30

Great Britain: to 1750

WITH Handel's appearance in England the violin finally ousted the viols, as the latter, with a few solitary exceptions of the use of the viol da gamba, found no place in his orchestra. When in 1714 Geminiani came to London and enthused his hearers by his playing of the compositions of his master Corelli, which had already gained a certain amount of popularity through Tom Britton's and J. Banister's concerts, the violin became the general favourite. Wm. Corbett and a few others went to Italy to study the instrument, while others studied it at home under Geminiani, whose two most eminent pupils, M. Festing and M. Dubourg, occupied leading positions in the musical life of England and Ireland respectively, where in their turn they trained a number of pupils who fostered not only the general interest in the violin but also the taste of good music. Dubourg's pupil John Clegg might even have risen to considerable heights as a virtuoso, had not the tragedy of his life prevented this. A great impetus was given to musical life in London by the brothers Castrucci, by Carbonelli, and Giardini, who all settled in London during the first half of the century.

An important event in the evolution of English violin playing was the publication of Geminiani's tutor, while the instruction books by John Lenton, Prelleur and Crome helped to further its popularity. During the second half of the century W. Cramer and Solomon acquainted the London public with the achievements of the Germans, especially the Mannheim school. No English violinist, however, arose in the 18th century who could be placed with the famous masters of this instrument.

JOHN RAVENSCROFT, *alias* REDERI INGLESE, d. London, 1745. A player of concertos (sonatas) by Corelli in Tower Hamlets and Goodman's Fields Theatre (Hawkins, v, 367). Composed Sonate (12) a 3, 2 violini e violone o Arcilento col. basso per l'organo, op. 1 (Roma, 1695, Mascardi); Sonate a 3, 2 violini e violone o Arcilento col. basso per l'organo (Amsterdam, Roger) (B. B.). Also a song, "The Foolish Woman." He was a very successful composer of hornpipes, which is probably the cause of a misunderstanding by Pougin, who describes him as equally clever as violinist and bagpipe (cornemuse) player.

JAMES SHERARD. An apothecary born about the end of the 17th century who calls himself on his works "Giacomo Sherard Filarmonico." He was an excellent violinist who wrote: Sonate a tre, 2 violini e violone col. basso per l'organo, op. 1 (Amsterdam, Roger); sonate a tre, doi violini, violoncello e basso, op. 2 (Ib., ca. 1725 or 1715). A copy of the sonatas in the Brit. Mus. belonged to Mr. Wm. Salter, apothecary and surgeon dentist in Whitechapel in 1789, who tells us in a note on the fly-leaf that: "Mr. Sherard was an apothecary in Crutched-Friars about the year 1735, performed well on the violin, was very intimate with Handel and other masters," and Hawkins says ("Hist. of Music") that he "played finely on the violin." Although "quite Corellian in style they are entirely different in character." His adagios show depth of thought and feeling, although they are not more developed in form than Corelli's, and in his quick movements there is a breezy vigour which often points to their parentage, although they are dressed in English fashion (*see* E. v. d. Str., "Eighteenth-Century Violin Sonatas," *The Strad*, Dec., 1917, Jan., 1918).

OBADIAH SHUTTLEWORTH, b. Spitalfields, London, towards the end of the 17th century; d. London, 1735. An excellent violinist and organist; 1st violin at the Swan Tavern concerts in Cornhill and at Thomas Britton's Club (E. v. d. Str., "Romance of the Fiddle"), London, from their foundation in 1728 until his death. He was also organist from 1724 at St. Michael's, Cornhill, and a few years later of the Temple church. His father lived in Spitalfields and had a trio for harpsichord, violin and gamba; he played the latter himself while his children, including Obadiah, played the violin and harpsichord; left 12 concertos and some sonatas for the violin in MS.; 2 concertos were published which were based upon sonatas by Corelli (Hawkins, v, 181). It appears that by making copies of the Corelli sonatas, which had then not yet appeared in print in England, he gained an appreciable addition to his otherwise meagre income, making it sufficient to bring up a numerous family.

MATTHEW DUBOURG, b. London, 1703; d. there, July 3, 1767; the natural son of Isaac, a dancing-master. He studied the violin under Geminiani. At the age of 9 he made his debut at Thomas Britton's concert, where he played a sonata by Corelli, standing on a stool that he might be seen by the audience, as his grandson G. Dubourg tells us in his "History of the Violin." On May 27, 1714, he had a benefit concert at Hickford's Room, and at the age of 12 he played solos at the great room in James's Street. He paid his first visit to Dublin in 1724. Mrs. Delaney, after hearing the music in honour of St. Cecilia, at the Crown Tavern, writes on Nov. 11, 1727: "Dubourg was the first fiddle, and everybody says he exceeds all the Italians, even his master Geminiani." On June 17 of that year he married Frances Gates (daughter of Bernard Gates, master of the Chapel Royal), at Stanmore, Middlesex. In 1728 he succeeded Cousser as master of the vice-regal band at Dublin, and composed many odes for Court festivals. In Nov., 1741, Handel went to Dublin and gave a series of concerts, culminating in the first performance of the "Messiah," on Apr. 13, 1742. Dubourg was leader of the orchestra, and while playing a cadenza to a ritornello of an air, he wandered about so long from one key into another, that when at length he had reached the final shake, Handel, who presided at the organ, called out, to the great amusement of the audience: "Welcome home, Monsieur Dubourg." In 1735 he was appointed chamber musician of the Prince of Wales, and in 1752 he succeeded Festing as leader of the King's band, while retaining his post in Dublin. In 1761 he became Master of Her Majesty's Private Musick, and in the same year Geminiani visited him and remained in Dublin until he died. In 1765 Dubourg returned to London and remained there to the end. As an executant he played an important part in the progress of violin playing in England, although he contributed nothing to its literature. A few pieces for flute, and trumpet tunes are contained in various collective works (*see* Grove).

RICHARD COLLET, b. ca. 1710. Appeared as violin virtuoso in London in 1751 (Pohl, ii, 270). Burney (vii, 663?) refers to him in 1744 as one of the best violinists of his time.

JOHN COLLET. Composed 6 solos for the violin with a thorough-bass for the harps (London, 1770).

JOHN CLEGG, b. in Ireland (?Mason Clarke), 1714; d. Bedlam, London, 1750. A pupil of Dubourg, afterwards of Bononcini. Made his debut in London at the age of 9, in 1723. The announcement says that "among various solos he will play a Concerto by Vivaldi." He speedily rose to the front rank of English players and is said to have surpassed all in beauty of tone and brilliance of technique. Handel chose him to succeed Castrucci (*see* the latter) and he was leader of his orchestra for a considerable time. He also was leader at the concerts at the Swan Tavern in Swan Alley, Cornhill. In 1742 he became mentally deranged, probably through excessive practice, and he was confined in Bedlam, where, according to Burney, it was long a fashionable though inhuman amusement to visit him, among other lunatics, in hopes of being entertained by his fiddle or his folly.

FRANCISCO GOODSENS, d. Jan., 1742. On Aug. 8, 1715, appointed violist(?) in Royal Chapel, London (Rimbault, 230). According to Viertelj. (viii, p. 521, etc.) he was solo violinist at the Royal "Kirchenkapelle" (Chapel Royal).

ROBERT BREMNER, b. in Scotland, 1720; d. London, May 12, 1798. One of the foremost music publishers of the 18th century. He was originally a pupil of Geminiani and commenced his career as a violinist and music teacher at Edinburgh. On Dec. 13, 1753, he gave a concert in the High School of Leith and an advertisement of July 11, 1754, shows that he had started a business as music seller and publisher, removing to London in 1762.

MICHAEL CHRISTIAN FESTING, b. (?) London; d. there, July 24, 1752. Son of the flautist of the same Christian names, who was a noted player in Handel's orchestra. He studied the violin under Rich. Jones and Geminiani, and made his debut as a soloist in 1724. In 1727 he became a member of Haymarket Theatre orchestra, and in 1737 (Grove: 1735) of the King's private band. In 1742 he became conductor at Ranelagh Gardens. He was one of the founders of the Royal Society of Musicians. During 1739–44 he gave regular subscription concerts. E. v. d. Str., "Romance of the Fiddle": He was leader of the Swan concerts in Cornhill which came to an end when the Swan Tavern burnt down in 1748. In 1737 he superseded Castrucci as leader in Handel's orchestra and Castrucci was jealous of Festing, which lead to amusing incidents (*see* Castrucci). He was also leader at the Academy of Antient Music, the concerts at the Castle Tavern in the City, and the subscription concerts in Hickford's Rooms, Brewer Street. One of his best pupils was Stephen Philpot. His first position was leader of the Philharmonic Society (Mason Clarke), 1737; he also became leader, Italian Opera (Riemann). He composed concerti grossi, sonatas for 1 and 2 violins with bass, 8 violin concertos, 14 double concertos for 2 violins (*see* Hawkins), also cantatas and songs. 1 sonata has been repub. by A. Moffat (*see also* Burney and E. v. d. Str., "Eighteenth-century Violin Sonatas").

PETER PRELLEUR. A French musician who settled in London at the beginning of the 18th century. He was successively a writing master in Spitalfields, organist at St. Alban (1728), accompanist at and composer for Goodman's Fields theatre, and organist at Christ Church, Spitalfields. He wrote a number of tutors, including "The Art of Playing on the Violin" (ca. 1730?, *see* E. v. d. Str., "Romance of the Fiddle"), at the end of which is an abridged history of music, extracted from Bontempi's book. After the closing of Goodman's Fields he was engaged at the newly opened "New Wells" in Leman Street, for which he wrote songs, etc. In a hymnbook, pub. 1758, to which he contributed, he is spoken of as dead.

CHARLES MACKLEAN. Known by 12 solos or sonatas for a violin and violoncello with a thorough-bass, op. 1 (Edinburgh, 1737). A collection of "Favourite Scots tunes with variations for the violin and a bass" (Edinburgh, by Charles MacLean) is considered doubtful as whether by the above.

CHARLES CLAUDIUS PHILLIPS, b. in Wales, 17..; d. Wolverhampton, 1732. Musician and violinist (Baptie).

NIEL GOW, b. Strathband, Perthshire, Mar. 22, 1727; d. Inver, near Dunkeld, Mar. 1, 1807. A Scottish violinist who in his time was unrivalled in the playing of the reels, strathspeys, etc., of which he published a large collection in 5 books (1784–1808). He possessed a technique particularly adapted for the playing of these tunes, which was traditional among the old Scotch fiddlers. NATHANIEL GOW, b. Inver, May 28, 1766; d. Edinburgh, Jan. 17, 1831 (*see* Brown), son of the above. Leader of the Fashionable concerts, Edinburgh. Composer of the song "Caller Herrin" (Stratton). Niel's other sons, WILLIAM, ANDREW and JOHN, were also Scottish fiddlers and composers of dance tunes.

WILLIAM JACKSON, b. Exeter, May, 1730; d. there, July, 1803. A pupil of John Sylvester and John Travers. In 1777 Mus.Bac., then organist and choirmaster of Exeter cathedral. He wrote 6 sonatas for harpsichord and violin which are above the average compositions of the time. He also composed operas, church music, etc., etc., and developed a considerable literary activity. He stood in friendly intercourse with most of the great men in arts and literature of his time.

RICHARD JONES. A distinguished English violinist-composer, who succeeded Carbonelli as leader of the band at Drury Lane Theatre, ca. 1730, and was in turn succeeded at that post by Charke and Michael Festing, his most talented pupil. Jones composed "Chamber Airs for a Violin and Through Bass, consisting Both of Double and Single Stops, Being a work very improving for that instrument." Alfred Moffat arranged a Sonata in D major from this work (Novello). Jones also wrote 6 solos or lessons for violin and thorough-bass, and a set of lessons for the harpsichord.

THOMAS ALEXANDER ERSKINE, EARL OF KELLIE, b. Castle Kellie, Fife, Scotland, Sept. 1, 1732; d. Brussels, Oct. 9, 1781. A pupil of the elder Joh. Stamitz at Mannheim, 1770. He was an excellent violinist; composed operas, symphonies, overtures, string trios, etc. His overture to "The Maid of the Mill" (1765) was a great favourite.

Great Britain: to 1750

ROBERT CROME. Was about the middle of the 18th century a violinist at Covent Garden Theatre, London. He wrote a tutor: "The Fiddle New Model'd . . ." pub. by Thompson, ca. 1740 (for particulars see E. v. d. Str., "The Romance of the Fiddle"). He also wrote a tutor for the violoncello, and songs.

PETER GILLIER. On Jan. 1, 1742, he was appointed violist in the Royal band (Rimbault, 233), also solo violinist in the Chapel Royal, London (Viertelj., viii, 530). Not to be confounded with Gillier, le Jeune.

WILLIAM MACGIBBON, d. as music teacher in Edinburgh, Oct. 3, 1756. Son of an oboist, and pupil of Corbett in London, leader of the orchestra in the Gentlemen's Concerts in Edinburgh. Wrote a collection of Scots tunes for the violin or German flute with a bass, with additions and variations (London, Brenner; New Ed., Preston); selection of Scottish reels or country dances (London, Preston); 6 sonatas or solos for a German flute or violin (Edinburgh, 1740) (see Grove).

JOHN ABRAHAM FISCHER, b. Dunstable, 1744; d. Dublin (Riemann: London), May, 1806. A pupil of Pinto. In 1763 he was in the King's Theatre, Haymarket, orchestra; in 1770 married Miss Powell and became Doctor of Music, Oxford, in 1777. He toured in Germany and Russia and in 1783 played in Leipzig and Frankfort a/M. (see Neefe's account in Gerber, i. or ii). Riemann says: "In the same year he appeared also in Vienna where, being then a widower, he married Anna Selina Storace, the famous operatic soprano, whose brother had brought out a comic opera in that town. He treated her with such cruelty that the emperor ordered his expulsion from Vienna in 1784. Finally he settled in Dublin as a teacher." Pohl, i, 169, gives an interesting account of his personal appearance, Neefe, in Gerber, of his playing. A list of works is in Gerber and Eitner (concertos, duets, solos, symphonies, etc., operas and songs). He combined a brilliant technique with fiery temperament but also with a strong admixture of charlatanry. He was of small stature and exceedingly vain. Pohl says: "A foreigner (black?, in brilliant livery) carried his violin in a crimson case, richly gilded. The famous virtuoso tip-toed behind, dressed in a brown silk camelot coat bound with scarlet and ornamented with bright buttons. His powdered and perfumed headdress was so high that his short figure appeared to be divided into two halves thereby. His breeches were fastened at the knees with diamond buttons. His rooms were filled with an atmosphere of perfume."

JOHN GEORGE FREAKE. Known by his "XII Solos for a Harpsichord, Violin, German Flute, etc., with a Thorough-Bass for the Harpsichord or Bass Violin" (London (1746) W. Smith) (*see* E. v. d. Str., "The Romance of the Fiddle").

WILLIAM MARSHALL, b. Dec. 27, 1748, at Fochabers, Scotland; d. Newfield, May 29, 1833. Scottish violinist and composer. In 1790 he lived in the house of the Duke of Gordon, became a farmer and factor of the Duke; ed. numerous Scottish airs and dances for pianoforte, violin and violoncello.

WILLIAM SHIELD, b. Swalwell, Durham, ca. 1748; d. London, Jan. 25, 1829. The son of a music teacher, who started his musical career as conductor of provincial theatres. Encouraged by Borgé (?) and Fischer, he entered the opera orchestra in London as violinist in 1772, and viola 1773. He studied for some time under Avison.

JAMES GEORGE. Composed 6 concertos in seven parts, 4 for violin, 1 for German flute, 1 for violoncello, with a tenor and thorough-bass for the organ or harpsichord (Bath, ca. 1750). Engraved and printed for the author (Brit. Mus.).

JEAN GEORGE. Wrote 2 concerti per il violino e orchestra (MS., Munich).

THOMAS WOODCOCK, d. ca. 1750. A violinist who played Corelli's solos in London coffee-houses and taverns, and is praised by Hawkins (v, 180).

PETER THOMPSON. The music publisher in Paul's Churchyard from 1751. He was violinist and oboist at St. Paul's Cathedral.

ABRAHAM BROWN, violinist and composer of the 18th century, who succeeded Festing at Ranelagh Gardens, about 1752 and at the aristocratic concerts in London. His tone was clear and loud but he played without expression (Eitner). He was a member of the King's band (Viertelj., viii, 519), and a violin virtuoso in London in 1758. About 1730 he was for some time leader of the concerts at the Swan Tavern, Cornhill.

Great Britain: to 1750

Burney tells us that Brown, Collet, and Festing were then the principal performers of the violin in London.

MAX HUMBLE. An 18th-century violinist and composer; 6 trios for 2 violins and bass (Berlin and Amsterdam, Hummel); 6 sonatas, 2 violins and thorough-bass for the harpsichord (London, Welcker); a favourite set of sonates for 2 violins (London) (B., Lpz.).

COLLARD. A noted 18th-century English violinist at King's Theatre, London, where he was together with Cobham, and Condell, ca. 1818 (Mason Clarke).

CHAPTER 31

Great Britain: to 1800

BENJAMIN BLAKE, b. Kingsland, 1751; d. London, 1827. Commenced the study of the violin in 1760. In 1768 he studied in London with Anton Thanmell, a celebrated Bohemian violinist. Later on he studied also the piano and received the advice of Clementi. From about 1775 till 1793 he was in the orchestra of the Italian theatre (opera?) and on leaving it he became professor at a school in Kensington, but was obliged to retire on account of illness in 1820. His pub. compositions include 3 books of 6 duets each for violin and viola, 1 duo for violin and viola, 6 easy sonatas for pianoforte and violin, 3 solos for viola and bass, sacred music with organ, etc. (Fétis).

WILLIAM DANCE, b. 1755; d. London, June 5, 1840. A pupil of Aylward, Baumgarten and Giardini. Violinist at Drury Lane Theatre, 1771-4; conductor at King's Theatre, 1775-93; leader at the Handel Festival, 1790. One of the founders of the Philharmonic Society, Jan. 17, 1813, and for a time its conductor and treasurer; also teacher of the pianoforte, for which he composed pieces and a sonata; he also composed songs, but of violin compositions nothing appears to be known.

JOHN HINDMARSH, b. ca. 1755; d. 1796. In 1792 a violinist and viola(?) player in London; pupil of Salomon (Pohl, ii, 731). One of his pupils was Dr. J. Jay.

CHARLES CLAGGET, b. Waterford, ca. 1755; d. 1820, London. 18th-19th-century London violinist. Wrote 6 solos, and 6 Scottish airs for the violin, op. 2 (London, Tompson & Son). Leader at a theatre at Dublin. Invented various instruments 1776-90, which he exhibited in London in 1791. Composed 6 duos for 2 violins; 6 duos for violin and violoncello, op. 6, etc.

Great Britain: to 1800

THOMAS LINLEY, JUNIOR, b. Bath, May, 1756; drowned at Ancaster near Grimthorpe, Lincs., Aug. 7, 1778. A pupil of his father and Dr. Boyce, and appeared as a boy as violin virtuoso. Went to Italy in 1770 and studied under Nardini; met with Mozart in Italy and they became close friends. In 1772 on his return he played with his father in the latter's concerts at Bath, went with him to London and joined the orchestra of Drury Lane Theatre (Grove; Stephen; Pohl, ii, 65 and 370). Only vocal compositions of his are known.

RICHARD CHARKE, b. London; d. Jamaica. He was violinist at Drury Lane Theatre, also actor and dancing-master; married the famous Charlotte Cibber. His debauchery and unhappy marriage caused him to flee in 1756 to the West Indies, where he died a few years later. He composed some violin pieces and was the first to write Medley overtures.

HENRY CONDELL, b. ca. 1757 in London (?); d. Battersea, London, June 24, 1824. Towards the end of the 18th century he was violinist at Drury Lane Theatre. In 1811 he gained a prize of the Catch Club. He wrote the 3-act opera "The Enchanted Island," performed in 1804; also overtures, songs, and pianoforte pieces, but apparently nothing for violin. According to Mason Clarke he was, together with Cobham and Collard, at the King's Theatre in 1818.

THOMAS PINTO, b. London, of Italian parents; d. in Ireland, ca. 1773 (Wki. 1780). From 1757 violinist at the Haymarket Theatre. His first wife was the German singer Sybilla. In 1766 he married Miss Brent, the famous vocalist, and lived alternately at Edinburgh and in Ireland. (Brown, and Burney, vii, 468; Pohl, i, 53 and 177, gives more particulars; also Eitner and Wki.) He possessed a considerable technique but inclined to charlatanry.

HAYES. Appeared in 1757 as violin virtuoso in London (Pohl, ii, 370).

WILLIAM FLACKTON. An 18th-century musician, who lived in Canterbury and wrote, among other pieces, 6 sonatas for 2 violins and a violoncello or harpsichord (Walsh, 1758).

RICHARDS. Appeared in London in 1759 as violin virtuoso (Pohl, ii, 370).

FREDERIC HILL, b. Louth, Lincs, ca. 1760; d. London. The son of an organist at Louth, he was a good organist, pianist and violinist. He began his career as organist at Loughborough, Leics, and afterwards settled in London. Composed for military band, also English airs with piano. He was also a noted harpist as well as organist.

FREDERIK NUSSEN. Lived during the second half of 18th century. Composed 6 solos for a violin, wind, and thorough-bass; 6 sonatas for 2 violins, wind, violoncello or harpsichord, op. 2 (*see* E. v. d. Str., "Eighteenth-Century Violin Sonatas," *The Strad*, Feb. and Mar., 1922); 6 sonatas for a violin tenor and violoncello, ca. 1760 (Welcker, London); musica da camera or some old tunes new set and some new ones composed for the harpsichord, op. 3. A GEORGE NUSSEN wrote the ballad "The Third Alliance," ca. 1800.

THOMAS MAZZINGHI, of a Corsican family; d. London, May 20, 1775, and was buried at St. Pancras. He was violinist at Marylebone Gardens, and composed solos for the violin with B.c., op. 1 (London, 1763).

JOSEPH MAZZINGHI, b. London, Dec. 25, 1765; d. there, 1839. Son of Thomas Mazzinghi; pupil of Joh. Chr. Bach, Bertolini, Sacchini and Anfossi. Appeared in public as a violinist at the age of 8, but afterwards he became chiefly known as organist, conductor and composer. He wrote for the violin: 3 sonatas for pianoforte or harpsichord with violin, op. 1 (London, 1788; Paris, 1790); 3 sonatas do. do. each, op. 2, 9, 10, 14 and 15, pub. between ca. 1792 and 1795. He wrote (mostly together with Reeve) 10 successful operas, ballets, melodramas, masses, pianoforte sonatas, etc. (Grove, iii, 357.)

THOMAS (COUNT) MAZZINGHI, b. London; d. Downside, near Bath, Jan. 15, 1844. Probably another son of Thomas Mazzinghi. A distinguished violinist who was raised to the rank of nobility in Italy in 1734 (biog. after his death in *Leipzig Zeitung*).

KARL WEICHSEL, JUNIOR, b. London, ca. 1764; d. Fulham, London, Mar. 26, 1811 (Mendel, Wki. and others say: b. London, ca. 1764; d. there, after 1830). (*Leipzig Musical Zeitung*, 41, 749.) Brother of Elizabeth, Mrs. Billington.

Great Britain: to 1800

He studied the violin under Wm. Cramer in London, and appeared as a soloist, ca. 1796. Composed sonatas for violin and bass, op. 1; 2 trios for 2 violins and bass, MS. (in Gerber, ii); an opera, "Orpheus" (pasticcio).

STEPHEN PHILPOT. English violinist of the mid-18th century, a pupil of M. Festing, and through him an outcome of the Geminiani School. He wrote a tutor, "An Introduction to the Art of Playing on the Violin on an Entirely New Plan," etc., by Stephen Philpot, of Lewes in Sussex, one of His Majesty's musicians in ordinary. London, printed and sold for the author by Messrs. Randall & Abell, successors to the late Mr. Walsh in Catherine Street in the Strand, etc., 1767. "Philpot's Dances, Rigadoons," etc., were pub. by John Johnson; also in Bremner's and Preston's lists.

THOMAS HAIGH, b. London, 1769; d. there, Apr., 1808. Violinist, pianist and composer. A pupil of Haydn in 1791 and 1792. Afterwards he lived at Manchester, but returned to London in 1801. He composed for the violin a concerto and 12 sonatas with pianoforte, apart from pianoforte sonatas, songs, and numerous arrangements.

GENERAL CHARLES ASHLEY, b. London, ca. 1769 near London; d. there, Aug. 28, 1818. Son of John Ashley. The first double bassoon player, who played at the Handel commemoration and followed Bates as conductor of Oratorio concerts. Ashley studied the violin under Giardini and Barthelemon and played on several occasions with Viotti the latter's symphonies concertantes. He succeeded his father as conductor of oratorios at Covent Garden, together with his brother Charles Jane Ashley. Of his compositions apparently nothing was pub.

JOHN GEORGE HENRY JAY (MUS.DOC.), b. Essex, Nov. 27, 1770; d. London, Sept. 17, 1849. Studied the violin under John Hindmarsh, went to London in 1800 and settled there as a teacher. In 1809 he took his degree of Mus.Bac. (Oxon.) and in 1811 that of Mus.Doc. (Camb.), and became an honorary member of the Academy of Music. He brought out pianoforte compositions. His son, JOHN JAY, was also a violinist; his elder daughter was a harpist, the younger a pianist (Grove).

JAMES LATES. A mid- or second-half 18th-century violinist. Was a teacher at Oxford ca. 1770. Composed 6 sonatas each flute, violin, and violoncello with thorough-bass, op. 3; 6 sonatas for 2 violins with a thorough-bass, op. 4; 6 trios for violin, violoncello, obbl. and bass with a thorough-bass for the harpsichord, op. 5. One sonata re-edited by A. Moffat (?Novello).

COBHAM, b. London, 1773; d. there, 1819. An excellent violinist, was with Collard and Condell at the King's Theatre, London, in 1818 (Mason Clarke).

ADOLPH FREDERIC, DUKE OF CAMBRIDGE, b. London, Feb. 25, 1774; d. there, 1847. Youngest son of George III. Amateur violinist; patron, pupil and friend of Viotti, who composed some charming violin duets for him, and was in regular correspondence with him.

WILLIAM FISCH, b. 1775 at Norwich; d. there, Mar. 15, 1866. A violinist and composer at the Norwich theatre, afterwards organist and teacher of Edw. Taylor and G. Perry. Some songs and pianoforte pieces by him in the Brit. Mus.

THOMAS POWELL, b. London, 1776; was living in Edinburgh, 1863. Violinist, harpist and pianist. He became a member of the Royal Society of Musicians, married in 1811 and settled at Dublin. Returned to London as violinist at the Haymarket Theatre and afterwards went, according to Fétis, to Edinburgh. Composed 15 violin concertos, duets for violin and violoncello, op. 1; 3 duets and a capriccio for violoncello, overtures for orchestra, pianoforte sonatas, etc. Some pieces signed "Powell" only in John Simpson's "Pocket Companion" (Brown, Fétis).

HENRY SMART, b. London, ca. 1778; d. Dublin, Nov. 23, 1823. A brother of Sir George Smart, and a pupil of Wilh. Cramer, conductor of Philharmonic Orchestra, Covent Garden Opera and other theatres. In 1820 he started a pianoforte factory. In order to support her concert there he went with a woman pupil to Dublin, where he died of typhus.

GEORGE AUGUSTUS POLGREEN BRIDGETOWER, b. Biala, Galicia, 1779 or 1780 (more probably in the British West Indies—see Grove); d. Peckham, London, Feb. 29, 1860. Son of an

African father and a white mother. According to Thayer (Beethoven, ii, appendix 6) the father received his name from the fact that he moved in high circles of society in London. The son was a violin prodigy who, according to Brenet ("Les Concerts en France"), made his debut at the Concert Spirituel, Paris, in the spring of 1789 with great success. On June 2, 1790, with the Viennese boy violinist, Franz Clement, he gave a concert in London, under the patronage of the Prince of Wales, after which he became a pupil of Gioronovichi and Barthelemon for the violin, and Attwood for composition, and afterwards became 1st violin in the Prince of Wales' private music. Apart from that he played at the Haydn-Salomon concerts. In 1802 he went to his mother in Dresden, where he gave concerts in July of that year and in Mar., 1803. On May 17 or 24 he gave a concert in Vienna, when he played the Kreutzer Sonata with Beethoven, who was pleased with his playing, which was full of temperament. In London his father was known as the "Abyssinian Prince." He composed violin concertos, etc. (*see* Eitner and Grove).

ARTHUR BETTS, b. at Stamford, Lincs, ca. 1780 (Brown and Stratton: 1774?); d. London, Sept., 1847, aged 73. His brother, JOHN BETTS, the famous violin maker, brought him to London, where he received the first lessons on the violin by Hindmarsh, an indifferent player, but after a few months he was taken up by Viotti, while Eley and Russell instructed him in harmony. Fétis says: "He numbers now among the ablest English teachers," and gives a list of his compositions, including 3 sonatas for pianoforte and violin, a divertissement for the same, and duets for violin and violoncello; 3 duets for violin and tenor are in the Brit. Mus.; songs, waltzes, etc. He was for forty-nine years a member of the Royal Society of Musicians, and was celebrated as a connoisseur of violins.

F. WARE. A pupil of W. Cramer. He appeared publicly in London as violin virtuoso in 1781 (Pohl, ii, 370; Ib., 371, in 1790 as viola player).

THOMAS SHAW. A violin virtuoso who appeared in London, 1781 (Pohl, ii, 370). Composed a violin concerto, a trio for 2 violins and violoncello; pianoforte sonatas; operatic music, etc.

NEVILLE BUTLER CHALLONER, b. London, 1784. Studied the violin under Cl. Jos. Dubroeck, at Brussels; made his first appearance as violinist in 1793 and became violinist at Covent Garden theatre, 1796, and at Richmond theatre, 1799. Afterwards he became leader at Birmingham, and Sadler's Wells theatre; then he became harpist at the Italian Opera and viola player at the Philharmonic Society. Finally he was a music seller. He wrote a method for violin, a number of pieces for harp, methods for various instruments, etc. (Brown and Stratton).

THOMAS GOODBAN, b. Canterbury, Dec. 21, 1784; d. there, May 4, 1863. THOMAS GOODBAN, b. Canterbury, July 28, 1816, violin player, was his son.

GEORGE FREDERIC PINTO, called Sanders (Saunders), b. Lambeth, London, Sept. 25, 1785; d. London, Mar. 23, 1806; grandson of Thomas Pinto. Was violin pupil of Salomon and acquired a remarkable technique combined with beauty and power of tone. Unfortunately his dissipated habits cut short a promising career; the immediate cause of his death was a cold contracted while giving a concert at Birmingham. Sandys and Forster enumerate him among the pupils of Viotti, but this statement appears open to doubt.

RICHARD CUDMORE, b. Chichester, 1787; d. Manchester, Jan., 1841. In his youth particularly, he was equally remarkable as a violinist, violoncellist and pianist. His first master was James Forgett, organist of Chichester. At the age of 9 he performed a violin concerto in public, and two years later, after a year's tuition from Reinagle, he played a concerto of his own composition. After that he was for two years a pupil of Salomon. At the age of 12 he was leader of the theatre orchestra at Chichester, and played a concerto at the benefit of the actor Suett. In the same year it is said that he came to London and played among the 1st violins at the Italian Opera. It is difficult to ascertain the actual facts of these reports. Certain it is, that after several years' residence at Chichester he went to London and studied the pianoforte under the famous Woelfl, and afterwards he played with great success a concerto first at Salomon's concerts and then at those of Mme Catalani. At another concert he played two concertos of his own composition, one for the violin and one for the pianoforte.

At Liverpool he played with equal virtuosity a violin concerto by Rode, a violoncello concerto by Cervetto, and a pianoforte concerto by Kalkbrenner. During the latter part of his life he was leader of the orchestra of the Gentlemen's Concerts at Manchester.

SCHÖNER. A violinist in London, 1788–ca. 1802 (Burney, iv, 682) (Gerber, ii, addition).

JOHN PHILIP DESAUBRYS. An English musician (violinist?) who composed 8 sonatas for 2 violins and violoncello and thorough-bass, London, pub. by J. Johnson for the author. Mendel says they were enumerated in Preston's catalogue of 1797, adding: "It cannot be ascertained whether he is identical with the violinist Aubry who was at the Comédie Française in 1798."

WILLIAM SHEPHERD. A Scottish violinist; d. Edinburgh, Jan. 19, 1812. He was teacher of music there and wrote "a collection of strathspeys, reels, etc., with a bass for the violoncello or harps," Edinburgh. Brown mentions a second collection for the pianoforte, violin and violoncello. Ib., in Brit. Mus., one song.

GEORGE VEAL. During the second half of the 18th century he was violinist in the orchestra of the Opera, London. He was not the author of the pamphlet against Burney, as stated in the catalogue of the Royal College of Music. The real author was John Laur. Bicknell (Eitner).

CHAPTER 32
Hungary

JOHANN LAVOTTA, b. Pusztafödémes, Hungary, July 5, 1764; d. Tálza, Aug. 10, 1820. Hungarian violinist who studied in Vienna and then toured throughout Hungary. He was a remarkable violinist and a very talented National composer who was the first to employ the Hungarian scale (harmonic minor with augmented fourth) in his compositions, based upon traditional Hungarian folk melodies.

JOHANN BIHARI, b. Gross-Abony, Hungary, 1769; d. Pesth, 1828. An eminent Hungarian gipsy fiddler who was unequalled in the expressive playing of Hungarian national songs and melodies. He formed a band of gipsy musicians which acquired a widespread reputation for being unique of its kind. Some pieces under his name are really by Lavoty (Lavota?) and Cérmák. The latter, although a Bohemian, vied with him in the playing of Hungarian popular music. An accident to his left arm in 1824 forced him to abandon violin playing. Bihari's violin and his portrait are in the National Museum at Pesth.

JOHANN TOST (1). During 1787-90 a violinist in the chapel of Prince Esterhazy; he stole Haydn's compositions and sold them to Schlesinger in Paris, and even gave out as Haydn's some compositions by Gyrowetz (Pohl, iv, 171). Reichardt (1789, 125) mentions a Tost, musician at Pressburg of Seipp's company, as the composer of some "Singspiele," possibly the above.

FRANZ GRILL, d. 1795 as chamber musician at Oldenburg, Hungary. Composed 3 sonatas, op. 4, Offenbach, André; 6 sonatas, op. 6, for harpsichord and violin, Livre 2, Offenbach, André; also sonates pour pianoforte et violon, Vienna, Hoffmeister (same?, Bruss. Cons.); 6 duos pour pianoforte ou clavecin et violon, Vienna, Hoffmeister (B.B. Schwerin F., Dresd. Mus.); also numerous quartets, etc.

Titles published by Travis & Emery Music Bookshop:

Bathe, William: A Briefe Introduction to the Skill of Song
Bax, Arnold: Symphony #5, Arranged for Piano for Four Hands by Walter Emery
Burney, Charles: An Account of the Musical Performances in Westminster-Abbey
Burney, Charles: The Present State of Music in France and Italy
Burney, Charles: The Present State of Music in Germany, The Netherlands …
Crimp, Bryan: Solo: The Biography of Solomon
Frescobaldi, Girolamo: D'Arie Musicali per Cantarsi. Primo Libro & Secondo Libro.
Geminiani, Francesco: The Art of Playing the Violin.
Hawkins, John: A General History of the Science and Practice of Music (5 vols.)
Herbert-Caesari, Edgar: The Science and Sensations of Vocal Tone
Herbert-Caesari, Edgar: Vocal Truth
Isaacs, Lewis: Hänsel and Gretel. A Guide to Humperdinck's Opera.
Isaacs, Lewis: Königskinder (Royal Children) A Guide to Humperdinck's Opera.
Lascelles (née Catley), Anne: The Life of Miss Anne Catley.
Mainwaring, John: Memoirs of the Life of the Late George Frederic Handel
Malcolm, Alexander: A Treaty of Music: Speculative, Practical and Historical
Mellers, Wilfrid: Angels of the Night: Popular Female Singers of Our Time
Mellers, Wilfrid: Bach and the Dance of God
Mellers, Wilfrid: Beethoven and the Voice of God
Mellers, Wilfrid: Caliban Reborn - Renewal in Twentieth Century Music
Mellers, Wilfrid: François Couperin and the French Classical Tradition
Mellers, Wilfrid: Harmonious Meeting
Mellers, Wilfrid: Le Jardin Retrouvé, The Music of Frederic Mompou
Mellers, Wilfrid: Music and Society, England and the European Tradition
Mellers, Wilfrid: Music in a New Found Land: … … American Music
Mellers, Wilfrid: Romanticism and the Twentieth Century (from 1800)
Mellers, Wilfrid: The Masks of Orpheus: …… the Story of European Music.
Mellers, Wilfrid: The Sonata Principle (from c. 1750)
Mellers, Wilfrid: Vaughan Williams and the Vision of Albion
Playford, John: An Introduction to the Skill of Musick.
Purcell, Henry et al: Harmonia Sacra … The First Book, [1726]
Purcell, Henry et al: Harmonia Sacra … Book II [1726]
Rastall, Richard: The Notation of Western Music.
Rubinstein, Anton : Guide to the proper use of the Pianoforte Pedals.
Simpson, Christopher: A Compendium of Practical Musick in Five Parts
Tans'ur, William: A New Musical Grammar; or The Harmonical Spectator
Tosi, Pier Francesco: Observations on the Florid Song.
Van der Straeten, Edmund: History of the Violoncello, The Viol da Gamba …
Van der Straeten, Edmund: History of the Violin, Its Ancestors… Vol.1.
Van der Straeten, Edmund: History of the Violin, Its Ancestors… Vol.2.

Travis & Emery Music Bookshop
17 Cecil Court, London, WC2N 4EZ, United Kingdom.
Tel. (+44) 20 7240 2129

© Travis & Emery 2009

www.ingramcontent.com/pod-product-compliance
Lightning Source LLC
Chambersburg PA
CBHW071644160426
43195CB00012B/1348